Handbook of

Christian Feasts
and Customs

FRANCIS X. WEISER

Handbook of
Christian Feasts
and Customs

The Year of the Lord
in Liturgy and Folklore

HARCOURT, BRACE & WORLD, INC.
NEW YORK

D.7.65

Library of Congress Catalog Card Number: 58-10908

Imprimi Potest: James E. Coleran, S.J., Provincial
Nihil Obstat: Michael P. Noonan, S.M., S.T.D., Diocesan Censor
Imprimatur: ✠ Richard J. Cushing, D.D., Archbishop of Boston
Date: February 6, 1958

Figures in parentheses after the names of persons indicate
the year of death.

Printed in the United States of America

TO MY TEACHER

JOSEPH A. JUNGMANN, S.J.

Preface

THOSE WHO wish to grow in knowledge and love of the Christian life will surely welcome Father Weiser's *Handbook of Christian Feasts and Customs*. For the casual reader, this new work presents an easy, convenient, genuinely entertaining approach to the thrilling story of Christian life in the liturgical calendar. For the discerning student, there is a wealth of reference material in the scholarly and exhaustive development of the ecclesiastical celebrations and of the folklore inspired by the liturgical feasts.

Each "Year of the Lord," with its feasts and celebrations, is the living voice of our Christian faith. There is no facet of Divine Revelation which is not somehow reflected in the Church calendar. Indeed, the passing seasons unfold a colorful tapestry in which are woven the strands of Church history, of Christian cult, of moral and dogmatic theology. And there is always fresh drama as each feast or season tells the ageless story of the life of Christ, or recalls the "fulness of Christ" in Mary and in other saints. All this, Father Weiser has captured for his readers in a truly remarkable work.

The faith of a people is eloquently expressed in folklore and in national customs and traditions. Nowhere will we find a more effective or more concise development of this theme than in this book. Present-day observances of the great Christian feasts have their roots in many lands. Father Weiser presents a fascinating study of this subject as he explores the origin and explains the significance of the popular customs and celebrations by which the central mysteries of the faith are brought close to the lives of millions.

The *Handbook of Christian Feasts and Customs* is destined to become a classic in its field. May it be for many the key to a devout and meaningful observance of the Year of the Lord.

✠ JOHN WRIGHT
Bishop of Worcester

March 31, 1958.

Foreword

THIS BOOK was written to explain the origin, history, development, and observance of our Christian feasts throughout the "Year of the Lord." In addition to the liturgical aspect of these feasts, their celebration in folklore is also presented. The radiation of liturgy has created many symbols, customs, and traditions that have enriched the observance of festive days and seasons in home and community, and remnants of pre-Christian lore have, in most cases, assumed new meanings and motivations through the influence of liturgical thought and celebration.

Classified within the vast field of knowledge, this book presents a compendium of heortology, the historical science that explains the origin and meaning of feasts. The word "heortology" is derived from the Greek *heorte* (feast) and *logos* (discourse). This work, then, is primarily intended as a historical explanation of general interest and as a source book of information.

The feasts of saints were selected on the basis of their celebration as holydays or holidays and because their folklore traditions are still alive in large groups of the population. Some purely liturgical feasts of recent date (Sacred Heart, Christ the King, Holy Name, Holy Family), which have not yet developed an established pattern of popular observance in homes or communities, have been omitted.

Writings on the liturgical year often employ, under the term "cycles," the twofold division that the Roman Missal and Breviary use in the arrangement of liturgical texts—the "temporal" cycle and the "sanctoral" cycle. This division of the official texts is based on the necessity of separating dated celebrations from those that are not held on the same calendar date. Actually, as Godfrey Diekmann, O.S.B., has pointed out, "there is only *one* cycle in the liturgical year, the cycle of Christ's redemptive work. Because of artificial divisions of terminology we are apt to consider the saints independently instead of being aware in every case that the Saint's Day is really a reflection and minor realization of the Passion and Resurrection of Christ."

The division into "cycles" is not used in this book. Its three parts represent merely external aspects in the observance of the one, and only, cycle of the liturgical year. The parts are: the celebrations based on natural time units and seasons of the year, the celebrations based on the commemoration of Christ's redemptive work, and the celebrations based on the result and fruit of the Lord's redemption in and through His saints.

The book combines material of three previously published works (*The Christmas Book, The Easter Book,* and *The Holyday Book*), augmented by a number of chapters and individual passages. The first part is almost entirely new. In most of the other chapters the passages on history and liturgy were enlarged by additional details, and the subject matter was rearranged to fit the purpose of a reference work. Popular items of restricted interest contained in the three books mentioned above, such as recipes, music, and poems, were omitted. Only those poems were retained that serve as examples for particular customs or liturgical celebrations.

Many details of religious and nonreligious folklore are given without reference to printed source material. This information the author has accumulated in the course of years through personal contact with experts on the folklore of various national groups. Much material was also collected through personal observation and study in central Europe, Italy, Ireland, and in the countries of the Near East.

A book like this must of necessity, and repeatedly, employ certain terms that are quite familiar to some readers and not so to others. For the convenience of the latter an alphabetical dictionary of terms may be found at the end of the volume. Reference notes will be found at the end of each chapter. The reader will also find occasional repetition of information or definition. This has been done to obviate the need for cross references and, therefore, to make the book easier to use as a reference work.

The author is gratefully indebted to His Excellency, Bishop John Wright of Worcester, Massachusetts, for the preface to the book. Acknowledgment for valuable help in the research on national folklore is due especially to Rev. Gregory Tom (Ukrainians), Rev. Claude Klarkowski (Poland), Rev. Vicente Beneyto, S.J. (Spain), Gediminas Kijauskas, S.J. (Lithuania), Sr. Marie Margarita, S.N.D. (France), Mrs. Hannah J. Ford (Ireland), Joaquin Herrero, S.J. (South America), Rev. Zeno Vendler, S.J., and Lajos A. Szathmáry (Hungary), Mr. and Mrs. Michael Topjian (Armenia), Stanley Marrow, S.J. (Near East), Rev. James L. Monks, S.J. (Eastern Churches), Rev. Richard Brackett, S.J., and Lars Lund (Scandinavia), Rev. John Correia-Afonso, S.J. (India). Acknowledgment is also due to Edward C. Currie and Rev. Martin F. McCarthy, S.J., for assistance in research on music, to Miss Anne Ford and Miss Margaret O'Loughlin for help in preparing the manuscript.

This book is dedicated, as a belated but sincere token of gratitude, to my former professor at the University of Innsbruck (Austria), the Rev. Joseph A. Jungmann, S.J. The lasting influence of his personality and example no less than his masterful teaching inspired me, as it did many others of his former students, to attempt a modest contribution to the great task of making the treasures of holy liturgy better known and appreciated. May this handbook not only be useful to anyone seeking information and understanding of our feasts and folklore, but also help toward a joyful and fruitful celebration in our churches, hearts and homes.

FRANCIS X. WEISER, S.J.

Weston College,
Weston, Massachusetts.

Contents

List of Abbreviations

Books and articles not listed here are quoted in full in the reference notes.

The notes, referred to by number throughout the text, are to be found at the end of each chapter.

AER   *American Ecclesiastical Review,* 1889 ff. (Vol. 1-113: *The Ecclesiastical Review*). New York, Philadelphia, Washington.

AP   *The Assisi Papers.* Proceedings of the first International Congress of Pastoral Liturgy. Collegeville, Minn., 1957.

Balt.   *Acta et Decreta Concilii Plenarii Baltimorensis Tertii,* ed. J. Cardinal Gibbons. Baltimore, 1886.

Barnett   J. H. Barnett, *The American Christmas: A Study in National Culture.* New York, 1954.

Benet   S. Benet, *Song, Dance and Customs of Peasant Poland.* New York, s.a.

BR   *Breviarium Romanum* (The Roman Breviary). Official book of the Divine Office (daily prayer-worship in liturgy).

CB   D. B. Wyndham Lewis and G. C. Heseltine, *A Christmas Book.* London, 1928.

Celano   T. de Celano, *Sancti Francisci Assisiensis Vita et Miracula.* Critical edition, revised by P. E. d'Alencon. Rome, 1906. (Quotations from this, Latin, edition translated by the author.)

Chambers   E. K. Chambers, *The Medieval Stage,* 2 vols. Oxford, 1925.

CIC   *Codex Juris Canonici.* Official codex of Canon Law.

CICI   *Corpus Juris Canonici.* Official collection of Canon Law before the present codex, ed. A. L. Richter, 2 vols. Leipzig, 1833-39.

Crippen   T. G. Crippen, *Christmas and Christmas Lore.* London, 1923.

CSEL   *Corpus Scriptorum Ecclesiasticorum Latinorum.* Vindobonae, 1866 ff.

CTD   *Carols for the Twelve Days of Christmas,* ed. P. M. Young. New York, s.a.

CwP   *Chrismas with the Poets,* ed. Ward, Lock, and Tyler. London, 1869.

DACL   *Dictionnaire d'Archéologie Chrétienne et de Liturgie,* ed. F. Cabrol and H. Leclercq. Paris, 1924-53.

Dawson   W. P. Dawson, *Christmas: Its Origins and Associations.* London, 1902.

Dur.   G. Durandus (Duranti), *Rationale Divinorum Officiorum,* ed. Lyon. 1592.

EC   *Enciclopedia Cattolica.* Vatican City, 1948 ff.

EI   *Enciclopedia Italiana di Scienze, Lettere ed Arti,* 35 vols. Roma, 1020-40.

ES   E. and M. A. Radford, *Encyclopedia of Superstitions.* New York, 1949.

EW   *Elsässische Weihnacht,* ed. J. Lefftz and A. Pfleger. Kolmar, 1011.

Franz   A. Franz, *Die kirchlichen Benediktionen im Mittelalter,* 2 vols. Freiburg, 1909.

Frazer   J. G. Frazer, *The Golden Bough. A Study in Magic and Religion.* New York, 1923.

Funk   F. X. Funk (ed.), *Patres Apostolici,* 2 vols. Tübingen, 1901.

Gaster   T. H. Gaster (ed.), *The Dead Sea Scrolls in English Translation.* Garden City, 1956.

Gelas.   *The Gelasian Sacramentary (Liber Sacramentorum Romanae Ecclesiae),* ed. H. A. Wilson. Oxford, 1894.

GH   *Der Grosse Herder. Nachschlagewerk für Wissen und Leben,* 12 vols. Freiburg, 1931-35.

Gugitz   G. Gugitz, *Das Jahr und seine Feste,* 2 vols. Wien, 1949-50.

Hackwood   F. W. Hackwood, *Good Cheer. The Romance of Food and Feasting*. New York, 1911.

HPEC   *The Hymnal of the Protestant Episcopal Church in the United States 1940*. New York, 1943.

HRL   J. Connelly, *Hymns of the Roman Liturgy*. London, 1957.

Jgn GK   J. A. Jungmann, *Der Gottesdienst der Kirche*. Innsbruck, 1955.

Jgn MS   J. A. Jungmann, *Missarum Sollemnia. Eine genetische Erklärung der Römischen Messe*, 2 vols. Wien, 1949.

Kellner   K. A. H. Kellner, *Heortology. A History of the Christian Festivals from Their Origin to the Present Day*. London, 1908.

LE   J. Lechner and L. Eisenhofer, *Liturgik des Römischen Ritus*. Freiburg, 1953.

Linton   R. and A. Linton, *We Gather Together. The Story of Thanksgiving*. New York, 1949.

LJ   *Liturgisches Jahrbuch*. Münster, 1951 ff.

LP   *Liber Pontificalis*, ed. L. Duchesne, 2 vols. Paris, 1886, 1892.

LThK   *Lexikon für Theologie und Kirche*, ed. M. Buchberger, 10 vols. Freiburg, 1930-38.

Mansi   J. D. Mansi (ed.), *Sacrorum conciliorum nova et amplissima collectio*, 31 vols. Florence and Venice, 1757-98.

MR   *Missale Romanum* (The Mass Book of the Roman Church).

Nilles   N. Nilles, *Kalendarium Manuale Utriusque Ecclesiae, Orientalis et Occidentalis*, 2 vols. Oeniponte (Innsbruck), 1896.

OF   *Orate Fratres. A Liturgical Review*. Collegeville, Minn., 1928-51. (Continued as *Worship*—see WOR.)

OiT   *Ostern in Tirol*, ed. N. Grass. Innsbruck, 1957.

PG   J. P. Migne (ed.), *Patrologia Graeca*, 166 vols. Paris, 1857-66.

PL   J. P. Migne (ed.), *Patrologia Latina*, 217 vols. Paris, 1844-55.

PW   Pauly—G. Wissowa (and W. Kroll), *Realenzyklopädie der klassischen Altertumswissenschaften*. Leipzig and Stuttgart, 1893 ff.

Raccolta *The Raccolta.* Official list of approved and indulgenced prayers and devotions, English edition. New York, 1943.

Rahner H. Rahner, *Griechische Mythen in Christlicher Deutung.* Zürich, 1945.

RCF F. X. Weiser, *Religious Customs in the Family.* Collegeville, Minn., 1956.

RR *Rituale Romanum* (The Roman Book of Rites).

Schuster I. Schuster, *The Sacramentary (Liber Sacramentorum),* 3 vols. New York, 1925.

Spamer A. Spamer, *Weihnachten in alter und neuer Zeit.* Jena, 1937.

SRC *Sacra Rituum Congregatio* (The Sacred Congregation of Rites).

SSP P. Geyser (ed.), S. *Silviae, quae fertur, Peregrinatio ad loca sancta,* in CSEL 39 (1898), 38-101.

StML *Stimmen aus Maria Laach. Katholische Blätter.* Freiburg, 1871-1915. (Continued as *Stimmen der Zeit*—see StZ.)

StZ *Stimmen der Zeit. Monatschrift für das Geistesleben der Gegenwart.* Freiburg, 1915 ff. (Formerly *Stimmen aus Maria Laach*—see StML.)

TCS *A Treasury of Christmas Songs and Carols,* ed. H. W. Simon. Boston, 1955.

TE V. Thalhofer and L. Eisenhofer, *Handbuch der katholischen Liturgik,* 2 vols. Freiburg, 1912.

TFB *The Trapp Family Book of Christmas Songs,* ed. F. Wasner. New York, 1950.

Thurston H. Thurston, *Lent and Holy Week.* London, 1904.

Trapp M. A. Trapp, *Around the Year with the Trapp Family.* New York, 1955.

VdM F. Van der Meer, *Augustinus als Seelsorger.* Köln, 1951.

VH H. Schauerte, *Die Volkstümliche Heiligenverehrung.* Münster, 1939.

VL L. A. Veit and L. Lenhart, *Kirche und Volksfrömmigkeit im Zeitalter des Barock.* Freiburg, 1956.

WC F. X. Weiser, *The Christmas Book.* New York, 1952.

WE F. X. Weiser, *The Easter Book.* New York, 1954.

WH F. X. Weiser, *The Holyday Book.* New York, 1956.

Wimmer O. Wimmer, *Handbuch der Namen und Heiligen.* Innsbruck, 1953.

WOR *Worship.* Collegeville, Minn., 1951 ff. (Formerly *Orate Fratres*—see OF.)

Young K. Young, *The Drama of the Medieval Church*, 2 vols. Oxford, 1933.

ZKTh *Zeitschrift für katholische Theologie.* Innsbruck, 1877 ff.

PART I

PART I

1

Sundays

HISTORY

OLD TESTAMENT · The system of dividing the moon month (twenty-eight days) into four parts and of keeping a day of rest in each period of seven days is of very ancient origin. At the time of Abraham it was generally observed among the Hebrews and other Semitic nations. The Bible reports the creation as taking place within six days; and the subsequent "resting" of the Lord on the seventh day reveals the Sabbath as instituted and sanctified by God (Genesis 2, 3). Consequently, the Sabbath rest was enjoined by the Law of Moses under severe sanctions. Daily labor for providing the necessities of life was to be laid aside. Travel and business transactions were not allowed, and no work could be done on farm or in garden or house. Even the food for the Sabbath meals had to be prepared on the preceding day. For this reason Friday came to be called "paraskeue" or day of preparation.[1]

Although additional acts of worship were not prescribed for the Sabbath, the custom developed in the later centuries of the Old Testament of doubling the official daily sacrifice in the temple on the Sabbath. People who lived outside Jerusalem attended the synagogues (meetinghouses) for religious instruction and common prayer.[2]

NEW TESTAMENT · In the New Testament there is no evidence that Christ or the Apostles immediately abolished the Sabbath. In fact, the Apostles for some years observed it along with other practices of the Old Testament (see Acts 18, 4), while at the same time they celebrated Sunday as the new Christian day of worship because it was the day of Christ's resurrection (Acts 20, 7). Saint Paul declared that the keeping of the Sabbath was not binding on the gentile Christians (Colossians 2, 16). It seems, however, that the converts from Judaism continued to observe

the Sabbath for quite some time. This custom prompted various
local churches of the Orient to keep both Saturday and Sunday
as holydays, until the Council of Laodicea in the fourth century
forbade this double observance.[3] The Greek Church preserves a
special distinction for Saturday even today: like Sunday, it is
always exempt from the law of fast or abstinence.[4]

MASS · In apostolic times the supreme act of Sunday worship, the
Sacrifice of the Mass, was held within the frame of a ritual meal
(the "Lord's Supper"). Imitating the example of Christ as closely
as they could, the Apostles seem to have followed the structure
of the traditional Sabbath meal of the Jews, with its prayers of
praise and thanksgiving and its religious-symbolic rite of distributing bread and wine to all present. As Christ had done, they
blessed the bread and wine and consecrated them by pronounc-
ing the words of the institution of the Holy Eucharist. (This
is still done at every Mass.) The meal was held on Saturday night
after sunset, when the "Day of the Lord" had started (1 Corinthians 11, 20).[5]

Soon after the close of the first century, the Eucharistic celebration was separated from the meal in many places, transferred
to the early-morning hours of Sunday, and made part of a service
according to the Jewish custom of worshiping on the Day of the
Lord. This service was held in the form of a "vigil" (night watch)
before dawn on Sunday, and usually consisted of a sermon,
prayers, singing of psalms, and readings from Holy Scripture.[6]
(This rite is still preserved in the prayers and readings of the
first part of the Holy Sacrifice, the "Mass of the Catechumens.")
Then followed, in the early morning, the main act of worship, the
Sacrifice itself (*Oblatio*).[7]

The earliest testimony concerning this Christian Sunday celebration comes from the pen of a famous pagan official and poet,
Pliny the Younger (113), who served as governor of Bithynia
under Emperor Trajan. In one of his letters to the emperor he
reported on the Christians in his province and, among other
things, in a description of their Sunday service said "that they
used to meet on a certain fixed day before dawn, and to recite
in alternating verses a hymn to Christ as to a god." [8]

A detailed description of the Sunday Mass may be found in

the *Apologia* of Saint Justine, the philosopher and martyr, a layman, born in Palestine and later living in Rome, who died for the faith about A.D. 165. He wrote his book (*The First Apology*) to defend the Christian faith against the calumnies and false judgments of his pagan fellow citizens in the Roman Empire. He says of Sunday:

On the so-called "Day of the Sun" all of us [Christians], both from the city and from the farms, come together in one place, and the memories of the Apostles or the writings of the prophets are read, as time will permit. (*Service of Reading*)

Then, when the reader has ceased, the one who presides speaks to us, admonishing and exhorting us to imitate the great things we have heard. (*Sermon*)

Afterwards we all rise and pray together. . . . When our prayer is finished, bread and wine and water are brought. (*Offertory*)

And he who presides offers prayers and thanksgivings [*eucharistias*] as best he can, and the people give their assent by saying "Amen." (*Canon*)

And a distribution and sharing of the Eucharistic oblations is made to each one; and to the absent ones a portion is sent through the deacons. (*Communion*)

Those who are well to do give voluntarily what they wish; and what has been collected is handed over to him who presides, and he will use it to help the orphans and widows, and those who are in need because of sickness or any other reason . . . in one word, he assumes the care of all who are in want. (*Charity Collection*) ⁹

In the same work Saint Justine further explains some important aspects of the Christian Sunday service, two of which deserve special mention:

Choice of the Day: We meet on Sunday because it is the first day, on which God created the world . . . [Gen. 1, 1-5], and because our Savior, Jesus Christ, rose from the dead on the same day.

Nature of the Eucharistic Oblations: This food is called by us the *Eucharist.* Nobody is allowed to receive it except who sincerely believes the truth of our doctrine and who was cleansed by the washing unto the remission of sins [baptism], and obtained the rebirth of life, as Christ has taught us. . . . Not as ordinary bread and drink do we receive this food; but as our Savior Jesus Christ was made flesh through the Word of God . . . so have we been taught *that this food is the flesh and blood of that same incarnate Jesus.*¹⁰

It is not difficult to recognize in this earliest document (from the second century) the essential structure and main parts of the Christian Sunday celebration through Mass and Communion. By the fourth century this morning celebration on Sunday had replaced in all Christian communities the original Saturday night meal and Mass.[11]

Despite the constant dangers in the times of persecution in those early centuries, the attendance at the Eucharistic Sacrifice was regarded as a duty of honor for all adult Christians. The Synod of Elvira in Spain, which was held during the great perse-cution at the beginning of the fourth century, expressed this duty for the first time by a formal law, imposing public penance on those who lived in the city and did not attend Mass for three successive Sundays.[12]

After the Church obtained her freedom under Emperor Constantine in 313 the hour of Sunday Mass was soon changed from dawn to nine o'clock in the morning. This was the time the Romans customarily assigned for "important business." It remained a general rule up to the late Middle Ages for Christians conscientiously to attend this official Sunday Mass of their own parish community. It was not until the fourteenth century that the ancient regulations were gradually loosened toward the present custom of allowing the faithful lawfully to attend Mass at other times and in other places.[13] In many countries, however, the official parish Mass is still distinguished from other Sunday Masses; it is a High Mass, often celebrated by the pastor himself, and canonical announcements (such as banns of marriage) are made. The liturgical rites assigned to certain feasts (such as blessings, processions) are also usually performed at this Mass.

NAMES

ANCIENT TERMS · Sunday in Jewish usage was "the first day after the Sabbath" (*prima Sabbati*), and is so designated in the Gospel reports of the Resurrection (Matthew 28, 1). Very soon the early Christians named it the "Day of the Lord" (*Kyriake, Dominica*) as may be seen in the Apocalypse of Saint John (1, 10). According to official Roman usage, the day was called "Sun Day" (*Dies Solis*), for the Romans had accepted the Egyptian custom of naming the seven days of the week after the sun, the moon, and the gods of the planets. Later, during the migrations, the Germanic nations substituted their own gods for those of the Romans, and thus came about our modern names of the weekdays: Sunday (sun), Monday (moon), Tuesday (Thiu), Wednesday (Woden), Thursday (Thor), Friday (Frija). Only Saturday retained its Latin name (Day of Saturn).[14]

It should be noted that in early Christianity *Kyriake* (Day of the Lord) meant primarily the day belonging to Jesus, "whom God has made both Lord [*Kyrios*] and Christ" (Acts 2, 36). The corresponding adjective (*kyriakos*) in those days was used by the Romans exclusively to denote the divine character of royal and imperial dignity. *Kyriake*, therefore, represented to the early Christians the day on which they gave solemn and joyful worship to Christ in the royal-divine glory of His resurrection.[15] The Christians also retained the use of the Roman popular term Sun Day. They did this to express the thought mentioned by many early Church Fathers that Christ is the true "Sun of Salvation." [16] Thus, the rising sun became a symbol of the Lord rising from His tomb.[17] The liturgical prayers in church were said for centuries in an "oriented" position, that is, clergy and people turned toward the rising sun, the east, as a symbol of the Risen Lord.[18]

LATER TERMS · The Latin nations kept the form "Day of the Lord" (*Dominica* in Italian and Portuguese, *Dimanche* in French, *Domingo* in Spanish, *Domineca* in Rumanian). The other form, "Day of the Sun," is used by the Germanic and Slavic nations (*Sunday* in English, *Sonntag* in German, *Sondag* in Scandinavian, *Nedelja* in Slavonic).

The Greek Church and its people still use the ancient term *Kyriake* (Day of the Lord). Another name for Sunday in the Greek liturgy is "Resurrection" (*Anastasis* in Greek, *Voskresenije* in Russian and Ukrainian).[19] The Arabic-speaking Christians retained the ancient Oriental custom, calling Sunday "the first day" (*Yom el-ahad*). Some nations of eastern Europe, having accepted Christianity at a later date, named the days of the week by numerals starting with Monday. Thus the Lithuanians call Sunday *Sekmádienis* (the seventh day).

"Eɪɢʜᴛʜ Dᴀʏ" · In early medieval times the term "eighth day" was often used for Sunday and may be found in the writings of the Fathers quite frequently. The thought behind this expression is that Sunday commemorates not only a beginning (first day of creation, beginning of Christ's risen life), but also an end and consummation (redemption and eternal glory).[20] Thus Sunday was considered both as the first and last day of the week. The popular custom still used in some European countries of calling a week "eight days" derives from this tradition.[21]

"Sᴀʙʙᴀᴛʜ" · At the end of the sixteenth century the Puritans (Presbyterians and other groups) originated the somewhat confusing practice of calling Sunday "Sabbath," a custom still prevalent in the literature and sermons of some Protestant denominations.

SUNDAY REST

Rᴇʟɪɢɪᴏᴜs Oʙsᴇʀᴠᴀɴᴄᴇ · Concerning Sunday rest, the early Church did not transfer the obligation of the Sabbath law to Sunday. It was generally understood, of course, that all work that would make attendance at divine worship impossible had to be discontinued. Beyond this necessary demand, however, no abstinence from any particular external occupation was required. The expression "to abstain from servile work" is found in the Old Testament with regard to Jewish feasts. Early Christian saints and writers often used this phrase, but only in a spiritual and allegorical sense. The *opus servile* (servile work) according to them is the "slavery of sin" from which Christians had to abstain not only on Sundays but every day. They expressly denied a strict obligation of resting from external work in the sense of the ancient Sabbath law.[22]

The Sunday rest of the early Christians was an *otium cordis* (rest of the heart), by which they meant the peace and joy of divine grace and of a good conscience. Saint Augustine (431) expressed this in one of his letters:

God prescribes a Sabbath rest for us. What kind of a rest? . . . It is internal. Our Sabbath is in the heart. There are many who idle, but their conscience is in turmoil. No sinful man can have Sabbath rest. Whoever has a good conscience is truly at peace; and it is this very tranquility in which consists the Sabbath of the heart.[23]

On the other hand, the solemn atmosphere of the Lord's day, the joyful participation in long church services (usually twice a day, morning and afternoon), and the practice of spiritual recollection naturally led to a general custom of abstaining more and more from strenuous and protracted occupations on Sunday. This trend was encouraged by civil legislation long before the Church authorities issued laws of their own in this matter. As early as 321, Emperor Constantine proclaimed a law of Sunday rest, which, however, did not include rural and agricultural work. About forty years later, the Council of Laodicea recommended some form of Sunday rest "as far as possible." [24]

The duty of complete Sunday rest, including rest from farm work, was not imposed until 650, when the Council of Rouen enjoined it for the Merovingian Church (France).[25] It is interesting to note that the words "servile work" in Canon 15 of this council are used, for the first time, with their Old Testament meaning: for laborious work such as was usually performed by slaves and servants. During the subsequent centuries this prohibition of servile work on Sunday was gradually adopted by the other European nations, and was finally incorporated into the body of Church law as a serious and general obligation for all Catholics.[26]

The practice of relieving slaves from work so they could attend worship and instruction, both in the morning and afternoon, had become universal among Christian Romans long before the laws of rest were issued; for it was not the aspect of rest as such but that of "freedom for worship" that inspired this practice. As early as the fourth century, many masters anticipated our modern weekend custom, for slaves were free even on Saturday, at least for the afternoon, in preparation for Sunday.[27]

In the High Middle Ages the obligation of resting from work began Saturday evening and was announced by the solemn ringing of church bells. Pope Alexander III (1181) declared that the time for Sunday rest could lawfully be reckoned from midnight to midnight.[28]

CIVIC OBSERVANCE · The first Christian emperor, Constantine, initiated the custom, which has continued through the centuries to the present day, of honoring Sunday as the Day of the Lord by state laws and regulations. In this he was not motivated by Church law (which did not yet exist), but by the desire of giving the Christian day of worship the same civic honors and privileges that were traditionally accorded to the pagan feasts. In 321 he forbade the sitting of courts and any legal action on Sunday.[29] He also allowed all Christian soldiers to be excused from duty in order to attend Sunday service, while the pagan soldiers had to assemble in camp, without arms, and offer a prayer which he himself had composed.[30]

The emperors Theodosius (in 386) and Valentinian II (in 425) suppressed circus games and all theatrical shows on Sundays. In 400, Honorius (for West Rome) and Arcadius (for East Rome) forbade horse races on Sunday because they kept people from attending divine service. Emperor Leo I (474) of East Rome went so far as to forbid musical performances, both private and public. This prohibition, though, was soon dropped from the lawbooks.[31]

In later times the rulers of all European nations continued the Roman practice of regulating Sunday observance. In 596, the Merovingian King Childebert of the Franks issued a strict code of Sunday laws for the population of his realm. So did King Ine of Wessex (726) and King Wihtred of Kent (725) in England. In Germany the prescriptions of Sunday rest were incorporated in the Frankish, Bajuvarian, and Salian collections of law, in the eighth and ninth centuries.

Prior to the Reformation, sports and popular amusements were allowed on Sundays in England and Germany. Similarly, the duty of attendance at Sunday services was not under the sanction of the civil law but its enforcement was left to the spiritual authority of the Church. After the Reformation, however, when the power over the Church was vested in parliament and rulers, attendance at Sunday worship came to be enforced by the state. In England, the first act of this kind was passed under Edward VI, in 1551. Under Queen Elizabeth I (1603) every adult citizen had to go to church on Sunday by order of the state or be fined a penalty of twelvepence. This law was not officially repealed until as late as 1846.[32]

The obligation of Sunday rest is still upheld by state law in all Christian countries. The legal tradition of England, which was also the basis for early American legislation, tended toward greater severity than the observance of other nations.

MODERN CHURCH LAW

Mass · The present demands of the Church regarding Sunday observance contain the grave obligation of attending Mass for all the faithful over seven years of age who are not excused by ill health or other sufficient reasons.[33]

Rest · The law of Sunday rest imposes the obligation of abstaining from servile work (nonessential labor in household, farm, trade, industry). Professional people, merchants, and civic officials are also required to abstain from their regular work. There are, however, many exemptions from the law because of present-day necessities, such as the duties of soldiers, policemen, firemen, doctors, nurses, officials, and workers in public utilities, communication, transportation, and similar occupations.[34]

The law does not apply to the so-called "liberal works" like study and writing, arts, music, sports, recreational activities, entertainment, nonlaborious hobbies, and similar pursuits.

Apart from these technical details of ecclesiastical law, the Church has always stressed the positive ideal of Sunday observance. The Day of the Lord, after the public worship, should be spent in works of piety and charity, in peaceful relaxation, in the happy union of family life.[35]

LITURGY

Sunday and Cycles · Sunday, together with Easter, forms the most ancient festive celebration in Christianity.[36] All other feasts came later. And as they were gradually introduced, Sunday acquired new aspects of its liturgical character through organic connection with the festive seasons and periods.[37]

Sunday is the keystone and foundation of all the Christian

festivals, for it constitutes the great day of worship recurring every week and thus fulfilling, with its sacred liturgy and other religious observance, the third commandment of the divine Decalogue. In this aspect it continues the celebration of the ancient Sabbath, but exceeds it in spiritual significance through the infinite nobility of its sacrificial worship.

This pre-eminence of Sunday within the temporal unit of the week was even more pronounced in the beginning of the Christian era, when Mass was not regularly celebrated on weekdays. Most likely it was also this aspect of Sunday, as a weekly holyday, that prompted the Apostles to adopt as part of its Christian celebration the structure and even, partially, the contents of the Jewish Sabbath service in temple and synagogue.[38]

In addition, Sunday is a solemn memorial of Christ's resurrection, a "little Easter" occurring every week. As such it commemorates the Lord's resurrection as well as all other mysteries of His life and redemption, and becomes in the fullest sense a "Day of the Lord" (Christ). Accordingly, every Sunday is a high-ranking feast of our Lord, a holyday of peace, consolation, and joy. The Church has always safeguarded this jubilant note in its Sunday liturgy.[39] The solemn Credo is recited on all Sundays, no fast is held, and people used to pray standing (instead of kneeling) on all Sundays just as they did at Easter time.[40] The Sundays outside the penitential seasons ring with the joyful song of the Gloria. The Sundays of Advent and Christmas season, of pre-Lent, Lent, and Easter season, also reflect in their Mass texts and other liturgical arrangements the particular character of each period.[41]

The direct association of Sundays with the feasts of saints often passes unnoticed. It does exist, however, in the form that the Mass texts of some Sundays are influenced by the proximity of certain saints' feasts.[42] Thus, the fourth Sunday after Pentecost has the Gospel of Saint Peter's miraculous catch (Luke 5, 1-11) because the Feast of Saints Peter and Paul usually occurs close by. The eighth Sunday after Pentecost contains the Gospel of the steward (Luke 16, 1-9) in honor of Saint Lawrence (August 10) who "made friends for himself in heaven" by distributing the Church goods to the poor. On the eighteenth Sunday after Pentecost the Gospel tells us of the cure of the paralytic (Matthew

9, 1-8) in honor of the two holy physicians and martyrs Cosmas and Damian (Sept. 27), who were highly venerated in Rome.[43]

An indirect connection of Sundays with festivals of saints occurs whenever a high feast of saints (Mary, Joseph, John the Baptist, Apostles, and Evangelists) falls on a Sunday. In such cases the Day of the Lord also assumes the character of a saint's feast both in Mass and Divine Office. It retains, however, its own liturgical commemoration.

There are, finally, a few Sundays, in addition to Easter and Pentecost, that have a special feast assigned: the Sunday between New Year's and Epiphany (Feast of the Holy Name of Jesus), the Sunday after Epiphany (Feast of the Holy Family), the Sunday after Pentecost (Feast of the Holy Trinity), and the last Sunday in October (Feast of Christ the King).

In various countries certain feasts falling on a weekday are celebrated again with public solemnity on the following Sunday, such as Corpus Christi (second Sunday after Pentecost), the Feast of the Sacred Heart of Jesus (third Sunday after Pentecost), the Feast of the Holy Rosary (first Sunday in October), and the feasts of local or national patron saints.[44]

The Greek Church celebrates a number of Sunday festivals, most of which are unfamiliar to Christians of the West, such as the Feast of the Second Coming of the Lord, the Feast of the Holy Fathers of the Ecumenic Councils, the Feast of the Holy Patriarchs, and the Feast of All the Ancestors of Christ.[45]

LITURGICAL TEXTS · In the calendar of the Western Church each Sunday has its own Mass formula. The oldest Masses are those of the Easter season, from the first Sunday of Lent to Pentecost. They are found in Sacramentaries (liturgical books) of the seventh century, and probably are of earlier origin. In subsequent centuries were added the Mass texts for the Sundays after Epiphany and the Sundays of Advent and pre-Lent. The twenty-four Sundays after Pentecost were first introduced in smaller groups (four after Pentecost, five after Peter and Paul, five after Lawrence, and six after Michael). The Ember Sundays, which had no Mass of their own (because the vigil Mass was celebrated before dawn on Sunday), acquired special texts when the vigil began to be anticipated on Saturday evening (in the sixth century).[46]

The Mass texts of the Sundays after Pentecost do not reflect any unified plan or central thought of liturgical commemoration. The Gospels are taken at random from the Synoptics. The Epistles, however, are selected in the order of the Biblical canon, starting with the letters of John and Peter (which in those days preceded the writings of Saint Paul), and followed by excerpts of Saint Paul's letters, from Romans to Colossians. The only exception is the eighteenth (Ember) Sunday, which received its Mass text independently, like all Ember Sundays.[47]

The Gloria in Excelsis Deo, which was used as a hymn in the Oriental Church as early as the fourth century, was very sparingly employed in the celebrations of the ancient Roman liturgy. Bishops alone had the privilege of inserting it in their Masses on Sundays and feast days; priests were allowed to intone it only on Easter Sunday. In the Frankish Church, however, it soon came to be recited by priests, too, on every Sunday outside of Lent and Advent. This custom was accepted by Rome in the tenth century, and subsequently became an established rule for the whole Western Church.[48]

The Credo recited every Sunday is called *Nicaeno-Constantino-politanum*, after the councils of Nicaea (325) and Constantinople (381), because it incorporates some important dogmatic formulations of these councils. It was originally used, in the Eastern Church, for the profession of faith in the rite of baptism; hence it is still recited in the singular. In the sixth century it was used in the Byzantine province on the eastern coast of Spain, and from there it spread through the whole of Spain. In later centuries it was introduced into Ireland and England. Abbot Alcuin (804) took it from England to the court of Charlemagne and inserted it into the liturgical books of the Carolingian Church.[49] Pope Benedict VIII (1024) finally adopted it for the Roman liturgy and prescribed it to be recited after the Gospel on all Sundays and on certain other feasts.[50]

It was a familiar thought in medieval times that Sunday commemorates in a special way the mystery of the Holy Trinity (the day on which God created Heaven and Earth, Christ rose from the dead, and the Holy Spirit descended upon the Apostles).

This thought prompted the introduction of the ancient "Preface of the Trinity" into the Sunday Mass—a custom that originated in the thirteenth century. Pope Clement XIII (1769) finally made it a law for all Sundays, except in Lent and those connected with great feasts.[51] The last Sunday of October (Feast of Christ the King) was given its own preface in 1925.

LITURGICAL COLORS · The use of liturgical colors for Sunday and other feasts developed gradually, from the ninth to the thirteenth centuries. It originated in the desire to express the mood of various celebrations by the display of symbolic colors that would inspire the faithful with that same appropriate spirit and mood. Of all the colors used in those centuries, Pope Innocent III (1216) mentioned only five: white, red, green, black, and purple. Obviously his list has helped to establish our present canon of colors. Blue and yellow, so generally favored in medieval times, have disappeared, but only after they were expressly forbidden by Rome. The exclusive and official use of the five colors dates from the time of Pius V (1572). The Eastern Churches have no established rules concerning liturgical colors.[52]

Green is the temporal color for Sunday as the weekly Day of Worship. All other colors proclaim a connection with special feasts and seasons of the liturgical year: white at Christmas and Easter, red at Pentecost, purple in Advent, pre-Lent, and Lent.

THE ASPERGES · The words of Saint Paul that through baptism we rise with Christ into the newness of life (Romans 6, 4-6) point to a special relation between the weekly memorial of the Resurrection and our own baptism. In the ninth century this thought seems to have prompted some bishops of the Frankish realm to introduce the custom of sprinkling holy water upon the faithful before Mass, to remind them of the grace of baptism. A century later the same practice was prescribed by Bishop Ratherius (974) at Verona in Italy; and soon afterward it was accepted by Rome. Thus the rite of the Asperges became a part of the solemn service on Sunday. In many places during the Middle Ages a procession around the church was held, and holy water was sprinkled upon the graves of the faithful.[53]

Sunday Vespers · In medieval times the general practice prevailed in most countries of people attending the solemn Vespers on Sunday afternoon. The recitation of the Divine Office, performed by the clergy, was followed by the singing of the Magnificat, while the altar was incensed. During the past few centuries this ancient custom has been gradually replaced in many sections by some popular devotion (prayers, hymns) followed by Benediction of the Blessed Sacrament. In many places of Europe, however, even these substitute devotions are still called "Vespers," and the light repast in the evening bears the name of "vesper meal" or simply "vesper" to this day.[54]

FOLKLORE

Religious Customs · A custom still practiced in many Catholic sections of Europe is the "praying around the church" on Sunday after the Mass. People go through the churchyard sprinkling the graves with holy water and saying prayers for the souls of the departed. This is a private and nonliturgical substitute for the ancient Asperges procession.

Another interesting Sunday custom prevalent in many countries is the "hearing" of the children at breakfast or dinner. During the meal the father gravely listens while the children repeat, as best they can, what the priest has preached in the Sunday sermon and what he has announced. If any corrections or explanations are in order, the mother usually provides them. Thus the parents make sure that the children have paid attention to the word of God and understand what was preached.

Finally, there is the widespread practice of wearing new clothes or shoes for the first time to Mass on Sunday, out of reverence for the Day of the Lord and to express due gratitude to God for granting us all good things. For a similar reason new loaves of bread are usually served on Sunday morning and the sign of the cross is made three times upon the loaf before it is cut.[55]

Legends and Superstitions · In the folklore and tradition of most Christian nations Sunday is a day of good luck and special blessing. From early centuries the faithful considered it particularly consecrated to the Holy Trinity, and in many places they still light a lamp or candle in their homes before the picture of the Trinity every Sunday. Children born on Sunday are said to be gifted with a cheerful and happy disposition and followed by good fortune throughout their lives. Superstitions ascribe all kinds of unusual powers to them, such as seeing angels and other spirits, great power of persuasion, finding hidden treasures, and freedom from accidents.[56]

On the other hand, people who violated the sanctity of Sunday were considered deserving of special punishment. Many legends of medieval times record such unusual happenings—Sunday violators being turned into stone, being frightened by a vision of the Devil, or being condemned to continue doing forever in the beyond what they had done while breaking the Sunday rest.

[1] H. Dumaine, *Les origines du Dimanche*, DACL, 4.1 (1920), 886 ff. [2] Kellner, 7. [3] Canon 24; Mansi, 2, 570. [4] Nilles, II, 87. [5] F. Cabrol, *Eucharistie*, DACL, 5.1 (1922), 656 ff. [6] SSP, 73 ff.; Schuster, 26 ff.; DACL, 15.2 (1953), 3108 ff. (*Vigiles*). [7] H. Leclercq, *Messe*, DACL, 11.1 (1933), 513 ff. [8] *Epistolae*, X, 96. [9] *Apologia Prima*, 66; PG, 6, 427. [10] Same, 67; PG, 6, 432. [11] H. Leclercq, *Agape*, DACL, 1.1 (1920), 775 ff. [12] Can. 21; Mansi, 2, 9. [13] CIC, 1249. [14] H. Dumaine, *Les noms de Dimanche*, DACL, 4.1 (1920), 858 ff. [15] Jgn GK, 258 ff. [16] H. Dumaine, *Le jour du soleil*, DACL, 4.1 (1920), 870 ff. [17] Rahner, 141 ff. (*Der Sonntag*). [18] H. Leclercq, *Orientation des fidèles*, DACL, 12.2 (1936), 266 ff. [19] S. Pétridès, *Anastasimos*, DACL, 1.2 (1924), 1926 ff. [20] J. A. Jungmann, *Beginnt die christliche Woche mit Sonntag?*, ZKTh, 55 (1931), 605 ff. [21] H. Dumaine, *Le huitieme jour*, DACL, 4.1 (1920), 879 ff. [22] F. Pettirsch, *Das Verbot der Opera Servilia*, ZKTh, 69 (1947), 257 ff., 417 ff. [23] *Epist.* 50, 10, 18; PL, 33, 212. [24] Can. 29; Mansi, 2, 570. [25] Can. 15; Mansi, 10, 1203. [26] See DACL, 15.1 (1950), 217 ff. (*Sabbatum*). [27] H. Leclercq, *Eslaves*, DACL, 5.1 (1922), 387 ff. [28] Kellner, 12. [29] T. Zahn, *Geschichte des Sonntags, vornehmlich in der alten Kirche*, Erlangen, 1894, 196 ff. [30] Eusebius, *Vita Constantini*, 4, 19; PG, 20, 1166 (Greek and Latin text of the prayer). [31] Kellner, 10. [32] W. Latey, "Sunday," Enc. Brit., 21 (1929), 565. [33] CIC, 1247, 1249. [34] CIC, 1248. [35] Balt., 58 (*De Observantia Diei Dominicae*). [36] Kellner, 37. [37] H. A. Reinhold, *How Many Cycles Has*

the Liturgical Year?, OF, 17 (1943), 102 ff.   ³⁸ Jgn MS, I, 27 ff.
³⁹ H. Dumaine, *Le jour de la résurrection*, DACL, 4.1 (1920), 884 ff.
⁴⁰ "On Sunday we consider it wrong to fast or to pray with bended
knees": Tertullian, *De corona militis*, PL, 2, 99.   ⁴¹ See Schuster, I,
319 ff., II, 30 ff.   ⁴² A. Vogel, *Der Einfluss von Heiligenfesten auf die
Perikopenwahl an den Sonntagen nach Pfingsten*, ZKTh, 69 (1947),
100 ff.   ⁴³ Jgn MS, II, 214.   ⁴⁴ CIC, 1247, 2.   ⁴⁵ Nilles, II, *passim*.
⁴⁶ LE, 167, 173.   ⁴⁷ Jgn GK, 239 f.   ⁴⁸ LE, 214; Jgn MS, I, 429.
⁴⁹ F. Cabrol, *Le Sacramentaire d'Alcuin*, DACL, 1.1 (1924), 1078 ff.
⁵⁰ LE, 224 ff.   ⁵¹ H. Leclercq, *Préface*, DACL, 14.2 (1948), 1704 ff.;
Jgn MS, II, 140 ff.   ⁵² TE, I, 496 ff.   ⁵³ Franz, I, 86 ff., 220 ff.   ⁵⁴ GH,
12 (1935), 298 (*Vesper*).   ⁵⁵ K. Hofmann, *Der Sonntag im religiösen
Brauchtum und Volksglauben*, LThK, 9 (1937), 669 f.   ⁵⁶ ES, 231;
VL, 137 ff.

CHAPTER

2   *Weekdays*

DAILY WORSHIP OF PRAYER

Christian prayer is the breathing of the Mystical Body of Christ,
the primary and most spontaneous manifestation of the supernatural life in the Church. God is adored and honored not only
through the Holy Sacrifice (which is itself imbedded in an exalted
ritual of prayer), but also through the private prayers of the
faithful and the official performance of the Divine Office by priests
and religious. This prayer life, by its very nature, is a daily task,
a duty of honor for all the faithful. The recital or chanting of the
Divine Office, moreover, binds those who are obliged to perform
it, under serious obligation each day.[1]

ORIGIN · In the Old Testament it was a custom among pious Jews
to pray three times a day: in the morning, in the afternoon at

three o'clock, and at night. This practice is mentioned in the Bible, which tells us that the prophet Daniel (sixth century B.C.) prayed three times every day "as he had been accustomed to do" (Daniel 6, 10).

A similar testimony has come to light in one of the famous Dead Sea scrolls. In the Hymn Book of the Qumran community (first century B.C.), the author mentions the daily exercise of prayer in the morning, about noon, and in the evening. In addition, he speaks of three additional prayer times during the night.[2] The Apostles seem to have kept this tradition even after Pentecost, for Peter and John are reported going into the temple "at the ninth hour of prayer" (Acts 3, 1).

The early Christians in the Roman Empire continued the ancient practice in the form of saying the Our Father three times a day, as the so-called *Teaching of the Twelve Apostles* (*Didache*), a book from the beginning of the second century, prescribed.[3] Soon, however, three more prayer times were added. Thus, at the end of the second century, we find the following hours of daily private prayer:

Midnight	(*Vigilia:* night watch)
Morning	(*Matutinum:* morning prayer)
Nine o'clock	(*Tertia:* prayer of the third hour)
Noon	(*Sexta:* prayer of the sixth hour)
Three o'clock	(*Nona:* prayer of the ninth hour)
Evening	(*Lucernarium,* from *lucerna,* lamp: the prayer at the time the lamps were lit) [4]

In the Christian empire in the fourth century two of these exercises began to be held in church. They consisted of readings from the Bible and chanting of psalms and other prayers: the *Matutinum* (our present Lauds) and the *Lucernarium* (our present Vespers). Thus the Church took over in the form of a liturgical service what up to then had merely been a private practice of the faithful; clergy and people, united in the house of God, performed these prayers together according to rules established by the ecclesiastical authorities.[5] The faithful were not strictly obliged to attend, but from ancient reports we know that they thronged the churches in good numbers for these daily morning and evening services.[6]

Saint Augustine reported that his mother (Saint Monica) most faithfully attended the daily *Matutinum* and *Lucernarium* in her church.[7] A noble Roman lady from southern Gaul, a nun by the name of Aetheria (Sylvia) who made a pilgrimage to the Holy Land about 395, vividly described these two services as they were held in Jerusalem at the end of the fourth century in the Church of the Holy Sepulchre (Anastasis), and how the many children present spontaneously cried "Kyrie eleison" in answer to the deacon's reading of commemorations.[8]

THE DIVINE OFFICE · From the beginnings of monastic life, the daily hours were kept by the monks in common, the psalms and many other prayers being chanted or recited in alternating groups (choir). Thus the basis was laid for the liturgical performance of the Divine Office. About the year 500 there appeared in the monasteries two additional prayer hours: the Prime (first hour, six o'clock in the morning) and the Compline (*completa:* finished, before retiring at midnight).[9]

For some centuries the *Opus Divinum* (Divine Work), as the Office used to be called, remained almost exclusively a task of monks, while the secular clergy continued to perform the two traditional public services (*Matutinum* and *Lucernarium*) together with their congregations in church.[10] From the eighth century, however, the recital of the whole Divine Office in common was also introduced among the secular clergy, who had started to live a community life in most places and were called *Canonici* (canons), from the canonical rules they followed.[11]

In the thirteenth century, when the secular clergy for the greater part had ceased to live in community, the *private* recitation of the Divine Office was enjoined as a daily duty on each clergyman, starting with the order of the subdeaconate. This law is still in force. The private recital is not necessarily bound to the official hours, but the whole Office must be performed every day.[12] In the monasteries the Office is still chanted in common, as of old, and at appointed hours.[13] Some changes and reforms have been made in the breviary (Book of the Divine Office) by various popes in the past centuries, with the purpose of removing less appropriate additions of later times and of adapting it to the conditions of priestly life in the modern age.

THE LAY PSALTER · During the seventh and eighth centuries the liturgical services of the *Matutinum* and *Lucernarium* gradually disappeared. The *Matutinum* was replaced by the introduction of daily Mass in the morning, and the *Lucernarium* was dropped because the faithful, especially in the northern countries, did not know Latin and were unable to take part. There was, however, a great desire on the part of the people to keep the official prayer hours with appropriate private devotions of their own. This desire, encouraged by the authorities of the Church, gave rise to a wealth of *horaria* (hour books, "prymers," *Stundenbücher*), which were in use all through the Middle Ages. They contained psalms, selections from the liturgical texts, and many other prayers of private origin.[14]

As the original "hours" in the ancient Church had usually been connected with particular commemorations of the mysteries of Christ's life and especially of His Passion, these medieval hour books also devoted each part of their daily reading to a certain event of the Saviour's life and Passion.[15] Great indulgences were granted by the popes for this pious exercise of daily hours in honor of the redemptive suffering of Christ. However, the books could serve only people who mastered the art of reading, and they were a minority in those days.

People who could not read, and among them especially the lay brothers in the monasteries, substituted for the written texts a certain number of familiar prayer formulas which they knew by heart. Thus, for instance, one hundred and fifty Ave Marias were substituted for the one hundred and fifty psalms, and the mysteries of Christ's life (taken from ancient responsories) were inserted in the Hail Marys. It was in this way that the rosary gradually developed during the High Middle Ages.[16] Saint Dominic (1221) is credited with the spreading of this particular exercise among the lay population of Italy.

At various times and in various centuries many such psalters were in use among pious lay people. In some places the Stations of the Cross were held within the frame of the ancient hour service. Finally, in the nineteenth century, an ancient custom was revived, of saying a short prayer every hour when the clock strikes and of accompanying this prayer with the sign of the cross in honor of the Lord's Passion.[17]

Protestant congregations kept the use of traditional hour books (with ancient liturgical texts) alive for quite some time. During the seventeenth and eighteenth centuries, however, both among Catholics and Protestants, a new kind of prayer book, containing instruction, meditation, litanies, prayers for "special occasions" like confession, communion, morning, and evening, gradually supplanted the psalters and hour books; thus the ancient devotion of daily hours became lost and forgotten in the minds of most modern Christians.[18]

Of late the Liturgical Movement in all parts of the world has endeavored to bring lay people back to the performance of "hours" through daily recital (in the vernacular) of liturgical hours from the Roman breviary. Whether this endeavor will be successful or not, and whether the practice will spread among the majority of the faithful, or merely remain a devotion of certain groups, only the future can tell.[19]

SIGNIFICANCE · Through the daily prayer of the Divine Office and the daily performance of the Holy Sacrifice, each weekday is sanctified and raised to the status of a true religious festival. Thus there is no "common" day in the whole Christian year, for the liturgical worship of the Mystical Body turns even the humblest day into a feast of great religious import. Although there was no Mass on weekdays in the early Christian centuries, perhaps a similar motivation (like the "newness of life" with the Risen Christ) prompted the Church from the beginning to call each weekday not simply *dies* (day), but *feria* (feast); for the word *feria* signified a religious feast among the ancient Romans.[20] Some scholars contend that the early Christians did not simply accept the Roman meaning but used the word *feria* as a translation for the Jewish "Sabbath" (Day of Rest).[21] Whichever the explanation, the significance remains the same; in the kingdom of Christ on earth every day of the year is a *feria* (holyday), a spiritual Sabbath.

MEMORIAL OF THE PASSION

There is clear proof from the earliest centuries of the Christian era that the second half of every week, from Wednesday to

Saturday, was devoted to a special commemoration of the Passion of Christ. Just as Sunday was the weekly memorial day of the Resurrection, so the preceding days quite naturally served to recall the Lord's sufferings by which He accomplished our redemption. In the first three centuries, however, it was not the Eucharistic Sacrifice, but the practice of fasting and prayer that expressed this commemoration.

FAST · The *Didache* (*Teaching*), written at the beginning of the second century, already mentioned Wednesday and Friday as weekly fast days.[22] The number of days was suggested by the ancient Jewish custom of fasting two days each week (Monday and Thursday). The Christian fast was put on Friday, as the day of Christ's death, and on Wednesday (from the third century on) because Judas made his contract of betrayal on that day (Luke 14, 1, 2, 10, 11). Thus the historical events of the redemption relived by the faithful every week formed a spiritual drama that comprised not only the Passion itself but also the decisions and actions of Christ's enemies that immediately led up to it.[23]

This Christian weekly fast was called "half fast" (*Semiieiunium*) because people were expected to fast only until three o'clock in the afternoon. Another name for it was "Station" (*statio:* standing), probably because the fast was concluded with prayer (in the church) performed standing. In later centuries, when Mass was usually celebrated on Station days, the word *statio* came to mean the *place* of the celebration on any day. (See the "Stations" in the Roman Missal.) [24]

The Station fast was accepted by newly converted nations and became so widespread in many countries that in Ireland, for instance, Thursday used to be called the "Day between the Fasts." [25] Even to this day the custom of voluntarily fasting or abstaining from certain foods on Wednesday is still alive; its motivation, however, has changed, for this pious practice is now usually held in honor of Saint Joseph.

In the fourth century, Saturday was added in Rome as one of the weekly fast days. This is explained as an extension of the Friday fast.[26] Pope Innocent I (417) motivated the Saturday fasting by the thought that on that day Christ had rested, a victim of death, in the tomb and that the Apostles had spent the day in sadness and fasting.[27] While this superimposed Saturday fast spread through the whole Latin Church, the Orientals never accepted it and have kept Saturdays free from any law of fasting. In the Western Church the original practice of fasting three days a week was later prescribed by law, but only for Ember weeks (apart from the special regulations for Lenten fast). For the rest of the year only Friday is still kept as a weekly day of prescribed abstinence, though not of fasting.

PRAYER AND MASS · On the weekly Station days the time of fasting (morning to early afternoon) was also devoted to private prayer, as far as possible. The author of *The Pastor of Hermas*, written at the beginning of the second century, described his own observance:

> I sat on some hill, fasting and *saying prayers of thanksgiving* to God for all the things He had done for me, when I suddenly saw the Pastor sitting at my side. He said: "Why did you come here so early in the morning?" I answered: "Because I am keeping the stations, Sir." "What is a 'station'?" he asked. "It means that I am fasting, Sir," I said.[28]

In many places the Station was originally concluded with a liturgical service in church, consisting of readings and prayers. Gradually, however, the Eucharistic Sacrifice began to be celebrated. By the second half of the fourth century this was an established custom in various parts of the Roman Empire (northern Italy, Africa, Palestine, Syria, Cappadocia).[29] In Rome, too, the Mass seems to have been customary, at least on Wednesday, after the fourth century.[30] For a long time, though, no Mass was held on Saturdays in the Latin Church, while the Eastern Churches celebrated it every Saturday from the fourth century on.[31]

MODERN OBSERVANCE · In medieval times the dramatic unity of this ancient observance from Wednesday (the betrayal of Judas) to Sunday (the Resurrection) was broken in favor of separate exercises in honor of the Passion. Saturday, now the weekly "Day of Mary," lost its memorial character of the Lord's rest in death. The conscious observance of Sunday as the weekly memorial of Christ's resurrection has also dwindled from the minds and hearts of most Christians in the West. However, the redemption is still honored by special weekly exercises, though in different setting and manner, mostly on Fridays, with Holy Hour, Stations of the Cross, ringing of bells at the "ninth hour," or various other forms of private or public devotions in honor of the Passion.

At the end of the eighth century, Friday began to be observed liturgically by various votive Masses, which priests were allowed to use in honor of the Passion of Christ whenever no higher feast occurred. Pope Pius V (1572), in his reform of the Roman Missal, suppressed most of these votive Masses, retaining only two for special use on Friday: the Mass of the Holy Cross and the Mass of the Passion. Both these Mass texts are still listed among the weekly votive Masses.[32]

FOLKLORE · The remembrance of the Lord's Passion by fasting, prayer, and other pious exercises made Friday a sacred and serious day in the minds of ancient and medieval Christians. Quite naturally it became a practice to avoid worldly pursuits and gainful enterprises as much as possible. Amusements and travel for pleasure were shunned. Whoever disregarded these restrictions imposed by popular piety was threatened with ill success and misfortune, as a punishment for his irreverent attitude. Thus originated our modern superstition of Friday, which still clings to its ancient objective (business pursuits, travel, and activities outside the home), being an "unlucky" day.[33]

OTHER WEEKLY COMMEMORATIONS

ORIGIN · It was customary from the early centuries for priests to say private Masses that did not constitute an official service for the community. In the beginning this was done only for the purpose of obtaining, through the Holy Sacrifice, God's mercy upon the souls of departed faithful. From the fourth century on, we also hear of private Masses celebrated for various reasons, either for the intention of the priest himself or of individuals and groups among the congregation. Because these Masses were offered ac-

cording to wish and request (*votum*), they were later called
votive Masses.[34]

The Church of the Carolingian Empire not only accepted the
ancient Roman texts of votive Masses, but Alcuin (704) also
wrote a new collection of such texts, which he called *Liber Sacramentorum*.[35] In it there appeared for the first time certain Mass
texts for every day of the week. Thus the custom was started of
devoting individual weekdays to the commemoration of religious
mysteries and sacred persons by means of the liturgical Mass
texts. As time went on, the number of such votive Masses grew
enormously. Pope Pius V (1572) reduced them to nine (for the
whole week). Their number has since been increased to eleven.
These votive Masses are allowed to be said whenever the respective weekday is "vacant," that is, when no other liturgical celebration is prescribed by the rubrics. Their choice was inspired
mostly by great popular devotions of medieval times, and has, in
turn, preserved and deepened these devotions.

HOLY TRINITY · At the beginning of the second millennium Sunday came to be considered in a special way as the "Day of the
Holy Trinity," not only in liturgical observance (through the preface of the Trinity and the Trinitarian "*Symbolum* of Saint
Athanasius" in the Divine Office), but also in popular piety.[36]
Following the trend of this devotion, the custom originated of
honoring each Divine Person separately on particular weekdays.
Sunday was kept mainly as the "Day of the Father," while Monday became the "Day of the Son," with a votive Mass in honor
of the Divine Wisdom (the second Person of the Trinity). Tuesday, also with a special Mass text, was celebrated as the "Day of
the Holy Ghost."

This manner of honoring each Divine Person by a separate
liturgical commemoration was declared inappropriate by many
theologians. The popes, too, did not formally approve it. Finally,
Pius V deleted the practice and provided only a votive Mass in
honor of the Holy Trinity, assigning it to Monday (where it is
still listed in the Missal). The Mass of the Holy Spirit he retained
(for Thursday) because it emphasizes not so much a separate
worship of the Third Divine Person but of His indwelling in the

Mystical Body. (The Mass prayers are not addressed to the Holy Ghost, but to the Father.)[37]

Holy Souls · In the early Middle Ages the common people and many theologians held the opinion that the souls in purgatory enjoyed a relief from their painful punishment every week from Saturday night until Monday morning, in honor of the Lord's Day.[38] It was not until Saint Thomas Aquinas (1274) treated the problem in his masterful way, and disproved such opinions, that this claim was finally abandoned.[39] While it lasted, however, popular piety inclined to help the holy souls in a special manner on Monday, since they were thought to return then from joy to suffering and, therefore, to need consolation and assistance more than at any other time. Without approving the popular belief, the Church facilitated this practice of prayer for the holy souls; hence the ancient rule that priests had to add a liturgical oration for the departed ones in their Masses on all "vacant" Mondays. This regulation was observed for many centuries, until the provisional reform of the rubrics (1955) under Pius XII discontinued it. The same reform, however, makes it possible now for priests to say Requiem Masses oftener than before.

Angels · In medieval times another votive Mass was provided for Monday: that of the Holy Angels. Some writers claim that Monday was chosen because the angels were the first fruit of divine creation, and thus should be venerated at the beginning of the week.[40] The actual reason, though, seems to be that the angels were considered to be the particular consolers and companions of the holy souls, and thus they were especially invoked and venerated on the "Day of Souls" (Monday).[41] The reform of the Missal under Pius V changed the assignment of this votive Mass from Monday to Tuesday, where it has remained up to now.

Apostles · Of all the votive Masses used in the Middle Ages to honor various saints, Pius V retained only two and assigned them to Wednesday: the Mass of Peter and Paul, and the Mass of the Apostles.

In the lore of the Germanic nations many traits that in pagan

times had been ascribed to the god Woden (such as guardian of
Heaven, protector of the harvest, and weather maker) were in
Christian times transferred to Saint Peter in the form of popular
legends. Thus, Peter acquired a particular connection with
"Woden's Day," on which he was especially invoked and ven-
erated in past centuries.[42] This popular veneration seems to ex-
plain the choice of Wednesday for the votive Mass of Saints
Peter and Paul and of the other Apostles.

SAINT JOSEPH · When the devotion to Saint Joseph spread in the
sixteenth and seventeenth centuries, Wednesday became associated with this great saint.[43] The reason for the choice seems to
be twofold. First, Wednesday was the only weekday dedicated
by the Church (in the votive Masses) to saints other than the
Blessed Virgin. Therefore, Saint Joseph obviously "belonged" on
Wednesday.[44] Second, in the popular mind ancient Station days
were considered of higher distinction and rank than the other
weekdays. This distinction was not based on any later practice or
ruling of the Church, but on the liturgical tradition that from
early times had actually singled out those three days for special
and solemn observance. Now, since Saturday was already devoted
to the Blessed Virgin, and Friday to the Passion of Christ, the
only day left on which to honor Saint Joseph in a special way
was Wednesday.

Whatever the reason, the custom was approved and confirmed
by the Church. Pope Pius X (1914), in 1913, put the Feast of
the Solemnity of Saint Joseph (now abrogated) on the third
Wednesday after Easter, and also assigned a Mass text in honor
of the saint for Wednesday among the weekly votive Masses of
the Roman Missal. Pope Benedict XV, in 1921, granted special indulgences to all faithful who perform some devout exercise in
honor of Saint Joseph on the first Wednesday of a month.[45]

BLESSED SACRAMENT · The weekly memory of the Last Supper,
with its institution of the Holy Eucharist, prompted the faithful
to accord special honors and veneration to the Blessed Sacrament
on Thursdays.[46] This custom, originating in the early centuries of
the second millennium, was accepted and approved in the reform

of Pius V, who inserted the Mass of the Most Blessed Sacrament among the weekly votive Masses. In many places it was custom. ary (and still is today in sections of central Europe) to celebrate this votive Mass whenever possible as a High Mass, which was attended by a large number of people (at least one member from every family of the parish).[47] The practice of holding a Holy Hour in honor of the Lord's agony on Thursday nights has spread of late in many countries.

Since 1937 a papal indult allows the celebration of a solemn votive Mass of "Christ, the eternal High Priest" on every first Thursday of the month. Its text was also put among the weekly votive Masses by Pius XI.

SACRED HEART OF JESUS · As a result of the revelations granted to Saint Margaret Mary Alacoque (1690), the practice developed from the seventeenth century on of devoting the first Friday of every month in a special way to the Sacred Heart of Jesus. Since 1889 a Roman indult has given this custom a liturgical expression through the "Mass of the Sacred Heart" which, under certain conditions, may be celebrated as a solemn votive Mass. Other liturgical devotions, too, have been provided for "First Friday"; they may be held in churches with the approval of the bishop and according to his regulations.

Through the pious exercises of the "Nine Fridays" and the "First Fridays," the custom grew in many places of performing on *every* Friday some devotion in honor of the Sacred Heart of Jesus, partly in church (by attendance at Mass, Communion, evening devotions), partly at home (by family prayer, burning of vigil lights before the Sacred Heart statue).[48]

BLESSED VIRGIN MARY · In the ninth century originated the popular veneration of Mary on Saturdays. This practice appears to have grown out of the ancient weekly memorial of Christ's Passion. The books of that time motivate it by the thought that while the Lord's body rested in death Mary alone did not doubt or despair, but firmly adhered to the faith in her Divine Son.[49] She was thus believed to deserve more devotion and honor on Saturday than on other weekdays. The authorities of the Church not only provided a votive Mass (which now has five different texts

according to the seasons of the ecclesiastical year), but also a
special Office in honor of Mary, to be recited on "free" Saturdays
(*Officium sanctae Mariae in Sabbato*).

[1] H. Leclercq, *Jours de la Semaine*, DACL, 7.2 (1927), 2736 ff.
[2] Gaster, Hymn 11, 182.   [3] Didache, 8, 2; Funk, I, 19.   [4] F. Cabrol,
Liturgical Prayer: Its History and Spirit, London, 1925.   [5] Schuster, I,
26 ff. (*Ecclesiastical Prayer in the Early Church*); J. Stadlhuber, *Das
Stundengebet der Laien im christlichen Altertum*, ZKTh, 71 (1949),
129 ff.   [6] Tertullian, *De Oratione*, 28; PL, 2, 1304.   [7] *Confess.*, 5, 9;
PL, 32, 714.   [8] SSP, 71 ff.   [9] F. X. Pleithner, *Älteste Geschichte des
Breviergebetes*, Kempten, 1887, 15 ff.   [10] SSP, 75.   [11] R. Capel, *Canons
Regular and the Breviary*, OF, 23 (1949), 246 ff.   [12] CIC, 135.
[13] CIC, 610.   [14] H. Leclercq, *Livres d'heurs*, DACL, 9.2 (1930),
1836 ff.; W. Busch, *The Origin of the Hour Prayers*, OF, 1 (1927),
327 ff.   [15] J. Stadlhuber, *Das Laienstundengebet vom Leiden Christi*,
ZKTh, 72 (1950), 282 ff.   [16] M. Gorce, *Le Rosaire et ses antécédents
historiques*, Paris, 1931, 11 ff.   [17] P. Singer, *Geistliche Betrachtung-
suhr*, Salzburg, 1889, 18 ff.   [18] See note 15, 320; Balt., 120 ff. (*De
Libris Precum*).   [19] L. C. Sheppard, *Divine Office and the Laity*, OF,
11 (1936-7), 107, 169, 214, 263, and ff.   [20] F. Cabrol, *Fêtes Chrétien-
nes: Feria*, DACL, 5.1 (1922), 1403 ff.   [21] LE, 134.   [22] Didache, 8,9;
Funk, 21.   [23] Jgn GK, 261. J. Cortes Quirant claims that the early
Christians fasted on Wednesday because Christ started His Passion
on that day: *La Nueva Fecha de la Ultima Cena*, in *Estudios Biblicos*,
XVII, Madrid, 1958, III and IV.   [24] H. Leclercq, *Stations liturgiques*,
DACL, 15.2 (1953), 1653 ff.   [25] Jgn GK, 260 f.   [26] Theodore Bal-
samon, *Comment. in can. 55 Conc. Trull;* PL, 137, 707 ff.   [27] *Epis-
tola* 25, 4; PL, 20, 556.   [28] *Hermae Pastor*, sim. 5, 1; Funk, 529.
[29] LE, 134.   [30] Innoc. I, *Epist.* 25; PL, 20, 555.   [31] SSP, 71-101,
passim.   [32] MR, *Missae Votivae, Feria Sexta.*   [33] ES, 126 (*Friday*);
VL, 142.   [34] LE, 188.   [35] F. Cabrol, *Le Sacramentaire d'Alcuin*,
DACL, 1.1 (1924), 1078 ff.   [36] Jgn MS, II, 151 (note 51).   [37] Jgn
GK, 262.   [38] VL, 138.   [39] *Comment. in Libr. Sent.*, D. XLV, Qu. II,
a. 2, qu. 1.   [40] Dur., IV, 1, 28.   [41] Jgn GK, 263.   [42] Gugitz, II, 3 ff.
[43] J. Kreuter, *St. Joseph in Literature and Devotion*, OF, 6 (1932),
255 ff.; F. L. Filas, *Joseph Most Just*, Milwaukee, 1956.   [44] VL, 141.
[45] Raccolta, 337.   [46] VL, 142.   [47] Jgn GK, 263.   [48] J. Stierli, *Die
Entfaltung der kirchlichen Herz-Jesu-Verehrung in der Neuzeit*, in
Cor Salvatoris, Freiburg, 1954, 137 ff.   [49] Jgn GK, 263; VL, 142.

CHAPTER

3   *Ember Days*

ORIGIN AND HISTORY

EARLY CENTURIES · The Romans, originally an agricultural people, had many nature gods and a goodly number of pagan religious nature festivals. Outstanding among them was the threefold seasonal observance of prayer and sacrifices to obtain the favor of the gods upon sowing and harvest. The first of these seasonal celebrations occurred at various dates between the middle of November and the winter solstice. It was a time of prayer for successful sowing (*Feriae Sementivae:* Feast of Sowing). The second festival was held in June or July for the grain harvest (*Feriae Messis:* Harvest Feast).[1] The third one came before the autumnal equinox (September) and was motivated by the wine harvest (*Vinalia:* Feast of Wine).[2]

The early Christians in the Roman Empire could not, of course, partake in such pagan celebrations in any way. On the other hand, the thought of prayer to God for His blessing upon sowing and harvest appealed as much, and even more so, to the Christians as it did to the pagans. Moreover, the Scriptures of the Old Testament mention "the fast of the fourth month, and the fast of the fifth, and the fast of the seventh, and the fast of the tenth" (Zechariah 8, 19). The Dead Sea scrolls, too, contain a clear reference to special prayer times at the beginning of the annual seasons.[3]

It is not surprising, then, that the Christians in Rome introduced such prayer seasons of their own at the time the empire was still pagan (third century). These prayer periods, although coinciding roughly with the pagan dates of celebration (because

of their natural background), did not imitate the heathen observance. Instead of the pagan feasting, the Christians fasted.
They offered the Eucharistic Sacrifice after having fasted the
whole of Saturday and having performed a long vigil service of
prayers and readings. The first regulations concerning this festival
of the "Three Seasons" are ascribed to Pope Callistus (222).[4]

Very early, probably during the fourth century, the Church
added a fourth prayer period (in March). This change seems to
have been motivated by the fact that the year contains four
natural seasons, and also by the mention of four fasting periods
in the Book of the prophet Zechariah. At about the same time,
each period was extended over the three traditional Station days
(Wednesday, Friday, Saturday). While the Station fast at other
times was expected but not strictly prescribed, this seasonal
observance imposed fasting by obligation. The vigil service from
Saturday to Sunday was retained as a full vigil, lasting the greater
part of the night.[5]

Pope Leo the Great (461) mentions these prayer periods, or
Ember Days, as an ancient traditional celebration of the Roman
Church. He even claims that they are of apostolic origin (which
may well be correct as far as the Jewish custom of seasonal
prayer times is concerned). He preached a number of sermons
on the occasion, stressing both the duty of imploring God's blessing and of thanking Him for the harvest by the tribute of a joyful fast before consuming the gifts of His bounty.[6] In subsequent
centuries, however, the Ember celebration lost a great deal of
its joyous and festive character, and the motive of penance was
stressed more and more.

Another historical event helped to overshadow the original
purpose and mood of Embertides. In 494 Pope Gelasius I prescribed that the sacrament of Holy Orders (deaconate, priesthood) be conferred on Ember Saturdays. Thus the prayer and
fasting of Ember week acquired added importance, for apostolic
tradition demanded that ordinations be preceded by fast and
prayer (Acts 13, 3). Not only the candidates fasted and prayed
for a few days in preparation for Holy Orders, but the whole
clergy and people joined them to obtain God's grace and blessing
upon their calling. It seemed natural, then, to put the ordinations

at the end of those weeks that already were established times of prayer and fasting.[7]

Thus the regulation of Pope Gelasius turned the Embertides into a general performance of spiritual exercises for all, similar in thought and purpose to our modern retreats and missions. The Holy Orders were then conferred before the Mass of Saturday, after the lessons which closed with the hymn *"Benedictus"* of the Old Testament (see Daniel 3, 52).[8]

The Embertides have remained official times of ordination ever since.[9] Candidates are still obliged to perform spiritual exercises in preparation; [10] however, these are now made privately, and not in union with the whole congregation, as was the case in ancient days. On the other hand, the Ember weeks have been stressed in recent centuries as a time of special prayer on the part of the faithful for vocations to priesthood and for the sanctification of priests.

MEDIEVAL TIMES · At the beginning of the sixth century the Ember Day celebration was well established at Rome in all its essential features. The only point that remained undetermined for a long time was the date of the Ember weeks in Advent and Lent. The ancient regulations only prescribed the "third week in December" and the "first week in March" without saying what should be done when the month started on a Monday or Tuesday or Wednesday.[11] This question was finally settled by Pope Gregory VII (1085), who decided on the following arrangement (which is still kept today): Embertides are to be celebrated in the weeks after the third Sunday of Advent, after the first Sunday of Lent, during Pentecost week, and in the week following the Feast of the Exaltation of the Cross (September 14).[12]

The Embertides spread slowly at first, and not without some popular resistance outside of Rome, for they were a typically local celebration of the city of Rome. The Diocese of Milan, for instance, did not introduce them for a thousand years, until the thirteenth century. They went to Spain through the acceptance of the Roman Missal in the eleventh century. Long before that, however, the Anglo-Saxons had adopted them in the eighth century by taking over the Roman rites as a whole at their conversion. In the Frankish kingdoms (France and Germany) they seem to have been introduced by Saint Boniface (754), but did not become established until Charlemagne prescribed them for the whole Frankish realm in 769. Their observance, though, had to be repeatedly enjoined by synods in France and Germany during the ninth century, until they finally became a universal and popular feature of ecclesiastical celebration.[13] The Eastern Churches do not observe Embertides, but have other periods of penance and fast besides Lent.[14]

NAMES · In the earliest liturgical books the Ember Days are simply called "the fast of the first, fourth, seventh and tenth month" (that is, March, June, September, December)—an interesting example of how the ancient practice of starting the year on March first, which had been officially abrogated by Julius Caesar, was still in vogue among the population of Rome centuries later.[15] During the sixth century the term *Quatuor Tempora* (Four Times or Seasons) was introduced, and has remained ever since as the official ecclesiastical name for the Embertides.[16]

From the Latin word most European nations coined their popular terms: *Quatretemps* in French, *Quatro Tempora* in Italian, *Las Temporas* in Spanish, *Quatember* in German, *Kvatri posti* among the southern Slavs, *Kántor böjtök* in Hungarian. The northern Slavs of the Latin Rite call the Embertides *Suche dni* ("Dry days") from the ancient custom of eating uncooked food during fasts. The English term Ember seems to derive from the Anglo-Saxon *ymbren* (season, period).

LITURGY

COMMON FEATURES · In early medieval days it was customary in Rome to hold a penitential procession which proceeded from the place of gathering (*collecta*) to the Station church for the services on Wednesdays, Fridays, and Saturdays of Ember weeks. The night from Saturday to Sunday was a major vigil. As at the Easter vigil, passages from the Bible were read in twelve long lessons, the last one always being the story of the three young men in the furnace (Daniel 3). Today there are only six lessons—considerably shortened—but closing, as of old, with the miracle of the furnace and the hymn of the three men (Daniel 3, 47-56).[17] The call *Flectamus Genua* (Let us bend our knees) has also been retained from the rite of major vigils in ancient times.

The Mass following the prayer service of the vigil stood for the Sunday Mass. Thus many old liturgical books carry the remark *Dominica vacat* ("the Sunday is vacant"), that is, it has no Mass text of its own. Only after the sixth century, when the vigil service and its Mass were anticipated on Saturday evening (and later on Saturday morning), did the Sundays receive texts of their own in the Missal.[18]

Besides some traces (in the lessons) of the original purpose, the Mass formulas of Ember Days mostly express the thoughts of the liturgical seasons in which they fall: expectation of the Lord in Advent; penance and prayer in Lent; the descent of the Holy Spirit at Pentecost. The Masses of the Embertide in September seem to have preserved features of the original celebration, since the lessons and prayers reflect the joy of a harvest festival.

It is an interesting fact that most of the Gospel passages on Ember Days (with the exception of those in Advent) relate or mention the expulsion of demons. This has been interpreted as an indication of how the Church consciously condemned and supplanted the pagan celebration of the seasonal *feriae,* which was not a service of the true God but a slavery of false gods whom the early Christians considered and called "demons." [19]

EMBERTIDE OF PENTECOST · This Embertide has assumed a special character which distinguishes it from all the others. Coinciding with the octave of Pentecost, it displays an interesting combination of penitential motives (in some of its Mass prayers) with the celebration of the great feast (Gloria, Credo, Alleluia, Sequence, Pentecostal orations, red vestments, omission of *Flectamus Genua*). Because of this joyful note it used to be called *Ieiunium Exultationis* (the Fast of Exultation) in the Middle Ages. Abbot Rupert of Deutz (1130) wrote about it as follows:

It is not a fast to make us sad or to darken our hearts, but it rather brightens the solemnity of the Holy Spirit's arrival; for the sweetness of the Spirit of God makes the faithful loathe the pleasures of earthly food.[20]

Saint Isidore of Spain (636), Doctor of the Church, relates
that for a time in the earliest centuries this fast was held right
after the Feast of the Ascension, in imitation of the Apostles'
prayerful retreat (Acts 1, 14). It was soon transferred to Pentecost week, however, because the practice of the Church did not
allow for fasting or penitential exercises between Easter and
Pentecost.[21]

FOLKLORE

RELIGIOUS CUSTOMS · Up to the late Middle Ages the Ember
Days were generally kept as holydays of obligation, with attendance at Mass and rest from work, and as weeks of penance and
fervent prayer. They were favored dates for the reception of
Holy Communion, a custom still alive in many Catholic sections
of Europe.

The practice of spiritual and temporal works of charity and
mercy, which had always been stressed by the Church in connection with Embertide fasting, produced the custom of devoting
the Ember Days to special prayer for the suffering souls in
purgatory, and of having Masses said for them during the Embertides. This tradition, too, is still frequently found in European
countries. Alms and food were given to the poor on Ember Days,
and warm baths provided for them (a popular work of Christian
charity in bygone centuries).

Since people in centuries past were more keenly aware of
the connection between Embertides and prayer for God's blessing
upon the functions and fruits of nature, they also included in
their petitions, and in a special way, the successful and happy
birth of their children. Thus the Ember Days became particular
occasions of prayer by and for pregnant mothers. Children born
during Embertides were considered as unusually blessed by God.
Popular superstition ascribed to them "good luck" for their whole
life, excellent health, and many favors of body and soul.

Finally, there is the ancient legend that many poor souls are
allowed to leave purgatory for a few moments every Embertide,
to appear in visible shape to those relatives and friends who
fervently pray for the departed ones, in order to thank them and
to beg for continued prayerful help for themselves and for those

holy souls who have nobody on earth to remember them. The laudable custom observed by many faithful in modern times of praying and having Masses offered for the "forgotten" souls in purgatory seems to be a happy relic of this medieval popular legend.[22]

QUARTER TERMS · From ancient Germanic usage the Ember weeks took over the character of "quarter terms," that is, the four seasonal periods of the year during which burdensome civic obligations had to be carried out, like the paying of debts, tithes, and taxes. From this practice the Ember weeks were called by the Persian-Latin term *Angariae* (Requisitions). The German word *Frohnfasten* is often explained as meaning the same as *Angariae*—the payment of what is owed to temporal lords. Actually, however, it means the "Fast of the Lord God," that is, a solemn, general, and holy fast in the service of God.[23]

[1] PW, 6.2, 2211 (*Feriae*); 2A.2, 1346 ff. (*Sementivae*).   [2] Pliny the Younger, *Epist.*, 8, 21.   [3] Gaster, Hymn 11, 182.   [4] LP, I, 141.   [5] LE, 135 f.   [6] See the sermons of Saint Leo in PL, 54, *passim* (1-3, 12, 13, 16-19, 51, 84, 87-94).   [7] H. Leclercq, *Quatre-Temps*, DACL, 14.2 (1948), 2014 ff.   [8] The ordinations are now conferred in separate rites after the various lessons of Ember Saturday.   [9] CIC, 1006, 2.   [10] CIC, 1001, 1.   [11] See the treatise by Abbot Berno of Reichenau (1048): *Qualiter quatuor temporum jejunia sint observanda;* PL, 142, 1087.   [12] Micrologus, 24 ff.; PL, 151, 978.   [13] DACL, 14.2 (1948), 2016.   [11] K. Holl, *Die Entstehung der vier Fastenzeiten in der griechischen Kirche*, in *Gesammelte Aufsätze zur Kirchengeschichte*, Tübingen, 1928, II, 155 ff.   [15] Kellner, 185.   [16] Nilles, II, 510 ff.   [17] MR, *passim* (*Sabbato Quatuor Temporum*).   [18] Jgn GK, 253.   [19] TE, I, 592.   [20] *De divin. officiis*, 10, 26; PL, 170, 289.   [21] *De eccles. officiis*, I, 1; PL, 38, 733.   [22] L. Eisenhofer, *Quatember*, LThK, 8 (1936), 581.   [23] Nilles, II, 512 ff.

CHAPTER

4   *Rogation Days*

ORIGIN AND HISTORY

LITANIES · The Jews in the Old Testament had a form of public
prayer in which one or more persons would pronounce invocations of God which all those present answered by repeating
(after every invocation) a certain prayer call, like "His mercy
endures forever" (Psalm 135) or "Praise and exalt Him above
all forever" (Daniel 3, 57-87).

In the New Testament the Church retained this practice. The
early Christians called such common, public, and alternating
prayers "litany," from the Greek *litaneia* (*lité*), meaning "a humble and fervent appeal." [1] What they prayed for is indicated in a
short summary by Saint Paul in his first letter to Timothy (2, 1-2).

The common and typical structure of the litany in the Latin
Church developed gradually, from the third century on, from
short invocations as they were used in early Church services.
It consisted of four main types, which were recited either separately or joined together. First, invocations of the Divine Persons and of Christ, with the response *Miserere nobis* (Have
mercy on us). Second, invocations of Mary, the Apostles, and
groups of saints, response: *Ora pro nobis* (Pray for us). Third,
prayers to God for protection from evils of body and soul, response: *Libera nos, Domine* (Deliver us, O Lord). Finally,
prayers for needed favors, response: *Te rogamus, audi nos* (We
beseech Thee, hear us). [2]

Many invocations of individual saints and special petitions
were added everywhere in later centuries, and popular devotion
increased their numbers to such an extent that Pope Clement

VIII, in 1601, determined the official text of the litany (called "Litany of All Saints") and prohibited the public use of any other litanies unless expressly approved by Rome.[3]

The invocation Kyrie eleison came from the Orient to Rome in the fifth century. It soon acquired such popularity that it joined (and even supplanted) the older form of litany in the Mass of the Catechumens.[4] Up to this day the Kyrie eleison and Christe eleison in the Mass remain as relics of the responses that the people gave to petitions recited by the deacon (before the readings) and by the celebrant (after the Gospel). Outside of the Holy Sacrifice, the Kyrie eleison was also added to the other types of litany prayers; it may still be found at the beginning and end of every litany. The Greek Rite still uses a number of actual litanies (*Ektenai*) in its liturgy (the Holy Sacrifice).[5]

Many and varied are the occasions on which litanies were in use among early Christians. Besides being a part of the Mass liturgy, a litany was recited before solemn baptism (as it is today in the liturgy of the Easter vigil) and in the prayers for the dying (where it is also still prescribed). Even more frequent, however, was the use of litanies during processions, because the short invocations and exclamatory answers provided a convenient form of common prayer for a multitude in motion.[6] This connection between litany and procession soon brought about the custom of calling both by the same term. From the sixth century on, *litania* was used with the meaning of "procession." The first Council of Orléans (511) incorporated this usage into the official terminology of the Church.[7]

Since the ancient Roman Church had many and divers kinds of processions, the litanies must have been a most familiar feature of ecclesiastical life. Litanies (processions) were held on Station days, every day in Lent, on many feasts, on Ember Days and vigils, and on special occasions (calamities and dangers of a usual or unusual kind) when God's mercy and protection was implored with particular fervor.[8] These latter occasions had already been observed in pagan Rome with processions to the shrines of gods at certain times of the year. Their natural features (dates, routes, motives) were part of the traditional community life. These features the Church retained in certain cases, filling them with the significance and spiritual power of Christian worship.

THE MAJOR LITANIES · The pagan Romans had two kinds of religious parades: the *amburbalia* (around the city) and *ambarvalia* (around the fields).⁹ The most important one of the rural processions every year (on April 25) walked along the Via Claudia to a place four miles outside the city. Its purpose was to obtain protection against frost and blight for the field fruits, especially grains. The Roman god responsible for this harvest was a bisexual divinity invoked either as male or female (Robigus, Robigo). He (or she) had the power to send blight upon the grains; and the procession was made to avert his "evil eye" from the fruits of human toil.¹⁰ At the fifth milestone, beyond the Milvian Bridge, was a grove which served as a shrine of Robigus. There the parade stopped, and the *Flamen* (pagan priest) sacrificed a sheep and a rust-colored dog, offering the entrails of these animals to the god. After the "service," young and old celebrated a kind of picnic with games, races, and amusements (some of which were not overly decent). In honor of the god the whole celebration was called *Robigalia*.¹¹

Christianity had no quarrel with the motive of such a procession (prayer for protection of the harvest) or with its traditional date and route. Thus, when the empire turned Christian in the fourth century and the pagan celebrations died a natural death, the Church took over this traditional observance, as a Christian rite, to pray for God's protection and blessing upon the fields. The pope with his clergy and a great crowd of people marched in solemn procession along the same route. They chanted the litany and repeated every invocation. After crossing the Milvian Bridge they did not, however, proceed to the place where the shrine of Robigus had been, but turned back and wended their way along the Tiber to the church of St. Peter at the Vatican. There the pope offered the Holy Sacrifice, and the multitude attended.¹²

When and how, after the pagan observance had stopped, the Church started this annual procession is not known. The first definite information is given in a sermon of Pope Gregory the Great (604), who called it a *Litania Major* (Greater Litany); and he speaks of the "return of this annual solemnity," which proves that it already was a traditional feature in his day.[13]

The name *litania major* was originally given to a number of solemn processions in Rome (such as those on April 25 and Ember Fridays).[14] Only later was it applied exclusively to the procession of April 25, and this term has remained in the liturgy ever since. There is no connection between the Major Litany and the Feast of Saint Mark the Evangelist, which is celebrated on the same day. The litany is of much earlier date, for the Feast of Saint Mark was not introduced until the ninth century.[15]

Shortly after the beginning of the Middle Ages, the Major Litany was adopted by other parts of the ancient empire, but not everywhere on the same date. It was only during the ninth and tenth centuries that the Roman date and ritual became those usually accepted. For the Frankish empire the observance in the Roman manner was prescribed by the Council of Aachen, in 836.[16] Today the liturgical books use the plural form in all cases, both for the prayers and the processions.[17]

THE MINOR LITANIES · In 470, during a time of unusual calamities (storms, floods, earthquakes), Bishop Mamertus of Vienne in Gaul originated an annual observance of penitential exercises for the three days before the Feast of the Ascension. With the cooperation of the civil authorities he decreed that the faithful abstain from servile work and that this triduum be held as a time of penance, with prayer and fasting. He also prescribed penitential processions (litanies) for each one of the three days. Thus the name "litanies" was given to the whole celebration.[18]

Very soon the other bishops of Gaul adopted the new observance. At the beginning of the sixth century it started spreading into neighboring countries. In 511 the Council of Orléans prescribed it for the Frankish (Merovingian) part of France.[19] The Diocese of Milan accepted the litanies, but held them in the week before Pentecost.[20] In Spain they were observed in the sixth century during the week after Pentecost.[21] The Council of Mainz (813) introduced them to the German part of the Frankish empire.[22]

Meanwhile, Rome had declined for centuries to adopt this custom because its liturgical character did not agree with the ancient practice of the Roman Church which excluded penitential rites on all days between Easter and Pentecost. Charlemagne and the Frankish bishops, however, urged Pope Leo III (816) to incorporate these litanies into the Roman liturgy.[23] The pope finally consented to a compromise: the observance of the fast was rescinded, but the penitential procession was approved. As Mass text, the formula of the Major Litany from the Roman liturgical books was taken. This approval was originally made only as an exception, for the litanies were not intended by Leo III as an established annual rite.[24] In return for the concession, the Frankish Church decreed, at the Council of Aachen (836), that these "minor litanies" should be held according to the Roman decision (without fast).[25]

During the subsequent centuries, however, the custom of holding these litanies became definitely established, even at Rome, as an annual feature of the liturgical year; it has remained so ever since in the whole Latin Church, and is now celebrated everywhere on the three days before the Feast of the Ascension. A memorable exception has been made recently: Pope Pius XII granted to some Catholic missions in the Pacific Islands the permission to celebrate both the major and minor litanies in October or November.[26]

NAMES · The litanies held on each one of the three days before the Feast of the Ascension are called "minor" because, in the Roman liturgy, they are of younger date than the Major Litany on April 25. In the early centuries they were also called "Gallican Litanies," because of their origin in Gaul.[27] The Major Litany was named "Roman" or "Gregorian" (after Gregory the Great, who first mentioned it). The popular term "Rogation Days" originated in the High Middle Ages. Another popular name, mostly used in central Europe, is "Cross Days" (from the crucifix that is carried in front of the procession).[28]

LITURGY

LATIN RITE · The Rogation Days are unique through their penitential nature (purple vestments, no Gloria) within the jubilant Easter season. Even the Major Litany, which in ancient times was a festive observance of joyful petition and confidence, became assimilated after the beginning of the tenth century, acquiring this note of mourning and penance.[29]

In the chanting of the litanies each invocation is repeated twice, first by the cantors, then by the people (choir). Some scholars explain this custom as a relic of the *Litania Septiformis* (Procession in Seven Columns) from the time of Pope Gregory the Great, who initiated this particular type of litany.[30] Another feature of the ancient Major Litany was the antiphons, which the cantors sang at the start of the procession. They unfortunately were discontinued centuries ago, so they are no longer found in our liturgical books.[31]

The litany used to lead directly into the Mass (as it still does on the vigil of Easter). The Rogation Mass, therefore, had neither Introit nor Kyrie of its own, but the priest concluded the litany by singing a Collect which also served as oration (prayer) of the Mass. The ten Collects used now in the litany are of later date, when the procession was severed from the Mass and held as a separate and isolated rite.[32]

There is no obligation now to conduct a procession. However, the rubrics of the Divine Office prescribe that on Rogation Days all those who are obliged to say the breviary must recite the Litanies of All Saints (with the psalm and prayers following it) whenever they have missed them before Mass.[33]

The Rogations must be commemorated in other Masses on Rogation Days (for instance, in the Mass of Saint Mark the Evangelist). If April 25 should happen to be Easter Sunday, the litanies are transferred to Tuesday in Easter week; apart from this exception, they are always to be held on their liturgical dates even if some other great feast should fall on one of their days.[34]

ORIENTAL RITES · Most of the Oriental Churches keep a triduum of fast and penitential prayer, comparable to the Rogations, shortly before the beginning of Lent. In the Greek Rite it is called the "Fast of Adam" in honor of the first law of abstinence which God gave to Adam and Eve in Paradise (Genesis 2, 17), and in preparation for the coming strict fast of Lent. About the same time of the year, the Syrians, Chaldeans, and Copts cele-

brate a three days' penitential season of prayer and fasting which
they call the "Fast of Indiction" (because God indicts man, and
punishes him through natural calamities) or "Fast of the Nine-
vites" (because the people of Nineveh averted God's punishment
through prayer and fasting; see Jonas 3, 5-10). The Armenians
term it *Aratshavor-atz,* which means "precursor" (a fast coming
before Lent).³⁵

FOLKLORE

RELIGIOUS OBSERVANCE · In the rural sections of Catholic countries the Rogations are still held in their full and original significance with many features of external solemnity. The church bells
ring while the procession slowly wends its way through the town
and out into the open. Religious banners are carried, the litanies
are chanted by choir and people, and the priest sprinkles the
fields, gardens, and orchards with holy water. After returning
to the church, a sermon is preached and the High Mass of the
Rogations is celebrated. Later in the day some time is spent by
many farmers with private little prayer processions around their
own homestead. Reciting traditional prayers, the whole family
asks for God's blessing upon house, barns, stables, and fields.³⁶

In some places the Rogations are held in a way that is strongly
reminiscent of the *Litania Septiformis* of ancient times. The inhabitants of villages surrounding some city or town will proceed
from their own churches in separate processions and converge
toward the big church of the city for the sermon and High Mass.
Afterward a market or fair is ready to serve their temporal needs
and interests.

The purpose and liturgy of the Rogations has for many centuries, up to our time, inspired a great number of semiliturgical
imitations and repetitions of its rite in the manifold smaller
processions which are held all through the summer months in
countless places of Europe. These prayer processions are customary whenever the harvest is in danger from frost, floods, hail,
drought, or the like.³⁷ Other such processions are steady features
of religious observance, and their main purpose is to pray for
the right kind of weather—a most important item on the prayer
list of agricultural populations.³⁸ In many sections of Europe a

"weather procession" is held around the church on every Sunday. Usually the priest sings the prologue of Saint John's Gospel (1, 1-14), which from the High Middle Ages has been considered as conferring a powerful blessing against all harmful trends of nature.[39]

PRE-CHRISTIAN ELEMENTS · The pre-Christian lore of averting harm from fields and homes by the magic power of "walking around" them (*circumambulatio, ambitus* in Latin and *umbigang* in old Germanic) still survives in many superstitious customs among the rural populations of Europe.[40] At the seasons of the year when the demons roam (before the winter solstice, on Walpurgis Night, around the middle of June, at Halloween), girls or young men must circle the fields and orchards, sometimes during the night and in a rhythmic dance step. Before Christmas the farmer goes around his buildings with incense and holy water. He must be careful to complete the round walk; otherwise "the blessing would not take hold." Here also belongs the superstition held in many places that visitors should leave the home by the same door through which they came (to "close the circle") in order to avoid misfortune and harm.[41]

---

[1] F. Cabrol, *Litanies,* DACL, 9.2 (1930), 1540 ff.   [2] Schuster, II, 359.   [3] CIC, 1259, 2.   [4] Jgn MS, I, 412 ff.   [5] Nilles, I, LXIII (*Ektenés*).   [6] J. A. Jungmann, *Beiträge zur Geschichte der Gebetsliturgie,* VII, ZKTh, 73 (1951), 347 ff.   [7] Can. 27; Mansi, 8, 355.   [8] Kellner, 189 ff.   [9] PW, I, 1796 (*Ambarvalia*), 1816 (*Amburbium*).   [10] M. T. Varro, *Antiquitates, De Rust.,* I, 1, 6.   [11] PW, IA.1, 949 ff.   [12] TE, I, 660.   [13] Letter without address; PL, 27, 1327.   [14] H. Grisar, *Das Römische Sacramentar,* ZKTh, 9 (1885), 585 ff.   [15] Kellner, 300.   [16] Cap. II, Can. 10; Mansi, 14, 678.   [17] H. Leclercq, *Procession de Saint Marc,* DACL, 10.2 (1932), 1740 ff.   [18] Gregory of Tours, *Historia Francorum* 2, 34; PL, 71, 231 ff.; Sidon. Apoll., *Epist.* 1; PL, 58, 563.   [19] Can. 27; Mansi, 8, 355.   [20] Kellner, 193.   [21] *Concil. Gerund.,* Can. 2; Mansi, 8, 549.   [22] Can. 33; Mansi, 14, 72.   [23] LE, 164.   [24] Schuster, II, 371.   [25] See note 16.   [26] W. van Bekkum, "The Liturgical Revival in the Service of the Missions," AP, 108.   [27] F. Cabrol, *Rogations,* DACL, 14.2 (1948), 2459 ff.   [28] OiT, 110.   [29] Schuster, II, 356.   [30] DACL, 10.2 (1932), 1740 (*Litania Septiformis*).   [31] Schuster, II,

358 (text of these ancient antiphons). [32] Schuster, II, 366. [33] BR, April 25 (*S. Marci Evangelistae*), rubric at the end. [34] MR, April 25 (*S. Marci Evangelistae*), rubric before Mass text. [35] Nilles, II, 6-11, 51, 646, 697. [36] OiT, 104 ff. (*Die drei Bittage vor Christi Himmelfahrt*). [37] B. Scholz, "The Sacramentals in Agriculture," OF, 5 (1931), 323 ff. [38] Franz, II, 71. [39] Jgn MS, II, 543. [40] Franz, II, 7, 68. [41] Koren, 129 ff.

PART II

Advent

HISTORY

ORIGIN · The celebration of Christ's nativity on December 25 was introduced as a special feast in Rome about the middle of the fourth century. It quickly spread through the Roman Empire of the West, and by the fifth century was already established in Gaul and Spain. Since it was one of the main feasts of the Christian year, a spiritual preparation soon began to be held. From the Church in Gaul comes the first news about a definite period prescribed for this preparation. Bishop Perpetuus of Tours (490) issued the regulation that a fast should be held on three days of every week from the Feast of Saint Martin (November 11) to Christmas.[1] The name Advent was not yet used for this preparatory period; it was called *Quadragesima Sancti Martini* (Forty Days' Fast of Saint Martin's).[2]

This practice of keeping a penitential season before Christmas spread all through France, Spain, and later also to Germany. The fast, however, was started at different times (September 24, November 1 or 11 or 14, December 1). For Mass texts on the weekdays of Advent the Church in Gaul simply used the Masses of Lent.[3]

In Rome the celebration of Advent originated considerably later, during the sixth century. There the season comprised only four or five Sundays. Pope Gregory the Great (604) preached a number of homilies on Advent.[4] Unlike the Gallic Church, Rome had no established fast (except, of course, in Ember week). Advent in Rome was a festive and joyful time of preparation for the Feast of the Lord's Nativity, without penitential character.[5]

When, in the eighth century, the Frankish Church accepted the Roman liturgy, the nonpenitential Advent of Rome clashed with the penitential observance of the much longer Gallic Advent. After a few centuries of vacillation there emerged a final structure of Advent celebration which combined features of both traditions. Rome adopted the fast and penitential character from the Gallic observance, while the Roman tradition of a four weeks' Advent and the Roman liturgical texts prevailed over the ancient Gallic custom of a seven or nine weeks' celebration. This compromise was completed in the thirteenth century. From that time, the liturgical observance of Advent has remained practically unchanged.[6]

FAST · The law of Advent fast was never as strict as that of Lent. It varied widely in different sections, both in content and in time. In most cases people were obliged to fast three days a week and to abstain from certain foods. Bishop Burchard of Worms (1025), for instance, issued the following regulation: "In the Quadragesima before Christmas you must abstain from wine, ale, honey-beer, meats, fats, cheese, and from fat fish." [7]

According to the penitential practice of those centuries, the faithful were also bound to abstain from weddings, amusements, pleasure travel, and from conjugal relations during the time of fasting.[8]

This observance of Advent fasting came from the North to Rome at the end of the first millennium. There it was quickly adopted by most monasteries, later also by the authorities of the Church, and finally prescribed for all the faithful. A letter of Pope Innocent III (1216) shows that in his time it already was a traditional part of the Advent celebration in Rome.[9] In subsequent centuries the obligation was gradually lessened by papal indults, the fast usually being restricted to two days a week (for example, Friday and Saturday in Italy, Wednesday and Friday in Austria), until the new Code of Canon Law (1918) completely abrogated it and only kept the fast of Ember week and of the Christmas vigil (and, lately, the vigil fast of the Immaculate Conception, December 7).

ORIENTAL CHURCHES · The Eastern Churches do not keep a liturgical season in preparation for Christmas, but they observe a fast. In the Byzantine Rite this fast has been customary from the eighth century. It begins on November 15 and lasts till Christmas. Its name is "Quadragesima of Saint Philip" (*Tessaran-themeron Philippou*) because it starts on the day after the Feast of the Apostle Philip. The Syrians of the Antiochene Rite also have a fast of forty days before Christmas, but the Catholic Syrians keep it, by papal indult, only for the last nine days before the Nativity. The Armenians now celebrate a fast of three weeks (instead of the original seven weeks), at the beginning, in the middle, and at the end of Advent. (Their Advent starts at the middle of November and runs until Epiphany.) The Copts, too, observe a fast, which is very strict, from November 24 (in upper Egypt) or from December 9 (in lower Egypt) until the Feast of the Nativity (which they celebrate on Epiphany). The Syro-Chaldeans begin their "Fast of the Nativity" or "Fast of the Annunciation" at the middle of November or, in some dioceses, on the Sunday nearest to December 1.[10]

LITURGY

SEASONAL CHARACTER · The liturgy of Advent is wanting in that harmony and unity which characterize the other seasons of the ecclesiastical year. Its features present a somewhat confused and unfinished aspect. Three factors are responsible for this. First, Gregory the Great, who had shaped the basic structure of the Roman Advent with the sure hand of an inspired leader, did not fill out the details himself.[11] Second, the original form of the Roman celebration was mixed and molded with the Gallic features into a "unit" that contained two somewhat opposite trends of thought (a season of joy and, at the same time, a season of penance). Finally, after the combination was made, no master appeared who could have shaped these elements into a celebration of unified harmony. Instead, the structure was prevented from further growth and development and preserved without change through the past centuries up to the present.[12]

Thus, to give but a few examples, Advent has no ferial Masses, as Lent has, but on "free" days the Sunday Mass is repeated. It has no preface of its own, but must continue (on Sundays) the preface of the Holy Trinity, which does not actually fit the season. (Lent, on the other hand, has two fitting seasonal prefaces.) In Advent the liturgy of the season must bow on most days to feasts of saints, while in Lent only March 19 and 25 take obligatory precedence. The orations in Advent express various trends and perspectives. Some of them speak of the coming of the Saviour at His birth, others of His coming at the end of time, and others again of a coming into the hearts of the faithful. Similarly, some lessons and Gospels clearly reveal the purpose of joyful preparation for Christmas, while others treat of the end of the world and the second coming of the Lord, not in the apostolic sense of jubilant expectation, but with the note of salutary fear and admonition to penance. In the Masses of the season (Sundays) the Gloria is omitted, and so is the *Te Deum* in the Divine Office; but the Alleluia is retained, and the third Sunday (*Gaudete*) bears a special character of joy.[13]

JOY AND PENANCE · In Rome, for almost a thousand years Advent was celebrated as a season of joyous preparation for the Feast of the Lord's Nativity.[14]

The Gospel of the first Sunday in Advent (Luke 21, 25-33), speaking of the end of the world, did not pertain to the original liturgy of Advent. Gregory the Great used it on a certain occasion when, at the end of November, a great storm had devastated Rome and killed many people. (Its descriptions read like modern reports of a hurricane.)[15] The pope wanted to console the people and explain to them the meaning of such natural catastrophes, hence he took the Gospel text that begins "And there will be signs in the sun and moon and stars, and upon earth distress of nations." After the reading of this Gospel, he preached a homily on it. Now the fact that the pope had used this particular passage on a Sunday around the beginning of December was duly noted in the manual of the Roman Church. In later times it was mistakenly assumed that Gregory had intended it as a regular Advent text, and thus it appeared in the Roman Missal as Gospel of an Advent Mass.[16]

As late as the beginning of the twelfth century the liturgical books of St. Peter's in Rome show the use of festive vestments, of the Gloria in the Mass and the *Te Deum* in the Divine Office for Advent. By the middle of the same century, however, the Frankish influence had caused the Roman authorities to make the change from a season of joy to one of penance: Gloria and *Te Deum* were dropped, and Advent soon acquired the traditional marks of a season of penance, similar to Lent. The color of liturgical vestments then was black (later changed to purple), the dalmatic (deacon's vestment) was prohibited because it represented a "gown of joy," celebration of weddings and organ playing in church were forbidden, and various penitential features were introduced into the Divine Office. In some places the sacred images were even veiled with purple cloth as they were in Lent.[17]

On the other hand, all these changes toward a penitential aspect remained more or less on the surface, for its innermost liturgical character distinguishes Advent very sharply from Lent. The texts of the Roman Missal, despite occasional motives of fear, penance, and trembling (which had been added from the Frankish liturgy), kept its basic note of joyful expectation of Christ's birth. Thus the liturgists, from the twelfth century on, have found no simple unity in the celebration of Advent, but have had to explain its character by a diversity of purposes. William Duranti (1296), Archbishop of Ravenna, one of the first to analyze the liturgical significance of Advent, expressed it in a formula which since then has been repeated in many books: Advent is partly a time of joy (in expectation of the Saviour's nativity) and partly a season of mourning and penance (in expectation of the judgment on the Last Day).[18]

SIGNIFICANCE · The name Advent (Coming) originally was used for the coming of Christ in His birth and was thus applied to Christmas only. After the sixth century various preachers and writers expanded its meaning to include the whole preparatory season, in the sense in which the word is now used. In the twelfth century it came to be interpreted as representing a two- or threefold "Advent" of Christ: His past coming, in Bethlehem; His future coming, at the end of time; and His present coming, through grace in the hearts of men.[19]

The present penitential character of Advent, although not consonant with the original celebration in Rome, still usefully fits the purpose of the season. By a spirit of humble penance and contrition we should prepare ourselves for a worthy and fruitful celebration of the great Feast of the Nativity. This penance is not as harsh as that of Lent—there is no prescribed fast— and the joyful note of the season helps people to perform penitential exercises in a mood of happy spiritual toil, to "make ready the way of the Lord" (Matthew 3, 3).[20]

THE SECOND COMING · There actually is a season of the year in which the Church draws our minds and hearts to the second coming of Christ. This season extends over the end of the ecclesiastical year through Advent and up to Epiphany. After having celebrated the events of the Lord's life on earth, His birth, Passion, resurrection, and ascension, and also the descent of the Holy Spirit and the life of Christ in His Mystical Body, the Church finally puts before our eyes a magnificent vision of eternal glory and reward: in the Lord Himself (Feast of Christ, the King), in His members who have already passed from this world (All Saints and All Souls), and in the events at the end of time when the remaining elect will be gathered into their glory (Gospel of the twenty-fourth Sunday after Pentecost; Matthew 24, 15-35).[21] Thus the ecclesiastical year, like a majestic symphony, ends on the powerful and triumphant strains of a final victory, not yet obtained by all, but assured and certain for those who remain "faithful unto death" (Apocalypse 2, 10). Then follows, in Advent, the thought of our own spiritual preparation for this glorious coming of the Lord at the end of time, and the humble security of our hope that His last coming will be consoling and joyful, just as His coming and His manifestation was in the first Christmas and the first Epiphany at Bethlehem.

FOLKLORE

THE ADVENT WREATH · The Advent wreath originated a few hundred years ago among the Lutherans of eastern Germany.[22] It probably was suggested by one of the many light symbols which were used in folklore at the end of November and beginning of December. At that season of the year our pre-Christian forefathers began to celebrate the month of Yule (December) with the burning of lights and fires.[23] The Christians in medieval times kept many of these light and fire symbols alive as popular traditions of ancient folklore. In the sixteenth century the custom started of using such lights as a religious symbol of Advent in the houses of the faithful. This practice quickly spread among the Protestants of eastern Germany and was soon accepted by Protestants and Catholics in other parts of the country.[24] Recently it has not only found its way to America, but has been spreading so rapidly that it is already a cherished custom in many homes.

The Advent wreath is exactly what the word implies, a wreath of evergreens (yew or fir or laurel), made in various sizes. It is either suspended from the ceiling or placed on a table, usually in front of the family shrine. Fastened to the wreath are four candles standing upright, at equal distances. These candles represent the four weeks of Advent.[25]

Daily at a certain time (usually in the evening), the family gathers for a short religious exercise. Every Sunday of Advent one more candle is lit, until all four candles shed their cheerful light to announce the approaching birthday of the Lord. All other lights are extinguished in the room, and only the gentle glow of the live candles illuminates the darkness. After some prayers, which are recited for the grace of a good and holy preparation for Christmas, the family sings one of the traditional Advent hymns or a song in honor of Mary.

The traditional symbolism of the Advent wreath reminds the faithful of the Old Testament, when humanity was "sitting in darkness and in the shadow of death" (Luke 2, 79); when the prophets, illumined by God, announced the Redeemer; and when the hearts of men glowed with the desire for the Messiah. The wreath—an ancient symbol of victory and glory—symbolizes the "fulfillment of time" in the coming of Christ and the glory of His birth.

In some sections of Europe it is customary for persons with the name of John or Joan to have the first right to light the candles on Advent wreath and Christmas tree, because John the Evangelist starts his Gospel by calling Christ the "Light of the World," and John the Baptist was the first one to see the light of divinity shining about the Lord at His baptism in the Jordan.[26]

CHILDREN'S LETTERS · This is an ancient Advent custom, widespread in Europe, Canada, and South America. When the children go to bed on the eve of St. Nicholas's Day (December 5), they put upon the window sills little notes which they have written or dictated, addressed to the Child Jesus. These letters, containing lists of desired Christmas presents, are supposed to be taken to heaven by Saint Nicholas or by angels. In South America the children write their notes to the "little Jesus" during the days from December 16 to 24 and put them in front of the crib, whence, they believe, angels take them to Heaven during the night.

PREPARING THE MANGER · This custom originated in France but spread to many other countries. It is the practice of having children prepare a soft bedding in the manger by using little wisps of straw as tokens of prayers and good works. Every night the child is allowed to put in the crib one token for each act of devotion or virtue performed. Thus the Christ Child, coming on Christmas Day, finds an ample supply of tender straw to keep Him warm and to soften the hardness of the manger's boards.

ADVENT CALENDARS · Originating in Germany, this custom has of late been spreading widely in other countries. A colored scene of the "Christmas House" printed on a large piece of cardboard is put up at the beginning of December. Every day one "window" of the house is opened by the children, revealing a picture or symbol that points toward the coming Feast of Christmas. Finally, on December 24, the "door" is opened, showing the Nativity scene. These calendars are a useful means of keeping the children's minds pleasantly occupied with the expectation of Christmas and with the spiritual task of preparing their souls for the feast.

NOVENA · In Central and South America, the nine days before Christmas are devoted to a popular novena in honor of the Holy Child (*La Novena del Niño*). In the decorated church, the crib is ready, set up for Christmas; the only figure missing is that of the Child, since the manger is always kept empty until Holy Night. The novena service consists of prayers and carol singing accompanied by popular instruments of the castanet type. After the novena service, the children roam through the streets of the cities and towns, throwing firecrackers and rockets, expressing their delight over the approach of Christmas.[27]

In central Europe the nine days before Christmas are kept in many places as a festive season. Since most of the religious observances were held after dark or before sunrise, people began to call this season the "Golden Nights." In the Alpine sections it is the custom to take a picture of the Blessed Virgin from house to house on these nine evenings (Carrying the Virgin). Every night the family and servants gather before the image, which stands on a table between flowers and burning candles. There they pray and sing hymns in honor of Mary the Expectant Mother. After the devotion, the picture is carried by a young man to a neighboring farm. The whole family, with torches and lanterns, accompanies the image, which is devoutly received and welcomed by its new hosts in front of their house.[28]

Meanwhile, schoolboys carry a statue of Saint Joseph every night to one of their homes. Kneeling before it, they say prayers in honor of the saint. On the first night, only the boy who carried the statue and the one to whose home it was brought perform this devotion. The following nights, as the statue is taken from house to house, the number of boys increases, since all youngsters who had it in their home previously take part in the devotion. On the evening of December 24 all nine of them, accompanied by nine schoolgirls dressed in white, take the image in procession through the town to the church, where they put it up at the Christmas crib. This custom is called *Joseph-stragen* (Carrying Saint Joseph).[29]

ADVENT PLAYS · A peculiar type of Advent play is the German *Herbergsuchen* (Search for an Inn). It is a dramatic rendition of the Holy Family's fruitless efforts to find a shelter in Bethlehem. Joseph and Mary, tired and weary, knock at door after door, humbly asking for a place to stay. Realizing that they are poor, the owners refuse their request with harsh words, until they finally decide to seek shelter in a stable.[30]

Usually the whole performance is sung, and often it is followed by a "happy ending" showing a tableau of the cave with the Nativity scene. There are scores of different versions, depending on the various songs and sketches provided in the text.

A similar custom is the Spanish *Posada* (the Inn), traditional in South American countries, especially Mexico. On an evening between December 16 and 24, several neighboring families gather in one house, where they prepare a shrine, and beside it a crib with all its traditional figures, but the manger is empty. After a procession through the house, pictures of Joseph and Mary are put on the shrine, venerated with prayer and incense, and all present are blessed by a priest. The religious part of the *Posada* is followed by a gay party for the adults, while the children are entertained with the *Piñata*. This is a fragile clay jar, suspended from the ceiling and filled with candy. The children, blindfolded, try to break the jar with a stick so the contents will spill, and everybody then rushes for some of its treasures.[31]

RORATE MASS · In the early mornings of the "Golden Nights," long before sunrise, a special Mass is celebrated in many places of central Europe. It is the votive Mass of the Blessed Virgin for Advent, called *Rorate* from the first words of its text (*Rorate coeli desuper:* Dew of Heaven, shed the Just One). By a special permission of Rome, this Mass may be sung every morning before dawn during the nine days preceding Christmas provided the custom existed in a place from ancient times.[32] The faithful come to the Rorate Mass in large numbers, carrying their lanterns through the dark of the winter morning.[33]

SAINT THOMAS'S DAY · In some parts of central Europe ancient customs of "driving demons aways" are practiced on the Feast of Saint Thomas the Apostle (December 21) and during the following nights (Rough Nights), with much noise, cracking of whips, ringing of hand bells, and parades of figures in horrible masks.[34]

In a Christianized version of this custom farmers will walk through the buildings and around the farmyard, accompanied by a son or one of the farm hands. They carry incense and holy water, which they sprinkle around as they walk. Meanwhile, the rest of the family and servants are gathered in the living room reciting the rosary. This rite is to sanctify and bless the whole farm in preparation for Christmas, to keep all evil spirits away on the festive days, and to obtain God's special protection for the coming year.[35]

CHRISTMAS EVE · Christmas Eve, the last one of the "Golden Nights," is the feast day of our first parents, Adam and Eve. They are commemorated as saints in the calendars of the Eastern Churches (Greeks, Syrians, Copts).[36] Under the influence of this Oriental practice, their veneration spread also in the West and became very popular toward the end of the first millennium of the Christian era. The Latin Church has never officially introduced their feast, though it did not prohibit their popular veneration. In many old churches of Europe their statues may still be seen among the images of saints. Boys and girls who bore the names of Adam and Eve (quite popular names in past centuries) celebrated their "Name Day" with great rejoicing. In Germany the custom began in the sixteenth century of putting up a "Paradise tree" in the homes in honor of the first parents. This was a fir tree laden with apples, and from it developed our modern Christmas tree.[37]

[1] Gregory of Tours, *Historia Francorum*, X, 31, 6; PL, 71, 231 ff. [2] J. A. Jungmann, *Advent und Voradvent*, ZKTh, 61 (1937), 341 ff. [3] *Conc. Matiscon.*, Can. 9; Mansi, 0, 088. [4] *Homil. in Evang.* (1, 6, 7, 29); PL, 76, 1078 ff. [5] Schuster, 1, 320. [6] LE, 169 ff. [7] *Decreta*, 19, 5; PL, 140, 951 ff. [8] DACL, 7.2 (1927), 2492 ff. [9] *Epist.*, 9, 3; PL, 215, 811. [10] Nilles, II, *passim*. [11] DACL, 6.2 (1925), 1776 ff.; on Saint Gregory's reform of the liturgy see also Schuster, I, 39 ff. [12] F. Cabrol, *Advent*, DACL, 1.2 (1924), 3223 ff. [13] See note 2, 369 ff. [14] DACL, 1.2 (1924), 3227. [15] *Sermo* I, 1; PL, 76, 1078 ff. [16] W. Croce, *Die Adventsliturgie*, ZKTh, 76 (1954), 273. [17] See note 2, 373 ff. [18] Dur., VI, 2, 6. [19] See note 16, 469 ff.; Saint Bernard, *Sermo* 3, 4; PL, 183, 45. [20] P. Parsch, "How To Interpret Seasons" (Advent), OF, 22 (1947), 1 ff. [21] See note 2, 387 ff. [22] GH, 1 (1931), 147. [23] Frazer, 638 ("The Midwinter Fires"). [24] See note 22. [25] Koren, 37. [26] RCF, 38 ff. [27] A. A. Marchant, "Christmas in Brazil," in *Bulletin, Pan-American Union*, Washington, December 1936. [28] Koren, 51; Geramb, 202. [29] Koren, 54; Geramb, 203. [30] VL, 144. [31] Crippen, 82 f.; see also NGM, December 1951, 799. [32] SRC, *Decretum*, December 10, 1718. [33] Koren, 35. [34] Geramb, 211. [35] VL, 148 f. [36] Nilles, II, 541 ff.; Spamer, 74. [37] Spamer, 73 ff. (picture opposite p. 92).

CHAPTER

6 *Feast of the Nativity*

HISTORY

ORIGIN · In the Roman Empire it was a general custom to celebrate the birthdays of rulers (see Matthew 14, 6) and of other
outstanding persons. Such birthdays often were publicly honored
even after the death of the individual. The day of the celebration
did not always coincide with the actual date of birth. The birthday of Plato, for instance, used to be celebrated on a feast of
the god Apollo.[1]

The early Christians, who attributed to Christ not only the
title (*Kyrios*) but also many other honors that the pagans paid
to their "divine" emperors, naturally felt inclined to honor the
birth of the Saviour. In most places the commemoration of
Christ's birth was included in the Feast of the Epiphany (Manifestations) on January 6, one of the oldest annual feasts.

Soon after the end of the last great persecution, about the year
330, the Church in Rome definitely assigned December 25 for the
celebration of the birth of Christ. For a while, many Eastern
Churches continued to keep other dates, but toward the end of
the fourth century the Roman custom became universal.[2]

No official reason has been handed down in ecclesiastical documents for the choice of this date. Consequently, various explanations have been given to justify the celebration of the Lord's
nativity on this particular day. Some early Fathers and writers
claimed that December 25 was the actual date of Christ's birth,
and that the authorities in Rome established this fact from the
official records of the Roman census that had been taken at the
time of the Saviour's birth. Saint John Chrysostom held this

opinion and used it to argue for the introduction of the Roman date in the Eastern Church.[3] He was mistaken, however, for nobody in Rome ever claimed that the records of the census of Cyrinus were extant there in the fourth century, and much less that Christ's birthday was registered in the lists.[4] In fact, it was expressly stated in Rome that the actual date of the Saviour's birth was unknown and that different traditions prevailed in different parts of the world.[5]

A second explanation was of theological-symbolic character. Since the Bible calls the Messiah the "Sun of Justice" (Malachi 4, 2), it was argued that His birth had to coincide with the beginning of a new solar cycle, that is, He had to be born at the time of the winter solstice. A confirmation of this opinion was sought in the Bible, by way of reckoning six months from the annunciation of John the Baptist (which was assumed to have happened on September 24) and thus arriving at March 25 as the day of the Incarnation. Nine months later, on December 25, would then be the birthday of the Lord. This explanation, though attractive in itself, depends on too many assumptions that cannot be proved and lacks any basis of historical certitude.[6]

There remains then this explanation, which is the most probable one, and held by most scholars in our time: the choice of December 25 was influenced by the fact that the Romans, from the time of Emperor Aurelian (275), had celebrated the feast of the sun god (*Sol Invictus:* the Unconquered Sun) on that day.[7] December 25 was called the "Birthday of the Sun," and great pagan religious celebrations of the Mithras cult were held all through the empire.[8] What was more natural than that the Christians celebrate the birth of Him Who was the "Light of the World" and the true "Sun of Justice" on this very day? The popes seem to have chosen December 25 precisely for the purpose of inspiring the people to turn from the worship of a material sun to the adoration of Christ the Lord. This thought is indicated in various writings of contemporary authors.[9]

It has sometimes been said that the Nativity is only a "Christianized pagan festival." However, the Christians of those early centuries were keenly aware of the difference between the two festivals—one pagan and one Christian—on the same day. The coincidence in the date, even if intended, does not make the two celebrations identical. Some newly converted Christians who thoughtlessly retained external symbols of the sun worship on Christmas Day were immediately and sternly reproved by their religious superiors, and those abuses were suppressed.[10] Proof of this are the many examples of warnings in the writings of Tertullian (third century) and the Christian authors of the fourth and fifth centuries, especially the sermons of Saint Augustine (430) and Pope Leo I (461).[11]

The error of confusing Yule (solstice) and Christmas (the "Mass of Christ"), as if both celebrations had a common origin, occurs even in our time. Expressions like "Christmas originated four thousand years ago," "the pagan origins of Christmas," and similar misleading phrases have only added to the confusion. While it is certainly true that some popular features and symbols of our Christmas celebration in the home had their origin in pre-Christian Yuletide customs, Christmas itself—the feast, its meaning and message—is in no way connected with any pagan mythology or Yule rite.

Christmas soon became a feast of such great importance that from the fifth century on it marked the beginning of the ecclesiastical year. After the tenth century, however, the season of Advent came to form an integral part of the Christmas cycle; thus the beginning of the ecclesiastical year was advanced to the first Sunday of Advent.[12]

Emperor Theodosius, in 425, forbade the cruel circus games on Christmas Day, and Emperor Justinian, in 529, prohibited work and public business by declaring Christmas a civic holiday. The Council of Agde (506) urged all Christians to receive Holy Communion on the feast.[13] The Council of Tours (567) proclaimed the twelve days from Christmas to Epiphany as a sacred and festive season, and established the duty of Advent fasting in preparation for the feast.[14] The Council of Braga (563) forbade fasting on Christmas Day.[15] Thus the groundwork was laid for a joyful celebration of the Lord's nativity, not only in the house of God but also in the hearts and homes of the people.

MIDDLE AGES · The great religious pioneers and missionaries who brought Christianity to the pagan tribes of Europe also introduced the celebration of Christmas. It came to Ireland through

Saint Patrick (461), to England through Saint Augustine of Canterbury (604), to Germany through Saint Boniface (754). The Irish monks Saint Columban (615) and Saint Gall (646) introduced it into Switzerland and western Austria; the Scandinavians received it through Saint Ansgar (865). To the Slavic tribes it was brought by their apostles, the brothers Saint Cyril (869) and Saint Methodius (885); to Hungary by Saint Adalbert (997).

Most of these saints were the first bishops of the countries they converted and as such they established and regulated the celebration of the Nativity. In England, Saint Augustine observed it with great solemnity. On Christmas Day in 598, he baptized more than ten thousand Britons.[16] In Germany, the observance of Christmas festivities was officially regulated by a synod in Mainz in 813.[17]

By about the year 1100, all the nations of Europe had accepted Christianity, and Christmas was celebrated everywhere with great devotion and joy. The period from the twelfth to the sixteenth centuries was the peak of a general Christian celebration of the Nativity, not only in churches and monasteries, but in homes as well. It was a time of inspiring and colorful religious services. Carols and Christmas plays were written. It was at this period, too, that most of the delightful Christmas customs of each country were introduced. Some have since died out; others have changed slightly through the ages; many have survived to our day. A few practices had to be suppressed as being improper and scandalous, such as the customs of dancing and mumming in church, the "Boy Bishop's Feast," the "Feast of the Ass," New Year's fires, superstitious (pagan) meals, impersonations of the Devil, and irreverent carols.[18]

DECLINE · With the Reformation in the sixteenth century there naturally came a sharp change in the Christmas celebration for many countries in Europe. The Sacrifice of the Mass—the very soul of the feast—was suppressed. The Holy Eucharist, the liturgy of the Divine Office, the sacramentals and ceremonies all disappeared. So did the colorful and inspiring processions, the veneration of the Blessed Virgin Mary and the saints. In many countries all that remained of the once rich and glorious religious festival

was a sermon and a prayer service on Christmas Day.[19] Although
the people kept many of their customs alive, the deep religious
inspiration was missing, and consequently the "new" Christmas
turned more and more into a feast of good-natured reveling.

On the other hand, some groups, including the German Lutherans, preserved a tender devotion to the Christ Child and
celebrated Christmas in a deeply spiritual way within their
churches, hearts, and homes.[20]

In England the Puritans condemned even the reduced religious
celebration that was held in the Anglican Church after the
separation from Rome. They were determined to abolish Christmas altogether, both as a religious and as a popular feast. It was
their contention that no feast of human institution should ever
outrank the Sabbath (Sunday); and as Christmas was the most
important of the non-Sunday festivals, they directed against it
all their attacks of fierce indignation. Pamphlets were published
denouncing Christmas as pagan, and its observance was declared
to be sinful. In this anti-Christmas campaign these English sects
were much encouraged by the example of similar groups in Scotland, where the celebration of the feast was forbidden as early
as 1583, and punishment inflicted on all persons observing it.[21]

When the Puritans finally came to political power in England,
they immediately proceeded to outlaw Christmas. The year 1642
saw the first ordinances issued forbidding church services and
civic festivities on Christmas Day. In 1644, the monthly day of
fast and penance was appointed for December 25.[22] The people,
however, paid scant attention to these orders, and continued
their celebrations. There was thus inaugurated a great campaign
of two years' duration (1645-1647). Speeches, pamphlets and
other publications, sermons and discussions were directed against
the celebration of Christmas, calling it "antichrist-Mass, idolatry,
abomination," and similar names. Following this barrage of
propaganda, Parliament on June 3, 1647, ordained that the Feast
of Christmas (and other holidays) should no longer be observed
under pain of punishment. On December 24, 1652, an act of
Parliament again reminded the public that "no observance shall
be had on the five-and-twentieth of December, commonly called
Christmas day; nor any solemnity used or exercised in churches
in respect thereof." [23]

Each year, by order of Parliament, town criers went through the streets a few days before Christmas, reminding their fellow citizens that "Christmas day and all other superstitious festivals" should not be observed, that market should be kept and stores remain open on December 25.[24]

During the year 1647 popular riots broke out in various places against the law suppressing Christmas, especially in London, Oxford, Ipswich, Canterbury, and the whole county of Kent. In Oxford there was a "world of skull-breaking"; in Ipswich the festival was celebrated "with some loss of life"; in Canterbury "the mob mauled the mayor, broke all his windows as well as his bones, and put fire to his doorsteps."[25] An ominous note was sounded against the republican Commonwealth at a meeting of ten thousand men from Kent and Canterbury who passed a solemn resolution saying that "if they could not have their Christmas day, they would have the King back on his throne again."[26]

The government, however, stood firm and proceeded to break up Christmas celebrations by force of arms. People were arrested in many instances but were not punished beyond a few hours in jail.[27] Anglican ministers who decorated their churches and held service on Christmas Day were removed from their posts and replaced by men of softer fiber.[28] Slowly and relentlessly, the external observance of Christmas was extinguished. December 25 became a common workday, and business went on as usual. But in spite of these repressive measures many people still celebrated the day with festive meals and merriment in the privacy of their homes.

REVIVAL IN ENGLAND · When the old Christmas eventually returned with the restoration of the monarchy in 1660, it was actually a "new" Christmas. The spiritual aspect of the feast was now left mostly to the care of the ministers in the church service on Christmas Day. What was observed in the home consisted of a more shallow celebration in the form of various nonreligious amusements and of general reveling.[29] Instead of the old carols in praise of the Child of Bethlehem, the English people observed Christmas with rollicking songs in praise of "plum pudding, goose, capon, minced pie and roast beef."[30] However, a spirit of good will to all and of generosity to the poor ennobled these more worldly celebrations of the great religious feast. Two famous descriptions of this kind of popular celebration are found in Charles Dickens's *A Christmas Carol* and in Washington Irving's *Sketch Book*.

The singing of hymns and carols, which had been suppressed by the Puritans, found only a slow and restricted revival in England. Even as late as 1823, an English collector of Christmas lore, William Hone (1842), wrote in his *Ancient Mysteries* that carols were considered as "something past" and had no place in the nineteenth century.[31] Meanwhile, a few religious carols had been written and soon became favorites among the English-speaking people. The most famous of these are "While shepherds watched their flocks by night" (Nahum Tate, 1715) and "Hark the herald angels sing" (Charles Wesley, 1788).

CHRISTMAS IN AMERICA · To the North American continent the Christmas celebration was brought by the missionaries and settlers from the various European nations. The Spaniards established it in their possessions in the sixteenth century, the French in Canada in the seventeenth century. The feast was celebrated with all the splendor of liturgical solemnity and with the traditional customs of the respective nationalities in Florida, on the shores of the Gulf of Mexico, in Canada, and in the territory of the present State of Michigan.

In the colonies of New England, however, the unfortunate and misdirected zeal of the Puritans against Christmas persisted far into the nineteenth century. Christmas remained outlawed until the second half of the last century.[32]

The Pilgrim fathers worked as usual on their first Christmas Day in America (1620), although they observed the most rigid Sabbath rest on the preceding day, which was Sunday.[33] December 25 until 1856 was a common workday in Boston, and those who refused to go to work on Christmas Day were often dismissed. In New England, factory owners would change the starting hours on Christmas Day to five o'clock in order that workers who wanted to attend a church service would have to forego it or else be dismissed for being late for work. As late as 1870, classes were held in the public schools of Boston on Christmas Day, and any pupil who stayed at home to observe the feast was gravely punished, even shamed by public dismissal.[34]

It was not until immigrants from Ireland and from continental Europe arrived in large numbers toward the middle of the last century that Christmas in America began to flourish. The Germans brought the Christmas tree. They were soon joined by the Irish, who contributed the ancient Gaelic custom of putting lights in the windows. All Catholic immigrants, of course, brought the crib, their native carols and hymns, the three Masses on Christmas Day, and the religious obligation of attending Mass and abstaining from work on the Feast of the Nativity.[35]

Very soon their neighbors, charmed by these unusual but attractive innovations, followed their example and made many of these customs their own. For some years, however, many clergymen continued to warn their congregations against celebrating Christmas with these "new" customs. But eventually a powerful surge of enthusiasm from people of all faiths swept resistance away. New Englanders especially were so won over by this friendly, charming way of celebrating Christmas that a revival of deeper and richer observance followed in many of their churches. One by one, the best of the old traditions were lovingly studied, revived, and became again common practice. Catholics and Protestants co-operated, uniting in a sincere effort to restore the beauties of a truly Christian celebration of the Nativity.[36]

NAMES AND GREETING

LITURGICAL NAMES · The original Latin names for Christmas are: *Festum Nativitatis Domini Nostri Jesu Christi* (the Feast of the Nativity of Our Lord Jesus Christ) and the shorter form, *Dies Natalis Domini* (the Birthday of Our Lord).

From these Latin names most nations obtained their popular terms for the Christmas feast: *Il Natale* in Italy, *La Navidad* in Spain, *Natal* in Portugal, *Nadal* in southern France, *Nadolig* in Wales (and probably the Gaelic *Nollaig*, as well). The Greek *Genethlia* means "Nativity," as do the names for Christmas in Hungarian (*Karácsony*) and in most of the Slavic languages: *Boze Narodzenie* (God's Birth) in Polish; *Rozhdestvo Khrista* (Christ's Birth) in Russian and Ukrainian.[37]

The French word *Noël* can be explained as either coming from the Latin *natalis* (birthday) or from the word *nowel* which means "news." In an old English Christmas verse the angel says:

> *I come from hevin to tell*
> *The best nowellis that ever befell.*

It is possible that both explanations are right. *Noël* and *nowel* may be words of different origin that have become identical in meaning because they are pronounced the same.[38]

POPULAR NAMES · The English word Christmas is based on the same pattern as the old names for other feast days in the liturgical year, such as Michaelmas, Martinmas, Candlemas. The first mention of the name, "Christes Maesse," dates from the year 1038. It means "the Mass of Christ." The English nation (as did all Christian nations at the time) acknowledged the Sacrifice of the Mass as the most important part of the Christmas celebration. For instance, the word in the Dutch language was *Kersmis* (the Mass of Christ); the old Dutch form is *Kerstes-misse* or *Kersmisse,* the German, *Christmesse.*

The German word for Christmas, *Weihnacht* or, in the plural form, *Weihnachten,* means "the blessed (or holy) night." Similar terms meaning "the holy night" are used in some Slavic languages (Czech, Slovak, Yugoslavian). The Lithuanian word *Kaledos* is derived from the verb *Kaledoti* (to beg, to pray) and has the meaning "Day of Prayer."

YULE · The origin of the word yule is disputed. Some scholars say it comes from the old Germanic word *Jol* (*Iul, Giul*), meaning a turning wheel (in this instance the sun wheel rising after the winter solstice). A better explanation, however, might be the Anglo-Saxon word *geol* (feast). Since the greatest popular feast in pre-Christian times was the celebration of the winter solstice, the whole month of December was called *geola* (feast month). This name was preserved in the English and German languages, and later applied to the Feast of Christmas: Yule in English, and *Jul* in German.[39]

MERRY CHRISTMAS · When this greeting was originally used, the word merry did not mean "joyful, hilarious, gay," as it does today. In those days it meant "blessed, peaceful, pleasant," expressing spiritual joys rather than earthly happiness. It was thus used in the famous phrase "Merry England."

The well-known carol "God rest you merry, gentlemen" is an excellent example of the original meaning of merry. The position of the comma clearly shows the true meaning (that the word is not an adjective describing "gentlemen"), and therefore is not "God rest you, joyful gentlemen," but "God rest you peacefully, gentlemen." [40]

LITURGY

THE VIGIL OF CHRISTMAS · The Mass of December 24 is not the original vigil Mass of the feast, but was inserted later, during the fifth century. The actual vigil Mass, following the night service of prayer, was the midnight Mass at St. Mary Major, which is now the first Mass of Christmas Day. Another unusual feature of this Mass is its joyful and festive character. Unlike the other vigils, in which the penitential note is stressed, the Mass of the Christmas vigil is jubilant, filled with holy joy. That the vestments are of penitential color appears almost an incongruity when one studies the Mass text. [41]

The spirit of this joyful and jubilant vigil has asserted itself in the observance of the faithful through all the past centuries. In the countries of central Europe people just could not see how this day should be as strict and painful a fast as other fast days of penitential character. While gladly keeping abstinence from meat all through the day, they felt justified in reducing the strictness of fasting as to the amount of food. Thus a legitimate custom of "joyful fast" (*jeiunium gaudiosum*) was established in such countries for this one day of the year. [42]

THREE MASSES · A custom that reaches back to the early centuries of Christianity is the celebration of three Masses on the Feast of the Nativity. It was originally reserved to the pope alone, and did not become universal until the end of the first millennium when the papal books of ceremonies had been adopted by the Frankish Church.[43]

The first Mass originally was connected with the vigil service at the chapel of the manger in the church of St. Mary Major in Rome.[44] There Pope Sixtus III (440) had erected an oratory with a manger, which was considered a faithful replica of the crib at Bethlehem.[45] The pope celebrated the Holy Sacrifice about midnight, in the presence of a small crowd, since the chapel could not hold many people.

The public and official celebration of the feast was held on Christmas Day at the church of St. Peter, where immense crowds attended the pope's Mass and received Communion. This was the third Mass as it appears in today's Missals. Under Pope Gregory VII (1085) the place of this Mass was changed from St. Peter's to St. Mary Major, because that church was nearer to the Lateran Palace (where the popes lived).[46]

In the fifth century, the popes started the custom of visiting at dawn, between these two services, the palace church of the Byzantine governor. There they conducted a service in honor of Saint Anastasia, a highly venerated martyr whose body had been transferred from Constantinople about 465 and rested in this church which bore her name. The whole Byzantine colony in Rome gathered at their church on Christmas Day for this solemn visit of the Holy Father. In later centuries, when the power and prestige of the East Roman Empire waned, the popular devotion of Saint Anastasia declined. The Station in her honor was still kept, however, and has been retained in Missals up to the present day. Instead of the original Mass in honor of Saint Anastasia, another Mass of the Nativity was substituted, in which the saint is now merely commemorated. This is the second one of the three Masses on Christmas Day.[47]

As the texts of the Roman Missal show, the first Mass honors the eternal generation of the Son from the Father, the second celebrates His incarnation and birth into the world, the third His birth, through love and grace, in the hearts of men. According to the contents of the respective Gospels, people came to call the first Mass "Angels Mass," the second "Shepherds Mass," and the third "Mass of the Divine Word." [48]

There are no special liturgical ceremonies other than the three Masses on Christmas Day. The feast, however, is usually celebrated with great splendor and solemnity in all churches. The color of the liturgical vestments is white, in token of its joyful and consoling character.

MIDNIGHT MASS · The first Mass is usually said at midnight on Christmas because of the traditional belief that Christ was born at that hour. There is, of course, no historical evidence to uphold this pious belief, which has its source in the following text from the Book of Wisdom (18, 14-15):

For while all things were in quiet silence, and the night was in the midst of her course, Thy almighty word leapt down from heaven from Thy royal throne, as a fierce conqueror into the midst of the land of destruction.

As the context shows, these words refer to the slaying of the first-born in Egypt; but the medieval theologians applied it as a prophetical reference to the Incarnation of the Divine Word. A beautiful Latin hymn of the fourth century, "*Quando noctis medium*," expresses this common belief in our Lord's birth at midnight:

> *When the midnight, dark and still,*
> *Wrapped in silence vale and hill:*
> *God the Son, through Virgin's birth,*
> *Following the Father's will,*
> *Started life as Man on earth.*[49]

In the liturgy of the Church, midnight is not assigned as the official time for the first Mass. It is merely prescribed that it be said *in nocte* (during the night). Hence in some places the first Mass is celebrated before dawn, at four or five in the morning. During earlier centuries (400-1200) the Roman regulations prescribed that the first Mass should be celebrated *ad galli cantum* (when the cock crows), which was about three o'clock in the morning.[50] A relic of this custom is found among the Spanish-speaking people, who even today call the midnight Mass *Misa de Gallo* (Mass of the Cock).

FOLKLORE

Legends · The sacred character of the night from December 24 to 25 has been acknowledged from ancient times by the term "Holy Night." Popular traditions of the Middle Ages ascribed to this night a hallowed and mysterious note of celebration and wondrous goodness. A spirit of peace and adoration was thought to prevail over the whole world, and nature was pictured as taking part in this joyful observance. Many of these legends are still alive today and form a charming part of the folklore of Christmas.

The cattle in the stables fall on their knees at midnight on Christmas; so do the deer in the forest.[51] The bees awake from sleep and hum a beautiful symphony of praise to the Divine Child; but only those can hear it who are dear to the Lord.[52] The birds sing all night at Christmas; their voices become sweeter and more melodious, and even the sparrows sing like nightingales. In the Orient there is a legend that during Holy Night all trees and plants, especially those on the banks of the Jordan, bow in reverence toward Bethlehem.[53]

On Christmas Eve the water in wells and fountains is blessed by God with great healing powers and heavenly sweetness. Mysterious bells are heard pealing joyfully from the depths of deserted mines, and cheerful lights may be seen blinking at the bottom of lonely shafts and caves.[54]

Other legends tell of how animals talk like humans at midnight. Their favorite language seemed to be Latin. In an old French mystery play the cock crows with a piercing voice, *"Christus natus est"* (Christ is born); the ox moos, *"Ubi?"* (Where?); the lamb answers, "Bethlehem"; and the ass brays, *"Eamus!"* (Let us go!).[55] In central Europe the animals in the stable are said to gossip about the public and hidden faults of those who listen in on their conversation.[56]

One of the oldest Christian legends is the charming story related by Saint Gregory of Tours (594) in his *Libri Miraculorum* (*Book of Miracles*) concerning the well of the Magi near Bethlehem. The people of Bethlehem made a practice of going there during Christmas week, bending over the opening of the well, and covering themselves and the opening with blankets or cloaks to shut out the light of day. Then, as they peered into the dark well, the star of Bethlehem, according to this pious legend, could be seen moving slowly across the water—but only by those who were pure of heart.[57]

Another legend inspired the popular belief that the power of malignant spirits, of ghosts and witches, was entirely suspended during the Christmas season. The mystical presence of the Christ Child made them powerless; no harm could be done to men or beasts or homes. Shakespeare has made this legend immortal by these familiar lines from Act I, Scene 1 of *Hamlet:*

> *Some say that ever 'gainst that season comes*
> *Wherein our Saviour's birth is celebrated,*
> *The bird of dawning singeth all night long:*
> *And then, they say, no spirit dare stir abroad;*
> *The nights are wholesome; then no planets strike,*
> *No fairy takes, no witch has power to charm,*
> *So hallow'd and so gracious is the time.*

It was an old and comforting belief that the gates of Paradise were open on Christmas at midnight, so that any person dying at that hour could enter Heaven at once.[58] Another legend considered every child born on Christmas especially blessed and fortunate. In addition to other gifts and privileges, such children were said to have the power of seeing spirits, and even of commanding them.[59]

There is the lovely medieval legend of the "Christmas angel." Every year—so the story goes—the Blessed Virgin Mary selects a number of angels and sends them out from Heaven into various parts of the world. Each angel awakens a little child from its first sleep and carries it to Paradise to sing a carol to the Christ Child. When the children afterward tell of their beautiful errand, some people will say it was just a dream; but those who know better will assure you that these children are chosen by God to be blessed with unusual favors.[60]

CHRISTMAS EVE · In many European countries, especially in central and northern Europe, the family celebration takes place on the evening of December 24. The common features of this cele-

bration are a festive meal in the evening, at which, besides
various native dishes, fish is the main fare, because, according
to canon law, Christmas Eve is a day of fast and abstinence
among all Catholic populations. Later in the evening the family
gathers to enter the festively decorated room where the Christmas tree and the presents are ready. The small children believe
that the Christ Child, accompanied by angels, has decorated the
tree and brought the gifts. A sign is given with a little bell, the
doors fly open, and the whole family enters the room. Standing
or kneeling in front of the Christmas crib, which is usually set
up under the tree, they pray and sing Christmas hymns. Then
they wish each other a blessed feast and proceed to open their
gift packages.[61]

The Slavic people, and also the Lithuanians, have a touching
and impressive custom which resembles the *Agape* (love meal)
of the early Christians in apostolic times. At the beginning of
the *vigilia* (the meatless Christmas Eve dinner) the father of
the family solemnly breaks wafers (*Oplatki*) and distributes
them, kissing each member of the household and wishing them
a joyful feast. In many places these wafers are blessed before-
hand by the priest.[62]

Another custom practiced among the Slavic people and other
nations of Europe (among them Hungarians and Lithuanians) is
the placing of straw under the tablecloth and the bedding of
small children on straw or hay during Holy Night, in memory
of the Lord's reclining on straw and hay in the manger.[63]

A very old and practical tradition made it obligatory on Christmas Eve to see that the house was thoroughly cleaned, all borrowed articles returned, all tools laid aside, no lint allowed "to
remain on rock or wheel," no unfinished work exposed to sight,
and no task started that could not be finished by nightfall.[64]

It was a widespread practice to be especially kind to animals
at Christmas and to allow them to share in the joy of the feast.
This tradition is still alive in northern and central Europe and
in Scandinavia. People put out sheaves of grain for the birds and
give their farm animals extra fodder on Christmas Eve.[65] This
custom was begun by Saint Francis of Assisi (1226). He admonished the farmers to give their oxen and asses extra corn
and hay at Christmas, "for reverence of the Son of God, whom

on such a night the blessed Virgin Mary did lay down in the stall between the ox and the ass." All creation, said he, should rejoice at Christmas, and the dumb creatures had no other means of doing so than by enjoying more comfort and better food. "If I could see the Emperor," he said, "I would implore him to issue a general decree that all people who are able to do so, shall throw grain and corn upon the streets, so that on this great feast day the birds might have enough to eat, especially our sisters, the larks." [66]

HOLY NIGHT · An inspiring and colorful sight are the Christmas fires burned on the peaks of the Alps. Like flaming stars they hang in the dark heavens during Holy Night, burning brightly, as the farmers from around the mountainsides walk through the winter night down into the valley for midnight Mass. Each person carries a lantern, swinging it to and fro; the night seems alive with hundreds of glowworms converging toward the great light at the foot of the mountain—the parish church. [67]

In some sections of England, Ireland, and Scotland, a quaint and unusually interesting custom was practiced in medieval times. One hour before midnight the big bell of the church would begin to toll its slow and solemn message of mourning, and it would thus continue for the whole hour, as if tolling for a funeral. But at the moment of midnight, just as the clock struck twelve, all the bells would suddenly ring out in a merry peal of Christmas joy. This tolling from eleven to twelve was called "the Devil's funeral," for according to the old legend, the Devil died when Christ was born. [68]

Another custom connected with midnight Mass is the ringing of church bells during the solemn service of Vespers, which is held in many places directly before the midnight service. [69] In America, chimes and carillons accompany or replace the bells in many churches, ringing out the tunes of familiar carols, especially the joyous invitation "O come, all ye faithful."

In Austria, Bavaria, and other countries of central Europe, carols are played from the church towers before midnight Mass; the tunes of traditional Christmas songs ring out through the stillness of the winter night, clear and peaceful, creating an unforgettable impression. [70]

In the Church of the Nativity in Bethlehem, the statue of the Divine Child is placed on the altar after the first Mass and then carried in procession to the crypt, where it is laid on the silver star that marks what is believed to be the actual spot of the Lord's birth. The Gospel of Saint Luke is sung, and when the deacon comes to the words "she laid him in a manger," the statue is lifted from the floor and placed in the rock-hewn crib next to the star.[71] A similar custom used to be observed in sections of central Europe, where the figure of the Christ Child was solemnly placed in the crib after the first Mass, while the people in church sang their ancient carols.[72]

Among the French people it is an old custom to hold a joyful family gathering and a traditional meal (*réveillon*) directly after midnight Mass. In Spain people promenade on the streets after the midnight Mass with torches, tambourines, and guitars, singing and greeting each other.[73]

[1] W. Schmidt, *Geburtstag im Altertum*, Giessen, 1908.   [2] Kellner, 127 ff.   [3] *Homil. in Diem Natal.*, 2; PL, 49, 552 ff.   [4] Kellner, 142; DACL, 12.1 (1935), 908 ff.   [5] Rahner, 190 ff. (*Das Weihnachtsfest*). [6] Kellner, 143 ff.   [7] DACL, 12.1 (1935), 915 ff. (*Natalis Invicti*). [8] H. Usener, *Das Weihnachtsfest*, Bonn, 1911.   [9] H. Rahner, *Die Gottesgeburt*, ZKTh, 59 (1935), 333 ff.   [10] Saint Leo I, *Sermo* 27, *In Nativ. Domini*, 7, 4; PL, 54, 218 ff.   [11] Rahner, 196 ff.   [12] F. Cabrol, *Advent*, DACL, 1.2 (1924), 3223 ff.   [13] Can. 18; Mansi, 9, 796. [14] Can. 27; Mansi, 9, 796.   [15] *Capit. contra Priscill.*, 4; Mansi, 9, 775. [16] Beda Ven., *App.*, VI; PL, 95, 316.   [17] Can. 36; Mansi, 14, 73. [18] W. P. Dawson, *Christmas: Its Origins and Associations*, London, 1902.   [19] VL, 1 ff.; K. Algermissen, *Konfessionskunde*, Celle, 1957, 573 ff.   [20] Barnett, 2 ff.   [21] Crippen, 87 ff.   [22] Crippen, 91.   [23] *The Flying Eagle Gazette*, London, December 25, 1652.   [24] Crippen, 91. [25] N. Doran, "The Ups and Downs of Christmas," in *The National Magazine*, London, December 1857.   [26] *The Declaration of Many Thousands of the City of Canterbury* (broadsheet), London, 1648 (British Museum).   [27] Crippen, 92.   [28] See note 18, 211 ff.   [29] Crippen, 93.   [30] From "Old Christmas Returned," a poem of about 1665; see CwP, 119.   [31] W. Hone, *Ancient Mysteries*, London, 1823, 23. [32] Barnett, 2 ff. ("Christmas in the Making").   [33] *Bradford's History "of Plymouth Plantation" from the Original Manuscript*, ed. Common-

wealth of Massachusetts, Boston, 1899, 107. [34] G. W. Curtis, "Christmas," in *Harper's New Monthly Magazine*, 68 (October 13, 1883). [35] Barnett, 6 ff. [36] K. L. Richards, *How Christmas Came to the Sunday-Schools*, New York, 1934, 71 ff. [37] Nilles, I, 363 ff.; Crippen, 11 ff. [38] Crippen, 48. [39] L. Hösl, *Julfest*, LThK, 5 (1938), 706. [40] CTD, 92. [41] Schuster, I, 356 ff. [42] H. Noldin and A. Schmitt, *Summa Theologiae Moralis*, Innsbruck, 1928, II, 633. [43] *Trina Celebratio*, DACL, 12.1 (1935), 934 ff. [44] Schuster, I, 361. [45] H. Leclercq, *Marie Majeure: L'Oratoire de la crèche*, DACL, 10.2 (1932), 2142 ff. [46] Schuster, I, 373 ff. [47] Schuster, I, 368; DACL, 12.1 (1935), 933 (*Anastasia*). [48] M. B. Hellriegel, "Christmas (The Three Masses)," OF, 19 (1944), 49 ff. [49] Trans. by the author. [50] TE, I, 676. [51] ES, 73. [52] ES, 32. [53] Crippen, 166. [54] ES, 77. [55] Koren, 57 ff.; R. J. Campbell, *The Story of Christmas*, New York, 1934, 40. [56] H. Mang, *Unsere Weihnacht*, Innsbruck, 1927; Benet, 94. [57] *Libri Miracul.*, I, 1; PL, 71, 707. [58] Crippen, 169. [59] ES, 37. [60] Crippen, 170. [61] Trapp, 52 ff.; Geramb, 212. [62] F. Tetzner, *Alte Gebräuche, Kleidung und Geräte der Litauer*, in *Globus*, 73 (1898), 110 ff. [63] Benet, 98 ff. [64] Crippen, 104. [65] Geramb, 221; Benet, 103. [66] Celano, 51, 199. [67] Trapp, 58. [68] Crippen, 68. [69] Geramb, 220. [70] Geramb, 216. [71] Crippen, 73. [72] CTD, 7, quoted in English trans. from the German of Naogeorgus (T. Kirchmeyer). [73] Crippen, 72.

CHAPTER

7

Christmas Hymns and Carols

HISTORY

THE WORD "CAROL" · A hymn is essentially solemn; a carol, in the modern sense, is familiar, playful, or festive, but always simple. The distinction between hymns and carols is often overlooked, and "carol" has come to denote all vernacular songs pertaining to Christmas.[1]

The word carol comes from the Greek word *choraulein* (*choros,* the dance; *aulein,* to play the flute), and referred to a dance accompanied by the playing of flutes. Such dancing, usually done in ring form, was very popular in ancient times among the Greek and Roman people. The Romans took the custom and its name to Britain.

In medieval England carol meant a ring dance accompanied by singing. The dancers would form a circle and, joining their hands, walk in rhythmic dance step while keeping the form of the circle.[2]

Gradually the meaning of carol changed, and the word was applied to the song. In an English-Latin vocabulary of 1440 the definition of a carol is given as "song, *psalmodium.*" [3]

ANCIENT HYMNS AND CAROLS · The first hymns in honor of the Nativity were written in the fifth century, soon after Christmas was fully established as one of the great annual feasts. These hymns, written in Latin, increased in number as time went on. Some of them were incorporated in the Divine Office and are still used at Christmas time in the daily prayers of the breviary, while others are sung by church choirs at liturgical services. Many Latin hymns of 1200 to 1700 were translated into various languages and have since become popular carols.[4]

The early Latin hymns of 400 to 1200 are profound and solemn, and dwell exclusively on the supernatural aspects of Christmas. Theological in text, they do not concern themselves with the human side of the Nativity. A few of the best-known early Latin hymns are:

> *Jesus refulsit omnium* (Jesus, light of all the nations), by Saint Hilary of Poitiers (368)
> *Corde natus ex Parentis* (Of the Father's love begotten), by Prudentius (405), a layman, government official of the Roman Empire, and great Christian poet
> *Agnoscat omne saeculum* (Let every age and nation know), by Venantius Fortunatus (602), Bishop of Poitiers.

A song of the ancient Greek Church which in English translation still survives is the hymn "O gladsome light" (*Phos hilaron*). It is used in many churches at Christmas candlelight services.

Other Latin hymns that were later translated and became popular carols are:

In hoc anni circulo (In the circle of this year)
Dies est laetitiae (O royal day of holy joy)
Flos e radice Jesse (A spotless rose is growing); this hymn of the sixteenth century was set to music—its present familiar tune—by Michael Praetorius (1621), a German priest.[5]

The birthplace of the true Christmas carol was Italy. There, in the thirteenth century, among the early Franciscans, Saint Francis of Assisi was the first to introduce the joyous carol spirit which soon spread all over Europe. He had a particular devotion and affection for the mysteries of the holy childhood of Jesus. His biographer, Thomas of Celano (about 1260), says, "The Child Jesus was forgotten by the hearts of many. But with the grace of God He was resurrected again and recalled to loving memory in those hearts through His servant, the Blessed Francis." [6]

Saint Francis wrote a beautiful Christmas hymn in Latin (*Psalmus in Nativitate*), but there is no evidence that he composed carols in Italian. His companions and spiritual sons, however, the first Franciscan friars, contributed a large number of lovely Italian Christmas carols. Here is an English translation of one of these thirteenth-century Italian carols.[7] The tune has become very familiar as the theme on which Handel developed his Pastoral Symphony in the *Messiah:*

> *In Bethlehem is born the Holy Child,*
> *On hay and straw in the winter wild;*
> *O, my heart is full of mirth*
> *At Jesus' birth.*

From Italy the carol spread quickly to Spain and France, and finally all over Europe.

In Germany in the fourteenth century a great many popular Christmas carols were written largely under the inspiration of the Dominican mystics John Eckhardt (1327), John Tauler (1361), and Blessed Henry Suso (1366), author of the famous carol *In dulci jubilo.*

The earliest-known English carol was written at the beginning

of the fifteenth century.[8] It is a lullaby of great simplicity and
tenderness:

> *I saw a sweet, a seemly sight,*
> *A blissful bird, a blossom bright,*
> *That mourning made and mirth among:*
> *A maiden mother meek and mild*
> *In cradle keep a knave* [boy] *child*
> *That softly slept; she sat and sung:*
> *Lullay, lulla, balow,*
> *My bairn, sleep softly now.*

These early English carols usually employed both rhyme and
alliteration. There followed a great number of English Christmas
poems in the next two centuries, most of them very tender and
devout, praising the Divine Child and His Virgin Mother.

MODERN HYMNS AND CAROLS · After the Reformation most of
the old hymns and carols were no longer sung, and consequently
were forgotten in many countries until their revival in the nineteenth century.

Christmas carols in general were discouraged by the Calvin-
ists, who substituted metrical psalms in their place. Carol singing was suppressed altogether by the Puritans. Following the
restoration of Christmas in England, however, there were numerous festive songs in praise of the feast, but very few religious
carols. One of the few, which has become a favorite among English-speaking nations, is the ballad "While shepherds watched
their flocks by night," written by Nahum Tate (1715).[9] Its familiar music was taken from the "Christmas melody" of Handel's
opera *Siroe,* and arranged in the present setting by Richard
Storrs Willis in 1850.

The Methodist revival in the eighteenth century, though, had
inspired a number of modern hymns, first used only in Methodist
churches, but gradually welcomed by all English-speaking people. The best-known of these is "Hark, the herald angels sing,"
written by Charles Wesley.[10] The music was adapted from Mendelssohn's *Festgesang* (written in 1840) by William H. Cum-
mings, organist at Waltham Abbey, England, in 1885.

Another popular English carol of the last century is the song

"Good King Wenceslaus." This is not a Christmas carol in the strict sense, but, rather, the poetic story of a famous miracle ascribed in medieval legend to Saint Wenceslaus, Martyr, Duke of Bohemia (935). The miracle, according to the poem, occurred "on the day of Stephen" (December 26), and thus became one of the English Christmas carols. The tune was originally a sixteenth-century spring canticle and the words were written by John M. Neale (1866).[11]

The carol "Joy to the world! The Lord is come" came from the pen of an English poet, Isaac Watts (1748). Lowell Mason (1872) of Medfield, Massachusetts, composed the music from tunes found in Handel's *Messiah*. This carol first appeared in print in 1839.[12] A recent English carol is "The world's desire" by G. K. Chesterton (1936).

The Lutherans in Germany wrote new hymns for their own use. Among these are some of the best modern carols, such as Martin Luther's delightful song *Vom Himmel hoch da komm' ich her* (From Heaven above I come to you), which he wrote in 1535.[13] Bach composed a harmonization for it in his Christmas oratorio.

Another carol ascribed to Martin Luther, and widely used in America, is the beautiful "Away in a manger." It is usually called "Luther's Cradle Hymn," though neither the text nor the music was written by him.[14] It might very well have been inspired, however, by the second part of the first stanza of Luther's hymn *Vom Himmel kam der Engel Schar,* which starts with the line *"Ein Kindlein zart, das liegt dort in der Krippen"* (Away there in the manger a little Infant lies). The familiar English text is of American origin, very likely written in one of the settlements of German Lutherans in Pennsylvania. The poem appeared in print in Philadelphia in 1885. Since then, forty-one settings have been written for this carol; the most popular ones are the tunes composed by James R. Murray (who, erroneously, ascribed the authorship of the poem to Luther) in 1887, and by William James Kirkpatrick (1921).[15]

Within the past two centuries a number of excellent carols have been written in Germany, and many have been adopted as popular church hymns. Some have become favorite songs in other countries. The best-known of these are:

O du fröhliche . . . (O, thou joyful Christmas time), a popular
carol written by Johann Falk in 1816; the tune was taken from
an old Sicilian Madonna hymn in Latin, *O Sanctissima* [16]

O Tannenbaum (O Christmas Tree), an early nineteenth-century
carol, familiar in the United States as the tune to which the
words of "Maryland, My Maryland" are set [17]

Ihr Kinderlein, Kommet (O come, all ye children), written by
Christoph von Schmid (1854) and sung to a tune composed
by Johann A. P. Schulz (1800), has become the favorite children's carol in Germany and is now frequently heard in
churches in this country.[18]

The first American carol was written by the famous missionary
to the Huron Indians, saint, and martyr John de Brébeuf, S.J.
(1649), who labored among the Hurons from 1626 until he was
captured and slowly tortured to death by the savage Iroquois
when they brutally attacked and destroyed the Huron mission
in 1649 and 1650.

Father Brébeuf wrote in the Huron language the Christmas
hymn *Jesous Ahatonnia* (Jesus is born), which he adapted from
a sixteenth-century French folk song. This hymn was preserved
by the Hurons who escaped the devastating attacks of the
Iroquois and were later settled by their missionaries on a reser-
vation at Loretto, near Quebec. There Father Etienne de Ville-
neuve recorded the words of the hymn; they were found among
his papers after his death (1794) and later published with a
French translation.[19]

In recent years Brébeuf's hymn has been reintroduced into
the treasury of American Christmas carols. J. E. Middleton, of
Toronto, wrote a free English translation to fit the ancient French
melody. The music was arranged by Edith Lovell Thomas, music
director at Radburn, New Jersey.

A great number of beautiful American carols were introduced
in the last century, inspired not only by the Methodist revival
but also as a result of the widespread renascence of Christmas
customs. These American carols are quite different from the
average English Christmas songs of the past centuries because
they reflect a religious spirit while most early English carols
praise only the external pleasures of feasting, reveling, and general good will, without direct reference to the nativity of Christ.

"It came upon the midnight clear" was written by Edmund H. Sears (1876), a Unitarian minister of Weston, Massachusetts, and set to music by Richard S. Willis (1900), a journalist and editor in Detroit, who in his youth was a personal friend of Mendelssohn.[20]

One of the most beloved of American carols is the famous "O little town of Bethlehem," written by Phillips Brooks (1893), rector of Trinity Church (Episcopal) in Boston, and later Episcopal bishop of Massachusetts. He visited the Holy Land, and the impression made on him by the Christ Child's birthplace inspired him to write this poem three years after his return, in 1865, to Holy Trinity Church in Philadelphia, where he was then stationed. Louis H. Redner (1908), the organist there and teacher in the church school, wrote the tune. It was first sung by the children of Holy Trinity Sunday School, on Christmas 1868.[21]

"We three kings of Orient are" was written and set to music in 1857 by John Henry Hopkins, Jr. (1891), an Episcopalian minister. It was published in 1883 and has been popular with children ever since.[22]

Another famous American carol is Henry Wadsworth Longfellow's poem entitled "Christmas Bells" ("I heard the bells on Christmas Day"). He wrote it for Christmas 1863.[23] The tune is called "Waltham" and was composed by the English organist John Baptist Calkin (1905).

A familiar carol in the United States is "Angels we have heard on high," most probably a translation of an old French or Flemish antiphon hymn of the sixteenth century. (An antiphon hymn is a free poetic translation, in the vernacular, of one or more antiphon verses in liturgical texts.) This particular hymn was probably inspired by the antiphons of the Lauds in the Divine Office of Christmas Day. The present version of the English text was written by Earl Marlatt, dean of the School of Theology at Boston University, in 1937; the arrangement for the "Gloria" was made by Edward Shippen Barnes in 1937.[24]

A startling example of nineteenth-century American folk music from the Kentucky mountains is the song "Christ was born in Bethlehem, and Mary was his niece." Another popular one, "The snow lay on the ground," is of uncertain origin. The melody was taken from an old Italian *pifferari* (pipers') melody. One of the favorites among many Negro contributions to American Christmas music is "Rise up, shepherd, an' foller." [25]

More recent contributions include *Gesu Bambino* with words by Frederick Marten and music by Pietro Yon (1943), organist and choirmaster of St. Patrick's Cathedral in New York. It is contrapuntal, in the pastoral manner, against the *Adeste Fideles* melody.[26]

The well-known Christmas song "O Holy Night" is of French origin. Adolphe Charles Adam (1856), professor at the Paris Conservatory of Music, wrote the tune to a poem (*Cantique de Noël*) of M. Cappeau de Roquemaure. The English translation was made by John Sullivan Dwight (1893).[27]

Despite the devoted research of musical scholars, the origin of the beloved Christmas hymn *Adeste Fideles* (O come, all ye faithful) is still shrouded in mystery. The original Latin poem is sometimes ascribed to Saint Bonaventure (1274), a Franciscan priest, later archbishop and cardinal. However, the original manuscripts, containing text and tune, date from the eighteenth century and are signed by John Francis Wade (1786), a music dealer of the English Catholic colony at Douay, France. Marcus Antonius de Fonseca (Portogallo), chapelmaster to the king of Portugal (1830), has also been mentioned as composer of the music. This tune is reported to have been sung at the Portuguese embassy chapel in London at the end of the eighteenth century. Dr. Frederick Oakely (1880), an Anglican minister and later Catholic priest, wrote the English version of the text in 1841.[28]

In Austria—especially in its Alpine provinces—many parishes had, and some still retain, local poets who continue to add new songs to the old treasury. In little towns and on the farms of the Alpine sections, men and women of "singing families" and rural choirs are continually improvising words and music, like minstrels of old. These simple folk have a native instinct for music and poetry. Many of them play instruments (violin, flute, zither, guitar), and improvise Christmas songs as they gather round the hearth. Any student of Christmas lore will find in Austria and Bavaria a rich treasury of popular carols, ancient and modern, hidden away in little country places. Most of them are as yet unknown to the world in general, though the famous

Trapp singers have brought many of them to this country and they are now included in many Christmas programs here.

One such familiar Austrian carol, written by a parish priest in the small town of Oberndorf, near Salzburg, in 1818, is the familiar *Stille Nacht, Heilige Nacht* (Silent Night, Holy Night).[29] It had been hidden among the manuscripts of the church choir for some time, until it was found by a music lover who brought it to the Rainers, a family of singers, in the Tyrol (Zillertal). They began to sing it at their concerts, and it gradually became widely used in Austria and Germany. On their American concert tour (1839-1843) they brought the new carol with them and sang it before large audiences.[30] Within a few years it conquered the hearts of the nation. Not only in America, but all over the world, "Silent Night" has become the most beloved of all carols, a truly international Christmas anthem.

Here is the legend of its origin: On Christmas Eve 1818, the parish priest of Oberndorf, Joseph Mohr, was notified that repairs of the church organ, which had broken down a few days before, could not be finished in time for midnight Mass. This was a great disappointment to the priest and his flock, since the music for the High Mass, which the choir had prepared, could not be sung. To lessen the disappointment, Father Mohr decided to surprise his people with a new Christmas song. He went to work immediately and wrote three stanzas of a carol, the first stanza of which was inspired by the sight of a baby whose ailing mother he had visited earlier in the day. Having finished the text, he took it to his friend Franz Gruber, teacher and organist in the nearby village of Arnsdorf. Gruber composed the tune within a few hours. At midnight Mass, the hushed congregation in the little church heard the first performance of *Stille Nacht*.[31]

Today a modest monument in Oberndorf perpetuates the memory of the men who gave us "Silent Night": the poet, Father Joseph Mohr (1848), and the composer, Franz Gruber (1863).

Stille Nacht was first performed to the accompaniment of a guitar. The composer later wrote an orchestration for strings, French horn, and organ. Father Mohr called it *Weihnachtslied* (Christmas song). It was first published at Leipzig in 1834. The commonly used English translation appeared in a Methodist

hymnal in Boston in 1871, and was compiled from various preceding translations. The name of the compiler is unknown.

In Latin countries, especially in rural sections of Spain and
South America, many towns have their traditional Christmas
carols which have now become part of American Christmas lore
in certain sections of the country. These are carols of childlike
simplicity, often humorous in parts, but always devout and tender. The local carol (*El Niño Jesús ha nacido ya*) of the town
Ocumare de la Costa in Venezuela, a jewel of popular Christmas
music, is a good illustration:

> *The little child Jesus is already here*
> *The Kings and the shepherds adore without fear*
> *There is much to behold for the wise and the fool:*
> *Saint Joseph, the Virgin; the ox and the mule.*
> *Let us adore the little child*
> *With pleasure and happy cheer;*
> *Let us adore as the Magi do*
> *As the Magi adore Him here.*[32]

CAROLING · The first mention of Christmas caroling in America
was recorded by Father Bartholomew Vimont, S.J., in his report
on the state of the Huron mission, dated Quebec, October 1,
1645. In it he described the zeal and devotion that the Christian
Hurons displayed in celebrating Christmas. Speaking of the Indians at Mackinac (now Macinaw, Michigan), one of the most
remote missions of New France, he said:

The savages have a particular devotion for the night that was enlightened by the birth of the Son of God. There was not one who
refused to fast on the day that preceded it. They built a small chapel
of cedar and fir branches in honor of the manger of the infant Jesus.
They wished to perform some penance for better receiving Him into
their hearts on that holy day, and even those who were at a distance
of two days' journey met at a given place to sing hymns in honor of
the new-born Child. . . . Neither the inconvenience of the snow nor
the severity of the cold could stifle the ardor of their devotion.[33]

This ancient custom of singing carols in public was revived
in America toward the end of the last century. In Boston the
first organized Christmas Eve caroling took place on the streets

of Beacon Hill in 1885.[34] In St. Louis caroling was started in 1909 by groups of young people who sang their carols before every house with a lighted candle in its windows. Organized groups of carol singers may now be found in thousands of American cities and towns.

In French Canada, the caroling is performed either a few days before Christmas or on New Year's Eve, by young men and women dressed in old-style country costumes (*La guignolée*), who go from house to house, singing and collecting gifts of food and clothes for the poor of the town.

In Hungary, in Poland, and in other Slavic countries singers go from house to house carrying a huge star, lighted inside. After their carols are sung, some of the groups enact scenes from the Nativity, the visit of the Magi, the court of King Herod, and other events. This custom is called *Kolednicy* in Polish, "Bethlehem" in Hungarian.

CLASSIFICATION OF CAROLS

NATIVITY CAROLS · This, the largest group, is made up of Christmas carols in the strict sense of the word, the main theme being the story of the Nativity itself. They reveal the religious feeling that the birth of Christ brings to the hearts of men, and usually express adoration, praise, love, gratitude, contrition, wonder, joy, and similar emotions, like this ancient English carol:

> *A child is born in Bethlehem;*
> *Rejoice, therefore, Jerusalem.*
> *Low in the manger lieth He,*
> *Whose kingdom without end shall be . . .*
> *All glory, Lord, to Thee be done,*
> *Now seen in flesh, the Virgin's Son.*[35]

PRAYER CAROLS · This is the group of Christmas songs that is directly addressed to the Holy Child in wonder, devotion, and admiration. Every Christian nation has its treasury of such prayer carols. The most famous of them is the Austrian carol "Silent Night." Another beautiful example is the poem *Tu scendi dalle stelle* (Thou camest from the heavens), written by Pope Pius IX (1878) and sung to a traditional melody:

> *Thou camest down, O heaven's King,*
>   *From starry sky,*
> *And in a cave so poor and cold*
>   *I see Thee lie.*
> *I see Thee tremble, blessed God;*
>   *Why should this be?*
> *Thy sacrifice, O love Divine,*
>   *Is all for me.*[36]

SHEPHERD CAROLS · These songs flourished in Germany, Austria, England, France, Ireland, Italy, Spain, as well as in the Slavic nations. They relate the message of the angel, the song of the heavenly hosts, the visit of the shepherds to the manger, and often describe their prayers and gifts. Many of these carols carry refrains imitating shepherds' instruments; for instance this English carol of the fifteenth century:

> *About the field they piped full right,*
> *Even about the midst of the night;*
> *They saw come down from heaven a light:*
> *Tirlè, tirlè—so merrily*
> *The shepherds began to blow.*[37]

NOELS · The noels are still another group of carols, of which we have many examples both in French and in English. The word "noel" or "nowell" is generally repeated as a refrain, in the same sense as "news." The familiar carol "The First Nowell" has become a favorite Christmas song among all English-speaking people.[38] An example of the noel refrain is these lines of another ancient English carol:

> *Noel, Noel, Noel,*
> *Tidings good I think to tell.*
> *The boar's head that we bring here,*
> *Betokeneth a prince without peer*
> *Is born today to buy us dear.*
> *Noel, Noel, Noel.*[39]

MACARONICS · A macaronic is a carol written partly in Latin, partly in the vernacular. There are many of these in French, English, and German. Here is the first stanza of Henry Suso's famous *In dulci jubilo,* a German macaronic of the fourteenth century, in English translation:

> In dulci jubilo
> *Sing ye, and gladness show!*
> *See our bliss reclining*
> In praesepio,
> *The very sun outshining*
> Matris in gremio.
> Alpha es et O,
> Alpha es et O.[40]

LULLABY CAROLS · These songs, as the classification suggests, make use of the lullabies of various countries, either picturing the Virgin Mary singing to the Holy Child or having the devout worshiper sing them directly to the Divine Babe, like this old Austrian carol:

> *Thy shining eyes, so blue and light,*
> *Thy tender cheeks, so soft and bright;*
> *I will remain forever Thine,*
> *O dearest Son, O child Divine. . . .*
> [lullaby humming] [41]

There is this endearing Czech lullaby, so typical of many similar songs among the Slavic nations. It is impossible to render in English the charming spirit of the original Czech text:

> Hajej, nynej, *Jesus dear,*
> *Sleep in peace, and do not fear.*
> *We shall bundle you to rest,*
> *Keep you close to our breast.*
> Hajej, nynej, *darling Child,*
> *Son of Mary, Saviour mild.*[42]

MYSTERY CAROLS · These carols form a large group of medieval Christmas songs delightfully describing all manner of legendary

events supposed to have happened to the Divine Child. One of
the most charming mystery carols is the old English "Cherrie
tree song." [43] It begins:

> As Joseph was a-walking,
>   He heard an angel sing:
> This night shall be born
>   Our heavenly king.
>
> He neither shall be born
>   In housen or in hall,
> Nor in the place of Paradise,
>   But in an ox's stall.
>
> He neither shall be clothed
>   In purple nor in pall,
> But all in fair linen,
>   As were babies all. . . .

COMPANION CAROLS · This is an interesting group of songs—
mostly German—wherein the singer represents himself as accompanying the shepherds, or as taking their place, addressing
the Child, or Mary and Joseph, in a simple, affectionate manner.
Often a broad local dialect is used, as in the old Austrian carol,
from the Tyrol, *Jetzt hat sich halt aufgetan das himmlische Tor*
(The gates of Heaven's glory did spring open suddenly). Here
is a rollicking, joyous stanza:

> So came we running to the crib,
>   I and also you,
> A beeline into Bethlehem,
>   Hopsa, trala loo:
> "O, baby dear, take anything
>   Of all the little gifts we bring:
> Have apples or have butter,
>   Maybe pears or yellow cheese;
> Or would you rather have some nuts,
>   Or plums, or what you please.
> Alleluja, alleluja;
>   Alle-, alle-, Alleluja." [44]

DANCE CAROLS · Dance carols, usually ring dances accompanied by singing, were greatly favored in medieval times. The altar boys, for example, in the Cathedral of Seville, Spain, used to dance before the altar on Christmas and other feast days, accompanied by song and the sound of castanets. In the Minster of York, England, until the end of the sixteenth century choirboys performed a dance in the aisle of the church after morning prayers on Christmas Day. In France it was customary to dance a *bergerette* (shepherd's dance) in churches at Christmas time. Dancing in churches was prohibited by an ecclesiastical council at Toledo in 590, but the custom had become so much a part of the Christmas festivities that in some places dancing survived until the thirteenth and fourteenth centuries; in England, right up to the Reformation, in Spain even longer.[45]

Christmas dancing is still practiced in the Scandinavian countries, where carols are sung as the people perform a ring dance around the Christmas tree. A popular dance carol is the Swedish *Nu ar det Jul igen* (Now it is Christmas again):

> *Now Christmas is here again,*
> *And Christmas is here again,*
> *And Christmas we'll have till Easter.*
> *Then Easter is here again,*
> *And Easter is here again,*
> *And Easter we'll have till Christmas.*
> *Now this will not be so,*
> *And this will not be so,*
> *For in between comes Lenten-fasting.*[46]

CRADLE-ROCKING · This word comes from the German *Kindelwiegen* (Rocking of the Child), a custom that originated in Germany and Austria in the fourteenth century. It became widespread as a substitute for the Nativity plays, after they were banned. A priest would carry to the altar a cradle with a figure of the Christ Child; there the cradle was rocked while the congregation sang and prayed. The service ended with the devotional kissing of the Christ Child at the altar rail.[47]

During the sixteenth century this custom, too, was forbidden in churches, but it survived for a long time as a devotional practice in many convents and in private homes. In the Tyrol, girls dressed in white carried the cradle from house to house, rocking it and singing carols. In other parts of Austria, and in Bavaria, mothers would rock the cradle to obtain the favor of having children, or to implore the Divine Child for special blessings upon their families.[48] The rocking was accompanied by songs written for this particular purpose, for instance, this German carol of the sixteenth century:

> *Joseph, dearest Joseph mine,*
> *Help me rock my baby fine!*
>   *What Gabriel foretold*
>   *Is now fulfilled,*
>   *Eia, Eia,*
>   *The Virgin bore a child*
>   *As the Father's wisdom willed.*
>   *Eia, Eia.*
> *Joseph, dearest Joseph mine,*
> *Help me rock my baby fine!* [49]

CHRISTMAS YODELING · Christmas yodeling is an old custom in the Austrian Tyrol, where it seems a natural way to honor the Divine Child. The mountaineers' song without words conveys deep feelings of devotion, love, and affection. This is, of course, the genuine yodel, not the modern hillbilly type so familiar to American radio fans. True Christmas yodeling is capable of great tenderness of voice and melody as the subtle changes from chest tones to head tones are delicately made by the yodelers.

They do this before the crib or in the open on mountain peaks during the holy season. It was performed in the churches during past centuries. Some yodels are based on old traditional tunes; others are improvised on the spur of the moment. Often the yodeling forms a background as Christmas carols are sung.

---

[1] Crippen, 41 ff.   [2] See Chaucer, *Romaunt of the Rose,* lines 798-804. [3] *Promptorium Parvulorum* (an English-Latin vocabulary for children), London, about 1440. See Crippen, 42.   [4] See H. Leclercq, *Hymnographie dans l'Eglise Latine,* DACL, 6.2 (1925), 2901 ff. [5] TCS, 85; TFB, 58; CTD, 52 (different English texts).   [6] Celano,

30, 86. [7] Crippen, 45. [8] Crippen, 49. [9] TCS, 154; CTD, 42. [10] TCS, 158; TFB, 42; CTD, 30. [11] TCS, 16; TFB, 38; CTD, 38. [12] TCS, 146. [13] Luther entitled this carol, "A children's hymn of the Christ Child for Christmas Eve": TCS, 150; TFB, 64; CTD, 58. [14] "It is to be hoped that . . . at last a stop will be put to the fiction that Martin Luther had a hand in the origin of this particular children's hymn": *Companion to the Hymnal of the Protestant Episcopal Church in the United States of America 1940*, New York, 1943, 34. [15] TCS, 166; TFB, 54; CTD, 48. [16] GH, 12 (1935), 803. [17] TCS, 164; TFB, 68. [18] TCS, 162; TFB, 72. [19] CB, 267 (Huron text and English trans.). See also Francis X. Curley, "St. John de Brébeuf's Christmas Carol," in *America*, vol. 90 (1958), 320 f. [20] TCS, 122; TFB, 48; CTD, 38. [21] TCS, 128; TFB, 50; CTD, 26. [22] TCS, 188; TFB, 52; CTD, 130. [23] TCS, 126. [24] TCS, 102. [25] TCS, 54. [26] Pub. J. Fischer Co., New York. [27] TCS, 197. [28] TCS, 82; TFB, 18; CTD, 82. [29] TCS, 58; TFB, 86; CTD, 24. [30] *The Trapp Family Singers*, New York, 1948, 4; also the article on the Rainer Singers by Hans Nathan, in *The Musical Quarterly*, New York, January 1946. [31] Stock-Klausner, *Silent Night*, Salzburg, s.a. [32] From the Spanish version as published in *Edasi* magazine, Caracas (Venezuela), 1949. Trans. by the author. [33] *The Jesuit Relations and Allied Documents*, ed. R. G. Thwaites, Cleveland, 1896-1901, Vol. 27 (1898), 210. [34] R. D. Kimball, *Christmas Eve on Beacon Hill*, Boston, 1918. [35] Crippen, 48. [36] TFB, 48. Trans. of foreign texts in this and the following carols by the author. [37] Crippen, 52. [38] TCS, 6; TFB, 25; CTD, 128. [39] CwP, 17. [40] Original text and ancient English trans. in CB, 9; also TCS, 76. [41] Trans. by the author from one of the Austrian dialect versions. [42] TFB, 118. [43] This poem is a part of the famous cherry tree carol, version of W. Hone, *Ancient Mysteries*, London, 1823, 90. [44] See note 41. [45] L. Gougard, *Dances populaires dans l'églises*, DACL, 4.1 (1920), 251 ff. [46] TCS, 168; TFB, 112. [47] CTD, 7; English trans. of the description of Cradle Rocking in *Pammachius* (1539) by Naogeorgus (T. Kirchmeyer, sixteenth century). [48] Gugitz, II, 264 ff. (*Das Christkindlwiegen*); VL, 149 ff. [49] See note 41.

CHAPTER

8   *Christmas Symbols and Customs*

THE CHRISTMAS CRIB

ORIGIN · The Child in the manger and various other representations of the story of Bethlehem have been used in church services from the first centuries. The earliest-known picture is the Nativity scene (about A.D. 380) that served as a wall decoration in the burial chamber of a Christian family in St. Sebastian's Catacombs, Rome, discovered in 1877.[1]

The crib in its present form and its use outside the church is credited to Saint Francis of Assisi. He made the Christmas crib popular through his famous celebration at Greccio, Italy, on Christmas Eve 1223, with a Bethlehem scene including live animals. His biographer, Thomas de Celano, writes:

It should be recorded and held in reverent memory what Blessed Francis did near the town of Greccio, on the feast day of the Nativity of our Lord Jesus Christ, three years before his glorious death. In that town lived a certain man by the name of John (Messer Giovanni Velitta) who stood in high esteem, and whose life was even better than his reputation. Blessed Francis loved him with a special affection because, being very noble and much honored, he despised the nobility of the flesh and strove after the nobility of the soul.

Blessed Francis often saw this man. He now called him about two weeks before Christmas and said to him: "If you desire that we should celebrate this year's Christmas together at Greccio, go quickly and prepare what I tell you; for I want to enact the memory of the Infant who was born at Bethlehem, and how He was deprived of all the comforts babies enjoy; how He was bedded in the manger on hay, between an ass and an ox. For once I want to see all this with my own eyes." When that good and faithful man had heard this, he departed quickly and prepared in the above mentioned place everything that the Saint had told him.

The joyful day approached. The brethren [Franciscan friars] were called from many communities. The men and women of the neighborhood, as best they could, prepared candles and torches to brighten the night. Finally the Saint of God arrived, found everything prepared, saw it and rejoiced. The crib was made ready, hay was brought, the ox and ass were led to the spot. . . . Greccio became a new Bethlehem. The night was made radiant like the day, filling men and animals with joy. The crowds drew near and rejoiced in the novelty of the celebration. Their voices resounded from the woods, and the rocky cliff echoed the jubilant outburst. As they sang in praise of God the whole night rang with exultation. The Saint of God stood before the crib, overcome with devotion and wondrous joy. A solemn Mass was sung at the crib.

The Saint dressed in deacon's vestments, for a deacon he was [out of humility, St. Francis never became a priest, remaining a deacon all his life], sang the gospel. Then he preached a delightful sermon to the people who stood around him, speaking about the nativity of the poor King and the humble town of Bethlehem. . . . And whenever he mentioned the Child of Bethlehem or the name of Jesus, he seemed to lick his lips as if he would happily taste and swallow the sweetness of that word.[2]

The animals in the crib—usually an ass and an ox—although not mentioned in the Bible, are traditionally now part of the picture.[3] Saint Francis was following tradition when he had these animals placed near the manger. As early as the fourth century they were represented in pictures of the Nativity. The custom originated because of two passages in the Old Testament that were applied to the birth of Christ: the words of Isaiah (1, 3), "The ox knoweth his owner, and the ass his master's crib; but Israel hath not known me and my people hath not understood"; and the verse of Habakkuk (3, 2) in the Itala version, "In the midst of two animals Thou shalt become known."

THE CRIB IN FOLKLORE · Since the time of Saint Francis, the Christmas crib has been a familiar sight in churches and homes all over the world. Farmers in the mountain provinces of central Europe spend the long winter evenings of Advent repairing and enlarging their beautiful cribs, which are sometimes made up of hundreds of figures, filling a whole room.[4]

Among the German sects that kept the custom of Christmas cribs even after the Reformation were the Herrenhuter, usually called Moravians. One small group of Moravian missionaries came to America and founded the town of Bethlehem, Pennsylvania, on Christmas Eve 1741.[5] The inhabitants of Bethlehem, and later those of other Moravian settlements in Pennsylvania, brought with them the custom of the crib. They called it *putz* (from the German *putzen:* decorate) and included not only the scene of the Nativity, but, in addition, all the charming details of a German *Krippe* (crib): dozens, sometimes hundreds, of figures, fanciful landscaping, waterfalls, houses and fences, bridges, fountains, villages, gardens, and groves. The custom of *putzing* and *putz* visiting has been preserved among them up to this day.[6]

LIGHTS AND FIRE

CHRISTMAS CANDLE · From the early centuries of Christianity it has been a religious practice to represent Christ the Lord by a burning candle, a custom still preserved in the liturgy of the Church—the Easter candle, for instance.

This symbolism of the liturgy was adopted by the faithful quite early. At Christmas, a large candle symbolizing the Lord used to be set up in homes on the eve of the feast. It was kept burning through Holy Night, and was lit, thereafter, every night during the holy season.[7]

The custom of the Christmas candle is still kept in its original form in some countries. In Ireland, the mother or the father of the household lights a large holly-bedecked candle on Christmas Eve while the entire family prays for all its dear ones, both living and departed.[8] Among the Slavic nations (Poles, Ukrainians, Russians) the large Christmas candle is put on the table after it has been blessed by the priest in church. The Ukrainians do not use candlesticks, but stick the candle in a loaf of bread.

In many sections of South America the candle is placed in a paper lantern with Christmas symbols and pictures of the Nativity decorating its sides. In England and France the Christmas light often consisted of three individual candles molded together at the base, in honor of the Holy Trinity. In Germany the Christmas candle used to be placed on top of a wooden pole decorated with evergreens (*Lichtstock*), or many smaller candles were distributed on the shelves of a wooden structure made in the form of a pyramid, adorned with fir twigs or laurel and draped with glittering tinsel (*Weihnachtspyramide*).[9] During the seventeenth and eighteenth centuries this pyramid was gradually replaced by the Christmas tree. In some sections of Germany, however, the Christmas pyramid has remained a traditional custom.[10]

LIGHTS IN THE WINDOWS · The custom of placing lighted candles in the windows at Christmas is of Irish origin. During the second half of the last century it was promoted by the carolers' groups in the Beacon Hill section of Boston. This tradition quickly spread to other cities and helped to establish a general custom in the United States.[11]

THE YULE LOG · At a time when coal and other modern heating fuels were unknown, the firewood to be burned during Holy Night and on Christmas assumed special significance. A huge log was selected and brought to the house with great ceremony in preparation for the festival. It was called the "Christmas log" or "Yule log," and was burned on the open hearth during the holy season. This custom became a tradition in most European countries, including the Latin nations.[12] In Italy the log was called *ceppo;* this name was later applied also to wooden structures (pyramids) that carried the Christmas lights.

In spite of modern heating, the Yule log has survived in many homes as an old and cherished Christmas tradition. Its origin is disputed. Some scholars trace it back to pre-Christian times, when the Germanic tribes used to burn large wooden logs during the Yule season.[13] There is no historical evidence, however, that the custom of the "Christmas log" existed before the sixteenth century.

In some places the log was the whole trunk of a tree, carefully selected on the preceding Feast of Candlemas and stored away to dry out during the summer.[14] Many popular customs and ceremonies were connected with the Yule log. The unburned parts were put aside and preserved because the new log of next year had to be kindled with wood from the old one.[15]

THE CHRISTMAS TREE

YULE TREES · Many writers derive the origin of the Christmas tree from the ancient Yule tree or from other light and fire customs of pre-Christian times.[16] These explanations, however, are based on mere guesswork and do not agree with the historical facts. It is true that people used to put up evergreen trees in their homes at Yule time, both in pre-Christian centuries and later, to reassure themselves that nature's life was not altogether dead under winter's ice and snow, and that spring would come again. The little evergreen tree in the home, staying bravely alive through the period of nature's "death," was a cheerful token and symbol of this assurance. The Yule tree had no direct pagan connotation, and never acquired any Christian religious meaning in later times. Decorations are alien to its symbolism, for its whole significance consists in remaining alive and green during the winter.[17]

Yule trees may still be found in some sections of central Europe, standing side by side with the Christmas tree in the homes of rural districts. Their symbolism has remained entirely separate and sharply distinguished from that of the Christmas tree. In fact, there is the general custom of putting up fir trees, without any decorations, in halls and even churches at Christmas time. These fir trees are not, of course, "Christmas trees"; but they are used at Christmas to make homes and halls and churches look more cheerful than at other times. They—and not the decorated Christmas tree—are the true descendants of the ancient Yule trees.

Surprising as it may seem, the use of Christmas trees is a fairly recent custom in all countries outside of Germany, and even in Germany it attained its immense popularity as recently as the beginning of the last century. It is completely Christian in origin. Historians have never been able to connect it with ancient Germanic or Asiatic mythology.[18] Its origin is due to a combination of two medieval religious symbols: the Paradise tree and the previously described Christmas light.[19]

THE PARADISE TREE · From the eleventh century on, religious plays used to be performed in churches or in the open in front of churches. One of the most popular of these "mystery plays," as they were called, was the Paradise play. It represented the creation of man, the sin of Adam and Eve, and their expulsion from Paradise. This play closed with a consoling promise of the coming Saviour and of His Incarnation. For this reason the Paradise play was a favorite pageant in Advent.[20]

The Garden of Eden was indicated by a fir tree hung with apples, from which Eve broke the fruit and gave it to Adam to eat. This "Paradise tree" attracted the attention of all, especially the children, since it was the only object on the stage.[21]

During the fifteenth century the mystery plays were gradually forbidden because abuses had crept in. The people, however, did not want to miss the Paradise tree. Since they could no longer see it in church, they started putting it up in their homes once a year, in honor of Adam and Eve on their feast day, which was December 24. The Latin Church has never officially celebrated Adam and Eve as saints, but the Eastern Churches do so, and from the East the custom came into Europe of keeping their feast. Thus, on December 24 one could see the Paradise tree in the homes of the faithful in various sections of Europe. It was a fir tree hung with red apples.[22]

Under the influence of medieval religious "mystery" pictures, the Paradise tree stood not only for the "Tree of Sin" but also for the "Tree of Life" (Genesis 2, 9). As such, it bore, besides the apples (fruit of sin), wafers representing the Holy Eucharist (fruit of Life).[23] These wafers were later replaced by little pieces of pastry and candy representing the sweet fruit of Christ's redemption.

THE CHRISTMAS LIGHT · The very same day on which people in western Germany had the Paradise tree in their homes (December 24), another custom was kept from ancient times in all Christian countries. It was the "Christmas light," a symbol for our Lord, the Light of the world that started shining at Bethlehem. This Christmas candle had been inspired by the liturgical usage of a burning candle to represent Christ. On Christmas Eve the large, decorated candle was lit while the whole family knelt in prayer, and was then kept burning through Holy Night.

In western Germany this Christmas light—in form of many smaller candles—used to be placed on the shelves or steps of a wooden structure in the shape of a pyramid. Besides the candles, this "Christmas Pyramid" also bore decorations of evergreen twigs, glass balls, tinsel, and the "star of Bethlehem" on its top.[24]

THE CHRISTMAS TREE · During the sixteenth century the people in western Germany, on the left bank of the Rhine, began to combine the two symbols they had in their homes on December 24—the Paradise tree with the Christmas light. Was not the Paradise tree itself a beautiful, live pyramid? Why not transfer the decorations from the lifeless wooden pyramid to the tree? This is exactly what they did. They took first the glass balls and tinsel from the wooden pyramid and put them on the Paradise tree (which already bore apples and sweets). The "star of Bethlehem" was transferred from the pyramid to the top of the tree; and the Christmas crib, which had been standing at the foot of the pyramid, was now put under the tree. During the seventeenth century the lights were also transferred to the tree. Thus our modern Christmas tree came into being; its particular features are all clearly explained as they developed through the combination of the two above-mentioned customs.[25] These findings of modern research are confirmed by many traditional facts, like the custom found in sections of Bavaria where fir branches and little trees, decorated with lights, apples, and tinsel, are still called *Paradeis.*[26] Another confirmation is the fact that the "fruits" on the Christmas tree traditionally are of round shape (apples, oranges, nuts, glass balls), thus retaining the symbolism of the fruit of the Paradise tree.

SPREAD OF THE CHRISTMAS TREE · It now seems quite certain that the original home of the Christmas tree was the left bank of the upper Rhine in Germany, where this transformation took place.[27] The first mention of the tree as it is now known (but still without lights) dates from 1521 in German Alsace.[28] A more detailed description is given in a manuscript from Strasbourg of 1605.[29] At that time the tree was widely accepted in those parts.

The first news of candles on the Christmas tree dates from the seventeenth century.[30] In the course of the following centuries it slowly became popular, first in southern Germany, then also in the north and east.[31] It was not until the beginning of the nineteenth century, however, that it spread rapidly and grew into a general German custom, which was soon accepted also by the Slavic people of eastern Europe.[32]

The Christmas tree was introduced into France in 1837 when Princess Helen of Mecklenburg brought it to Paris after her marriage to the Duke of Orléans. It went to England around the middle of the last century when Prince Albert of Saxony, the husband of Queen Victoria, had a tree set up at Windsor Castle in 1841. From the royal court the fashion spread, first among the nobility, then among the people in general, until by the second half of the last century it was very much a part of the English Christmas celebration.[33]

The tree arrived in America as a cherished companion of the German immigrants. The first wave of German immigration, about 1700, brought thousands of Protestant farmers from the Rhine provinces, the Palatinate, who, after much suffering and many adventures in the colony of New York, finally settled in western Pennsylvania. The descendants of these early immigrants still inhabit the Lebanon valley and keep most of their ancient customs.

The second wave of German immigration began about 1830. These people, made up of both Catholic and Protestant groups, settled in New York, New England, and on the farms of Ohio and Wisconsin, and other parts of America. Through them the Christmas tree was brought to the attention of their neighbors, and soon became a much admired and familiar sight in all the churches of German settlements and in the homes of German-Americans.[34]

In spite of the official suppression of Christmas in New England, the custom of the Christmas tree spread. The fact that royalty in England had adopted it did much to make it fashionable in the homes of Americans of English descent.

The tree, which in 1850 had been called "a new German toy" by Charles Dickens, was termed "old-fashioned" by President Benjamin Harrison in 1891 when, on December 22 of that year, speaking to reporters about the Christmas celebration at the White House, he said, "And we shall have an old-fashioned Christmas tree for the grandchildren upstairs." [35]

America has added one new feature to the traditional use of the tree. It was in Boston that the custom originated (in 1912), of setting up lighted trees in public places. This custom spread rapidly all over the country and found its way to Europe after World War I, where it became quite general shortly before World War II.

LEGENDS · Innumerable are the legends connected with the origin and symbolism of the Christmas tree. Those legends which purport to explain its origin are, of course, merely etiological; they give a fictional explanation of origin for an already existing custom. Thus the "origin" of the tree is sometimes ascribed to Saint Boniface or Saint Ansgar or to the Christ Child Himself. Among Protestants a legend attributes the origin of the Christmas tree to Martin Luther. There is, of course, no historical basis for any of these legends.

THE "FIRST" TREE IN AMERICA · Many places in the United States claim the honor of having had the "first" Christmas tree in America. Such claims can never be truly substantiated, because it will remain impossible to prove that there was no Christmas tree in any other place before. As a matter of fact, German immigrants, especially those from the upper Rhine, are most likely to have set up the first Christmas trees in America as early as 1700. They lived in settlements of their own, and thus their trees probably did not come to the knowledge of their fellow citizens of other nationalities. It is reported that the Hessian soldiers in George Washington's army used Christmas trees.[36]

SYMBOLISM · Considering the historical facts, the meaning and message of the Christmas tree appear completely and deeply religious. It stands in the home at Christmas time as a symbol and reminder that Christ is the "Tree of Life" and the "Light of the World." Its many individual lights might be explained to the children as symbols of His divine and human traits and virtues. The glittering decorations indicate His great glory. The fact that it is evergreen is an ancient symbol of eternity.

In keeping with this historical symbolism, the decorations of the Christmas tree should remain appropriate and traditional. Silly "decorations" of modern manufacture which disturb the dignified aspect of the tree should not be used. Sensational features like "swirling" candles, animal figures, and dolls do not fit its purpose and meaning. In radiant beauty and quiet solemnity it should proclaim in the Christian home the very message of holy liturgy that has inspired its origin: *Lumen Christi*—the Light of Christ.

PLANTS AND FLOWERS

The custom of decorating homes on festive days is world-wide. It is neither pagan nor Christian in itself, but, rather, a natural expression of joy mingled with solemnity. It has been practiced in all parts of the world for thousands of years. After the time of the persecutions the Church soon approved and accepted the practice of decorating both the house of God and the Christian home with plants and flowers on the Feast of the Lord's Nativity. Pope Saint Gregory I (604) in a letter to Saint Augustine of Canterbury advised him to permit, and even to encourage, harmless popular customs which in themselves were not pagan, but natural, and could be given Christian interpretation.[17]

The plants used traditionally as Christmas decorations are mostly evergreens: first, because they were the only ones available in the winter season; second, because from ancient times evergreens have been symbolic of eternal life.

THE MISTLETOE · The mistletoe was a sacred plant in the pagan religion of the Druids in Britain. It was believed to have all sorts of miraculous qualities: the power of healing diseases, making poisons harmless, giving fertility to humans and animals, protecting from witchcraft, banning evil spirits, bringing good luck and great blessings. In fact, it was considered so sacred that even enemies who happened to meet beneath a mistletoe in the forest would lay down their arms, exchange a friendly greeting, and keep a truce until the following day. From this old custom grew the practice of suspending mistletoe over a doorway or in a room as a token of good will and peace to all comers. A kiss under the mistletoe was interpreted as a sincere pledge of love and a promise of marriage, and, at the same time, it was an omen of happiness, good fortune, fertility, and long life to the lovers who sealed and made known their engagement by a kiss beneath the sacred plant.[38]

After Britain was converted from paganism to Christianity, the bishops did not allow the mistletoe to be used in churches because it had been the main symbol of a pagan religion. Even to this day mistletoe is rarely used as a decoration for altars. There was, however, one exception. At the Cathedral of York at one period before the Reformation a large bundle of mistletoe was brought into the sanctuary each year at Christmas and solemnly placed on the altar by a priest. In this rite the plant that the Druids had called "All-heal" was used as a symbol of Christ, the Divine Healer of nations.[39]

The people of England then adopted the mistletoe as a decoration for their homes at Christmas. Its old, pagan religious meaning was soon forgotten, but some of the other meanings and customs have survived: the kiss under the mistletoe; the token of good will and friendship; the omen of happiness and good luck and the new religious significance:

> *The mistletoe bough at our Christmas board*
> *Shall hang, to the honor of Christ the Lord:*
> *For He is the evergreen tree of Life. . . .*[40]

THE HOLLY · To the early Christians in northern Europe this plant was a symbol of the burning thorn bush of Moses and the flaming love for God that filled Mary's heart. Its prickly points and red berries, resembling drops of blood, also reminded the faithful that the Divine Child was born to wear a crown of thorns.[41]

When the earth turns brown and cold, the holly, with its shiny green leaves and bright red berries, seems to lend itself naturally to Christmas decoration. Its appearance in the homes of old England opened the season of feasting and good cheer. Today holly is not only hung at doors and windows, on tables and walls, but its green leaves and red berries have become the universal symbol of Christmas, adorning greeting cards, gift tags and labels, gift boxes, and wrapping paper at Christmas time.

Medieval superstition in England endowed holly with a special power against witchcraft; unmarried women were told to fasten a sprig of holly to their beds at Christmas to guard them throughout the year from being turned into witches by the Evil One. In Germany, branches of holly that had been used as Christmas decoration in church were brought home and superstitiously kept as charms against lightning. Another superstition claimed that holly brought good luck to men, and that ivy brought it to women. The holly, therefore, is always referred to as "he," while the ivy is the distaff plant.[42]

In the United States the native holly has almost disappeared because of the selfishness of careless holly hunters at Christmas time. What is used here now is the European variety, with larger leaves and berries, which is commercially grown by farmers in this country. The California holly (Toyon) grows along the Pacific coast and has extra-brilliant flaming-red-colored berries, which are placed in Christmas wreaths of evergreen for decorations.

THE IVY · In pagan Rome the ivy was the badge of the wine god Bacchus, and was displayed as a symbol of unrestrained drinking and feasting. For this reason it was later banished from Christian homes. The old tradition in England ruled that ivy should be banned from the inside of homes and should be allowed to grow only on the outside. Accordingly, the use of ivy as a Christmas decoration was opposed by most people in medieval England. On the continent of Europe it was hardly ever used for that purpose. But a symbolism of human weakness clinging to divine strength was frequently ascribed to the ivy, and this prompted some poets in old England to defend ivy as a decoration at Christmas time.[43]

The delicate little ground ivy, "which groweth in a sweet and shadowed place," was at all times a favorite plant of the English home; it used to be kept in pots and displayed around the house not only at Christmas, but all year round as well. Many of the pioneer settlers coming to the shores of the New World brought pots of such ground ivy with them. Today it is a popular indoor as well as outdoor plant in most parts of America.

THE LAUREL (BAY) · As an ancient symbol of triumph, the laurel is aptly used for Christmas decorations, to proclaim the victory over sin and death that Christ's birth signifies. It was greatly cherished as a Christmas plant in bygone centuries. In fact, laurel was the first plant used as Christmas decoration; the early Christians at Rome adorned their homes with it in celebration of the nativity of Christ.[44]

The modern custom of hanging laurel wreaths on the outside of doors as a friendly greeting to our fellow men comes from an old Roman practice. The wreath was their symbol of victory, glory, joy, and celebration.[45] The Christmas wreath seems to have been introduced to the United States by immigrants from England and Ireland, and gradually became part of the American Christmas scene.

THE ROSEMARY · This delicate plant has been connected with Christmas since time immemorial. According to an old legend, it was honored by God in reward for the humble service that it offered to Mary and her Child. On the way to Egypt, so the charming story goes, Mary washed the tiny garments of Jesus and spread them over a rosemary bush to dry in the sun. Since then the rosemary has delighted man by its delicate fragrance.

In other medieval legends this plant is pictured as a great protection and help against evil spirits, especially if it has been used in church as a decoration on Christmas Day.[46]

THE CHERRY · It is customary among the Czechs and Slovaks, and also in Austria and some other sections of central Europe, to break a branch off a cherry tree on Saint Barbara's Day (December 4), place it in a pot of water in the kitchen and keep it in warm air. The twig would then burst into blossom at Christmas time, and made a very festive decoration. Such cherry branches, brought to flowering at Christmas, were considered omens of good luck—for instance, the girl who had tended the twig would find a good husband within the year if she succeeded in producing the bloom exactly on Christmas Eve.[47]

THE POINSETTIA · This native plant of Central America is now widely used in churches and homes at Christmas, because the flaming star of its red bracts resembles the star of Bethlehem. The poinsettia was named for Dr. Joel Roberts Poinsett (1851), who served as United States ambassador to Mexico. Upon his return, in 1829, he brought this flower with him to his home in South Carolina, where it flourished.[48]

The people of Mexico call the poinsettia the "flower of Holy Night." A charming Mexican legend explains its origin: On a Christmas Eve, long ago, a poor little boy went to church in great sadness because he had no gift to bring to the Holy Child. He dared not enter the church, and, kneeling humbly on the ground outside the house of God, prayed fervently and assured our Lord, with tears, how much he desired to offer Him some lovely present. "But I am very poor and dread to approach You with empty hands." When he finally rose from his knees, he saw springing up at his feet a green plant with gorgeous blooms of dazzling red. His prayer had been answered; he broke some of the beautiful twigs from the plant and joyously entered the church to lay his gift at the feet of the Christ Child. Since then the plant has spread over the whole country; it blooms every year at Christmas time with such glorious abandon that men are filled with the true holiday spirit at the mere sight of the Christmas flower, symbolic of the Saviour's birth.[49]

GREETING CARDS

ORIGIN · In the middle of the nineteenth century, when postal rates became cheaper, people began to send written greetings and good wishes to their relatives and friends before the Feast of Christmas. It is claimed that the first Christmas greeting card was engraved in 1842 by a sixteen-year-old London artist, William Maw Egley. Some years later, special cards were privately printed in Britain by a few individuals who designed them for their personal use. It was many years before the manufacture and sale of cards was commercialized. By 1860 they were on the market, and were quite common by about 1868.[50]

In America, the printing of Christmas cards was introduced by the Boston lithographer Louis Prang, a native of Breslau,

Germany. Prang offered them to the public for sale in 1875. Since the present popular designs of Christmas symbols were not yet known in the United States, he adorned his cards with Killarney roses, daisies, geraniums, apple blossoms, and similar floral motives. These first American Christmas cards, like all other products of Prang's lithographic art, are still famous among collectors because of their exquisite design and craftsmanship.[51]

PRESENT CUSTOM · Within the last few decades, the sending of Christmas cards has become more a burden of social amenity than a token of affection. At present, two billion greeting cards are mailed annually at Christmas in the United States—an average of fifty cards per family. Though many of the modern cards do not have appropriate Christmas designs, there is a tendency of late to return to the genuine spiritual tone of the season.[52]

It is interesting to note that traditional Christmas cards show wintry landscapes, with ice and snow, even in countries of the Southern Hemisphere (South America, Australia, Africa), where December is the warmest month of the year.

CHRISTMAS PAGEANTS

ORIGIN · In early centuries, the story of the Nativity was dramatized in churches within the framework of so-called "miracle plays." These semidramatic services consisted in pious representations of the "mystery" of Christ's birth, accompanied by song, prayer, and other acts of devotion. (Mystery, in this connection, is the religious term for any episode of Christ's life related in the Gospels.) In those days, of course, books and pictures were not available to most of the common people, so these plays served not only as acts of worship, but also as a means of religious instruction. They soon became very popular in all Christian countries.[53]

There is a touching note of childlike piety and devotion in these early church plays, revealing the deeply religious manner in which plays were used to help in divine service. From such beginnings grew that bewildering number of mystery plays which flourished in all parts of Europe from the eleventh to the fifteenth centuries. As time went on, the plays became more elaborate and covered more details of the Biblical story. Fictional and legendary scenes were added, and the congregation was allowed to take part.[54]

SUPPRESSION · As a natural, but unfortunate, result of these changes, many abuses appeared, such as irreverence, comedy, improper behavior of clergy and laymen, sensational effects, and similar aberrations. The authorities of the Church protested against such scandal; but things had gone too far for correction and change. Under the pretext of tradition, the warnings and admonitions of the bishops were ignored or neglected. After all efforts had failed to restore the plays to their original character, the whole institution was gradually suppressed and finally forbidden during the fourteenth and fifteenth centuries, and miracle plays were no longer performed in churches.[55]

This banishment, however, brought about an indirect blessing. In order to survive outside the church, the plays were purged of their abuses and were able to employ many dramatic effects that formerly had been impossible in church plays. There subsequently developed a rich growth of religious drama, which flourished up to the Reformation and continued to flourish long after in many countries.[56] The schools of the Jesuit Fathers were centers of this drama movement until the order was suppressed in 1773.[57]

REVIVAL. · The restoration of Christmas customs in the last century also brought about a revival of Nativity plays—not the long and tiresome seventeenth- and eighteenth-century morality plays, but simple, devotional plays of an earlier type. In fact, these old plays, in simplified form and with certain restrictions, had never ceased to exist in some sections of Germany and Austria, even in churches.

It was from Germany that the Nativity pageant found its way into America. As far as is known, the first such play in this country was performed in the German Catholic church of the Holy Trinity in Boston, Massachusetts, on Christmas 1851.[58] The children of the parish, dressed as Oriental shepherds, carrying bundles of food, linen, and other gifts, marched in solemn procession to the crib in front of the altar, singing Christmas carols.

They honored the Divine Child by offering their presents, reciting prayers, and chanting hymns. The parish priest accepted the offerings, which were afterward distributed to the poor. The children in their Oriental costumes, their hands folded devoutly, left the church in a street procession after the service. This performance attracted such attention and admiration that it had to be repeated twice during Christmas week upon the urgent request of both Catholics and Protestants from all over the city who were anxious to witness the "new" pageant. This procession at Holy Trinity Church, Boston, has been held every year since then, though of late in simplified form, without costumes.

GIFTS AND GIFT-BRINGERS

CHRISTMAS PRESENTS · Christmas is the season for exchanging presents. It is not difficult to understand why people should be filled with good will on the Christ Child's birthday. "As long as you did it for one of these, the least of my brethren, you did it for me" (Matthew 25, 40).

The practice of giving presents was also an old Roman custom, called *strenae*. On New Year's Day the people of ancient Rome exchanged gifts of sweet pastry, lamps, precious stones, and coins of gold or silver, as tokens of their good wishes for a happy year.[59] This custom and even its name (*étrennes*) have been preserved among the French people to the present day. In most countries, however, the present-giving has become a part of the actual Christmas celebration.

In Germany the packages of Christmas gifts were called "Christ bundles." They contained candy, sugar plums, cakes, apples, nuts, dolls, and toys; useful things like clothes, caps, mittens, stockings, shoes and slippers; and things "that belong to teaching, obedience and discipline," such as ABC tables, paper, pencils, books; and the "Christ rod." This rod, attached to the bundle, was a pointed reminder for good behavior.[60]

Another form of presenting gifts was the old German custom of the "Christmas ship," in which bundles for the children were stored away. This was adopted in England to some extent, but never attained general popularity, though special carols for the occasion were sung in both countries.[61]

A popular Christmas custom in Britain is "boxing" on the feast of Saint Stephen, December 26. It originated because in medieval times the priests would empty the alms boxes in all churches on the day after Christmas and distribute the gifts to the poor of the parish. In imitation of this practice, workers, apprentices, and servants kept their own personal "boxes," made of earthenware, in which they stored savings and donations throughout the year. At Christmas came the last and greatest flow of coins, collected from patrons, customers, and friends. Then, on the day after Christmas, the box was broken and the money counted. This custom was eventually called "boxing" (giving and accepting presents). Each present is a box, and the day of present-giving is Boxing Day.[62]

A similar custom prevailed in Holland and some parts of Germany, where children were taught to save their pennies in a pig-shaped earthenware box. This box was not to be opened until Christmas, and consequently was called the "feast pig."

THE CHRIST CHILD · In most European countries the Child Jesus is the gift-bringer. The children believe He comes with angels in the evening, trimming the tree and putting the presents under it. Sometimes the Divine Child was impersonated by a girl dressed in white, but this custom was never widespread. The general practice has the Christ Child arrive unseen by the children; helped by the parents, He prepares the tree and distributes the gifts. When everything is ready, a little bell is rung and the anxious children enter the room where all the presents are spread out before their shining eyes. But the Child Jesus, with His angels, has already left for some other home. The reading of the Christmas Gospel, a prayer before the crib, and the singing of a hymn unite the whole family in the Christmas spirit before the gifts are opened in the late evening of December 24.

This custom still survives in some parts of Germany, Austria, and other countries of central Europe, as well as in France, French Canada, Spain, Central and South America. In Spain and Spanish-speaking countries the Child Jesus (el Niño Jesús) brings the Christmas gifts for the children during Holy Night. Since the crib has been set up for nine days with an empty manger, the children are familiar with it. On Christmas morning, however, they find the Holy Child in the crib and the gifts arranged in front of it.

The German name of the Christ Child is *Christkind,* commonly used in its diminutive form *Christkindel* (both i's are short). When German immigration to New York and other eastern cities of the United States increased after the middle of the last century, the word *Christkindel* of the immigrants was adopted in the form of Kris Kringle by their fellow countrymen, but was identified with Santa Claus.[63]

OTHER GIFT-BRINGERS · In Rome and other cities of Italy an unusual figure impersonates the gift-bringer for children. It is the "Lady Befana" (or Bufana), a sort of fairy queen. The day she distributes presents is January 6 (Epiphany), when the children roam the streets, happily blow their paper trumpets, and receive the gifts that Lady Befana has provided for them. The name comes from the word epiphany.[64]

The gift-bringer in Russia is a legendary old woman called Babushka (Grandmother). She is said to have misdirected the Magi when they inquired their way to Bethlehem. According to another version she refused hospitality to the Holy Family on its way to Egypt. Whatever her fault, she repented of her unkindness, and to make reparation for her sin she now goes about the world on Christmas Eve looking for the Christ Child and distributing gifts to children.[65]

After 1660 the custom originated in England of impersonating the spirit of the feast by a figure called "Father Christmas." This legendary Christmas man was pictured as a heavily bearded, furclad, friendly individual, symbolizing and bestowing the mood of merry celebration. He did not usually bring the presents, however, and thus held no special appeal to the affection of children. A similar figure is the Christmas Man of northern Germany (*Knecht Rupprecht*).[66]

SANTA CLAUS · After the Reformation, the feast and veneration of Saint Nicholas, the patron of little children, were abolished in many countries. Soon people in those countries forgot the saint who had once been so dear to them. Only here and there a trace of him would linger on, as, for example, in the pageant of the "Boy Bishop" in England, and in the name *Pelznickel* (Fur Nicholas), which many people in western Germany gave to their Christmas Man (*Pels-nichol* now among the Pennsylvania Dutch).

When the Dutch came to America and established the colony of New Amsterdam, their children enjoyed the traditional "visit of Saint Nicholas" on December 5, for the Dutch had kept this ancient Catholic custom even after the Reformation.[67] Later, when England took over the colony and it became New York, the kindly figure of Sinter Klaas (pronounced like Santa Claus) soon aroused among the English children the desire of having such a heavenly visitor come to their homes, too.[68]

The English settlers were glad and willing to comply with the anxious wish of their children. However, the figure of a Catholic saint and bishop was not acceptable in their eyes, especially since many of them were Presbyterians, to whom a bishop was repugnant. In addition, they did not celebrate the feasts of saints according to the ancient Catholic calendar.

The dilemma was solved by transferring the visit of the mysterious man whom the Dutch called Santa Claus from December 5 to Christmas, and by introducing a radical change in the figure itself. It was not merely a "disguise," but the ancient saint was completely replaced by an entirely different character.[69] Behind the name Santa Claus actually stands the figure of the pagan Germanic god Thor (after whom Thursday is named). Some details about Thor from ancient German mythology will show the origin of the modern Santa Claus tale:

Thor was the god of the peasants and the common people. He was represented as an elderly man, jovial and friendly, of heavy build, with a long white beard. His element was the fire, his color red. The rumble and roar of thunder were said to be caused by the rolling of his chariot, for he alone among the gods never rode on horseback but drove in a chariot drawn by two white goats (called Cracker and Gnasher). He was fighting the giants of ice and snow, and thus became the Yule-god. He was said to live in the "Northland" where he had his palace among icebergs. By our pagan forefathers he was considered as the cheerful and friendly god, never harming the humans but rather helping and protecting them. The fireplace in every home was especially sacred to him, and he was said to come down through the chimney into his element, the fire.[70]

Here, then, is the true origin of our "Santa Claus." It certainly was a stroke of genius that produced such a charming and attractive figure for our children from the withered pages of pagan mythology. With the Christian saint whose name he still bears, however, this Santa Claus has really nothing to do.[71]

The fairy tale of Santa Claus will not be abolished easily, despite the efforts of well-meaning people [72]—nor does it seem necessary. Children do like fairy tales, and Santa Claus is one of the most charming of them. Parents can use it without harm provided they apply some safeguards to avoid an undue overstressing of the Santa Claus figure. The descriptions of great disappointment and psychological conflicts occurring when children find out that there is no Santa Claus apply only to families where parents have misled their children in the first place by allowing Santa to take the central place instead of Christ, Whose birthday is the only reason for the feast.

[1] H. Leclercq, *Crèche*, DACL, 3.2 (1948), 2021 ff.   [2] Celano, 199, 84.
[3] F. E. de Uriarte, *El buey y el asno testigos del naciamento de nuestro Señor*, in *La ciencia christiana*, Madrid, Vol. 12 (1879), 260 ff. and Vol. 13 (1880), 64 ff., 167 ff.   [4] G. Hager, *Die Weihnachtskrippe*, München, 1902.   [5] F. Klees, *The Pennsylvania Dutch*, New York, 1951, 347 ff.   [6] G. E. Nitzsche, "The Christmas Putz of the Pennsylvania Germans," in *Publications of the Pennsylvania German Folklore Society*, 6.1 (1941), 1 ff.   [7] Crippen, 114 ("Christmas Candles").
[8] Crippen, 115.   [9] See pictures of Christmas pyramids in Spamer, 40-41 and 85.   [10] O. Huth, *Der Lichterbaum*, Berlin, 1943, 68 ff.   [11] R. B. Kimball, *Christmas Eve on Beacon Hill*, Boston, 1918, 2 ff.
[12] Gugitz, II, 248 ff.   [13] Frazer, 636 ff.   [14] Crippen, 108.   [15] Crippen, 110; Frazer, 638 ff.   [16] See A. Tille, "German Christmas and the Christmas Tree," in *Folklore*, 3 (1892), 166 ff.   [17] L. Hosl, *Julfest*, LThK, 5 (1938), 706.   [18] R. Hindringer, *Christbaum*, LThK, 2 (1931), 902 f.   [19] A. Pfleger, *Die Wiege des Christbaumes*, EW, 56.
[20] H. Craig, "The Origin of the Old Testament Plays," in *Modern Philology*, 10 (1912-13), 473 ff.; *Le Mystère d'Adam*, ed. P. Studer, Manchester, 1918.   [21] Koren, 61.   [22] Spamer, 73 f. (picture opposite p. 92); Gugitz, II, 277. About the Paradise Tree on Christmas Eve in the Tyrol see A. Dörrer, *Tirol hat die älteste Weihnachtsbaumtradition*, in *Tiroler Tageszeitung*, Innsbruck, December 1957, 4. See also the account on Christmas pyramids among the German settlers

at Bethlehem, Pa. (in 1747) in *Publications of the Pennsylvania German Folklore Society,* 6 (1941), 13 ff. [23] EW, 56. See picture of Paradise Tree (with crucifix) bearing the apples of sin and the wafers of life (symbolizing the Eucharist) in Rahner, 99. [24] See many pictures of Christmas pyramids in O. Huth, *Der Lichterbaum,* Berlin, 1943, 72 ff.; also Spamer, 85 and 92. [25] A. Jacoby, *Der Ursprung des Christbaums,* in *Hessische Blätter für Volkskunde,* 1928, 134 ff. [26] GH, 3 (1932), 317. [27] A. Pfleger, *Die Wiege des Christbaumes,* EW, 51 ff. [28] EW, 52 (text of the original manuscript). [29] EW, 53 (text of the original manuscript). [30] EW, 55. In Graz, Austria, the Paradise tree bore not only apples, but also lights, as early as 1603: F. Popelka, *Geschichte der Stadt Graz,* Graz, 1936, II, 420. [31] VL, 81; EW, 51. [32] L. Mackensen, *Geschichte des Weihnachtsbaumes,* in *Deutscher Kulturatlas,* Berlin-Leipzig, 1919 (detailed report on the spread of the Christmas tree, with maps and statistics). [33] Koren, 65. [34] Barnett, 13 f. [35] Dawson, 313. [36] See A. M. Sowder, "Christmas Trees," in *Yearbook of Agriculture,* Washington, 1949, 245 ff. [37] Saint Gregory addressed this instruction to Saint Augustine through the Frankish Abbot Mellitus: *Epist. 76 ad Mellitum Abbatem;* PL, 77, 1215. [38] Frazer, 658 ff.; ES, 175. [39] Dawson, 240 ff. [40] Crippen, 24. [41] Crippen, 15. [42] Crippen, 17. [43] Crippen, 14 ff. [44] Tertullian, *Liber de Idololatria,* 15; PL, 1, 684. [45] N. Fiebiger, *Corona,* PW, 4, 1636. [46] ES, 205. [47] Cugitz, II, 217 ff. (*St. Barbara mit dem Lebenszweig*); Koren, 38. [48] Enc. Brit., 18 (1929), 116 f. [49] WC, 133. [50] J. K. Arthur, "A Century of Christmas Cards," in *American Home,* December 1946, 15 ff. [51] Barnett, 18; E. D. Chase, *The Romance of Greeting Cards,* Boston, 1926, 6 ff. [52] Barnett, 123 ff. ("Christmas Cards"). [53] M. Böhme, *Das lateinische Weihnachtsspiel,* Leipzig, 1917. [54] Young, II, 14 ff. [55] A. Dörrer, *Geistliche Schauspiele,* LThK, 9 (1937), 223 f.; Young, II, 416 ff. [56] G. Cohen, *Le Théâtre en France au Moyen Age,* Vol. I (*Le Théâtre religieuse*), Paris, 1928. [57] J. Müller, *Das Jesuitendrama,* Freiburg, 1930. [58] Notes of the pastor (Gustave Eck), 1851, manuscript, parish archive, Holy Trinity Church, Boston. [59] PW, 4A.II, 351 (*Strena*). [60] Crippen, 147. [61] Crippen, 155. [62] Crippen, 157 ff. [63] Barnett, 11. [64] Crippen, 195. [65] Crippen, 146. [66] Spamer, 62 ff. [67] Barnett, 24 ff. [68] M. J. Lamb, "Christmas Season in Dutch New York," in *Magazine of American History,* 10 (December 1883), 471 ff. [69] Barnett, 27 ("Transition"). [70] H. A. Grueber, *Myths of Northern Lands,* Vol. I, New York, 1895, 61 ff. [71] On Thomas Nast as creator of the modern Santa Claus picture, see Barnett, 28 ff. [72] Barnett, 36 ff. ("For and Against Santa Claus").

CHAPTER

9   *Christmas Foods*

SEASONAL BAKING

FERTILITY RITES · In pre-Christian times the winter solstice was celebrated for ten or twelve days in December. One of the main features of the celebration consisted of rituals expressing reverence for the gift of bread, thereby winning the favor of the field gods for the new year of planting and reaping. Agricultural fertility cults were universal among the ancient nations of Europe. Invocations, display of wheat in the homes, baking of special kinds of bread and cakes, symbolic actions to foster the fertility of the soil, honoring the spirits of ancestors who had handed down the fields and pastures were all part of their ritual.[1]

With the coming of Christianity many of these practices were discontinued; many others, however, were never relinquished and were more or less incorporated into the celebration of Christmas, usually assuming Christian symbolism.

This dual origin of many Christmas customs has been preserved most clearly in the agricultural nations of eastern Europe, especially among the Ukrainians, whose country still is regarded as the "bread basket" of Europe. To a Ukrainian peasant, Christmas was, and still is, what Thanksgiving Day is to us, a day on which he offers thanks to God for a good harvest and invokes divine blessing for his fields in the coming year.

On Christmas Eve, the father of the Ukrainian family brings into the home a sheaf of wheat from the barn, placing it upright in a corner of the room. This sheaf is called "Forefather," symbolizing those forefathers of the nation who first tilled the land. The floor is strewn with hay and straw; there is hay even on the table, on which two loaves of fragrant white bread are placed, one on top of the other, with a Christmas candle stuck in the upper loaf. The first and most important dish of the solemn dinner on Christmas Eve is Kutya, consisting of boiled wheat with honey and poppy seed. The head of the family, after blessing this dish, takes a spoonful of it and throws it against the ceiling—an ancient symbol of thanksgiving that has survived from the pre-Christian era.

In Poland, sheaves of wheat or grain from the harvest are placed in the four corners of the principal room on Christmas Eve. Straw is spread on the floor and laid on the dining table, and a clean white cloth put over it. The table, bearing the Christmas candle and dishes with traditional pastry, is placed in front of the family shrine—usually a statue of Christ or the Blessed Virgin.[2]

BREADS AND CAKES · In most countries the Christmas cakes, which were baked on the eve of the feast and eaten during the season, were said to bring special blessings of good luck and health.[3] In Ireland, England, and Scotland cakes were baked on Christmas Eve for every member of the household. These were usually circular in shape and flavored with caraway seeds. The Irish people have a Gaelic name for Christmas Eve, *Oidhche na ceapairi*, which means "Night of Cakes." [4] In Germany and France, Christmas cakes were often adorned with the figure of the Holy Child, made of sugar. The Greek Christmas cakes had a cross on top, and one such cake was left on the table during Holy Night in the hope that Christ Himself would come and eat it. The Christmas loaf (*Pain calendeau*) is still made in southern France; it is quartered crosswise and is eaten only after the first quarter has been given to some poor person. In central and eastern Germany a special bread (*Christstollen*) is made of wheat flour, butter, sugar, almond, and raisins.

Slavic people (Poles, Russians, Slovaks) and other nations of eastern Europe prepare, in addition to their Christmas loaves, thin wafers of white flour which are blessed by the priest and eaten, often with syrup or honey, before the main meal on Christmas Eve. The Lithuanians call these wafers "bread of the angels," the Poles *oplatki* (offerings). Various scenes of the Nativity are

imprinted on them, and the head of the household distributes
them among his family, as a symbol of love and peace. In Russia,
Saint Nicholas (Kolya) puts wheat cakes on the window sills
during Holy Night. Among the nations of central Europe fruit
bread (*Kletzenbrot*) and fruitcake are favorite Christmas dishes.
In France and French Canada housewives bake a large batch
of small round loaves (*pain d'habitant*) in honor of the feast.

SWEETS AND PASTRIES · Even more abundant and varied are the
many forms of Christmas pastries, cookies, and sweets that have
survived to the present and, in some countries, as a substitute
for the ancient cakes. In Germany, Austria, Switzerland, and
other regions of central Europe, the Christmas pastry *Weih-
nachtsgebäck* has various forms, different in shape and composition. Christmas tree pastry (*Christbaumgebäck*) is made of a
white dough and cut in the shape of stars, angels, flowers, and
animals. It was, and still is, hung on the tree and eaten by the
children when the tree is taken down. The honey pastry (*Honig-
backwerk*) is made of flour, honey, ginger and other spices, and
is a favorite Christmas dish all over Germany as *Lebkuchen*,
Pfefferkuchen, Pfeffernüsse. Another pastry, baked very hard,
is the South German *Springerle*, cookies rectangular in shape
with pictures, such as flowers, animals, dancing figures, and many
Christmas symbols stamped on them.

The Scandinavians bake their Christmas pastry in the form
of a boar or he goat (*Juleber, Julgat*). It is served at Christmas
with the other dishes but not eaten until January 19, the feast
day of Saint Canute (Martyr, King of Denmark, died 1086). A
familiar Spanish Christmas sweet is the *dulces de almendra*, a
pastry made of sugar, flour, egg white, and almonds. Similar
almond pastries are used during this season in Portugal and Italy.
Central and South American people enjoy an unusual pastry,
buñuelos, baked of white flour, very crisp and brittle, and eaten
with syrup or honey. In Venezuela the *hallaca* is the national
Christmas dish. It is a pie of chopped meat wrapped in a crust
of corn pastry. The French and French Canadians have dough-
nuts (*beignes*) made of a special dough, also fruitcake and white
cream fudge (*sucre à la crème*), and a cake of whole wheat,
brown sugar, and dates (*carreaux aux dattes*). The Lithuanian

people eat little balls of hard and dry pastry (*Kukuliai*) which are softened in plain water.

THE CHRISTMAS DINNER

Christmas, among Latin Catholics and all Eastern Rites, still is, preceded by a day of fasting and abstinence, in preparation for the Lord's nativity. But on Christmas Day, ever since the feast was established, a great dinner was held. Naturally in the course of time each nation developed its own treasured customs in connection with the Christmas meal.

THE FESTIVE MEAL · The traditional American Christmas meal is English in origin, although the English "Christmas bird" (usually goose or capon) was supplanted by turkey and cranberry sauce. The boisterous Christmas dinners of the English nobility and gentry in ancient times, with many guests and gluttonous eating and drinking, have never found their way into the New World and have long since disappeared in Britain.

The typical English Christmas dinner in medieval times, in castle and manor, started with the serving of the boar's head, which was brought in solemn procession by the chief cook, accompanied by waiters, pages, and minstrels to the tune of the old carol, "The boar's head in hand I bear." [5] Then followed other courses in bewildering variety: roast boar, beef, pork, venison, lamb, capon, goose, duck, swan, pigeon, and others.[6]

Among the common people, a large bird was the standard fare at Christmas dinners: goose, capon, bustard, or chicken; and, after 1530, turkey, which had been brought from Mexico to Europe at the beginning of the sixteenth century and was soon domesticated in Spain, France, and England.[7] It was this traditional festive meal of the common people which set the style of the American turkey dinners at Christmas and Thanksgiving.

MINCE PIE · Mince pie on the Christmas table is an old English custom.[8] When the Puritans in New England tried to supplant Christmas with Thanksgiving (and almost succeeded for a time), they also transferred the English Christmas dinner of "a bird" and mince pie to their new feast day.

The British had various kinds of "minc'd pie" long before it became a part of the Christmas meal. The Christmas pie originated when the Crusaders, returning from the Holy Land, brought along all sorts of Oriental spices, and the Feast of the Lord's Nativity came to be celebrated with a pie containing the spices from His native land.

A Christmas mince pie of the seventeenth century, according to Robert Herrick, was filled with beef tongues, chopped chicken, eggs, raisins, orange and lemon peelings, sugar, and various spices. In this recipe it is not difficult to recognize the basic pattern of modern mince pie.[9]

Before the Reformation, in honor of the Saviour's humble birth, the mince pies were made in oblong form, representing the manger; and sometimes, in the slight depression on top of the pie was placed a little figure of the Child Jesus. Thus the pie was served as an object of devotion as well as a part of the feast.[10] The "baby" was removed and the "manger" was eaten by the children. This custom was suppressed by the Puritans when they came to power in the seventeenth century; and the pie was henceforth made in circular shape.[11]

PLUM PUDDING · A national Christmas dish in England was, and with variations still is, the famous plum pudding. It was bound up in a cloth, boiled on Christmas morning, and served with great ceremony, often saturated with alcohol and set aflame while being borne into the dining room. The name dates from the end of the seventeenth century. Before that time it was called "hackin" because its ingredients were hacked or chopped before being mixed into the pie.[12]

CHRISTMAS DRINKS · Christmas has always been a favorite occasion for drinking, especially so in recent times, when hard liquor often replaces the sweet ciders and light wines of more temperate days. The Latin nations enjoyed, and still do, their customary wine with the Christmas meal. In northern Europe, beer was a favorite drink; in England, ale.

A Christmas drink peculiar to the English was the "wassail," always served in a large bowl. The word comes from the Old Saxon and used to be a drinker's greeting (*Was haile:* Your

Health). It usually consisted of ale, roasted apples, eggs, sugar, nutmeg, cloves, and ginger, and was drunk while hot. From this custom of drinking the wassail, the English derived the word wassailing for any kind of Christmas revels accompanied by drinking.[13]

It was not until the eighteenth century that the mild wassail drink was gradually supplanted by a punch made of stronger spirits. The punch bowl finally replaced the wassail bowl and is now a popular feature of the Christmas celebration in many homes. Another traditional English drink was "Lamb's wool," made of ale and the juice of roasted apples, heated, and spiced with nutmeg.

[1] See R. Wossidlo, *Erntebrauche*, Hamburg, 1927; G. Jarosch, *Erntebrauch und Erntedank*, Jena, 1937. [2] Benet, 98 ff. [3] M. Höfler, *Weihnachtsgebäcke*, Wien, 1905. [4] Also *"oidche nam bannag"*; see *The Illustrated Gaelic Dictionary*, ed. E. Dwelly, Fleet, Hants, 1930, 66. [5] TCS, 18. [6] W. Hone, *Table Book*, London, 1825, II, 506. [7] Crippen, 119. [8] Hackwood, 196. See "The Battle of the Mince Pie," WC, 147. [9] Crippen, 123. [10] Hackwood, 197. [11] T. K. Hervey, *The Book of Christmas*, Boston, 1888, 159. [12] Hackwood, 195 ff. [13] Crippen, 99 ff.; ES, 75.

CHAPTER

10   *Christmas Week*

HISTORY AND LITURGY

OCTAVE · Easter was observed from the first with an eight days' celebration (in keeping with the Jewish custom of an eight days' Pasch), and the eighth day was called "octave" (*dies octava*). By

the end of the seventh century the Feast of Epiphany had such
an octave, too. Thus it seemed fitting to provide Christmas with
the same distinction. The eighth day after the Lord's nativity
bore the name "Octave of the Lord" (*Octava Domini*) in the
liturgical books of the eighth century.[1]

SAINTS' DAYS · On the intervening days, however, the feasts of
great saints had been celebrated from earlier centuries, and these
feasts have remained to our day: Saint Stephen on December 26,
Saint John the Evangelist (originally also his brother James) on
December 27, and the Holy Innocents on December 28. In most
of the Eastern Churches, December 28 was reserved for the solemn commemoration of Peter and Paul, and the Innocents' feast
was held either on December 27 or 29.[2]

The reason these particular saints had their feasts assigned
immediately following Christmas was the desire of honoring
them because of their special connection with the Lord: Stephen,
the first martyr of the New Testament; John, the Apostle "whom
Jesus loved" (John 21, 20); the Holy Innocents, so closely connected with the events of Christ's nativity and infancy; Peter and
Paul, the princes of the Apostles. Duranti calls these saints the
"companions of Christ" (*comites Christi;* the word "*comes*," from
which we got our word "count," also connotates aristocracy or
nobility).[3]

December 29, the Feast of Saint Thomas Becket, Archbishop
of Canterbury, who was martyred in his cathedral by the soldiers
of Henry II in 1170, is the true anniversary date of his death.
Because of the great shock and sensation that this martyrdom
caused at a time when all of Europe was Catholic, the Roman
authorities, in the thirteenth century, deemed it appropriate to
assign the celebration of his feast within the privileged days of
Christmas week, thus adding him to the group of "Christ's nobility." [4]

On December 31 the liturgy honors the great pope Sylvester I
(335), under whose pontificate the Church began to enjoy the
precious freedom given her by Constantine, which gradually
spread over the whole Roman Empire.[5]

With the liturgical celebration of these feasts is connected
the daily commemoration of the Nativity, not only in the usual

orations of the Mass and Divine Office, but also in the second Vespers, which take their psalms and antiphons from Christmas Day.

SUNDAY · In the ancient lectionaries (reading lists) of the Roman Church, the Sunday of Christmas week was called the "First Sunday after the Nativity of the Lord." In the eighth century, when the octave had been introduced, the title was changed to "Sunday within the Octave of the Nativity." A Station is not indicated, probably because on Sundays of lesser liturgical rank (of which this is one) the popes celebrated the Mass in their palace chapel and therefore no station procession took place in the city.[6]

The liturgical texts of the Mass reflect the joy of Christmas and the thought of the newborn Saviour's divinity and glory. The Gospel (Mark 2, 33-40) relates the prophecy of the old man Simeon and the meeting of the prophetess Anna with the Divine Child. The prayers of the breviary are entirely the same as on Christmas Day, except for the lessons of the Matin and the oration.

The three days after Christmas precede this Sunday in liturgical rank. Thus, if December 25, 26, 27, or 28 falls on a Sunday, the respective feast is celebrated and the Sunday Mass is transferred to December 30.

FOLKLORE

RELIGIOUS OBSERVANCE · In the Middle Ages, Christmas week also assumed the note of a hallowed time within the homes of the faithful. Many observances of a religious character were introduced locally and spread over large sections of the Christian population of Europe. For the farmers and their animals it was a time of rest and relaxation from laborious work; only the necessary chores were done in stable and barn. Thus the whole week became a series of holidays. More time than usual was spent on prayer and religious exercises. It is still the custom in many sections of Europe to light the candles of the Christmas tree every night while the whole family says the rosary or performs some other devotion, followed by the singing of carols.

Carol singing from house to house is an ancient tradition in central Europe on the twelve nights between Christmas and Epiphany. The Poles call these nights the "Holy Evenings" (*Swiete Wieczory*). Another widespread practice is the performance of religious plays portraying events of the Christmas story (such as the Nativity, the visit of the Magi, the flight into Egypt, and the massacre of Bethlehem). In southern Germany and Austria many such plays are still performed in rural communities.[7] Among the northern Slavs (Poles, Ukrainians, Czechs, Slovaks) a puppet theater (*szopka*) is in vogue; its religious scenes alternate with secular dramatic exhibits. In the cities of Poland children put on Christmas dramas (*jaselka*).[8] A similar performance (*Bethlehemes játék*) is done by children in Hungary; a representation of the manger is carried from house to house, little dramatic plays are enacted and carols sung.

In many Catholic sections of Europe a daily church service is held on these evenings, gathering the children around the crib to honor the Divine Child with prayers and hymns (Manger Service). In the church of Ara Coeli on the Capitoline Hill in Rome little children preach and recite poems in honor of the Child Jesus before a large crowd of adults in front of the shrine of the *Bambino* (a statue of the Holy Child, carved from wood, wrapped in linen, and adorned with a crown).[9]

PRE-CHRISTIAN TRADITIONS · The days after the winter solstice bore the character of an exciting and decisive struggle in the folklore of the Indo-European races. The demons of winter and death were believed to fight against the increasing length and light of the day. It was a time when all the evil spirits freely roamed the world, when the souls of the dead returned to haunt the humans, when the giants of snow, ice, and storm endeavored to extinguish the growing flame of light and life in nature.[10]

In order to protect themselves and to frighten the demons away, people roamed the open spaces disguised by horrible masks of weird aspect and fantastic shape, emitting loud cries and imprecations, and making all kinds of frightening noises. At the same time, to encourage the good spirits of growth and harvest, they practiced all their traditional fertility rites (such as the touch with the Rod of Life, sprinkling with water, and magic incantations).[11]

Each one of these pre-Christian traditions has survived as an external feature of the celebration of Christmas week in the folklore of rural populations in central and eastern Europe. Parades of horrible masks (*Perchten*) still traditionally roam the streets and the countryside with loud cries and weird songs, to the noise of drums and the discordant blasts of trumpets. Farmers crack their whips and mortars and rifles are fired every night, but especially on New Year's Eve. Girls and women are "spanked" with branches and twigs, and water or grain is thrown upon boys and girls. The trees in the orchards, the barren fields, and the snow-covered gardens receive imploring or threatening incantations to insure their fertility for the coming spring.[12]

To these nature rites of northern Europe was added a second element of celebration in the countries of Roman tradition: a festival of reveling and unrestrained rejoicing, which had come down from the ancient custom of the *Calendae Januariae* (New Year's feast).[13] This feast, being mostly a civic celebration, was allowed to continue in the Christian empire of Rome. It contained, however, some of the popular features (drinking, gambling, masquerading in costumes of the opposite sex) that had been practiced during the Saturnalia (December 17).[14] The Church had forbidden and suppressed the Saturnalia because of their pagan background and objectionable aspects. As it happened, some of these customs slipped into the *Calendae* celebration after the prohibition of the Saturnalia, and this caused the Church authorities much trouble and worry for centuries.[15]

Another detail of the Roman *Calendae* celebration came from the Orient: the custom of putting up a "King of Fools," who served as the center of wild nonsense and childish folly.[16] Bishop Asterius of Amaseia (410) described in one of his sermons such a "fools' king" festival among Roman soldiers.[17] Saint John Chrysostom (407) preached in sharp and powerful words against the excesses of the New Year's night at Constantinople.[18] Ever since, the ecclesiastical authorities had to warn, admonish, and threaten punishment against similar excesses of reveling, drinking, and immodest behavior which were practiced in medieval times during Christmas week and culminated in the celebration of New Year's night. Our modern New Year's celebration, although quite refined compared to the ancient practice, still exhibits the basic features (and excesses) of the Roman *Calendae* festival.

THE FEAST OF FOOLS · In order to keep at least the clergy from the accustomed practice of reveling and masquerading during Christmas week, the authorities of the Church introduced, in the eleventh century, special feast days for the various ranks of clerical communities: Saint Stephen's for the deacons, Saint John's for the priests, the Feast of the Innocents for choirboys and students, and New Year's Day or Epiphany for the subdeacons.[19] This well-meant effort, however, had an unexpected adverse effect. Instead of keeping the clergy from joining the silly revels of the laity, it gradually occasioned the identification of these clergy feasts with the very abuses they were to prevent. In France especially, the clergy feasts turned into a Festival of Fools (*Festum Fatuorum, Fête des fous*) which invaded the very house of God. One from the ranks was chosen as "Bishop of Fools" or "Pope of Fools." [20] Dressed in the respective pontifical regalia he presided for one or more days during Christmas week over the recitation of the Divine Office in the choir.[21] All kinds of jokes and tricks were played on him, and by him on others. These abuses, connected with reveling, dancing, mumming, and banqueting, became so traditional that some priests would leave money in their testaments for the upkeep of these revels.[22]

As early as 1199 Archbishop Odo (Eudes) de Sully of Paris issued regulations to restrict the abuses of these clergy feasts. The Council of Basle, in 1435, reiterated the prohibition. Such edicts, however, had no lasting effect. In 1444 the theological faculty of the University of Paris came out with a stern condemnation of the Feast of Fools. In the following year King Charles VII forbade the practice in his whole realm. Backed by the power of secular punishment, he finally succeeded in stamping out the abuse. The last occasional remnants of the Feast of Fools disappeared everywhere when in 1748 Pope Benedict XIV in his encyclical *Super Bacchanalibus* ("Concerning Revels") reiterated the condemnation of New Year's and Carnival excesses.[23]

FEAST OF THE ASS · One may call this "festival" a by-product of the Feast of Fools in medieval France (and some places outside of France). Compared to the excesses of the Feast of Fools, the Feast of the Ass (*Festum Asinarium, Fête de l'âne*) was harmless and not as objectionable as the other features of the Christmas week celebration.[24] It consisted originally of a performance representing, after the style of mystery plays, the famous donkeys connected with events of the Bible. The place of honor, of course, was given to the donkey of the Holy Family, for it had stood at the manger of the Lord and carried Him and His Mother into Egypt.[25] Of the songs that were used in this play, a Latin poem later became the opening "hymn" during the procession of the clergy or students when they approached the church on the Feast of Fools in some cities of France.[26] Here is the first stanza in Latin and in English:

> Orientis partibus
> Adventavit asinus,
> Pulcher et fortissimus,
> Sarcinis aptissimus.
> Hez, Sir asne, hez!

> *From Oriental country came*
> *A lordly ass of highest fame,*
> *So beautiful, so strong and trim,*
> *No burden was too great for him.*
> *Hail, Sir Donkey, hail.*

The Feast of the Ass disappeared gradually, together with the Feast of Fools of which it had been a part, during the second half of the fifteenth century. It is hard for modern man to understand the appeal and attraction such a "feast" exerted on clergy and lay people in the Middle Ages. Perhaps they had, beneath the apparent lack of reverence and good taste, a spark of the genuine spirit of Saint Francis of Assisi.

MUMMING · In countries outside of France the Feast of Fools was mostly confined to revels of the laity. Kings and princes took part in them, and the celebration sometimes reached startling dimensions. Under the direction of the "Master of Revels," a grand mumming was performed by the citizens of London as early as 1377, for the amusement of Richard, son of the Black Prince. On that occasion over one hundred and thirty gentlemen, disguised as emperors, popes, and cardinals, with their retinue of knights, squires, and servants, rode to the palace of the young prince at Kensington. They were all well mounted, wearing visors and armor, and attended by numerous torchbearers and musicians. At the palace they played games with dice, reveled with much feasting, drinking, and dancing, and finally departed "in order as they came" with all the splendor of their mummery.[27]

While the higher classes thus enjoyed a well-ordered pageant of mumming, the common people were content with a more humble performance.[28] They went from house to house during Christmas week, their faces blackened with soot or covered with paint and the men frequently dressed in female costumes, making merry among their friends and neighbors.[29]

SAINTS' DAYS

SAINT STEPHEN (December 26) · The story of this saint can be found in the Acts of the Apostles (6-7). He is usually pictured in deacon's vestments, with a palm branch, the symbol of martyrdom, in his hand, and sometimes with a stone in his left hand, to indicate his death by stoning. Many images show him wearing a wreath, which is an allusion to his name, for the Greek word *Stephanos* means "wreath." [30]

From early times this saint was venerated as patron of horses. A poem of the tenth century pictures him as the owner of a horse and dramatically relates how Christ Himself miraculously cured the animal for His beloved Disciple. Though there is no historical basis for this association with horses in the life of Saint Stephen, various explanations have been attempted. Some are founded on ancient Germanic ritual celebrations of horse sacrifices at Yuletide. Others use the fact that in medieval times "Twelfth Night" (Christmas to Epiphany) was a time of rest for domestic animals; and horses, as the most useful servants of man, were accorded at the beginning of this fortnight something like a feast day of their own.[31]

It was a general practice among the farmers in Europe to

decorate their horses on Stephen's Day, and bring them to the house of God to be blessed by the priest and afterward ridden three times around the church, a custom still observed in many rural sections.[32] Later in the day the whole family takes a gay ride in a wagon or sleigh (St. Stephen's ride). In Sweden, the holy deacon was changed by early legend into the figure of a native saint, a stable boy who is said to have been killed by the pagans in Helsingland. His name—Staffan—reveals the original saint. The "Staffan Riders" parade through the towns of Sweden on December 26, singing their ancient carols in honor of the "Saint of Horses." [33]

Horses' food, mostly hay and oats, is blessed on Stephen's Day. Inspired by pre-Christmas fertility rites people throw kernels of these blessed oats at one another and at their domestic animals. In sections of Poland they even toss oats at the priest after Mass. Popular legends say this custom is an imitation of stoning, performed in honor of the saint's martyrdom. The ancient fertility rite, however, can still be clearly recognized in the Polish custom of boys and girls throwing walnuts at each other on Saint Stephen's Day.[34]

In past centuries water and salt were blessed on this day and kept by farmers to be fed to their horses in case of sickness. Women also baked special breads in the form of horseshoes (St. Stephen's horns: *podkovy*) which were eaten on December 26.[35]

In some parts of the British Isles, Saint Stephen's Day is the occasion for boys (the Wren Boys) to go from house to house, one of them carrying a dead wren on a branch decorated with all kinds of gay, streaming ribbons. Stopping in front of each door they sing a song and receive little gifts in return. The wren is "stoned" to death in memory of Saint Stephen's martyrdom. Actually, though, this represents a relic of the ancient Druidic sacrifice of wrens at the time of the winter solstice.[36]

SAINT JOHN THE EVANGELIST (December 27) · This favorite Disciple of Christ was Bishop of Ephesus in Asia Minor and died around the year 100. His grave was a goal for many pilgrimages in the early centuries, and countless legends were told about his tomb. People claimed they saw the earth on top of his grave move up and down, indicating his breathing, and believed he did not really die but only slept in the grave. Another legend claimed that his body was taken up to Heaven after he had "slept" in the tomb for some years. All these stories, of course, are traced to the saint's own report of what Christ said: "If I wish him to remain until I come, what is it to thee?" (John 21, 23), a statement the Apostles even then had misinterpreted to the effect that John would not die.[37]

Saint John's Day was a general holyday in medieval times, not only as the third day of Christmas but also in its own right (as the feast of an Apostle). The significant part of the traditional celebration was the blessing and drinking of wine, called the "Love of Saint John" (*Johannesminne; Szent János Aldása*) because, according to legend, the saint once drank a cup of poisoned wine without suffering harm.[38] The prayer of this blessing can be found in the Roman ritual (Blessing of Wine on the Feast of Saint John the Evangelist).[39] In central Europe people still practice the custom of bringing wine and cider into the church to be blessed. Later, at home, some of it is poured into every barrel in their wine cellars.[40]

People take Saint John's wine with their meals on December 27, expressing the mutual wish: "Drink the love of Saint John." It is also kept in the house throughout the rest of the year. At weddings, bride and bridegroom take some of it when they return from the church. It is also considered a great aid to travelers and is drunk before a long journey as a token of protection and safe return. A sip of Saint John's wine is often used as a sacramental for dying people after they have received the sacraments. It is the last earthly drink to strengthen them for their departure from this world.[41]

In the beginning of his Gospel, Saint John proclaims with great beauty of expression that Christ is the Light of the World. For this reason it was, and still is, the custom in many places at Christmas time, when all the lights in the home express this symbolism, to allow children with the name of John or Joan the privilege of lighting the candles on the Advent wreath and the Christmas tree. Even if the name is taken from John the Baptist, the privilege still holds because the Baptist had been the first one to see the light of divinity shining about the Lord at the baptism in the Jordan.[42]

THE HOLY INNOCENTS (December 28) · King Herod (4 B.C.) is considered one of the cruelest tyrants in history. In the course of his reign, it is reported, he drowned his brother-in-law, a youth of sixteen, who was high priest of Israel; he killed his uncle Joseph, his wife, Mariamne, and his mother-in-law, Alexandra. His brother-in-law, Kostobar, together with several members of his family, was killed by his order. A few years before the birth of Christ, Herod murdered his two sons, Alexander and Aristobulus, and had three hundred officials slain whom he accused of siding with the two young men. In the year 4 B.C., only five days before his death, he had his first-born son, Antipater, executed.

Like all tyrants, he killed thousands of innocent people whom he suspected of plotting against him. He was so suspicious of his own subjects and terrified at the thought of rebellion that he ordered the people by special decrees to keep busy at all times. He forbade them to meet together, to walk or eat in groups, and he had his spies everywhere, in both the city and rural districts, watching every move of the citizens. Public and private executions of countless victims took place in his citadel of Hyrcania, overlooking the Dead Sea.[43]

This is the man, Saint Matthew reports, who "sent and slew all the boys in Bethlehem and its neighborhood who were two years and under" (2, 16). How many children were killed? At times their number has been wildly exaggerated as hundreds, even thousands. An approximate figure might be estimated, however, because at the time of Christ, Bethlehem was a small town or village. Assuming a population of two thousand souls, the number of boys of two years and under might be around thirty. Most modern scholars consider even this figure too high and put the number at fifteen or twenty victims.[44] In the martyrologies (catalogues of saints' feasts) of the Greek Rite the number of Innocents is still officially given as 14,000. [45] This is clearly due to legends or to uncritical assumptions of medieval writers, for the oldest lists (of the first millennium A.D.) make no mention of the number of babies who were killed. The fact, however, that they truly died for Christ and deserved the honor and title of martyrs is already proclaimed in the writings of Saint Irenaeus (about 200) and Saint Cyprian (258).[46]

In the West, the Feast of the Nativity very soon occasioned the solemn memory of the Innocents on December 28. The earliest recorded mention of their feast is found in the church calendar of Carthage of the end of the fourth century.[47] The words of Jeremiah quoted by Saint Matthew (2, 18) about "Rachel weeping for her children" inspired the celebration of Innocents' Day as a feast of mourning; the Church, as a second Rachel, would lament the massacre of its little ones. Hence the penitential character of the liturgy (except on Sunday): purple color, no Gloria, no Alleluia. In the early centuries the Christians in Rome were expected to fast on this day by abstaining from meat and from foods cooked in fat.[48]

In contrast to this note of mourning, the octave day of the Innocents (now abolished) on January 4 was dedicated to the thought of their glory, the Mass being celebrated in red, with Gloria and Alleluia.

CUSTOMS OF INNOCENTS' DAY

FEAST OF THE BOY BISHOP · Pope Gregory IV (844) declared his predecessor Saint Gregory I (604) the patron of schools and choirs, and his feast day (March 12) as a holyday for all students and choirboys.[49] During the following centuries the custom developed that one of the boys, dressed in pontifical robes, would impersonate the patron saint. He was usually accompanied by two other boys serving as "chaplains." The celebration originally consisted of a devotional service at which the boy bishop presided and preached a sermon. Soon there was added a "chapter" ceremony; the boy bishop would examine his fellow students and also the adult audience with questions on religious doctrine, give praise or reproach, and distribute presents or punishments.[50]

From the eleventh century on, the Boy Bishop's Feast was transferred in most countries to December 28, for by that time Innocents' Day had become the official feast of students and choirboys. Unfortunately, it was soon identified with the Feast of Fools in many places, and for a long time reflected some of the irreverent abuses of that strange celebration. In the four-teenth century, however, it began to be purged of those alien elements and was moved to December 5, the eve of the Feast of Saint Nicholas, who was the patron saint of children.[51] Thus, when the Feast of Fools was finally suppressed in the fifteenth century, Boy Bishop's Day was already safely out of the way and escaped annihilation. Gradually the impersonation changed from the original one of Saint Gregory (which had been forgotten long before) to that of Saint Nicholas. In many countries of the conti-nent the role of the bishop was assumed by adults. Representing Saint Nicholas, the venerable figure now paid an annual visit to children on the eve of "his" feast. Thus originated the charming celebration that is still held in the Catholic countries of central Europe and in Holland on the eve of St. Nicholas's Day.[52]

OTHER FOLKLORE · During the past centuries, and up to the pres-ent, Innocents' Day was the traditional feast of the young ones in many religious communities. The novices had the privilege of sit-ting in the first places at meals and meetings. In many convents and monasteries the last one to have taken vows was allowed to act as superior for the day. The youngest members of the com-munity received congratulations, enjoyed a holiday, and baby food was served them at dinner.

In central Europe, Innocents' Day is one of the traditional "spanking" days of the ancient fertility cult. Groups of children go from house to house with branches and twigs, gently striking women and girls while they recite an old verse that contains the original wish of this pre-Christian practice:

> *Many years of healthy life,*
> *Happy girl, happy wife:*
> *Many children, hale and strong,*
> *Nothing harmful, nothing wrong,*
> *Much to drink and more to eat;*
> *Now we beg a kindly treat.*[53]

In German-speaking countries a strange legend and supersti-tion originated from a combination of the Christian festival with the pre-Christian belief that the souls of the dead roamed the earth after the solstice of winter. During the night of December

28, so the story goes, the souls of children who have died without baptism wander through the open spaces around farms and villages, led by their frightening custodian, Lady Hel (who was the Germanic goddess of the underworld; hence our word "hell"). Each child carries a pitcher filled with the tears that it shed during the past year in the solitude and anguish of Hel's dungeon.[54]

Now God in His mercy allows these children to be saved on Innocents' Day. If a human discerns their gentle cries through the howling storm of the winter night, and if he sees the formless shape of such a ghost child fluttering in the dark, then he must quickly call it by a Christian name. Thus the child can be released from the power of Lady Hel and, bearing a "baptismal" name, it may join the Holy Innocents in the bliss of eternal happiness.[55]

[1] Kellner, 163.   [2] LE, 171.   [3] Dur., VII, 42, 1.   [4] Schuster, I, 391. [5] H. Leclercq, *Constantine et le pape Silvester*, DACL, 3.2 (1948), 2683 ff.   [6] Schuster, I, 388.   [7] Geramb, 215 ff.   [8] Benet, 105 ff. [9] Personal observation of author; Crippen, 86.   [10] See S. K. Meisen, *Vom Wütenden Heer und Wilden Jäger*, Münster, 1935; Frazer, 561 ff. [11] Koren, 73.   [12] Gugitz, II, 312; Benet, 103 ff.   [13] H. Leclercq, *Calendes des Janvier*, DACL, 7.2 (1927), 2147 ff.   [14] PW, 2A.I, 202 ff.; Frazer, 583 ff.   [15] John Chrysostom, *In Kalendas*, 1; PG, 48, 953.   [16] PW, 10.II, 1562.   [17] *Advers. Kal. Festum*, 4; PL, 40, 221. [18] See note 15.   [19] J. Buchberger, *Narrenfest*, LThK, 7 (1935), 442. [20] Chambers, I, 274 ff. ("Feast of Fools").   [21] L. Lefebre, *L'évêque des fous et la fête des innocents*, Lille, 1902.   [22] G. M. Dreves, *Zur Geschichte der Fête des Fous und Fête de l'âne*, StML, 47 (1894), 571 ff.   [23] Text in Nilles, II, 65 ff.   [24] Kellner, 164 (footnote).   [25] H. Leclercq, *L'âne de la Fuite en Egypte*, DACL, 1.2 (1924), 2059 ff. [26] See note 22; Chambers, II, 279 ("The Prose of the Ass").   [27] CwP, 64.   [28] Crippen, 94; Chambers, II, 205 ff.   [29] See note 27.   [30] Schuster, I, 378; H. Leclercq, *Etienne*, DACL, 5.1 (1922), 624 ff.   [31] Gugitz, II, 280 (*Der Hl. Stephan und die Pferde*).   [32] Koren, 70; R. Hindringer, *Weiheross und Rossweihe*, München, 1932, 140 ff.   [33] See note 31, 281.   [34] Benet, 108 ff.   [35] See note 31, 286.   [36] Frazer, 536 ff.; R. Gibbings, *Sweet Cork of Thee*, New York, 1951, 86 ff.   [37] Schuster, I, 381.   [38] Franz, I, 294 ff. (*Johanneswein und Johannesminne*). [39] RR, *Benedictio vini in festo S. Joannis Ap. et Ev.*   [40] Gugitz, II, 290 ff. (*Johannissegen*).   [41] Koren, 72.   [42] RCF, 40.   [43] Jos. Flavius,

The Jewish Antiquities, XV, 10, 4. [44] G. Ricciotti, *The Life of Christ,* Milwaukee, 1947, 255 ff. [45] Nilles, I, 371. [46] Irenaeus: PG, 7, 924; Cyprian: PL, 4, 354. [47] PL, 13, 1228. [48] Schuster, I, 385 ff. [49] R. Hindringer, *Kinderbischof,* LThK, 5 (1933), 955. In the Alpine sections of Austria Saint Gregory's Day remained a feast day for school children into the twentieth century; see OiT, 6 ff. and Gugitz, I, 114. [50] Koren, 73 ff. [51] Gugitz, II, 312 ff. (*Tag der Unschuldigen Kinder*); Koren, 43 ff. [52] See K. Meisen, *Nikolauskult und Nikolausbrauch im Abendlande,* Düsseldorf, 1931. [53] Gugitz, II, 315. [54] ES, 71; Gugitz, II, 312. [55] G. Graber, *Volksleben in Kärnten,* Graz, 1934, 196 ff.

CHAPTER

11   Feast of the Circumcision

HISTORY AND LITURGY

LATE ORIGIN · Since the Gospel reports the fact of Christ's circumcision on the eighth day after His birth (Matthew 2, 21), a feast of the liturgy in commemoration of that event might have suggested itself as soon as Christmas was established on December 25. It took four centuries, however, until this feast was actually introduced into the Roman liturgy, and then it came from the outside, from the churches in France that had already celebrated it for two hundred years. In the East, too, the Feast of the Circumcision is not mentioned in any calendar before the eighth century.[1]

This reluctance to introduce a feast the object and date of which were so clearly given in the Bible might have been due in some degree to the fact that circumcision had been replaced by the sacrament of baptism in the New Testament.[2] The main reason, however, doubtlessly was the secular New Year's celebration that took place in the whole Roman Empire on January

1, and which contained so many objectionable elements that the
Church authorities did not want to make that day an official feast
and thereby encourage the holiday mood of the faithful. This is
indicated by the fact that in the early centuries January 1 was
kept as a day of fasting and penance.[3] "During these days, when
they [the pagans] revel, we observe a fast in order to cry and
pray for them," said Saint Augustine in a sermon on New Year's
Day.[4]

Not only in Rome, but also in Gaul, Spain, and Greece the
calends of January presented great problems of religious discipline to the authorities of the Church. During the sixth and
seventh centuries various councils in France strictly forbade
participation in those revels. Such prohibitions had to be repeated
many times by the bishops in their respective dioceses.[5] The
faithful were told to hold private penitential processions
(*litaniae*) in penance and atonement for the excesses and sins
committed by so many.[6] In Spain, the fourth Council of Toledo
(633) prescribed a strict fast and abstinence for January 1, and
the Alleluia was omitted from the liturgical texts in token of
penance.[7]

As late as the eighth century, the people in Rome spent New
Year's night reveling and dancing in the streets, thereby scan-
dalizing the pious pilgrims from northern countries.[8] If so much
public rejoicing happened at a time when Rome was completely
Christian, it is no wonder that in earlier centuries the popes
would not hold a solemn feast, with its customary Station processions, on January 1 when crowds of pagans, and some irre-
sponsible Christians, roamed the city with frivolous dancing, wild
carousing, and indecorous masquerades.[9]

OCTAVE OF THE NATIVITY · While the popes and bishops in the
Christian empire of Rome abstained from introducing a solemn
feast on the calends of January, there was a strong inclination to
distinguish the day not only by fasting but also by a prayerful
and official celebration in church. Since the people by tradition
were in a festive mood, it seemed appropriate to gather them
for a special service in the house of God to direct their hearts
and minds to the Lord in a devout and quiet, but impressive, way.
Saint Augustine had already felt this when he beheld a large con-

gregation gathered in church on January 1: "I see that you have come here as if we had a feast today." [10]

When the last remnants of paganism had disappeared, January 1 was made a ranking liturgical feast, shortly after the beginning of the seventh century, probably under Pope Boniface IV (615). In imitation of the Easter, and Epiphany, Octave it became the "Octave Day" of Christmas. This distinction, however, was applied in a lesser degree, since the eighth day as such, and not the whole week, as at Easter, received the liturgical character of the main feast. Of the ancient liturgical books, the *Sacramentarium Gelasianum* (seventh century) contains the first entry of this feast under the simple title *Octava Domini* (Octave Day of the Lord). [11]

FEAST OF MARY · Soon after the Octave of Christmas had been introduced, the celebration of January 1 assumed a Marian character. This was due to the Station of the papal service, which was the church of St. Mary beyond the Tiber, the oldest Roman church dedicated to the Mother of God. Thus New Year's Day became a special memorial of Mary. In the old Roman calendars it is called *Natale Sanctae Mariae*. (The word *natale* here means simply "feast".) In a certain sense this was the earliest feast of our Lady in the Latin Church. [12] Interesting is the emphasis placed on Mary's maternity, that she is truly the Mother of Him Who was made flesh for our salvation. The character of January 1 as a feast of Mary is still preserved in the Station title; the Mass prayers, too, and the texts of the Divine Office reflect the Marian note of the feast up to this day. [13]

CIRCUMCISION · The celebration of our Lord's circumcision started in the Church of Gaul, where we find the earliest records of this feast about the middle of the sixth century. [14] From Gaul it spread to Spain and into the Frankish empire, and from there to Rome in the ninth century. [15] In the Greek Church it had already been introduced during the eighth century. Today all Eastern Rites celebrating the Nativity on December 25 also keep a Feast of the Circumcision on January 1. [16]

The new celebration soon overshadowed the Octave of Christmas in the Roman liturgy, but did not entirely supplant it. Up to this day the official title (in the Latin Church) is a combination of both liturgical festivals: "The Circumcision of Our Lord and Octave of the Nativity."

Because the Divine Child received the name Jesus at the circumcision, this day was also connected in the Middle Ages with special devotions in honor of the holy name. Saint Bernard (1444), by both word and example, promoted the veneration of the sacred name of Jesus with great zeal. The famous hymn *Jesu Dulcis Memoria* (How sweet the thought of Jesus), which he composed, is still used in the Divine Office.[17] In 1721 Pope Innocent III established a separate feast in honor of the holy name of Jesus. Pope Saint Pius X (1914) fixed its present date: on Sunday between January 1 and 6, or on January 2 if no Sunday occurs. The Catholics of the Greek-Slavonic and Armenian Rites have kept January 1 as the Feast of the Holy Name in addition to the Circumcision.[18]

NEW YEAR · The liturgical texts take no notice at all of January 1 as the beginning of a new civic year. This is probably due to the pagan and objectionable character of the ancient Roman New Year's celebration, which prevented the authorities of the Church from even mentioning that aspect in the sacred service of divine worship. In the Diocese of Toledo, Spain, however, January 1 bore the official title *Caput Anni* (Beginning of the Year) in the liturgical books of the seventh century.[19]

FOLKLORE

RELIGIOUS OBSERVANCE · The end of the old and the beginning of a new year was, and still is, marked by popular devotional exercises. Special services are held in many churches on the eve of New Year's to thank God for all His favors in the past year and to implore His blessings for the new one. In rural sections of central Europe many families spend the minutes around midnight saying the rosary or other prayers, and all the church bells peal "to ring out the old and ring in the new year." [20]

In France and French Canada a custom coming down from medieval times is the blessing of the family. The father makes the sign of the cross on the foreheads of his kneeling family, wife and children, in token of God's blessing for the new year. In other Catholic sections of Europe parents bless their children with the sign of the cross at midnight. This custom of parental blessing, which is practiced also on many other occasions during the year, was a universal tradition in all countries before the Reformation.[21]

In the towns of the Alpine sections of Austria and Germany it is a widespread custom for a little brass band to play Christmas carols and other religious hymns from the tower of the local church, or for groups of carol singers to go from street to street and "sing in the new year." In some places these carol singers are mounted on horses, riding from farm to farm during New Year's night.[22]

SYLVESTER CELEBRATION · The popular festival on New Year's Eve is called "Sylvester" in many countries. The word is derived, of course, from the liturgical observance of December 31, the Feast of Saint Sylvester. Besides the traditional and familiar reveling celebration in our modern cities, many ancient customs are still practiced in European countries.[23] In Spanish-speaking sections it is an old tradition to eat twelve grapes at midnight, one at each stroke of the tower bell. In central Europe the new year is greeted with the cracking of whips, shooting of rifles and mortars, and with banging and clanging noises in the home. This is a relic of the pre-Christian ritual of "driving demons away"; its original significance, however, has been forgotten, and it is now practiced as a salute to the new year.[24]

Sylvester Night is one of the great nights for all kinds of traditional oracle games to find out what the year will bring. Tea leaves are read in many places. In central Europe spoonfuls of molten lead are poured into water, and the fantastic shapes of the congealing metal are supposed to reveal or symbolize events of the coming year. Girls especially are looking for apparitions and oracles disclosing the young man who will come to love and marry them. Superstitions claim that his likeness will show through the mirror in the darkened room at midnight, or that he will appear to them in a dream.[25]

These oracles are usually connected with Saint Sylvester, thus giving them the character of a devotional practice rather than a mere superstition. The saint is asked in traditional rhyme prayers to exercise his patronage and provide a husband. And it is from his kindly favor that girls expect to see the picture in their dreams or in the mirror.[26]

PRESENT-GIVING · The old Roman practice of giving presents at the beginning of a new year (*strenae*) has survived in all Latin countries, and so has the name (*étrennes* in France, *estrenas* in Spain).[27] The date, however, is now January 6 in Italy and in Spanish-speaking countries; only in France has January 1 been retained as the day of giving presents to children.

A general custom in many countries is the giving of money or presents on, or after, New Year's Day to persons who make regular deliveries to the home (such as the milkman, letter carrier, and paper boy).[28] A recent practice, which started spontaneously some years ago and may be found in many cities of Europe, is the custom among motorists of leaving presents at the stands of traffic policemen. These packages are then taken to the police station and distributed among the families of all traffic policemen within the precinct.

[1] Kellner, 163 ff.   [2] LE, 171.   [3] DACL, 8.1 (1928), 623 ff.   [4] *In Psalm*. 98; PL, 37, 1262.   [5] Chambers, II, 290 ff. ("Winter Prohibitions").   [6] Kellner, 164.   [7] Can. 11; Mansi, 10, 621.   [8] See note 6.
[9] Schuster, I, 395.   [10] *Sermo ad Kal. Jan.*, 1; PL, 38, 1024.   [11] Gelas., 9.   [12] Jgn GK, 236.   [13] Schuster, I, 396.   [14] LE, 171.   [15] Kellner, 165.   [16] Nilles, I, 46 ff.   [17] Matins and Lauds of the Feast of the Holy Name of Jesus.   [18] Nilles, I, 47.   [19] Kellner, 166.   [20] Koren, 75.   [21] RCF, 27 ff.   [22] Geramb, 17 ff.   [23] Chambers, I, 249 ff.; Barnett, 135 ff.   [24] Gugitz, II, 327 ff.   [25] J. Hösl, *Klöpfelnächte*, LThK, 6 (1934), 47.   [26] Gugitz, II, 330.   [27] PW, 4A.II, 351 (*Strena*).   [28] Gugitz, I, 6.

CHAPTER

12 *Feast of the Epiphany*

HISTORY AND LITURGY

ORIGIN · The term *Epiphaneia* (manifestation) designated in the Greek-Roman world an official state visit of a king or emperor to some city of his realm, and especially the occasions on which he publicly showed himself to the people. The Apostles applied this term to Christ manifesting Himself as our Divine Saviour: "He manifested his glory, and his disciples believed in him" (John 2, 11).[1] Since in the ancient pagan world people believed that gods, too, did sometimes "appear" on earth and show themselves in human form, the word theophany was applied to such events (*theophaneia*: manifestation of a god). The early Church, in both the East and the West, often used this meaningful term of theophany for the Feast of the Epiphany.[2]

The liturgical feast of Christ's "manifestation" originated in the Orient, in Egypt, during the third century. Modern scholars explain the date (January 6) by the fact that the Egyptians celebrated on this day their great festival of the winter solstice in honor of the sun god.[3] The Church authorities opposed this pagan observance with a feast of the true manifestation (nativity) of the Divine Saviour King. This Christian feast, in turn, occasioned among the heretical Gnostics a feast of Christ's baptism, celebrated on the same day.[4] According to their false doctrine, Jesus was a mere human until His baptism in the Jordan. On that day, they claimed, the Divinity united itself with the man Jesus, and therefore the first truly divine manifestation of Christ could not happen at His birth but only at His baptism.[5]

Epiphany, then, started as a feast of the Lord's nativity cele-

brated on the day of the winter solstice in Egypt, which was
twelve days behind the Julian calendar.[6] This festival also
included the commemoration of the Magi's visit and adoration.
In Egypt (and a century later in the whole East Roman Empire)
a commemoration of Christ's baptism was added, to stress the
true character of this manifestation against the Gnostic "birth
of divinity" doctrine regarding Christ's baptism.[7]

In the Greek Church Epiphany is still named *Theophaneia*
(the appearing of God). In a similar sense the Syrians call it
"coming forth" (*denho*) of the Saviour; and the Armenians use
the term "God's manifestation" (*Hajdnuthiún*).[8]

From the Orient Epiphany came to Europe during the fourth
century, about the same time as the new Feast of Christmas
took root in the Roman liturgy. In many places (Spain, Gaul,
upper Italy) Epiphany was established first. In Milan it was
solemnly observed as early as 353, but it still commemorated
mainly the nativity of the Lord.[9] Soon, however, Christmas
spread from Rome through the whole Latin Church, and toward
the end of the fourth century into the Greek Church as well, and
the Nativity was now celebrated everywhere on December 25.
This caused a change in the liturgical objective of Epiphany.
In the Western Church, Epiphany had as its main objective the
adoration of the Magi. The baptism of Christ and the miracle of
Cana were also commemorated, but only in a subordinate manner. In the East, however, the visit of the Magi was celebrated
together with Christmas on December 25, and Epiphany soon
became the great feast of Christ's baptism.[10]

Epiphany has always remained one of the greatest feasts of the
liturgical year. As early as A.D. 400 Emperor Honorius (for West
Rome) and Arcadius (for East Rome) forbade horse races and
circus games on January 6 because they kept people from attending divine service. Justinian (565) made it a full civic holyday. During the Middle Ages it had a vigil with fast and abstinence. The solemn octave was abrogated by Pope Pius XII in
1955 (for the Latin Church).[11]

In the new Code of Canon Law (1918), Epiphany has been
retained as a holyday of obligation for the whole Church.[12] The
United States, however, and some countries in western Europe

(France, Belgium, Holland) are dispensed from this obligation by the Holy See.[13]

Among the Greeks, too, it is one of the highest feasts, and as such bears the official notation in the calendar "Day of rest and solution from everything" (meaning all penitential fasting: *Argia kai katalysis eis panta*).[14] The Armenians keep it as one of their five *Daghavár* (Greatest Festivals) with a week's fast in preparation and a solemn octave following, of which the second day is also a feast of obligation.[15]

NATIVITY OF CHRIST · That Epiphany originated as a celebration of Christ's nativity and was kept as such for over two hundred years is evident from many historical sources. In one of his sermons, Saint John Chrysostom called it "Day of the Nativity" (*hemera genethlios*).[16] Similar references to the birth of the Saviour may be found in the writings of other early Fathers in the Orient.[17] One of the most interesting accounts of this nativity celebration on January 6 in Bethlehem and Jerusalem is preserved in the diary of Aetheria (from the end of the fourth century). She vividly described the joyful splendor and fervent devotion of the Christian community in Jerusalem, and all their liturgical services performed during the eight days of the Epiphany celebration in honor of the Lord's nativity.[18]

In our present Mass text there is a trace left of this nativity celebration. The Preface of the Mass, which was taken from an older prayer (*ektenia*) of the Greek liturgy of Epiphany, speaks of God's only-begotten Son "appearing in the substance of our mortality." The original Greek version had "thy only-begotten Son, co-eternal with thee in thy glory, appeared among us in a visible body like unto our own" (which clearly refers to Christ's birth).[19]

BAPTISM OF CHRIST · The celebration of Christ's baptism by the Gnostics as His "birth of divinity" prompted the Eastern Church to commemorate that event in its true and historical meaning, as one of the manifestations of the Divine Saviour, together with His first and basic epiphany at Bethlehem.[20] This commemoration was also suggested by the fact that the baptism of the faithful is their true birth to supernatural life. And since Epiphany was the birthday of the "Sun of Justice" (replacing a pagan light feast), the thought naturally occurred that at baptism each soul is illumined with the Light of Christ, the Divine Sun. For this reason the Greek Church used the word illumine (*photizesthai*), rather than the term washing (*baptizesthai*), to designate baptism. And Epiphany, as the feast of our Lord's baptism, became the "Feast of Light" (*photismos; ta phota*). Saint Gregory of Nazianz (390), preaching on Epiphany, called it "the holy Light of the Manifestations" (*hagia phota ton Epiphaneion*).[21]

Very soon Epiphany not only commemorated Christ's baptism in the Jordan, but also became the great annual day of the solemn baptism of the faithful (as Easter vigil is in the Latin Church). The Slavs of the Greek Rite still call Epiphany the "Feast of Light" (*Prosveszenije*) or "Feast of Baptism" (*Krescenije*).[22]

In the Latin Church, since 1955, the baptism of Christ in the Jordan is commemorated also by a special feast on January 13. The Mass text used is the same as that of the former Octave of Epiphany.

ADORATION OF THE MAGI · In the Latin Church this event (Matthew 2, 1-12) forms the main object of the Epiphany celebration. All the texts of the Mass refer to it, and so do the prayers and hymns of the Divine Office. Only in the antiphons for the *Benedictus* (Lauds) and *Magnificat* (Vespers) is mention made of the two other manifestations included in the liturgy:

Three miracles adorn the sacred day which we celebrate: Today, the star led the Magi to the manger. Today, water was turned into wine at the wedding. Today, Christ willed to be baptised by John in the Jordan, in order to save us. Alleluia.[23]

In the Greek Church this "adoration of the Magi" (*proskynesis ton Magon*) is not celebrated on January 6, but is commemorated on Christmas Day. For the night Office an *eikon* (picture) showing the Infant in the manger, adored by the shepherds, is put up for veneration. At the Office during Christmas Day this picture is replaced by another one representing the visit and adoration of the Magi, thus reminding clergy and people of the twofold epiphany in their Christmas celebration.[24]

MIRACLE OF CANA · The celebration of this miracle as one of the manifestations of Christ is probably due to the fact that the Gospel uses the very word "manifest" (*ephanerosen*) in connection with it (John 2, 11). Some scholars claim it was also occasioned by a pagan Egyptian legend that at the time of the winter solstice celebration (January 6) the gods turned water into wine, and that the Church wished to replace that pagan fiction by the memory of the historic miracle of Christ at Cana.[25] Saint Paulinus, Bishop of Nola, in Italy (431), already mentions it as one of the "three manifestations" of Christ.[26]

In holy liturgy this commemoration presents a spiritual comparison of great depth, namely of Christ's "wedding" to His spouse, the Church—a picture based on many texts of a similar marriage symbolism between God and His people in the Old Testament.[27] "Today, the Church is wedded to her heavenly bridegroom, after Christ has washed away her sins in the Jordan." [28]

THE FINAL MANIFESTATION · There was a trend among many pious authors in medieval times of adding other manifestations to those officially mentioned in the liturgy, such as the multiplication of loaves, Christ walking on the waters, and the raising of Lazarus.[29] It is true that all these events, and many similar ones, could rightly be considered as epiphanies of the Lord. The liturgy, however, has never officially included more than the four events of the Nativity, the adoration of the Magi, the baptism of Christ, and the miracle of Cana.

There is an exception, though, and a very significant one. Although not expressly mentioned in the liturgical texts of Epiphany, the thought of Christ's last and greatest manifestation in His coming at the end of time (*parousia*) stands like a radiant beacon behind the liturgical celebration of His coming in the past.[30] Through the whole season of Advent and Christmas—in fact, through the whole ecclesiastical year—the liturgical prayers have stressed the preparatory character of all the celebrations on earth: they are to lead the faithful to the joyful and everlasting reunion with Christ at the end of time.

"Behold, the Lord will come, and all his saints with him; and on that day there shall be a great light. Alleluia." [31] These words of the Advent liturgy seem to come to a symbolic fulfillment on Epiphany. As the Lord truly manifested Himself on earth, so He will manifest Himself in that last and greatest epiphany when all things will find their fulfillment in Him.

Saint John Chrysostom proclaims this very thought in one of his sermons on Epiphany:

There are two manifestations of Christ, not only one. The first is the one which has already happened, His epiphany in the present. The second is the one of the future which will come at the end of time with great splendor and glory. You have heard read today what St. Paul writes to Titus about both these epiphanies. Concerning the first he says, "The grace of God our Savior has appeared to all men. . . ." About the second he writes, "We look for the blessed hope and glorious coming of our great God and Savior, Jesus Christ" (Titus 2, 11-13).[32]

FEAST OF THE THREE KINGS · In the High Middle Ages popular devotion turned to the Magi themselves on January 6. They are called "saints" for the first time in the writings of Archbishop Hildebert of Tours (1133).[33] In the twelfth century their veneration spread over all of Europe. The authorities of the Church did not prohibit this cult, and Epiphany acquired the popular name of "Feast of the Three Holy Kings" in most countries of Europe.[34]

The name Magi is not a Hebrew word, but of Indo-European origin, and means "great, illustrious." Saint Matthew mentioned the term without explanation because it was well known to the people of Palestine. The Magi originated in Media (Persia), and their caste later spread to other Oriental countries. They were a highly esteemed class of priestly scholars, devoting themselves not only to religion but also to the study of natural sciences, medicine, mathematics, astronomy, and astrology. In several countries they were members of the king's council.[35]

Where did the Magi come from? Saint Matthew gives a general answer: "Wise men from the East." Speaking in modern terms, it could have been from any one of the countries of Arabia, Iraq, Iran, Afghanistan, or India. It has never been exactly determined from which of these countries they came.

Quite early in the Christian era a popular tradition conferred on them the title of "kings." This tradition became universal at the end of the sixth century. It was based on Biblical prophecies which described the conversion of the pagans and, although not referring to the Magi, were applied to their visit:

The kings of Tharsis and the islands shall offer presents: the kings of the Arabians and of Sheba shall bring gifts. (Psalms 71, 10)

The kings shall walk in the brightness of thy rising. . . . They all shall come from Sheba, bringing gold and frankincense. (Isaiah 60, 3-6)

The Gospel does not tell us how many they were. The Christians in the Orient had an old tradition of twelve Magi. In early paintings and mosaics they are represented as two, three, four, and even more. In the occidental Church a slowly spreading tradition put their number at three. It does not seem to have any historical foundation, but was probably based on the fact of the threefold presents.[36] Another reason for the number three was the early legend that they represented all humanity in its three great races. Thus one of them was pictured as a member of the black race, and this choice seemed to be confirmed by the Bible:

Let the great ones come forth from Egypt,
let Ethiopia stretch out her arms to God. (Psalms 67, 32)

The book *Collectanea et Flores*, ascribed to Saint Bede the Venerable (735), records an earlier legend of their names and appearance:

The first was called Melchior; he was an old man, with white hair and long beard; he offered gold to the Lord as to his king. The second, Gaspar by name, young, beardless, of ruddy hue, offered to Jesus his gift of incense, the homage due to Divinity. The third, of black complexion, with heavy beard, was called Baltasar; the myrrh he held in his hands prefigured the death of the Son of man.[37]

There is an old legend that when many years had passed the Magi were visited by Saint Thomas the Apostle, who, after instructing them in Christianity, baptized them. They were then ordained to the priesthood and made bishops. It is said that once more the star of Bethlehem appeared to them and reunited them toward the end of their lives. "The city of Sewa in the Orient" is given as the place of their burial.[38]

The legendary relics of the Magi were brought from Constantinople to Milan in the sixth century. In 1164 Emperor Frederick Barbarossa obtained them from the archbishop of Milan and transferred them to Cologne. Their shrine in Cologne was, and still is, the center of many pilgrimages.[39]

PROCLAMATION OF FEASTS · One of the special traditions connected with Epiphany was the publication on January 6 of the annual letter of the patriarch of Alexandria announcing the date of Easter for the current year (*epistola festalis*).[40] The scholars of Alexandria were considered most competent to make the difficult computations and observations necessary to determine this date, and thus the whole East followed their findings, which were sent to all churches by the patriarch. In the sixth century, the fourth Council of Orléans (541) ordered the same procedure in the West.[41] During the Middle Ages the dates of other movable feasts used to be added to the date of Easter and be solemnly read to the people on Epiphany Day. This ancient custom is still observed in some cathedrals as a traditional solemnity on January 6 at the end of the pontifical Mass.[42] With the introduction of modern calendars the announcing of the Easter date and other feasts has been discontinued. Instead, the bishops now issue pastoral letters before Lent, including the regulations for fast and abstinence.

SOLEMN BLESSING OF WATER · With the commemoration of Christ's baptism there was associated in the Orient from ancient times not only the custom of blessing baptismal water in the churches but also of solemnly blessing a nearby river or fountain in honor of the Lord's baptism.[43] In Palestine it was the Jordan, of course, that received this blessing in a most colorful and solemn ceremony. Thousands of pilgrims would gather on its shores to step into the water after the rite, submerging three times to obtain the great blessing. In Egypt the Nile was thus blessed for many centuries; the whole Christian population, and even many Mohammedans, would plunge into its floods three times, then drive their domestic animals into the river, and also dip pictures, statues, and crosses to obtain the Epiphany blessing.[44]

In the cities of East Rome, Epiphany water was blessed in the church and given to the people to take home. Saint John Chrysostom claimed that this water was known to stay fresh throughout the whole year and even longer.[45]

The Russians and other Slavs of the Greek Rite observe the "blessing of water" on the twenty-fifth day after Easter (always a Wednesday) which they call "Mid-Pentecost." Priests and people walk in procession to a well or river, the water is solemnly blessed, and the faithful fetch a goodly supply to keep during the year.[46]

In the Latin Church this blessing of water was introduced in the fifteenth century. The present rite of solemn blessing is to be performed on the vigil of Epiphany. The prayers, replacing older formulas, date from the year 1890.[47] After the texts of the blessing the Roman ritual gives the following instruction: "This blessed water should be distributed to the faithful, to be devoutly used by them in their homes, and also for the sick ones." [48]

BLESSING OF HOMES · The Roman ritual also provides a beautiful and impressive rite of blessing the homes of the faithful on the Feast of the Epiphany. This blessing is usually given by the pastor.[49] After reciting the *Magnificat,* the priest sprinkles the rooms with holy water and incenses them, then recites the prayers. Here, in English translation, is the actual prayer of blessing:

Bless, O Lord, almighty God, this house, that therein be found good health, chastity, the power of spiritual victory, humility, goodness and meekness, the plenitude of the Law, and thanksgiving to God, the Father, Son and Holy Spirit: and may this blessing remain on the house and on its inhabitants. Through Christ our Lord. Amen." [50]

After the blessing the initials of the legendary names of the Magi—Gaspar, Melchior, Baltasar—are written with white chalk on the inside of the door, framed by the number of the year, and all symbols are connected by the cross: 19+G+M+B+—. To sanctify even the chalk for this writing, there is a special "Blessing of Chalk on the Feast of the Epiphany" in the ritual.[51]

FOLKLORE

MAGI PLAYS · A favorite mystery play in medieval times was the "Office of the Star," a pageant of the Magi's visit on the Feast of the Epiphany. Like the Nativity play, this originated as a part of the liturgical service in church (in the eleventh century, probably in France) and soon spread into all European countries. However, from a devout religious ceremony it degenerated into a boisterous affair, due to the appearance of King Herod, who was introduced into the play as a raging maniac, throwing a wooden spear around, beating clergy and laity alike, creating havoc in both sanctuary and church by his antics.[52]

Because of these abuses, the "Office of the Star" was soon abolished as a part of the liturgical service. In its place appeared very early the "Feast of the Star," an Epiphany play performed partly outside the church, partly inside, but in no way connected with the Mass or the liturgical Office. One of the earliest reports of this pageant is in Milan, 1336, where it was directed by the Franciscan friars as an inspiring religious ceremony. The "Three Kings," crowned and richly clad, appeared on horseback with a large retinue, bearing golden cups filled with myrrh, incense, and gold. They rode in state through the streets of the city to the church of St. Eustorgius where they dismounted, entered in solemn procession, and offered their gifts at the Christmas crib.[53]

These Epiphany plays spread quickly through all of Europe; the interest in them was heightened because the Crusaders had brought back tales and Oriental customs from the Holy Land.[54] They were gradually prohibited after the Reformation and completely discarded as religious pageants in many countries, degenerating into wild Dragon plays, "Thre Kynges" puppet shows, and other demonstrations.[55] In more religious communities they kept their original character, somewhat simplified like the *Sternsingen* in Germany and the festival of *Los Tres Rejes* (The Three Kings) among Spanish-speaking nations.[56]

EPIPHANY CAROLS · These carols tell the story of the three Magi, their journey to Bethlehem, the adoration, the presents offered, and other details, including sentiments of prayer and devotion.

Many of them are like ballads and of considerable length. Here is the beginning of an old English Epiphany carol:

> *Three kings came out of Indian land*
> *To see the wondrous Infant bent,*
> *With rich presents in their hand;*
> *Straightly a star before them went.*
> *A wondrous thing it was to see:*
> *That star was more than other three. . . .*[57]

An Epiphany song of deep devotion is the old Portuguese carol *Os Reis* (The Kings):

> *Out of the Orient they came ariding*
> *Three noble kings, of humble heart and mild;*
> *They came to see the Blessed Lord of Heaven*
> *Descend to earth, to be a little child.*
> *Precious gifts of gold and myrrh and incense,*
> *Bringing God the gifts which God had made:*
> *Low the kings in homage bowing,*
> *At the feet of Mary laid.*[58]

STAR CAROLS · These songs are sung by young people who go from house to house at Epiphany, carrying a pole with the "star of Bethlehem," and impersonating the Magi, reporting the adventures of their journey and wishing all a happy and holy Christmas. This custom, a simplified form of the ancient Epiphany plays, was widespread in England, Holland, France, Austria, and Germany from the end of the fourteenth century until the Reformation. It is still practiced in Austria, Bavaria (*Sternsingen*), and the Slavic countries.[59]

> *We are the three Kings with our star,*
> *We bring you a story from lands afar:*
> *And so, dear people, we say to you—*
> *It might sound strange, but is really true—*
> *That something happened in the Holy Land;*
> *We went there, all three, by God's command,*
> *And in Bethlehem's stable we found a child:*
> *Our new-born Saviour, sweet and mild. . . .*

PRESENT-GIVING · In Italy and in the Spanish-speaking countries January 6 is the day of giving presents to children. In Rome and other cities of Italy an unusual figure impersonates the gift-bringer for children. It is the "Lady Befana," a sort of fairy queen. She has to atone, according to the legend told to the little ones, for having treated Jesus and Mary in an unfriendly manner on their journey to Egypt. Now that Christ is no longer on earth, she tries to make children happy in His honor by giving them presents. The name comes from the word epiphany.

In Spain and South America the present-giving (*estrenas*) is done not only at Christmas, but also by the Magi (*Los Tres Rejes Magos*). During the night of January 6, little gifts are deposited in the children's shoes by the Magi; and on the feast day, after Mass, the children receive them. Often the Magi leave presents for them at the house of the grandparents as well, where they go on the afternoon of Epiphany. In some cities of Spain the custom recently developed of three men (usually employees of toy stores) impersonating the Magi and delivering the presents on Epiphany Day "in person."

KINGS' CAKE · An old tradition in most countries of Europe was the festival of the "Kings' Cake" (*Dreikönigskuchen, Gâteau des Rois*), which was baked on Epiphany in honor of the Magi and eaten at a special party in the home on the afternoon of the feast.[60] Often a coin was put in the dough before baking, and the person who found it was the "king." In Austria, Germany, France, and England, and also in Canada, this cake contained a bean and a pea, making the respective finders "king" and "queen" of the merry party.[61]

This custom has been explained as a relic of the ancient games of chance at the Roman Saturnalia. However, there is no proof of this connection; the first reports about the "Kings' Cake" date from the end of the fourteenth century.[62] Also, the wild and excessive reveling of the Saturnalia or *Calendae* was never a feature of this festival. It was an old custom in France to put a big piece of the cake aside "for our Lord" and to give it to some poor person after the feast. Another tradition in France demanded that rich people help collect a goodly sum of money by giving a substantial donation in return for their piece of the cake.

This money was deposited on a tray and was called "the gold of the Magi." It was afterward used to pay the cost of higher education for some talented poor youngster.[63]

A canon of the cathedral of Serles, Jean Deslion, wrote a whole book against the Kings' festival in the seventeenth century. He erroneously identified it with the Feast of Fools.[64] He probably stopped some abuses, for which credit is due him. The custom itself, however, lived on and is still practiced in sections of France, England, and French Canada.

[1] See also 2 Timothy 1, 10; Titus 2, 11; 3, 4.   [2] Nilles, I, 56 ff.   [3] Jgn GK, 230 ff.   [4] Clem. Alex., *Stromatum Liber*, I, 21; PG, 8, 888.   [5] K. Holl, *Der Ursprung des Epiphaniefestes*, in *Gesammelte Aufsätze zur Kirchengeschichte*, Tübingen, 1928, II, 123 ff.   [6] Rahner, 177 ff.   [7] M. Noirot, *Epiphanie (Liturgie)* in *Catholicisme*, IV (1956), 324 ff.   [8] Nilles, I, 56, II, 555.   [9] LE, 172.   [10] B. Botte, *Les origines de la Noël et de l'Epiphanie*, Louvain, 1932.   [11] SRC, *Decr.*, March 22, 1955.   [12] CIC, 1247, 1.   [13] *Responsum*, December 31, 1885; Balt., CV.   [14] Nilles, I, 56.   [15] Nilles, I, 58. About the celebration of the Octave of Epiphany in ancient Jerusalem see SSP, 76 ff.   [16] *Homil. in Pentec.*, 1; PG, 50, 454.   [17] H. Rahner, *Die Gottesgeburt*, ZKTh, 59 (1939), 333 ff.   [18] SSP, 75.   [19] Schuster, I, 404.   [20] H. Leclercq, *Epiphanie*, DACL, 5.1 (1922), 197 ff.   [21] *Orat.* 39; PG, 36, 335.   [22] Nilles, I, 58.   [23] BR, *In Epiphania Domini, II Vesp., Ant. ad Magnificat.*   [24] N. Nilles, *Zur Darstellung der Hirten und Weisen in der christlichen Kunst*, ZKTh, 6 (1882), 580 ff.   [25] W. O'Shea, "The Feast of Christmas," in *American Ecclesiastical Review*, 137 (1957), 361 ff.   [26] *Poema*, 27; PL, 61, 649.   [27] D. N. Stanley, "Cana as Epiphany," WOR, 32 (1058), 83.   [28] BR, *In Epiphania Domini, Ant. ad Bened.*   [29] Kellner, 169.   [30] K. Prümm, *Der christliche Glaube und die altheidnische Welt*, Leipzig, 1935, II, 208 ff.   [31] BR, *Dom. I Adventus, Ant. III ad Laudes.*   [32] *De Bapt. Christi*, 1; PG, 49, 365.   [33] *In Epiphania Sermo*, I; PL, 171, 407.   [34] See H. Kehrer, *Die Hl. Drei Könige in Literatur und Kunst*, 2 vols., Leipzig, 1908.   [35] G. Ricciotti, *The Life of Christ*, Milwaukee, 1947, 249 ff.   [36] D. Nestle, *Einiges über Zahl und Namen der Weisen aus dem Morgenland*, Tübingen, 1893; DACL, 10.1 (1931), 985 ff. and 1061 ff. (*Les Noms des Mages*).   [37] *De Collect.* IV; PL, 94, 541.   [38] BR, *Proprium of the Archdiocese of Cologne*, Feast of the Translation of the Magi (23 July), second Nocturn.   [39] B. Filalete, *I Magi Evangelici e le loro Reliquie*, Milano,

1914.   [40] Kellner, 171.   [41] Can. 1; Mansi, 9, 111.   [42] F. Cabrol, *L'Annonce des Fêtes dans la Liturgie Romaine actuelle*, DACL, 1.2 (1924), 2238 ff.   [43] P. de Puniet, *Bénédiction de l'eau en la fête de l'Epiphanie chez les Orientaux*, DACL, 2.1 (1925), 698 ff.   [44] Nilles, I, 59; H. Leclercq, *Bénédiction de l'eau du Nil*, DACL, 4.1 (1920), 2560 ff.   [45] *De Bapt. Christi*, 2; PG, 49, 366.   [46] N. Nilles, *Mitte-Pfingsten*, ZKTh, 19 (1895), 169 ff.; Ukrainians: Sr. Josepha, "Feast of the Epiphany," in *The Ark*, I (1946), 4 ff.   [47] F. Cabrol, *L'usage de l'eau bénite en Orient et en Occident*, DACL, 4.1 (1920), 1685 ff.; Koren, 81 ff.   [48] RR, *Bened. Aquae in Festo Epiphaniae*.   [49] CIC, 452, 6.   [50] RR, *Bened. Domorum in Festo Epiphaniae*.   [51] RR, *Bened. Cretae in Festo Epiphaniae*; Koren, 81 ff.; Geramb, 18.   [52] J. Sondheimer, *Die Herodespartieen im lateinischen liturgischen Drama und in den französischen Mysterien*, Halle, 1912.   [53] Young, II, 29 ff.   [54] K. A. M. Hartmann, *Ueber das altspanische Dreikönigsspiel*, Bautzen, 1879; H. Anz, *Die lateinischen Magierspiele*, Leipzig, 1905; Chambers, II, 41 ("Liturgical Plays").   [55] VL, 78.   [56] Geramb, 20 (*Sternsingen*).   [57] Crippen, 53.   [58] WC, 74.   [59] H. Moser, *Geschichte des Sternsingens*, in *Bayerischer Heimatschutz*, 31, München, 1935.   [60] Hackwood, 199 ("Kings' Cake").   [61] Gugitz, I, 8 (*Bohnenkönig*).   [62] G. Marsot, *Epiphanie* (Folklore) in *Catholicisme*, 4 (1956), 329 ff.   [63] See note 62.   [64] *Discourse ecclesiastique contre le paganisme des roys de la Fêve et du roy boit*, Paris, 1664.

CHAPTER

13   Pre-Lent

HISTORY AND LITURGY

The liturgical preparation for the greatest feast of Christianity—Easter—proceeds in five periods of penitential character. As the observance of this preparation approaches the feast, the penitential note grows progressively deeper and stricter. The first period is the season of pre-Lent, from Septuagesima Sunday to Ash Wednesday; the second extends from Ash Wednesday to Passion Sunday; the third comprises Passion Week; the fourth includes the days of Holy Week up to Wednesday; the fifth consists in the Sacred Triduum (Holy Thursday, Good Friday, Holy Saturday). In these three days, which are devoted entirely to the commemoration of the Lord's Passion, the penitential observance reaches its peak, until it ends (at the Easter Vigil) in the glorious and joyful celebration of the Resurrection.[1]

ORIGIN · The three Sundays preceding Lent are called Septuagesima (seventieth), Sexagesima (sixtieth), and Quinquagesima (fiftieth). Actually they are *not* the seventieth, sixtieth, and fiftieth days before Easter, as their names would indicate. These titles seem to have been arbitrarily chosen for the sake of round numbers, in keeping with the much older term of Quadragesima (fortieth), which denotes the first Sunday of Lent.[2]

This preparatory time of pre-Lent in the Latin Church was suggested by the practice of the Byzantine Church, which started its great fast earlier, because their "forty days" did not include Saturdays. Saint Maximus (465), Bishop of Turin, mentioned the practice in one of his sermons. It is a pious custom, he said, to keep a fast of devotion (not of obligation) before the start of Lent.[3]

The immediate occasion, however, for introducing the liturgical observance of pre-Lent seems to have been the frequent public calamities of the sixth century, especially the invasion of the Langobards, who devastated Italy and threatened Rome. This danger prompted the pope (Pelagius I or John III) to set these weeks (during which many people already fasted) aside for a general penitential observance. The liturgical texts of the Sunday Masses still exhibit traces of this origin.[4]

Since the time of danger and need endured through many years, the celebration became established in Rome as a traditional annual observance. From Rome it spread to other parts of the Western Church. We find the pre-Lenten Sundays mentioned as early as 541, in the fourth Council of Orléans.[5]

The penitential character of pre-Lent is usually motivated by the thought of "preparing for Lent." Fasting was never prescribed but was highly recommended in past centuries.[6]

LITURGY · At the time of Pope Saint Gregory I (604) the Masses of the pre-Lent Sundays were already celebrated in Rome with the same liturgical texts that are used today.[7] The spirit of this season is one of penance, devotion, and atonement, the liturgical texts and rules reflecting this character. The Gloria is omitted in the Mass, the *Te Deum* in the Divine Office, purple vestments are worn, and the altars may no longer be decorated with flowers.[8]

The Mass prayers of Septuagesima Sunday reflect most clearly the anguished cry for the Lord's help that rose from the heart of Saint Gregory and his people at sight of the misery and desolation that filled all Italy and threatened Rome:

The groans of death surrounded me, the sorrows of hell encompassed me: and in my affliction I called upon the Lord, and he heard my voice from his holy temple. (Psalms 17. Introit)

O Lord, we beseech thee, graciously hear the prayers of thy people, that we, who are justly afflicted for our sins, may for the glory of thy name be mercifully delivered. (Collect)

Sexagesima Sunday still bears the character of its original celebration in honor of Saint Paul. It probably was an annual feast on January 25 (Translation of St. Paul) which, being transferred to this Sunday, perpetuated the Roman celebration and extended it to the whole Church. The Mass text is a combination of penitential prayers with notes of rejoicing in honor of the Apostle of the Gentiles.[9]

The Mass prayers of Quinquagesima Sunday exhibit the note of penance and remind us of the approaching obligatory fast. In the Tractus of the Mass the Church breaks out in a jubilant prayer of praise, as if assured that her fervent appeals for God's help during the season of pre-Lent had been mercifully heard and heeded by the Lord.

FAST AND PENANCE · In the Latin Church many priests and people, as well as the religious, fasted voluntarily during the latter part of pre-Lent, especially from Quinquagesima Sunday on.[10] In the Byzantine Church this fasting was officially regulated from early times. They started abstaining from meat on Sexagesima, which is therefore called "Meatless" (*apokreo* in Greek; *miasopust*, in Slavic). With Quinquagesima the Eastern Church began (and still begins) the abstinence from butter, cheese, milk, and eggs. Thus in eastern Europe that day is called "Cheeseless Sunday" (*syropust*).[11]

In preparation for Lent the faithful in medieval times used to go to confession on Tuesday before Ash Wednesday. From this practice, that day became known as "Shrove Tuesday" (the day on which people are shriven from sins).

FAREWELL TO ALLELUIA

Alleluia, or *hallelujah*, is one of the few Hebrew words adopted by the Christian Church from apostolic times. It means "Praise the Lord!"

On Saturday before Septuagesima Sunday (the third Sunday before Lent) this ancient and hallowed exclamation of joy and praise in the Christian liturgy is officially discontinued in the Western Church to signify the approach of the solemn season of Lent.[12] According to the regulation of Pope Alexander II (1073) the Alleluia is sung twice after the prayers of the Divine Office,[13] and not heard again till the solemn vigil service of Easter, when it once more is used as a glorious proclamation of Easter joy. The Greek Church, however, still retains the Alleluia even in Lent.

USAGE OF THE WORD · Saint John the Evangelist mentioned *alleluia* in his Apocalypse (19, 1-6), and the early Church accepted the word from the beginning. From Jerusalem the custom of using it spread with the expanding Church into all nations. It is interesting to note that nowhere and at no time was any effort made to translate it into the vernacular, as Saint Isidore of Seville (636) mentioned in his writings.[14] He explains this by the reverence for the hallowed traditions of the apostolic Church.

In addition to the official liturgy, as early as the third century the Christian writer Tertullian said in his treatise on prayer that the faithful of his time used to insert many alleluias in their private devotions.[15] Saint Jerome (420) praised the pious farmers and tradesmen who used to sing it at their toil, and the mothers who taught their babies to pronounce "alleluia" before any other word.[16]

In the Roman Empire the Alleluia became the favorite prayerful song of oarsmen and navigators. Saint Augustine (430) alluded to this custom, saying, "Let the Alleluia be our sweet rowing-song!" [17] And some years later, the Roman poet and bishop Sidonius Apollinaris (480) described how the river banks and shores of Gaul resounded with the Alleluia song of the rowing boatmen.[18] Even the Roman soldiers fighting against pagan barbarians used it as battle cry and war song. Saint Bede the Venerable (735), in his history of England, reported such an "Alleluia victory" won by the Christian Bretons over the Picts and Scots in 429.[19]

Finally, the expression "Alleluia, the Lord is risen" became the general greeting of Christians in early medieval times on the Feast of the Resurrection. Apart from these popular usages the Alleluia has at all times found its primary and most meaningful application in the official liturgy. In the early centuries, the Roman Church used it only during Easter time, but it soon spread over the rest of the ecclesiastical year, except of course, during Lent. It used to be sung even at funerals and burial Masses as an expression of the conviction that for a true Christian the day of death was actually the birthday of eternal life, a day of joy.[20] The Eastern Churches have preserved this custom in their Masses for the dead up to now.

FAREWELL CUSTOMS · The *depositio* (discontinuance) of the Alleluia on the eve of Septuagesima assumed in medieval times a solemn and emotional note of saying farewell to the beloved song. Despite the fact that Pope Alexander II had ordered a very simple and somber way of "deposing" the Alleluia, a variety of farewell customs prevailed in many countries up to the sixteenth century.[21] They were inspired by the sentiment which Bishop William Duranti (1296) voiced in his commentaries on the Divine Office: "We part from the Alleluia as from a beloved friend, whom we embrace many times and kiss on mouth, head and hand, before we leave him." [22]

The liturgical office on the eve of Septuagesima was performed in many churches with special solemnity, and alleluias were freely inserted in the sacred text, even to the number of twenty-eight final alleluias in the church of Auxerre in France. This custom also inspired some tender poems which were sung or recited during Vespers in honor of the sacred word. The best known of these hymns is, *Alleluia, dulce carmen* (Alleluia, Song of Gladness), composed by an unknown author of the tenth century. It was translated into English by John Mason Neale (1866) and may be found in the official hymnal of the Protestant Episcopal Church.[23]

In some French churches the custom developed in ancient times of allowing the congregation to take part in the celebration of a quasi-liturgical farewell ceremony. The clergy abstained from any role in this popular service. Choirboys officiated in their stead at what was called "Burial of the Alleluia" performed the Saturday afternoon before Septuagesima Sunday. We find a description of it in the fifteenth-century statute book of the church of Toul:

On Saturday before Septuagesima Sunday all choir boys gather in the sacristy during the prayer of the None, to prepare for the burial of the Alleluia. After the last *Benedicamus* [*i.e.*, at the end of the service] they march in procession, with crosses, tapers, holy water and censers; and they carry a coffin, as in a funeral. Thus they proceed through the aisle, moaning and mourning, until they reach the cloister. There they bury the coffin; they sprinkle it with holy water and incense it; whereupon they return to the sacristy by the same way.[24]

In Paris, a straw figure bearing in golden letters the inscription "Alleluia" was carried out of the choir at the end of the service and burned in the church yard.

With the exception of these quaint aberrations, however, the farewell to alleluia in most countries was an appropriate addition to the official ceremonies of the liturgy. The special texts (hymns, responsories, antiphons) used on that occasion were taken mostly from Holy Scripture, and are filled with pious sentiments of devotion, like the following unusual personification collected from a farewell service of the Mozarabic liturgy of Spain (ninth or tenth century):

Stay with us today, Alleluia,
  And tomorrow thou shalt part.
When the morning rises,
  Thou shalt go thy way.
Alleluia, alleluia.

The mountains and hills shall rejoice, Alleluia,
  While they await thy glory.
Thou goest, Alleluia; may thy way be blessed,
  Until thou shalt return with joy.
Alleluia, alleluia, alleluia.[25]

Thus the Alleluia is sung for the last time and not heard again
until it suddenly bursts into glory during the Mass of the Easter
Vigil when the celebrant intones this sacred ⁺word ⸱after the
Epistle, repeating it three times, as a jubilant herald of the
Resurrection of Christ.[26]

MAN AND NATURE

Just as many Christmas customs and similar observances had
their origin in pre-Christian times, so, too, some of the popular
traditions of Lent and Easter date back to ancient nature rites.
The "spring lore" of the Indo-European races is their source in
this case. From Yule to the summer solstice (which was celebrated on June 24), a continuous tradition of spring rites and
symbolic fertility cults was practiced among our forefathers.[27]

THE FIGHT AGAINST WINTER · These activities began at the winter
solstice, when the day was shortest in the year, and lasted until
April or May. In order to frighten the demons of winter away,
and at the same time to hide their own identity, the participants
in this "fight" were disguised in wild and strange costumes. Wearing masks of horrible size and shape, they ran shouting and
screaming through the open spaces around their homes.[28]

Mummers' and carnival masquerades of later times and the up-
roarious celebrations on various days between Christmas and
Easter have their origin in this "fight." In southern Germany, in
Austria, and among the Slavic nations such mummers' (*Perchten*)
parades are still held every year. Dressed in ancient costumes

and masks, the paraders follow traditional routes, accompanied by the loud and discordant noise of drums, cowbells, crude trumpets, and the cracking of whips or the shooting of mortars (*Böller*).[29]

Another rite of "frightening the winter away" was the setting of fires between Yule and May. Attached to wooden rings or wheels, brands were sent rolling down the meadows from the hilltops. In southern Germany the first Sunday of Lent is still called *Brandsonntag* (Fire Sunday), when many such burning wheels move, sparkling in the dark night, on the hillsides and from the mountain peaks. In France the same Sunday was called *Fête des brandons* (Feast of Torches) because on that day young people ran through the streets with firebrands to chase the winter away.[30]

As the spring advanced and days grew warmer, the people celebrated "winter's burial." Sometimes with mock sadness, more often, however, with wild and joyous abandon, they dragged a ragged straw figure, often of giant size, through the village, accompanied by a large crowd of "mourners" in masquerade. Popular funeral rites were held, and the huge figure, dressed in white to symbolize the snow, was either buried or "executed" by quartering, drowning, burning, or hanging, with the lusty approval and acclaim of the onlookers. In the sixteenth century they started in many places to stuff the figure with powder and fireworks, so that the heat of the flames would make it explode with a thunderous crash.[31]

Such burials of winter are still held in many countries. Very often, however, the ceremony has come to be interpreted as the "burial of carnival," or the "burning of Judas" on Holy Saturday.[32]

The climax of these rites was the play depicting "winter's defeat." The actors, impersonating with appropriate dress the figures of summer and winter, would carry on a verbal battle in which winter, defeated, conceded the victory to summer.[33]

FERTILITY RITES · While the struggle between summer and winter went on (December to April), many symbolic celebrations were held to demonstrate how anxious people were for the coming warm season and to insure as well the blessings of fertility (the important second part of these ancient rites).

The joy over the appearance of new plants and flowers in spring prompted man to attribute to them a special power of protection and healing. People planted special spring flower gardens; they brought branches of early-blossoming plants, like pussy willows, into their homes; they decorated themselves and their living rooms with wreaths of flowers and clusters of blossoms. A striking Christian variation of these nature rites was the medieval custom of planting "Mary gardens," which were made up of all the flowers and herbs that are ascribed by love and legend as a special tribute to the Blessed Virgin. This charming tradition has recently been revived in many places.[34]

Another fertility rite was the symbolic "plowing" of the earth in early spring, with a real plow or a wooden log, to make the soil fertile. It was done with elaborate ceremonies, often connected with a mummers' parade. In Germany and eastern Europe it became a part of the carnival celebration (*Blochziehen*). In England it was held in January, and the Monday after Epiphany (January 6) acquired from this ancient custom the name "Ploughmonday." The original fertility cult is still preserved in the superstition that maidens who draw the plow or sit on it or touch it will soon be married and will be blessed with healthy offspring.[35]

Chemistry and physics as we know them, of course, were a mystery to our pre-Christian forefathers. From constant observation, however, they knew only too well the effects of rain, or lack of rain, on vegetation and life. Water, therefore, assumed in their minds a magic role of producing fertility, health, and new life. This is the basis of the many ancient "water rites."[36] It was the fashion among all nations of Europe to sprinkle women and girls with water, thus to insure them the blessings of fertility and good health. This custom is still preserved in European countries, where during carnival time or at Easter the boys sprinkle or splash water on the girls, and the girls retaliate on the following day. In cities perfume is often used instead of water.

In the Middle Ages the Feast of Christ's Resurrection became the favorite time for such ancient water rites. In many parts of central and eastern Europe, and also in France, girls and women wash their faces in brooks and rivers on Easter Sunday morning (*Osterwaschen*). It is a widespread legend that on Easter Day all running water is especially blessed because the Risen Lord sanctified all life-giving elements and bestowed upon them special powers for the one great day of His resurrection.

Similar customs prevail in French Canada, where people wash themselves with water taken from rivers or fountains on Easter Sunday. They also preserve it in bottles, and it is said to remain fresh until the following Easter, being credited with great healing powers. In Germany and Austria bridegroom and bride sprinkle each other with such water before going to church on their wedding day. Domestic animals, too, are believed to benefit from the power of Easter water. In many parts of Europe farmers sprinkle them with water drawn from brooks or springs during Easter night. In some sections of Germany horses are ridden into a river on Easter Sunday to obtain for them protection and good health.[37] Irish legends attribute to water fetched on Easter Day magic powers against witches and evil spirits.

Among the Slavic nations the men in rural districts will rise at midnight on Holy Thursday and walk to the nearest brook to wash themselves. They do this in honor and imitation of Christ who, according to an old Oriental legend, fell into the river Cedron on His way to the Passion.

The Church has provided a Christian version of the ancient water rite by blessing and distributing Easter water on Holy Saturday, thus elevating the pre-Christian symbolism of nature into a Christian sacramental. It is customary for millions the world over to obtain for their households the Easter water blessed on Holy Saturday.

Another rite of fertility was the touch with the "rod of life" (*Lebensrute*).[38] A few branches were broken from a young bush, and any maiden touched or hit by this rod was believed to obtain the blessings of health and fertility. This symbolism was incorporated in the mysteries of the Roman goddess Libera, in which young matrons were initiated into childbearing and motherhood by a ritual of flagellation to insure fertility.

All through Europe this custom is found at carnival time or Eastertide. Girls and women are tapped with leaved rods or pussy willow branches, which are often decorated with flowers and ribbons. A familiar relic of this tradition seems to be the modern practice of throwing the bridal bouquet at weddings. It reveals its ancient symbolism by the claim that the girl who catches the bouquet (thus being touched by the rod of life) will be the next one to marry.

The greater part of the pre-Christian usage and meaning of the rod of life was transferred in medieval times to the Christian symbolism of the "palms" which the Church blesses on Palm Sunday.

SPRING FESTIVAL · When the victory of spring was fully won and winter had disappeared, our forefathers used to celebrate by dancing around a gaily decorated tree (maypole), cleared of branches except on its top. The tree itself was a symbol of nature's triumph, a tribute to the power of new life.[39] In medieval times maypoles were erected in every community. In rural towns of the Austrian Tyrol the inhabitants still observe the appealing custom of planting a maypole, at any time of the year, in front of houses where newly wed couples live; there the gay symbol remains until the night after the birth of the first child, when the young men of the village silently take it down.[40]

The crowning of the "May Queen" is another ancient rite which has been practiced by Indo-European peoples for thousands of years. One of the girls, chosen by a vote of young men, was led in procession to the place of the spring festival, where she presided over the celebration. She was often accompanied by a young man who was called the "May King." Both were dressed in festive robes, wore wreaths of flowers on their heads, and held in their hands a wooden scepter (the rod of life) adorned with flowers and ribbons.[41]

The final victory over winter was also celebrated with the setting of "bonfires" on hills and mountain peaks in all countries of northern Europe during pre-Christian times. The Easter fires and Saint John's fires are still a cherished part of the annual folklore in many sections, especially the Alpine provinces.[42]

Thus the religious celebration of the sacred seasons of Lent and Easter is accompanied by many popular traditions of ancient origin which have added a charming touch to the supernatural meanings of the season. Under the guiding inspiration of the Church a popular observance was molded, in which most of the natural customs were ennobled through the spiritual power of Christianity.

CARNIVAL CELEBRATION

NAMES · In ancient times, when the law of abstinence was much stricter and included many other foods besides meat, the clergy and a good number of the laity started abstaining progressively during the pre-Lenten season, until they entered the complete fast on Ash Wednesday. After Quinquagesima (the Sunday *before* Lent) this voluntary fasting began with abstinence from meat; consequently, this Sunday was called *Dominica Carnevala* from the Latin *carnem levare* (*carnelevarium*), which means "withdrawal" or "removal" of meat.[43]

The German word for this time of carnival is *Fassnacht,* or *Fasching,* which probably comes from the ancient *vasen* ("running around crazily"). It was adopted by the Slavic nations (as *fasiangy*) and by the Hungarians (as *farsang*). Another German word of later origin is *Fastnacht* (Eve of the Fast). The Lithuanians call the carnival season *Uzgavenes* (Pre-Lent).

Carnival celebrations are still held in most countries of central and western Europe and among the Latin nations of Europe and America.

CARNIVAL FOODS · The primary reason for carnival celebrations is the feasting, rejoicing, and reveling before the imminent season of fast and abstinence. It is a trait of human nature to anticipate approaching privations by greater or lesser excesses. The intensity of this urge, however, should not be judged from the mild Lenten laws of today, but from the strict and harsh observance of ancient times, which makes modern man shiver at the mere knowledge of its details. No wonder the good people of past centuries felt entitled to "have a good time" before they started on their awesome fast.

Another reason for the feasting, and a very practical one, was the necessity for finishing those foods which could not be eaten during Lent, and which, in fact, could not even be kept in homes during the fast—meat, butter, cheese, milk, eggs, fats, and bacon. This meant an increased consumption of rich foods and pastries the week before Ash Wednesday. Hence have come the names "Fat Tuesday" (*Fetter Dienstag* in German; *Mardi gras* in

French); "Butter Week" (*Sedmica syrnaja*) in Russia and other Slavic countries; and "Fat Days" (*Tluste Dni*) in Poland.

In the northern counties of England, the Monday of carnival week is "Collop Monday" (from the Latin *colpones*, cut pieces). Collops consist of sliced meat or bacon, mixed with eggs, and fried in butter.[44] In Scotland people eat "Crowdie," a kind of porridge cooked with butter and milk. On Tuesday, England enjoys her famous Shrove Tuesday pancakes. The Germans have pastries called *Fassnachtstollen,* the Austrians *Faschingskrapfen.*[45]

Fastelavnsboller are sold in Norway in great quantities during carnival time. Resembling our muffins, these "bollers" are sold throughout the whole year plain, but at carnival time they are filled with whipped cream and coated with sugar and frosting.

Russia, before the present regime, attached a national and strictly regulated importance to the several seasons of carnival, Lent, and Easter. Carnival or "Butter Week" was a general holiday. As in the western countries, there are pre-Christian relics in the Russian festival too. In the country districts a fantastic figure called *Masslianitsa* (Butter Goddess) is gaily decorated and driven about on a sledge while the peasants sing special songs and *horovode* (folk choruses). At the end of the week it is burned, and a formal farewell is bidden to pleasure until Easter. Rich but unsweetened pancakes (*blinni*) are served in every household at carnival time.

CARNIVAL FROLICS · Since carnival is a time of feasting and reveling, it was only natural that many elements of the pre-Christian spring lore should have become part of the celebration. Lent excluded the boisterous practices of mumming and masquerading, so what better time could be found for it than the gay days of the carnival? All the familiar features of our modern carnival celebrations are firmly rooted in a tradition that actually dates from about the fourteenth century.

The pre-Christian element of the carnival frolics in the Latin countries seems to be a growth of the Roman Saturnalia, a pagan feast in honor of the field god Saturnus held annually in December.[46] Northern countries have adopted customs and rites from the much older Indo-European spring lore.[47]

The popes, as temporal rulers of their state, acknowledged the carnival practice in Rome by regulating its observance, correcting its abuses, and providing entertainment for the masses. Paul II (1471) started the famous horse races which gave the name *Corso* to one of Rome's ancient streets, the former *Via Lata* (broad street). He also introduced the carnival pageants for which the Holy City was famous.[48] Within the past few centuries other cities, too, have developed their own special features of carnival celebration, like the famed carnival of Cologne, the parade of gondolas in Venice, the carnival balls of Vienna, the floats and parades in the cities of South America, and the mummers' parade in Philadelphia. The best-known celebration of carnival in America is the famous Mardi Gras in New Orleans, which takes its name from the day on which it is annually held.

FORTY HOURS' DEVOTION · In order to encourage the faithful to atone in prayer and penance for the many excesses and scandals committed at carnival time, Pope Benedict XIV, in 1748, instituted a special devotion for the three days preceding Lent, called "Forty Hours of Carnival," which is held in many churches of Europe and America, in places where carnival frolics are of general and long-standing tradition. The Blessed Sacrament is exposed all day Monday and Tuesday, and devotions are held in the evening, followed by the Eucharistic Benediction.[49]

---

[1] TE, I, 598. [2] Jgn GK, 204, note. [3] *Homil.* 36; PL, 57, 301. [4] TE, I, 600. [5] Can. 2; Mansi, 9, 113. [6] H. Leclercq, *Septuagésime*, DACL, 15.1 (1950), 1262 ff. [7] L. Eisenhofer, *Septuagesima*, LThK, 9 (1937), 481. [8] D. Tucker, "The Vestibule of Lent," OF, 3 (1929), 65 ff. [5] Schuster, II, 33. [10] Schuster, II, 36. [11] Nilles, II, 19 ff., 50 ff. [12] Pope Gregory I prescribed the use of Alleluia on all days except from Septuagesima to Easter. See DACL, 15.1 (1950), 1264 f. [13] BR, *Sabbato ante Septuages., ad Vesp.* [14] *De eccles. offic.*, I, 13; PL, 83, 750. [15] *Liber de Orat.*, 27; PL, 1, 1194. [16] *Ad Marcell. epist.*, 46; PL, 22, 491. [17] *De cant. novo*, 2; PL, 50, 680. [18] *Epist. Liber* II, 10; PL, 58, 488. [19] *Hist. Gentis Anglor.*, I, 20; PL, 95, 49. [20] Saint Jerome, *De morte Fabiolae, ep.* 77; PL, 22, 697. [21] H. Leclercq, *Le Départ de l'Alleluia*, DACL, 15.2 (1953), 2178 ff.; M. B. Hellriegl, "Alleluia, Farewell," OF, 19 (1945), 97 ff. [22] Dur., VI, 24, 18. [23] HPEC, hymn

54.   [24] Young, I, 552 (Latin text).   [25] C. Blume, *Des Alleluia Leben, Begräbnis und Auferstehung,* StML, 52 (1897), 429 (Latin text). [26] P. Botz, "Alleluia: Our Easter Song," OF, 20 (1946), 241 ff.   [27] These "fertility cults" are *not* the Greek cults of the same name, but a part of the general practice of nature lore among the Indo-Europeans. On the background of ancient spring lore, see Frazer, *passim,* and E. Dietrich and E. Fehrle, *Mutter Erde,* Berlin, 1925, 92-115.   [28] A. Spamer, *Deutsche Fastnachtsgebräuche,* Jena, 1936.   [29] Koren, 97. [30] Nilles, II, 118 ff.; Frazer, 609 ("Lenten Fires").   [31] Frazer, 301 ff.; Geramb, 45 ff.   [32] Gugitz, I, 86 ff. (*Faschingsbegraben*).   [33] See text of such a dialogue in WE, 18.   [34] D. J. Foley, "Mary Gardens," in *The Herbarist,* Boston, 1953, No. 9.   [35] Geramb, 38 ff. (*Blochziehen und Pflugziehen*).   [36] Frazer, 341 f.   [37] Benet, 57; E. Fehrle, *Deutsche Feste und Volksgebräuche,* Leipzig, 1927, *passim.*   [38] Nilles, II, 333; G. Graber, *Der Schlag mit der Lebensrute,* Klagenfurt, 1910. [39] Frazer, 120 ff., 314 ff.   [40] Geramb, 84.   [41] Frazer, 131.   [42] Frazer, 614 ff. ("The Easter Fires"); Geramb, 69 (*Die Osterfeuer*).   [43] Nilles, II, 55 ff.   [44] Hackwood, 201.   [45] Gugitz, I, 27 ff. (*Der Faschingskrapfen*).   [46] R. Corso, *Carnevale,* EI, 9 (1931), 98 f.   [47] G. Schierghofer, *Fastnacht,* LThK, 4 (1929), 896.   [48] Enc. Brit., 4 (1949), 896; EC, 3 (1949), 903 ff.   [49] Nilles, II, 64 ff.

CHAPTER

14   *Lent*

HISTORY AND LITURGY

GENERAL FEATURES · Within the liturgy of the Church Lent is the season of penitential and prayerful preparation for the great feast of Easter. This penance was practiced from the earliest times by strict fasting, additional prayer services, and by other penitential exercises which were of obligation for those who had committed public sins and crimes, and in which the other faithful joined more and more during medieval times in token of humble, voluntary penance.[1]

The external manifestation of the penitential character of Lent is apparent in the liturgical color (purple), and in the discontinuance of Alleluia, Gloria, and *Te Deum* in all seasonal Masses and Offices starting with Septuagesima. From Ash Wednesday on, organs remain silent, solemn weddings and other joyous celebrations in church are prohibited.[2]

In the ancient Church Lent was also the season of immediate preparation for baptism (*scrutinia:* investigations). The catechumens were not only instructed but also frequently questioned about their knowledge and understanding of what they had been taught. A public scrutiny took place, in which the bishop carefully ascertained whether they had given up all habits of sinful living. They had to produce witnesses who would testify as to their sincerity and purity of motive.[3]

The thought of Christ's Passion, which now is predominant in popular devotion all through Lent, is reflected in the liturgy only during the last two weeks of the season (Passiontide).[4]

The Mass texts of Lent are of very early origin; they go back before the time of Gregory the Great (604). Only the Thursday Masses are of later date; Gregory II (731) introduced them.[5] A unique feature of these weekday masses is the *Oratio super populum* (Prayer over the People) after the *Postcommunio.* This prayer used to be recited in every Mass throughout the year in the fifth and sixth centuries, but was later replaced by the "Blessing of the Faithful," which came into the Roman liturgy from the Gallic-Frankish observance. Only in Lent has it been retained up to the present.[6]

FAST · From the time of the Apostles the Church has singled out two days of the week for special observance: in honor of Christ's resurrection, Sunday replaced the ancient Sabbath as the new "Day of the Lord," while in memory of His death, Friday became a weekly day of fast. In addition, a strict two-day fast was kept from Good Friday to Easter Sunday by many early Christians who did not eat or drink at all during that period. The practice of this "Passion fast" was based on the Lord's word: "The days will come when the bridegroom shall be taken away from them, and then they will fast on that day" (Mark 2, 20).[7]

Eventually, a longer period of fasting was introduced in preparation for Easter, although its observance varied widely in the early centuries. Some churches fasted only in Holy Week, others for two or more weeks. Sunday was always excepted from the fast (in the Eastern Churches, Saturday as well). During the third and fourth centuries most churches gradually adopted a forty days' fast, in imitation of Christ, Who had fasted forty days in the desert (Luke 4, 2). Saint Athanasius (373), Patriarch of Alexandria, after having traveled to Rome and over the greater part of the Roman Empire in Europe, wrote in the year 339 that ."the whole world" fasted forty days.[8]

How did the Christians fast in times past? The various forms of fast and abstinence in the first centuries made for confusion, but gradually there emerged general rules which eventually became the accepted practice of the whole Church. In a letter to Saint Augustine of Canterbury (604), Pope Saint Gregory the Great announced the final form of abstinence which soon became the law: "We abstain from flesh meat and from all things that come from flesh, as milk, cheese, eggs" (and butter, of course).[9] For almost a thousand years this remained the norm of abstinence for all except those who were excused for reasons of ill health. In fact, the Eastern Churches (and many pious people among the Slavic nations of the Latin Church) still keep their fast in this manner; they don't touch meat or eggs or butter all through Lent, not even on Sundays.

The observance of Lent also includes the *jejunium* (fast in the strict sense). Its early practice consisted of eating only once a day, toward evening; nothing else except a little water was taken all day. After the eighth century, the time for this one and only meal was advanced to the hour of the None in the liturgical prayer (meaning the ninth hour of the Roman day, which is three o'clock in the afternoon). This meal was gradually transferred to the middle of the day (hence our word noon, from None). The noonday meal did not become a general practice until the fourteenth century.[10]

Saint Basil the Great (379), Archbishop of Caesaria in Asia Minor, vividly described in one of his sermons the widespread

observance of the fast in the fourth century (and by "fasting"
he meant only *one* meal a day):

There is no island, no continent, no city or nation, no distant corner of the globe, where the proclamation of Lenten fast is not listened
to. Armies on the march and travelers on the road, sailors as well as
merchants, all alike hear the announcement and receive it with joy.
Let no man then separate himself from the number of fasters, in
which every race of mankind, every period of life, every class of
society is included.[11]

The severity of the ancient rule was applied very sensibly at
all times by the Church authorities. Saint John Chrysostom (407),
Patriarch of Constantinople, gave this instruction: "If your body
is not strong enough to continue fasting all day, no wise man
will reprove you; for we serve a gentle and merciful Lord who
expects nothing of us beyond our strength." [12] Pope Saint Leo I
(461) pointed out that fasting is a means and not an end in
itself; its purpose is to foster pure, holy, and spiritual activity.
He coined the famous phrase which a thousand Christian writers
have not ceased to reiterate: "What we forego by fasting is to be
given as alms to the poor." [13]

It was not until the ninth century, however, that less rigid laws
of fasting were introduced. It came about in 817 when the monks
of the Benedictine order, who did much labor in the fields and
on the farms, were allowed to take a little drink with a morsel
of bread in the evening. This extremely light refreshment they
took while they listened to the daily reading of the famous
Collationes (collected instructions) written by Abbot Cassian
in the fourth century. Our modern word collation, meaning a
slight repast, comes from this.[14]

Eventually the Church extended the new laws to the laity
as well, and by the end of medieval times they had become universal practice; everybody ate a light evening meal in addition
to the main meal at noon. The present custom of taking some
breakfast on fasting days is of very recent origin (the beginning
of the nineteenth century).

Abstinence from *lacticinia* (milk foods), which included milk,
butter, cheese, and eggs, was never strictly enforced in Britain,
Ireland, and Scandinavia because of the lack of oil and other

substitute foods in those countries. The Church using common sense granted many dispensations in this matter in all countries of Europe. People who did eat the milk foods would often, when they could afford it, give alms for the building of churches or other pious endeavors.[15] (One of the steeples of the Cathedral of Rouen in France is still known for this reason as "butter tower.") In past centuries the Western Church increasingly allowed the consumption of *lacticinia* until the new Code of Canon Law (1918) omitted them entirely from the list of abstinential foods.[16]

During the Reformation some of the Protestant churches retained the Lenten fast, but not for long. In England, the government issued a series of proclamations and statutes enjoining the duty of Lenten fast. It was announced by the town criers on order of Parliament and changed all the time. The Puritans substituted monthly fast days. After the Restoration (1660), the Lenten laws were generally neglected, although they remained on the statute book until 1863, when Parliament finally repealed them. On the other hand, while the observance of Lent was no longer kept, many members of the Protestant clergy (among them John Wesley) personally kept the fast and also recommended it to their congregations. The growth of the Oxford Movement revived the practice of Lenten fasting in some Protestant groups, who now observe it according to the spirit of the universal Christian tradition.[17]

Among the Eastern Rites, many people still retain the old and strict routine, refusing to avail themselves of dispensations, although such are readily granted.[18] In the Near East numerous priests keep a total fast for two days and eat only every third day all through Lent. Among the Russians, Ukrainians, and other Slavic nations, it is common practice to fast until three in the afternoon, while children, though not obliged to, fast voluntarily until noon.

PREPARATION FOR BAPTISM · In the first centuries after the persecutions in the Roman Empire, Lent was not only a time of fasting and public penance but also the annual season of "preparation for baptism." [19] Those who had proved themselves serious applicants and had received preliminary instructions for many months would be admitted to the baptismal rites at the beginning of Lent. While the details of this practice varied locally, it was everywhere a somewhat hard school for the catechumens (candidates for baptism). If they were married, they had to live in continence all through Lent. They were not allowed to bathe and had to keep a complete fast every day until sunset.[20] Above all, however, they had to practice fervent prayer and sincere contrition for their past sins. Separated from the faithful, they stood in church at every service, weak from hunger, and constantly admonished by the bishop, "harshly scourged with regulations and catechetical instructions," as Saint Augustine observed.[21]

Standing barefoot on old rags or goat skins (symbolizing the godless world), they were exorcized in a special ceremony at the start of Lent. The bishop would breathe on them with a hiss and utter the command addressed to the Devil, whose slaves they had been in idolatry: "Depart, thou accursed one!"[22] At another ceremony, they listened for the first time to the Apostolic Creed, named *symbolum* (probably meaning handclasp; contract). Each candidate solemnly affirmed his belief in the sacred truths, and was then obliged to memorize the Creed, in order to "return the handclasp" (*reddere symbolum*) by public recitation on Holy Saturday.

A week later (usually on Palm Sunday), the bishop entrusted them with the sacred words of the Lord's Prayer, the "Our Father." Finally, on Holy Thursday, they interrupted the fast and took a welcome bath at the public bathhouses, which were still in use in Roman cities and towns.[23] The rest of the ceremonies, familiar from the ritual of baptism, were performed at the solemn Easter Vigil.

NAMES · The official term of the forty days' fast, Quadragesima (fortieth), is first mentioned in the fifth canon (decree) of the Council of Nicaea (325), although its reference to Lent is not yet certain; at the time of Saint Gregory (sixth century), however, the word was clearly applied to the period of Lenten fast.[24] The same word was also applied to the Sunday on which the fast began at that time (the first Sunday of Lent). In about 600 A.D. the period of fasting was made to begin four days earlier by Saint Gregory in order to establish the exact number of forty days, and since that time Lent has begun on the Wednesday before Quadragesima Sunday. (Only the Diocese of Milan in Italy still adheres to the ancient custom of starting the fast on the first Monday in Lent.) [25]

The names for Lent in all Latin countries come from the word Quadragesima. The Greek word for it is *Tessarakoste,* and the Slavonic, *Chetyridesnica.*[26] Our English term refers to the season of the year, sometimes explained as coming from the old Anglo-Saxon *Lengten-tide,* springtime, when the days are lengthening. The German *Fastenzeit* means "fasting time." The Hungarians call it the "Great Fast" (*Nagy-böjt*), and in Arabic-speaking countries they say the "Big Fast" (*Sawm al-Kabir*). The Christian population of Malta has adopted the Moslem term *Randan* for Lent.

ASH WEDNESDAY · The first day of Lent is called "Ash Wednesday" in all Christian countries of the Western world from the ceremony of imposing blessed ashes in the form of a cross on the foreheads of the faithful while the priest pronounces the words *"Memento homo quia pulvis es et in pulverem reverteris"* (Remember, man, that thou art dust, and to dust thou shalt return) (Genesis 3, 19).[27] The name "Ash Wednesday" (*Feria quarta cinerum*) was officially introduced by Pope Urban II (1099); prior to that the first day of Lent was called "Beginning of the Fast" (*initium jejunii*).[28]

The ashes used are obtained from burning the blessed palms of the previous Palm Sunday. They are also given a special blessing before being distributed on Ash Wednesday. The four prayers employed in the Roman Missal for this ceremony date back to the eighth century.[29]

PUBLIC PENANCE · The use of ashes as a token of penance and sorrow is an ancient one, often mentioned in the Scripture of the Old Testament (for example, in Jonas 3, 5-9 and Jeremias 6, 26 and 25, 34). Christ, too, refers to this custom, in Matthew 11, 21. The Church accepted it from Jewish tradition and preserved its original meaning.[30] The early Christian writer Tertullian (third century) mentions the imposition of ashes as one of the external marks of Christian penance.[31] Persons who had committed serious public sin and scandal were enjoined on Ash Wednesday with the practice of "public penance." [32] The period of this penance lasted until Holy Thursday, when they were solemnly reconciled, absolved from their sins, and allowed to receive Holy Communion. Since it extended through forty days, its observance was called "quarantine" (forty).[33] This word was also accepted into general use to denote a separation or expulsion from human contact in the case of infectious diseases.

The imposition of public penance on Ash Wednesday was an official rite in Rome as early as the fourth century, and soon spread to all Christianized nations. Numerous descriptions of this ancient ceremony have been preserved in medieval manuscripts and, in every detail, breathe a spirit of harshness and humility really frightening to us of the present generation.

Public sinners approached their priests shortly before Lent to accuse themselves of their misdeeds, and were presented by the priests on Ash Wednesday to the bishop of the place. Outside the cathedral, poor and noble alike stood barefoot, dressed in sackcloth, heads bowed in humble contrition. The bishop, assisted by his canons, assigned to each one particular acts of penance according to the nature and gravity of his crime. Whereupon they entered the church, the bishop leading one of them by the hand, the others following in single file, holding each other's hands. Before the altar, not only the penitents, but also the bishop and all his clergy recited the seven penitential psalms.[34] Then, as each sinner approached, the bishop imposed his hands on him, sprinkled him with holy water, threw the blessed ashes on his head, and invested him with the tunic of sackcloth.

After this ceremony the penitents were led out of the church and forbidden to re-enter until Holy Thursday (for the solemn rite of reconciliation). Meanwhile, they would spend Lent apart from their families in a monastery or some other place of voluntary confinement, where they occupied themselves with prayer, manual labor, and works of charity. Among other things they had to go barefoot all through Lent, were forbidden to converse with others, were made to sleep on the ground or on a bedding of straw, and were not allowed to bathe or to cut their hair.[35]

PRIVATE PENANCE · Although the imposition of ashes originally applied only to public sinners, many devout people soon voluntarily submitted to it, so that by the end of the eleventh century it had become general in all European countries. The popes, too, adopted it for their personal use. In medieval times they walked barefoot on Ash Wednesday to the church of Santa Sabina, accompanied by their cardinals (also barefoot), where the pope received the ashes from the oldest cardinal-bishop, and afterward distributed them to all the cardinals.[36]

After the Reformation, the imposition of ashes was discontinued in most Protestant churches, but was kept alive for a time in the Church of England by special proclamations of the government in 1538 and 1550, which reaffirmed it. It was gradually neglected, and completely forgotten in England by the seventeenth century. Today the Anglican Church keeps a relic of the ancient character of Ash Wednesday in a special service of "Commination," a solemn avowal of God's anger and justice against sinners. In recent years, some Protestant churches have returned to the practice of imposing ashes.[37]

Among the members of the Oriental Churches, Ash Wednesday is not observed. Their Lent begins on Monday before Ash Wednesday, which they call "Clean Monday" because the faithful not only cleanse their souls in penance but also wash and scrub their cooking utensils very thoroughly to remove all traces of meat and fat for the penitential season.[38]

LENTEN CLOTH · An interesting symbol of penance, used from Ash Wednesday until Wednesday in Holy Week, was the "Lenten Cloth," a common tradition in England, France, and Germany from the eleventh century on.[39] In Germany it was also called by the popular name of "Hunger Cloth" (*Hungertuch, Schmachtlappen*). It was composed of an immense piece of cloth suspended in front of the sanctuary, and parted in the middle, which symbolized the outcasting of the penitent congregation from the sight of the altar.[40] It was purple or white in color and decorated with crosses or scenes from Christ's Passion, was drawn back only for the main parts of the Mass, and remained suspended all through Lent until the words were read in the Passion Gospel of Wednesday before Easter (Holy Week). "And the curtain of the temple was torn in the middle" (Luke 23, 45).[41]

LAETARE SUNDAY

DAY OF JOY · The fourth Sunday in Lent (Mid-Lent) derives its Latin name from the first word of the Mass text, *Laetare Jerusalem* (Rejoice, O Jerusalem). It is a day of joy within the mourning season. The altars may be decorated with flowers, organ playing is permitted, and rose-colored vestments may be worn instead of purple ones.

The historical background of this sudden joyful note during the penitential season lies in the ancient practice of the *traditio symboli* ("handing over" of the *symbolum*, the Apostolic Creed). The catechumens received the sacred text for the first time on Wednesday after the fourth Sunday in Lent.[42] Soon afterward, the "Our Father" was also given to them. These ceremonies formed the last and decisive step toward baptism for those who had successfully stood the tests and scrutinies and proved themselves worthy to be admitted into the Church. Thus already at the beginning of the week (Laetare Sunday) the exultation of Mother Church over the approaching increase of her children (through baptism) manifested itself in the above-mentioned liturgical expressions of joy.[43]

The Station of the fourth Sunday was held at the church of Santa Croce in Gerusalemme (called simply "Hierusalem" in ancient books).[44] Hence the repeated mention of Jerusalem in the liturgical texts. The holy city is taken as a type of the New Testament "Jerusalem," the Church, who is our Mother (Galatians 4, 26), giving supernatural birth to us in baptism.

In later centuries, when the original practice of the *traditio* on Wednesday in Mid-Lent had been discontinued (being connected with the baptismal ceremony into one rite), the true reason for the Sunday's liturgical character of joy was forgotten, and other reasons were often given. Thus Pope Innocent III (1216) said in one of his sermons:

On this Sunday, which marks the middle of Lent, a measure of consoling relaxation is provided so that the faithful may not break down under the severe strain of Lenten fast but may continue to bear the restrictions with a refreshed and easier heart.[45]

THE GOLDEN ROSE · As a symbol of joy on Laetare Sunday the popes used to carry a golden rose in their right hand when returning from the celebration of Mass. Originally it was a natural rose, but from the eleventh century on it was made of gold. This custom seems to derive from an ancient popular spring celebration in Rome, at which people carried blossoms or flowers.[46]

Since the fifteenth century this golden rose consists of a cluster or branch of roses wrought of pure gold and set with precious stones in brilliant workmanship by famous artists. The popes bless it every year, and often they confer it upon churches, shrines, cities, or distinguished persons as a token of esteem and paternal affection. In case of such a bestowal, a new rose is made during the subsequent year.

The meaning and symbolism of the golden rose is expressed in the prayer of blessing. It represents Christ in the shining splendor of His majesty, the "flower sprung from the root of Jesse." From this ecclesiastical custom Laetare Sunday acquired its German name, *Rosensonntag* (Sunday of the Rose).[47]

MOTHERING SUNDAY · In England a popular observance developed toward the end of the Middle Ages. On Laetare Sunday, boys and girls who lived away from home (as apprentices and servants) were given leave to go home to visit their "mother church" in which they had been baptized and had worshiped as children. They always carried with them gifts to put on the altar. This custom, of course, was based on the liturgical significance of the Church as the "New Jerusalem." It was also the custom for the boys and girls to visit their own mother on the same day. They brought her flowers and simnel cakes (a rich plum cake; from *simila*, fine flour) and would do all the housework for her. This old custom still survives in certain parts of England, and the cakes are sold in London as well as provincial towns.[48] Hence the name "Mothering Sunday" and the famous old saying, "He who goes amothering finds violets in the lane." An ancient carol entitled "Mothering Sunday" (It is the day of all the year) may be found in the *Oxford Book of Carols*.[49] The tune is taken from an old German song of the fourteenth century.

PASSIONTIDE

PASSION SUNDAY · The fifth Sunday in Lent, called "Passion Sunday" (*Dominica Passionis*) since the ninth century, occurs two weeks before Easter and inaugurates Passiontide, the final and particularly solemn preparations for the great feast.[50] As a liturgical season, Passiontide is older than Lent, having been established by the Church as a period of fasting as early as the third century. During the first four weeks of Lent the spirit of personal penance prevailed, but these last fourteen days were devoted entirely to the meditation of Chirst's Passion. Among the Slavic nations Passion Sunday is also called "Silent Sunday" and "Quiet Sunday." [51]

In the Divine Office of Passiontide the famous hymns of the Holy Cross (*Vexilla regis* and *Pangue lingua, gloriosi lauream*) are sung or recited. Psalm 42 (*Introibo*) is omitted at the Mass, as is the Gloria Patri in the Divine Office. These changes, however, are probably due to reasons other than the liturgical memory of the Lord's Passion.[52]

On the eve of Passion Sunday the crucifixes, statues, and pictures in the churches are draped in purple cloth as a sign of mourning. This custom originated in Rome, where in ancient times the images of the papal chapel in the Vatican used to be shrouded when the deacon sang the concluding words of the Sunday Gospel, "Jesus hid himself and went out of the temple" (John 8, 59).[53] The liturgical services of Passiontide are based on what happened to our Lord during the last days before His death, leading up to the mysteries of the Passion. (Mystery, in this connection, is the religious term for any episode of Christ's life related in the Gospels.) The Mass texts are dominated by the thought of the Just One, persecuted by His enemies, as He approaches the supreme sacrifice on Golgotha.[54]

FEAST OF THE SEVEN SORROWS · On Friday after Passion Sunday the Church celebrates the Feast of the Seven Sorrows of the Blessed Virgin, commemorating events of pain and suffering in

her life, as recorded in the Gospels. The devotion to the sufferings
of Mary was very popular and widely practiced in medieval times.
In 1423, a synod at Cologne introduced a Mass text and prescribed a feast in honor of the Seven Sorrows to be annually
held in western Germany.[55] In 1727, Pope Benedict XIII (1730)
extended this feast to the whole Church.[56]

As sequence (hymn after the Gradual of the Mass) the Church
employs the famous Latin poem *Stabat Mater Dolorosa,* which
originally was written as a prayer for private devotion by an
unknown author (probably a Franciscan) in the thirteenth century. It is often attributed to the Franciscan Jacobus de Benedictis
(1306), better known under his popular name Jacopone da Todi.
His authorship, however, is still not certain.[57]

The *Stabat Mater* has been translated from the Latin into the
vernacular among all Christian nations, and is a greatly cherished
Lenten hymn everywhere.

In Latin countries, especially in Spain and South America, the
Feast of the Seven Sorrows is a great day of popular devotions.
Thousands throng every church to visit the shrine of the Sorrowful Mother, which is radiant with many lights and richly decorated with flowers, palms, and shade-grown clusters of pale young
wheat. In central Europe, where the feast is called "Friday of
Sorrows" (*Schmerzensfreitag*), popular devotions are held, and
for dinner a soup is served consisting of seven bitter herbs.[58]

DEVOTIONS AND HYMNS

STATIONS OF THE CROSS · The prevailing popular devotion in
Lent is, quite naturally, the veneration of the suffering Lord and
the meditation on His Passion and death. Both the Eastern and
Western Churches practice the touching devotion of the fourteen
Stations of the Cross, which originated in the time of the Crusades, when the knights and pilgrims began to follow in prayerful
meditation the route of Christ's way to Calvary, according to the
ancient practice of pilgrims. This devotion spread in Europe and
developed into its present form through the zealous efforts of
the Franciscan friars in the fourteenth and fifteenth centuries.
As custodians of the shrines in the Holy Land, the Franciscans

are still entrusted with the official erection and blessing of new Stations.[59]

LENTEN HYMNS · Most of the medieval Lenten songs are translations or adaptations of Latin hymns used in the Divine Office. The poem of Saint Gregory the Great (604) *Audi benige conditor* (Kind maker of the world, o hear) is recited during Vespers in Lent.[60] It inspired many popular Lenten songs during the Middle Ages. In the English language alone, more than twenty translations are known.

Another hymn ascribed to Saint Gregory is *Clarum decus jejunii* (The sacred time of Lenten fast). An English translation, with a melody by Johann Sebastian Bach (1750) may be found in the Protestant Episcopal hymnal.[61] Other Latin hymns include *Ex more docti mystico* (By mystical tradition taught), which is recited daily at the Office of the Matins; its authorship is also ascribed to Saint Gregory. *O sol salutis* (O Jesus, saving sun of grace), by an unknown author of the seventh or eighth century, is used at Lauds during Lent.

PASSION HYMNS · The most important hymns in honor of the Redeemer's Passion are used in the liturgical office of Passiontide. From early centuries translations of these hymns have also served as popular Lenten songs. At Matins, in Passiontide, the Church intones the famous song *Pangue lingua gloriosi lauream certaminis* (Praise, o tongue, the victory of the glorious battle), written by Venantius Fortunatus (602), Bishop of Poitiers.[62] This is frequently sung in choral groups all over the world.

At Vespers, in Passiontide, another hymn by Venantius Fortunatus is heard: *Vexilla Regis prodeunt* (The royal banners forward go). He composed it in 569, when the relics of the true cross, sent by Emperor Justinian II of East Rome, arrived at the monastery of Poitiers. Of this hymn, about fifty English translations since the fourteenth century are known.

An old German song, *O Haupt voll Blut und Wunden* (O bleeding Head, so wounded), written by Paul Gerhardt in 1656, was often translated into English; it is sung both in Catholic and Protestant churches during Lent. The tune is taken from an old German folk song composed by Hans L. Hassler and published in 1601. Johann Sebastian Bach employed the melody repeatedly in his *Saint Matthew Passion*.

Of modern Passion hymns, the most famous is the American Negro spiritual "Were You There When They Crucified My Lord?" It was first published in 1899, and has since become a favorite song in many churches. The traditional melody was arranged by the Reverend Charles Winfred Douglas (1944), and made famous by the Negro tenor Roland Hayes.

There are numberless ancient English poems written in honor of Christ's Passion which at one time probably served as church hymns but are forgotten today.

FOLKLORE

MOURNING · A character of mourning was always an important feature of the season of Lent. Church and state laws forbade public entertainments and festivities.[63] In medieval times people would also forego all private entertainments at home that were of joyous and hilarious nature.

At the royal courts in past centuries, Lent was an official period of mourning. The monarchs and their households dressed in black, as did most of the nobility and people in general. England remained loyal to this custom even after the Reformation; Queen Elizabeth I (1603) and the ladies of her court wore black all through Lent. In Russia, up to the twentieth century, all secular music ceased in Lent. During the first and last weeks all public amusements were forbidden. Women dressed in black and laid their ornaments aside. In the rural sections of Poland, dancing and singing still cease on Ash Wednesday. Both men and women don clothes of dark and somber color; the girls relinquish their finery and multicolored ribbons, and an atmosphere of devout recollection descends over the entire village. In many countries the expressions of mourning are now restricted to the last days of Holy Week, as in the Latin nations, where women dress in black on Good Friday. In Malta, the men, too, wear black.

EASTER CONFESSION · The Church imposes on its members the duty of receiving the sacraments of Penance and Holy Communion at least once a year.[64] Though most of the faithful approach the sacraments oftener, the "Easter confession" is still singled out in various countries as a solemn rite. It is usually made in Lent, and the Church provides special services of preparation, such as annual missions for the congregations. These services are very popular in the Latin countries. They are called *misiones* in the Spanish-speaking parts, *esercizi* (spiritual exercises) in Italy, *retraites* (retreats) in France and Canada. The original purpose of the Lenten missions was to help people prepare for a good confession.

In Russia, the faithful kept a specially strict fast during the whole week preceding their Easter confession. Starting on Monday, they attended two services a day. On Saturday, before going to confession, they would bow deeply to each member of their household, including the servants, and utter the age-old phrase "In the name of Christ, forgive me if I have offended you." The answer was "God will forgive you." Thus prepared, they made their confession on Saturday, and went to Communion on Sunday. Coming home from Mass and Communion, they again faced their whole family; but this time everyone embraced them with smiles and congratulations, flowers decorated the room and the breakfast table, and the entire household shared in the joy of the one who had received his Easter Communion. Similar traditions are still observed among the other Slavic nations. It was a custom in Austria for men and boys coming home from their Easter confession to decorate their hats with flowers and distribute pretzels to all in the house while receiving congratulations and good wishes.[65]

LENTEN FOOD · A most interesting survival of early Christian Lenten fare is a certain form of bread familiar to all of us. The Christians in the Roman Empire made a special dough consisting of flour, salt, and water only (since fat, eggs, and milk were forbidden). They shaped it in the form of two arms crossed in prayer, to remind them that Lent was a season of penance and devotion. They called these breads "little arms" (*bracellae*).[66] From the Latin word the Germans later coined the term *Brezel* or *Prezel*, from which comes our word pretzel. The oldest known picture of a pretzel may be seen in a manuscript from the fifth century in the Vatican.[67]

All through medieval times and into the present, pretzels remained an item of Lenten food in many parts of Europe. In Germany, Austria, and Poland, they made their annual appearance on Ash Wednesday; special vendors (*Brezelmann*) sold them on the streets of cities and towns.[68] People would eat them for lunch, together with a stein of their mild, home-brew beer. In Poland they were eaten in beer soup.

In the cities pretzels were distributed to the poor on many days during Lent. In parts of Austria, children wore them suspended from the palm bushes on Palm Sunday. With the end of Lent the pretzels disappeared again until the following Ash Wednesday.[69] It was only during the last century that this German (actually, ancient Roman) bread was adopted as an all-year tidbit, and its Lenten significance all but forgotten.

In Russia, the Lenten fare is the most meager of all European nations. Rigidly observed by the faithful far into the twentieth century, the traditional fast is still kept by old people: no meat, no fish, no milk (nor anything made of milk), no butter, no eggs, no sugar or candy. The diet during this period consists of bread made with water and salt, vegetables, raisins, honey, and raw fruit.[70]

The Polish people's main staples in Lent include herring (smoked or cooked), and *zur,* a mush made of fermented rye meal and water, which serves as a base for some Lenten soups.[71]

Among the Ukrainians, neither meat nor dairy products are used by those who keep the strict fast. During Lent meals are never cooked, only vegetables, fruit, honey, and special bread are eaten.

Mid-Lent · The week from the Wednesday before to the Wednesday after Laetare is called "Mid-Lent" in most countries. It is a time of many popular customs and traditions, most of them connected with ancient spring lore. In Germany and among the northern Slavic nations the "burial of winter" is celebrated in rural sections. In Poland children carry the effigy of a stork through the village; thus they greet the return of the bird as a harbinger of the approaching summer. In France and Canada, Mid-Lent is kept with a joyous meal and entertainment in the home. A rite performed in central and southern Europe is the decoration of wells and fountains with branches and flowers, to celebrate their final liberation from winter's ice. Laetare Sunday is called *Fontana* (Sunday of Fountains) in parts of Italy because of this.[72]

In Germany, Austria, and among the western Slavs, Laetare Sunday used to be the day of announcing the engagements of young people (*Liebstatt Sonntag; Druzebna*).[73] In Bohemia the boys would send messengers to the homes of their girl friends to deliver the solemn proposal. In Austria the girls of the village lined up in front of the church after Mass; their boy friends would take them by the hand and lead them back into the house of God, and thus "propose" to them by a silent act of religious import. After having prayed together, the couple would seal their engagement with a special meal. It is a curious fact that these engagement customs were called "Valentine," although they did not take place on Saint Valentine's Day. The name is explained by the fact that Saint Valentine was the heavenly patron of young lovers and engaged couples.[74]

In Ireland not only Mid-Lent but the whole season of Lent is the traditional time of matchmaking (*cleamhnas*). The older people visit each other's homes to discuss the possibilities of matching their sons and daughters. Among the young generation, there is much fun poked at those not yet married. In some parts of Ireland weddings are held only on Easter Sunday, after the last preparations have been made during Lent.

[1] E. Vagandard, *Carême*, DACL, 2.2 (1925), 2139 ff.; E. and J. Winter, "Lent in the Home," WOR, 31 (1957), 178 ff. [2] LE, 139. [3] SSP, 96 f. [4] LE, 139. [5] LP, I, 402. [6] Jgn MS, II, 517 ff. [7] Kellner, 90. [8] Letter quoted by Saint Jerome; PL, 22, 773. On the ancient practice of Lenten fast in Jerusalem see SSP, 80 ff. [9] *Epist. ad Augustinum Angl. Episc.*; PL, 77, 1351. [10] F. X. Funk, *Die Entwicklung des Osterfastens,* Paderborn, 1897. [11] *De Jejunio Hom.*, II, 2; PL, 31, 186. [12] *Gen. Hom.*, X, 1; PG, 53, 82. [13] *Sit abstinentia jejunantis refectio pauperis, Sermo* 13; PL, 54, 172. [14] A. Sturm, *Collatio*, LThK, 2 (1931), 1013 f. [15] DACL, 2.2 (1925), 2149. [16] CIC, 1250. [17] Enc. Brit., 13 (1949), 923. [18] Nilles, I, 62 f. [19] P. de Puniet, *Catéchuminat*, DACL, 2.2 (1925), 2579 ff.; Schuster, I, 12 ff. ("Initiation"). [20] *Conc. Carthag. IV, can.* 83; Mansi, 3, 958. [21] VdM, 420. [22] Saint

Augustine, *Sermo 216, ad Competentes;* PL, 38, 1076 ff.   [23] VdM, 424.   [24] Can. 5; Mansi, 2, 670.   [25] DACL, 2.2 (1925), 2145.   [26] Nilles, II, 75.   [27] F. Cabrol, *Mercredi des Cendres,* DACL, 2.2 (1925), 3040 ff.   [28] Franz, I, 462; DACL, 2.2 (1925), 2134 ff. (*Caput Jejunii*).   [29] Franz, I, 463 ff.   [30] F. Cabrol, *Les cendres dans l'antiquité,* DACL, 2.2 (1925), 3037 ff.   [31] *De Penit.,* XI; PL, 1, 1246.   [32] J. A. Jungmann, *Die lateinischen Bussriten,* Innsbruck, 1932; Schuster, II, 38 f.; VdM, 447 ff.   [33] DACL, 2.2 (1925), 2158 (*Carena*).   [34] Psalms 6, 31, 37, 50, 101, 129, 142.   [35] Thurston, 60 ff.   [36] *In S. Gregorii libr. Sacram.,* notae; PL, 78, 1070.   [37] Enc. Brit., 9 (1949), 106 ("Fasting"); 2 (1949), 512 ("Ash Wednesday").   [38] Nilles, II, 86 f.   [39] A. E. Rientjes, *Over het gebreuk van vasten- of hongerdock in Nederland,* in *Eigen Volk,* 8 (1935), 73 ff.; OiT, 17 (*Vom Fasten-oder Hungertuch*).   [40] Thurston, 100 ff.   [41] J. Braun, *Hungertuch,* LThK, 5 (1932), 200.   [42] Schuster, II, 129.   [43] LE, 142.   [44] Schuster, II, 114.   [45] Sermo 18; PL, 217, 393.   [46] LE, 143.   [47] L. Eisenhofer, *Goldene Rose,* LThK, 4 (1932), 567; Thurston, 180 ff.; Nilles, II, 143 f.   [48] Enc. Brit., 13 (1949), 923.   [49] *The Oxford Book of Carols,* ed. P. Dearmer, London, 1941, 292.   [50] Amalarius, *De ord. antiphon.,* 43; PL, 105, 1291.   [51] Nilles, II, 188 f.   [52] LE, 143.   [53] F. Ravanat, *Del velo delle croci ed imagini nel tempo di passione,* in *Perfice Munus,* 2 (1927), 499 ff.   [54] Schuster, II, 145; Kellner, 102 f.   [55] Can. 11; Mansi, 28, 1057.   [56] TE, 705.   [57] G. De Luca, *Stabat Mater,* EI, 32 (1949), 432.   [58] OiT, 22 (*Vom Schmerzensfreitag*).   [59] B. Mathes, *Kreuzweg,* LThK, 6 (1934), 261 ff.   [60] HRL, 74 f. For the following two hymns see 76, 78.   [61] HPEC, hymn 61.   [62] HRL, 82 f.; *Vexilla Regis,* 80 f.   [63] DACL, 2.2 (1925), 2151 f.   [64] CIC, 906.   [65] OiT, 24 ff. (*Osterbeicht*).   [66] The word pretzel does *not* derive from *pretiolum* (little prize) as often claimed. See R. Hindringer, *Fastenbrezel,* LThK, 3 (1931), 968.   [67] Codex no. 3867, Vatican Library.   [68] Gugitz, I, 113 (picture of pretzel vendor).   [69] OiT, 12 ff.   [70] See note 18.   [71] Benet, 48.   [72] Nilles, II, 144 ff.   [73] *Ibid.* (*Neděle družebná*).   [74] Gugitz, I, 77 f.

CHAPTER

15 *Holy Week*

THE GREAT AND SACRED WEEK

NAMES · In the Greek Church Holy Week bears the solemn title the "Sacred and Great Week" (*IIe hagia kai megale hebdomas*). In the Latin Church the official term is the "Greater Week" (*hebdomada major*). The popular names are "Great Week" among the Slavic nations, and "Holy Week" in other countries. The German name *Karwoche* means "Week of Mourning." In ancient times Holy Week was also called "Week of Remission," since the public sinners were absolved on Maundy Thursday. Another name was "Laborious Week" (*semaine peineuse*) because of the increased burden of penance and fasting. The faithful of the Eastern Churches also call it the "Week of Salvation." [1]

OBSERVANCE · From the very beginning of Christianity it has always been devoted to a special commemoration of Christ's Passion and death through the practice of meditation, prayer, fasting, and penance. After the great persecutions, the Christian emperors of both the East and West Roman Empires issued various decrees forbidding not only amusements and games, but also regular work in trade, business, professions, and courts. The sacred days were to be spent free from worldly occupations, entirely devoted to religious exercises. Every year during Holy Week an imperial edict granted pardon to a majority of those detained in prison; in the courts many charges were withdrawn in honor of Christ's Passion.

Following this custom, kings and rulers in medieval days retired from all secular business during Holy Week to spend the time in recollection and prayer, often within the seclusion of a monastery. Farmers set aside their plows, artisans their tools, schools and government offices closed, and courts did not sit. Popular feeling caused the banning not only of music, dancing, and secular singing but also of hunting and any other kind of sport. It was truly a "quiet" and "holy" week even in public life.[2]

The Sacred Triduum of Holy Week (Thursday, Friday, Saturday) was a time of holyday obligation all through the Middle Ages. The Christian people, freed from servile work, were all present at the impressive ceremonies of these days. Due to the changed conditions of social life, however, Pope Urban VIII, in 1642, rescinded this obligation. Since then the last three days of Holy Week have been classified as working days, despite the sacred and important character they bear, which was powerfully stressed by the renewal of the liturgical order of Holy Week in 1955.[3]

EASTER CLEANING · According to an ancient tradition, the three days after Palm Sunday are devoted in many countries to a thorough cleaning of the house, the most vigorous of the whole year. Carpets, couches, armchairs, and mattresses are carried into the open and every speck of dust beaten out of them. Women scrub and wax floors and furniture, change curtains, wash windows; the home is buzzing with activity. No time is wasted on the usual kitchen work; the meals are very casual and light. On Wednesday night everything has to be back in place, glossy and shining, ready for the great feast.[4] In Poland and other Slavic countries people also decorate their homes with green plants and artificial flowers made of colored paper carrying out ancient designs.[5]

This traditional spring cleaning is, of course, to make the home as neat as possible for the greatest holidays of the year, a custom taken over from the ancient Jewish practice of a ritual cleansing and sweeping of the whole house as prescribed in preparation for the Feast of Passover.[6]

PALM SUNDAY

LITURGY · As soon as the Church obtained her freedom in the fourth century, the faithful in Jerusalem re-enacted the solemn entry of Christ into their city on the Sunday before Easter, holding a procession in which they carried branches and sang the "Hosanna" (Matthew 21, 1-11).[7] In the early Latin Church, people attending Mass on this Sunday would hold aloft twigs of olives, which were not, however, blessed in those days.

The rite of the solemn blessing of "palms" seems to have originated in the Frankish kingdom. The earliest mention of these ceremonies is found in the Sacramentary of the Abbey of Bobbio in northern Italy (at the beginning of the eighth century). The rite was soon accepted in Rome and incorporated into the liturgy. A Mass was celebrated in some church outside the walls of Rome, and there the palms were blessed. Then a solemn procession moved into the city to the basilica of the Lateran or to St. Peter's, where the pope sang a second Mass. The first Mass, however, was soon discontinued, and in its place only the ceremony of blessing was performed.[8]

Everywhere in medieval times, following the Roman custom, a procession composed of the clergy and laity carrying palms moved from a chapel or shrine outside the town, where the palms were blessed, to the cathedral or main church. Our Lord was represented in the procession, either by the Blessed Sacrament or by a crucifix, adorned with flowers, carried by the celebrant of the Mass. Later, in the Middle Ages, a quaint custom arose of drawing a wooden statue of Christ sitting on a donkey (the whole image on wheels) in the center of the procession. These statues (Palm Donkey; *Palmesel*) are still seen in museums of many European cities.[9]

As the procession approached the city gate, a boys' choir stationed high above the doorway of the church would greet the Lord with the Latin song *Gloria, laus et honor*. This hymn, which is still used today in the liturgy of Palm Sunday, was written by the Benedictine Theodulph, Bishop of Orléans (821):

> *Glory, praise and honor,*
> *O Christ, our Savior-King,*
> *To thee in glad Hosannas*
> *Inspired children sing.*[10]

After this song, there followed a dramatic salutation before the Blessed Sacrament or the image of Christ. Both clergy and laity

knelt and bowed in prayer, arising to spread cloths and carpets
on the ground, throwing flowers and branches in the path of the
procession. The bells of the churches pealed, and the crowds sang
the "Hosanna" as the colorful procession entered the cathedral for
the solemn Mass.

In medieval times this dramatic celebration was restricted
more and more to a procession around the church. The crucifix
in the churchyard was festively decorated with flowers. There
the procession came to a halt. While the clergy sang the hymns
and antiphons, the congregation dispersed among the tombs,
each family kneeling at the grave of relatives. The celebrant
sprinkled holy water over the graveyard, the procession formed
again and entered the church. In France and England the custom
of decorating graves and visiting the cemeteries on Palm Sunday
is still retained.[11]

Today the blessing of palms and the procession are usually
performed within the churches. The new liturgical arrangements
made by Pope Pius XII have restored the original solemnity of
the procession, and the members of the congregation now take
active part again in the sacred ceremonies of Palm Sunday. The
blessing of palms, however, is now very short and simple compared to the former elaborate ritual.[12]

NAMES · The various names for the Sunday before Easter come
from the plants used—palms (Palm Sunday) or branches in general (Branch Sunday, *Domingo de Ramos, Dimanche des
Rameaux*). In most countries of Europe real palms are un-
obtainable, so in their place people use many other plants:
olive branches (in Italy), box, yew, spruce, willows, and pussy
willows.[13] In fact, some plants have come to be called "palms"
because of this usage, such as the yew in Ireland and the willow
in England (palm willow) and in Germany (*Palmkätzchen*).
From the use of willow branches Palm Sunday was called "Willow
Sunday" in parts of England and Poland, and in Lithuania *Verbu
Sekmadienis* (Willow Twig Sunday). The Greek Church uses
the names "Sunday of the Palm-carrying" and "Hosanna Sunday."

Centuries ago it was customary to bless not only branches but
also various flowers of the season (the flowers are still mentioned
in the first antiphon of the procession). Hence the name "Flower

Sunday," which the day bore in many countries—"Flowering Sunday" or "Blossom Sunday" in England, *Blumensonntag* in Germany, *Pâsques Fleuris* in France, *Pascua Florida* in Spain, *Virágvasárnap* in Hungary, *Cvetna* among the Slavic nations, *Zaghkasart* in Armenia.[14]

The term *Pascua Florida*, which in Spain originally meant just Palm Sunday, was later also applied to the whole festive season of Easter Week. Thus the State of Florida received its name when, on March 27, 1513 (Easter Sunday), Ponce de Leon first sighted the land and named it in honor of the great feast.

THE PASSION · In the new liturgical order of Holy Week, Palm Sunday bears the official title "Second Sunday of the Passion, or Palm Sunday." Thus the Church enhances the significance of this Sunday as a memorial of Christ's sufferings, which are commemorated by the reading of the Passion. The word Passion in this connection means those passages of the Gospels which report the events of Christ's suffering and death. The Passions of all four Gospels are read or chanted in all Catholic churches during the liturgical services on certain days of Holy Week, and observed in varying degrees in many Protestant churches. On Palm Sunday, the Passion of Saint Matthew (26, 36—27, 54) is solemnly sung during Mass, in place of the usual Gospel.

The ancient liturgical rules prescribe that three clergymen of deacon's rank, vested in alb and stole, chant the sacred text. They are to alternate in contrasting voices. One (tenor) represents the Evangelist narrator; the second (high tenor) chants the voices of individuals and crowds; the third (bass) sings only the words of Christ.[15]

The melodies prescribed for the liturgical chanting of the Passion are among the most impressive examples of Gregorian chant, and for many centuries remained the only Passion music, until the nonliturgical works on the Passion were written.

THE PALMS · In central Europe, large clusters of plants, interwoven with flowers and adorned with ribbons, are fastened to the top of a wooden stick. All sizes of such palm bouquets may be seen, from the small children's bush to rods of ten feet and more.[16] The regular "palm," however, consists in most European countries of pussy willows bearing their catkin blossoms. In the Latin countries and in the United States, palm leaves are often shaped and woven into little crosses and other symbolic designs. This custom was originated by a suggestion in the ceremonial book for bishops that "little crosses of palm" be attached to the boughs wherever true palms are not available in sufficient quantity.[17]

In the spirit of this blessing, the faithful reverently keep the palms in their homes throughout the year, usually attached to a crucifix or holy picture, or fastened on the wall.[18] In South America they put the large palm bouquets behind the door. In Italy people offer blessed palms as a token of reconciliation and peace to those with whom they have quarreled or lived on unfriendly terms. The Ukrainians and Poles strike each other gently with the pussy-willow palms on Palm Sunday; this custom, called *Boze Rany* (God's Wounds) they interpret as an imitation of the scourging of our Lord.[19]

In Austria, Bavaria, and in the Slavic countries, farmers, accompanied by their families, walk through their fields and buildings on the afternoon of Palm Sunday. Praying and singing their ancient hymns, they place a sprig of blessed palms in each lot of pasture or plowland, in every barn and stable, to avert the punishment of weather tragedies or diseases, and to draw God's blessing on the year's harvest and all their possessions.[20]

HOLY THURSDAY

NAMES · Holy Thursday bears the liturgical name "Thursday of the Lord's Supper" (*Feria Quinta in Coena Domini*). Of its many popular names the more generally known are:

Maundy Thursday (*le mandé;* Thursday of the *Mandatum*). The word *mandatum* means "commandment." This name is taken from the first words sung at the ceremony of the washing of the feet, "A new commandment I give you" (John 13, 34); also from the commandment of Christ that we should imitate His loving humility in the washing of the feet (John 13, 14-17). Thus the term *mandatum* (maundy) was applied to the rite of the feet-washing on this day.[21]

Green Thursday. In all German-speaking countries people call
Maundy Thursday by this name (*Gründonnerstag*). From Germany
the term was adopted by the Slavic nations (*zeleny ctvrtek*) and in
Hungary (*zöld csütörtök*). Scholars explain its origin from the old
German word *grunen* or *greinen* (to mourn), which was later corrupted into *grün* (green). Another explanation derives it from *carena*
(*quadragena*), meaning the last day of the forty days' public
penance.[22]

Pure or *Clean Thursday.* This name emphasizes the ancient tradition that on Holy Thursday not only the souls were cleansed through
the absolution of public sinners, but the faithful in all countries also
made it a great cleansing day of the body (washing, bathing, shav-
ing) in preparation for Easter. Saint Augustine (430) mentioned this
custom.[23] The Old English name was "Shere Thursday" (meaning
sheer, clean), and the Scandinavian, *Skaer Torsdag.* Because of the
exertions and thoroughness of this cleansing in an age when bathing
was not an everyday affair, the faithful were exempted from fasting
on Maundy Thursday.[24]

Holy or *Great Thursday.* The meaning of this title is obvious since
it is the one Thursday of the year on which the sacred events of Christ's
Passion are celebrated. The English-speaking nations and the people of
the Latin countries use the term "Holy," while the Slavic populations
generally apply the title "Great." [25] The Ukrainians call it also the
"Thursday of the Passion." In the Greek Church it is called the "Holy
and Great Thursday of the Mystic Supper." [26]

MASSES · In the early Christian centuries the bishop celebrated
three Masses on Maundy Thursday. The first (Mass of Remission) for the reconciliation of public sinners; the second (Mass
of the Chrism) for the blessing of holy oils; the third (Mass of
the Lord's Supper) in commemoration of the Last Supper of
Christ and the institution of the Eucharist.[27] This third Mass was
celebrated in the evening, and in it the priests and people received Holy Communion. It is interesting to note that in ancient
times Holy Thursday was the only day of the year when the faithful could receive the Blessed Sacrament at night after having
taken their customary meals during the day (since it was not a
fast day).

Today the Mass of the Chrism is still solemnly celebrated in
every cathedral. During this Mass the bishop blesses the holy
oils (oils of the sick, holy chrism, and oil of the catechumens).[28]

In the evening the Mass of the Lord's Supper is celebrated in all churches. It is one of the most solemn and impressive Masses of the year, since the very "birthday" of the Holy Sacrifice is commemorated in it. The altar is decorated, crucifix and tabernacle are veiled in white, and the priests wear rich vestments of white, the liturgical color of joy. At the beginning of the Mass the organ accompanies the choir, and through the Gloria a jubilant ringing of bells proclaims the festive memory of the institution of the Blessed Sacrament. After the Gloria the bells fall silent and are replaced by a wooden clapper and not heard again till the Gloria of the Easter Vigil is intoned on Holy Saturday.[29]

Only one priest celebrates Mass in each church on Holy Thursday; the other priests and the lay people receive Communion from his hand, thus representing more vividly the scene of our Lord's Last Supper. The faithful are expected and invited (but not strictly obliged) to attend this Mass and receive Holy Communion.

REPOSITORY · After the Mass, the Blessed Sacrament is carried in solemn procession to a side altar, richly decorated with candles and flowers, where it is kept in the tabernacle until the Good Friday service. This "repository" altar is a highly venerated shrine in every church, visited by thousands of people. A popular custom in cities is to visit seven such shrines. Throughout the night, in many countries, groups of the clergy and laymen keep prayerful watch in honor of the agony of Christ.

In the Latin countries of Europe and South America the Maundy Thursday shrine is called *monumento*. It is much more elaborate than the shrines of other nations. Usually a special scaffolding with many steps, representing a sacred hill, is erected, so high that it almost reaches to the ceiling. On the top of this the Sacrament is elevated, raised above a glorious forest of candles, palms, orchids, lilies, and other decorations. Dressed in black, the city people visit at least seven such *monumentos*, which, in many places, are open through the night. On their way from church to church they say the rosary.

DENUDING OF ALTARS · After the Mass and procession on Holy Thursday, the altars are "denuded" in a ceremony of deep significance. Priests robed in purple vestments remove the altar linen, decorations, candles, and veils from every altar and tabernacle except the repository shrine. Robbed of their vesture, the bare altars now represent the body of Christ, Who was stripped of His garments. In medieval times the altars used to be washed with blessed water and wine, the priests using bundles of birch twigs or palms to cleanse and dry them. In the Vatican this ceremony is still performed by the canons of St. Peter's on Holy Thursday.[30]

MANDATUM · Finally, there is the ancient rite of the *Mandatum,* the washing of the feet. It is prescribed by the rules of the Roman Missal as follows:

After the altars are denuded, the clergy shall meet at a convenient hour for the Mandatum. The Gospel *Ante diem festum* (John 13, 1-17) is sung by the Deacon. After the Gospel the prelate puts off his cope and, fastening a towel around him, he kneels before each one of those who are chosen for the ceremony, washes, wipes and kisses the right foot.

From ancient times, all religious superiors, bishops, abbots, and prelates, performed the Maundy; so did the popes at all times. As early as 694 the Synod of Toledo prescribed the rite.[31] Religious superiors of monasteries washed the feet of those subject to them, while the popes and bishops performed the ceremony on a number of clergy or laymen (usually twelve). In medieval times, and in some countries up to the present century, Christian emperors, kings, and lords washed the feet of old and poor men whom they afterward served at a meal and provided with appropriate alms.[32]

In England, the kings used to wash the feet of as many men as they themselves were years old. After the Reformation, Queen Elizabeth I still adhered to the pious tradition; she is reported to have used a silver bowl of water scented with perfume when she washed the feet of poor women on Maundy Thursday. Today, all that is left of this custom in England is a distribution of silver coins by royal officials to as many poor persons as the monarch is years old.[33]

The washing of feet is still kept in many churches.[34] In Mexico and other sections of South America the Last Supper is often re-enacted in church, with the priest presiding and twelve men or boys, dressed as Apostles, speaking the dialogue as recorded in the Gospels. In Malta, a "Last Supper Table" is richly laden by the faithful with food that is later distributed to the poor.

RECONCILIATION OF PENITENTS · An ancient rite of Maundy Thursday now totally extinct was the solemn reconciliation of public penitents. As on Ash Wednesday, they again approached the church dressed in sackcloth, barefoot, unshaven, weak, and feeble from their forty days' fast and penance. The bishop led them into the house of God, where he absolved them from their sins and crimes after the Gospel of the Mass of Reconciliation.

With his blessing they joyfully hurried home after the Mass to bathe, shave, and cut their hair in preparation for Easter, and to resume their normal dress and routine of daily life, which had been so harshly interrupted during the time of their public penance.[35]

ROYAL HOURS · The Greek Church celebrates a night vigil from Holy Thursday to Good Friday, in which the texts of the Passion, collected from the Bible and arranged in twelve chapters (called the "Twelve Gospels") are sung or read, with prayers, prostrations, and hymns after every chapter. In the cathedral of Constantinople, the East Roman emperors used to attend this service; hence it was called the "Royal Hours." [36] Its original name is *Pannuchida* (All-Night Service). In Russia people would carry home the candles that they had used in this vigil, and with them they would light the lamps that burned day and night before the family *ikons* (holy pictures). The Ukrainians celebrate the "Royal Hours" on Good Friday morning.[37]

FOLKLORE · Many popular customs and traditions are connected with Maundy Thursday. There is, above all, the universal children's legend that the bells "fly to Rome" after the Gloria of the Mass. In Germany and central Europe the little ones are told that the church bells make a pilgrimage to the tomb of the Apostles, or that they visit the pope, to be blessed by him, then sleep on the roof of St. Peter's until the Easter Vigil.[38] In France the story is that the bells fly to Rome to fetch the Easter eggs that they will drop on their return into every house where the children are good and well behaved.

In some Latin countries sugared almonds are eaten by everybody on Maundy Thursday. From this custom it bears the name "Almond Day" in the Azores. In central Europe the name "Green Thursday" inspired a tradition of eating green things. The main meal starts with a soup of green herbs, followed by a bowl of spinach with boiled or fried eggs, and meat with dishes of various green salads.[39]

Following the ecclesiastical custom, the bells on farm buildings are silent in Germany and Austria, and dinner calls are made with wooden clappers. In rural sections of Austria boys with clappers go through the villages and towns, announcing the hours, because the church clock is stopped. These youngsters (*Ratschenbuben*) sing a different stanza each hour, in which they commemorate the events of Christ's Passion.[40]

GOOD FRIDAY

From the earliest centuries, Good Friday was universally celebrated in the Church as a day of sadness, mourning, fasting, and prayer. The Apostolic Constitutions (fourth century) called it a "day of mourning, not a day of festive joy." Saint Ambrosius (397), Archbishop of Milan, mentioned Good Friday as a "day of bitterness on which we fast." [41]

NAMES · The liturgical title in the Western Church is "Friday of the Preparation" (*Feria sexta in Parasceve*). At the time of Christ, the Jews used the Greek word *Paraskeue* (getting ready) for Friday, meaning the day of preparation for the Sabbath. This word is now used both in the Oriental and Occidental Churches. Popular names are "Holy Friday" among the Latin nations, "Great Friday" among the Slavic peoples (*petok veliki*) and Hungarians (*nagypéntek*), "Friday of Mourning" in German (*Karfreitag*), "Long Friday" in Norway (*Langfredag*), and "Good Friday" in English and Dutch.

The early Church, following apostolic tradition, employed the hallowed term "Pasch" (from Hebrew *pesach,* passover) both to

Good Friday and Easter Sunday. Thus Good Friday is called the "Pasch of Crucifixion" (*pascha staurosimon*), Easter the "Pasch of Resurrection" (*pascha anastasimon*), and the Eastern Church has kept these names up to our day.[42]

SERVICE OF READING AND PRAYER · The first part of the Good Friday service is the only example of an ancient Roman *Synaxis* (prayer meeting without Mass) that has survived to the present. It consists of a silent prostration before the altar, followed by lessons (readings from the Bible), chanting of the Passion of Saint John, prayers, and the solemn Collects for all classes of men and for the needs of the Church, the celebrant starting every invocation with the words *"Oremus, dilectissimi nobis"* (Let us pray, dearest brethren).

ADORATION OF THE CROSS · After the *Synaxis* one of the most moving ceremonies of the year takes place, the Adoration of the Cross. (The word adoration in this instance is a translation of the Greek *proskunesis,* which meant a tribute of the highest honor, performed by a prostration to the ground.) In medieval England and Germany the ceremony was called "creeping to the Cross" (*zum Kreuz kriechen*).

The celebrating priest unveils the crucifix in three stages, singing "Behold the wood of the Cross, on which hung the Salvation of the world"; to which the choir and people, kneeling and reverently bowing, answer "Come, let us adore!" Then the crucifix is placed on a pillow in front of the altar. The priest and his assistants approach it, genuflecting three times, and devoutly kiss the feet of the image. The rest of the clergy and the lay people follow, performing the same humble act of veneration. Meanwhile, the choir sings the ancient *Improperia* (complaints) of Christ:

> *My people, what have I done to thee?*
> *Or in what have I grieved thee? Answer me!*
>
> *I brought thee out of the land of Egypt:*
> *And thou hast prepared a cross for thy Saviour.*
>
> *For thy sake I scourged Egypt and its first-born:*
> *And thou didst scourge me and deliver me to death.*

In answer the choir sings the invocation called *Trisagion* (thrice holy) in Latin and Greek:

> *O holy God,*
> *O strong, holy One,*
> *O holy, immortal One, have mercy on us.*

The Adoration of the Cross was adopted by the Roman **Church** from Jerusalem, where the true Cross of Christ was thus venerated every year on Good Friday as early as the fourth century. Aetheria, after her pilgrimage to the Holy Land about A.D. 395, left in her diary the first description of this ceremony. It is of special interest that, according to her report, not only the Cross, but also the title board bearing the inscription (John 19, 19-22) was presented to the pilgrims. They were allowed to kiss, but not to touch, the sacred objects.[43] When the Mohammedans conquered Jerusalem under Sultan Saladin, in 1187, they took the relics away, and no trace of them was ever found. Fortunately, a piece of the true Cross was brought to Rome in the fourth century, and from it many churches in all countries have received small particles as relics.[44]

COMMUNION SERVICE · After the solemn veneration of the cross, the Blessed Sacrament is carried in procession from the repository shrine (where it was placed the day before) to the main altar. Then the Communion service is celebrated. It is a solemn rite presenting some ceremonies of the Mass, but not the Divine Sacrifice itself. On the day on which Christ offered Himself on the Cross for the redemption of the world, the Church reverently abstains from performing the same sacrifice, in its unbloody repetition, which otherwise is offered every day according to His command (1 Corinthians 11, 23-26). The faithful are encouraged to receive Holy Communion at this service.[45]

After the solemn ceremonies of Good Friday, the altar is stripped again, the tabernacle is left open, no lights burn in the sanctuary. Only the crucifix, now unveiled, takes the place of honor in front of the empty tabernacle. The faithful, however, practice various additional devotions on Good Friday. In all countries such devotional exercises are now held with traditional piety.

HOLY SEPULCHER · The most ancient and impressive of these extraliturgical rites is the shrine of the Holy Sepulcher, a custom that derived from the practice of the early Church in Jerusalem, where the faithful kept a devout prayer vigil at the tomb of the Lord from the evening of Good Friday until the start of the Easter services.[46] Unfortunately, this practice was not incorporated in the Roman liturgy. It would give a liturgical inspiration and significance to the evening of Good Friday and to Holy Saturday, which now are utterly aliturgical.

This tradition of a vigil at the Holy Sepulcher was brought from Jerusalem to Europe and spread in the form of a semi-liturgical practice through many countries.[47] In past centuries it was a universal tradition in England and France. The rite was performed with liturgical texts and ceremonies. In some countries a crucifix or the Blessed Sacrament (or both together) were borne in solemn procession to a shrine called the Sepulcher. There the priest deposited them in a sort of tabernacle shaped like a tomb chamber. The faithful visited the shrine all through Good Friday and Holy Saturday.[48]

Today, the custom of the Holy Sepulcher is still observed in central and eastern Europe and in the Latin countries. After the liturgical service, the priests carry the Blessed Sacrament in splendid procession to the side altar. The monstrance in which the Sacrament is borne is covered with a transparent veil of white lace to symbolize the burial shroud of Christ. A representation of the Lord's tomb, showing an image of the Saviour resting in death, awaits the procession. This shrine is decorated with many candles, palms, flowers, and lights. There the Blessed Sacrament is exposed on a throne for the veneration of the faithful. All through Good Friday and Holy Saturday, people come in great numbers, kneel in devout prayer before the Eucharistic Lord, actually a spiritual "wake" of devotion and adoration. In Austria it is a traditional custom for soldiers of the army, in parade uniform, with steel helmets and fixed bayonets, to man a guard of honor at the shrine, and thus atone for the irreverent guard of Roman soldiers at the tomb of Christ.[49]

In Spanish-speaking countries of Europe and South America the *monumento* is taken down on Good Friday and in its place a representation of Calvary is erected, with life-size figures of

Christ on the Cross, the Blessed Mother, Saint John, and Mary Magdalen. After the service, the priest mounts a ladder to detach the body of Christ from the Cross. He takes it down and places it in the shrine of the Sepulcher. There the faithful visit and pray all through the evening and on Holy Saturday. It is customary to recite thirty-three Credos in honor of the years of our Lord's life.

In the Byzantine Church, on the afternoon of Good Friday, the elders of the parish carry a cloth containing a picture of our Lord's body resting in death. Followed by the priest, they walk in procession to the shrine of the Sepulcher, where the cloth is placed on a table to be venerated by the people. The entire ceremony and the shrine are called *Platsenitsia* (winding sheet) by the Ukrainians and other Slavs of the Oriental Church.

In Russia a silver coffin bearing a cross was placed in the center of the church and surrounded with lights and flowers. One after another the faithful, creeping on their knees, approached to kiss the cross and to venerate the image of Christ's body painted on the "winding sheet."

ORIGIN OF THE FORTY HOURS' DEVOTION · Usually the origin of the Forty Hours' Devotion is ascribed to the city of Milan, where, in 1527, in a time of war and calamities, the faithful were invited to visit the exposed Blessed Sacrament four times a year and to pray to the Eucharistic Lord, imploring His mercy and help. The dates for this devotion, which was called "Forty Hours' Prayer," were Easter, Pentecost, Feast of the Assumption, and Christmas.[50]

It is interesting to note that the church where this devotion was to be held bore the name Church of the Holy Sepulcher. The duration, forty hours, points far back into the earliest centuries of Christianity, when the faithful honored our Lord's rest in the tomb by a fast and prayer of forty hours. "From the moment of Christ's death to the morning of His resurrection it is forty hours," said Saint Augustine (430).[51] By the second century it was a widespread custom for people to fast day and night for forty hours, from Good Friday afternoon until Easter Sunday morning, according to the word of Saint Irenaeus (202) recorded in the history of Eusebius.[52]

To the fast of forty hours there was added a forty hours' prayer at the Holy Sepulcher, as Aetheria reported in her diary.[53] Fasting and prayer at the shrine of the Sepulcher remained through all the centuries of the Middle Ages, and in some countries even the latter is still kept. Liturgically speaking, however, only the fasting is provided in the Roman Rite, while the Eastern Rites have a "burial" service and a symbolic shrine of the Sepulcher in their Good Friday ritual.[54] The practice of prayerful watch at the tomb of Christ, which would admirably fit the liturgical meaning of Holy Saturday, has never been officially introduced in the Latin Church. Instead, the Forty Hours' Devotion, which grew out of the ancient forty hours' "wake," was separated from its original place and officially established as a liturgical devotion at various other times of the year. This lack of a liturgical ritual for Holy Saturday has become more apparent since the renewal of the Holy Week order (1955).[55]

THREE HOURS' DEVOTION · A very well-known Good Friday service is the Devotion of the Three Hours (*Tre Ore*). It was first performed in Lima, Peru, by Father Alphonso Messia, S.J. (1732), and quickly spread to all the Latin-speaking countries.[56] In Italy it was introduced with special enthusiasm, and from there went to England and America, where in recent years it has grown in popularity also in many Protestant churches. It consists of sermons on the seven last words of Christ, alternating with hymns and prayers. In most countries of Europe the Three Hours' Devotion is hardly known. Instead, oratorios on the seven words are often presented by church choirs in a musical service on Good Friday night. Such musical programs are also observed in many Protestant churches, both in Europe and America.

PROCESSIONS · A famous feature of Good Friday is the popular procession in the Latin countries. Such public processions were also held in most countries of central and western Europe up to the nineteenth century.[57] In many regions, especially in Spain, the confraternities (*confradias*) of lay people, wearing hoods and carrying lighted candles, walk through the streets in religious parades. Images of the suffering Christ and the Blessed Virgin are conveyed in a pageant of magnificent splendor. The statues,

borne on huge platforms, are beautifully decorated and surrounded by a multitude of burning tapers. In Malta the bearers
wear Oriental robes, and many go barefoot in observance of vows.

This Spanish custom of the *confradia* processions, especially
the famous tradition of the city of Seville, has also found its way
into the Spanish-speaking countries of the New World. Among
the most impressive celebrations of this kind is the annual *Semana
Santa* (Holy Week) observance in Mexico City. There a funeral
procession (*el santo entierro*) is held with a touching scene in
which the Mother of the Lord meets the lifeless body of her Son
(*el pésame*). The Stations of the Cross are often dramatically
represented in a passion play outside the church, followed by
sermon and prayer. In parts of South America a procession, carrying the empty cross and many statues, moves slowly through
the crowded church while the people pray and sing. In Caracas,
Venezuela, this service is supposed to last four to five hours; and
in order to fill the time, the procession not only moves very slowly
but proceeds in a quaint manner, walking three steps forward
and two steps backward.

In India the native Christians accompany the "funeral" of
Christ, which is met outside the church by a statue of the sorrowful Virgin. A sermon is preached, and both statues together
are taken into the church. There the people perform the purana,
a service of wailing, at which they sing hymns to their ancient,
plaintive tunes. The early missionaries to India were Portuguese,
and they took these customs with them.

MUSIC · Following the Reformation, the practice grew in Germany of presenting, on Good Friday afternoon, in place of the
ancient liturgical service, musical settings of the parts of the
Gospel narrating the Passion and death of Christ. One of the
earliest works of this kind is the composition of Antonio Scandello
(1580), choir director of the court chapel at Dresden. He wrote
a *St. John's Passion* that follows the traditional recitative of the
liturgical chant in the solo part (evangelist). He was the first
composer to set the story of the Passion to music in oratorio form,
and it became the model for most of his successors for hundreds
of years.

Heinrich Schuetz (1672) set to dramatic music all four Gospel narrations of the Passion. They all close with a devotional chorus in motet style based on some familiar church hymn.

The best known and perhaps the greatest of all are the two immortal compositions of Johann Sebastian Bach, *Saint John Passion* and *Saint Matthew Passion.* The *Saint John Passion* was first performed on Good Friday, 1723, at Leipzig. Its first complete American performance was given by the Bach Choir of Bethlehem, Pennsylvania, in 1888. The *Saint Matthew Passion,* somewhat longer, was also produced for the first time in Leipzig, in 1729. During Passiontide throughout the world many performances of both these famous compositions are heard by thousands, especially since the advent of radio and television.

While Handel, in 1704, at the age of nineteen, wrote a Passion, far better known is his inspired *Messiah.* The latter half of this gigantic oratorio deals with the Crucifixion and Resurrection.

A composition called the *Seven Last Words* for solo, chorus, and orchestra was written by Franz Josef Haydn (1809) at the request of the cathedral chapter of Cadiz, Spain, to be performed at the Three Hours' Devotion, and is being heard rather frequently in recent years.

The *Christus am Oelberg* (Christ on the Mount of Olives) by Beethoven, Charles Gounod's *Seven Last Words,* César Franck's *Redemption,* with a text by Eduard Blau, are some of the many works of music for Passiontide. Gounod's *Seven Last Words* is often performed in both Catholic and Protestant churches on Good Friday.

A composition that in recent years has become a favorite with church choirs is the dramatic setting of the Seven Last Words, with a Latin text, by the French organist and composer Theodore Dubois (1924). It was first performed in Paris in 1869, and is now often given as a sacred concert on Palm Sunday evening or at some other time during Holy Week.

Some of the best-known works of English composers often heard in Protestant churches during Holy Week include: Maunder's *Olivet to Calvary,* Gaul's *Holy City,* and Stainer's *Crucifixion.*

Parsifal, by Richard Wagner (1883), based on a folklore interpretation of the search for the Holy Grail, is an opera frequently heard in Holy Week, and the music for the "Good Friday

Spell" from it is usually played by symphony orchestras here and in Europe during that period.

POPULAR OBSERVANCE · Following the spirit of the liturgy, the faithful everywhere keep Good Friday as a day of strictest fast, often far beyond the obligation of the law. Many people take nothing but a little bread and water all day. In some counties of England plain rice cooked in milk is the traditional Good Friday meal. The Irish people hold a "black fast," which usually means that they take only water or tea on that day. In central Europe it is the custom to eat just vegetable soup and bread at noon, and some cheese with bread in the evening. Both meals are taken standing and in silence. No noisy tasks are performed, people refrain from joking and laughing, and children abstain from their usual games.[58]

In many countries, pious legends have inspired popular practices that are widely observed, mostly in a spirit of true reverence, some of which, however, have given rise to superstitions. Among farmers, Good Friday is considered a lucky day for sowing, since Christ blessed and sanctified the soil by His burial. On the other hand, craftsmen must be careful not to swing a hammer or drive a nail on the day on which Christ was nailed to the Cross; carpenters, plumbers, blacksmiths rest from their usual work. No washing is done by women, since the Lord's blood stained the linen and clothes on Good Friday. A familiar superstition is that if a woman washes on Good Friday, she will find the laundry spotted with blood, and ill luck will befall her all through the year.[59]

A deeply impressive practice among the Christian Syrians and Chaldeans is the fact that they do not use their customary greeting, *Shlama* ("Peace be with you") on Good Friday and Holy Saturday, because Judas Iscariot saluted Christ with these very words when he betrayed Him. Instead, they substitute on these two days, as mutual greeting, the phrase "the Light of God be with your departed ones."

In many parts of Europe people who die on Good Friday are considered highly fortunate, since they are believed to share in the privilege of the Good Thief, and to be given the grace of salvation and a speedy entry into Heaven.

It was a universal custom (and still is in Catholic countries) to mark a new loaf of bread with the sign of the cross before cutting it, in order to bless it and thank God for it. On special occasions the cross was imprinted on the loaf before baking, as on the Christmas loaves in southern France and in Greece, the *Kreuzstollen* (cross loaf) in Germany, the cross bread of Mid-Lent among the Slavs. On Good Friday, loaves bearing an imprinted cross (*Karfreitaglaib*) are eaten in Austria. In England, from the end of the fourteenth century, buns were baked with a cross marked on them. They are said to have originated at Saint Alban's Abbey in 1361, where the monks distributed them to the poor. Whatever their origin, these "hot cross buns" became a famous Good Friday feature in England and Ireland, and later in this country. They were made of spiced dough, round in shape, with a cross made of icing on the top. In recent times these cross buns are sold not only on Good Friday but all through Lent.

The hot cross buns were considered blessed and powerful against all kinds of sickness and dangers. Eating them on Good Friday was said to protect your home from fire. People would keep them through the year, eating them as medicine or wearing them as charms against disease, lightning, and shipwreck.[60]

HOLY SATURDAY

NAMES · The English title for the day before Easter, Holy Saturday, is a translation of its official name in the Western Church—*Sabbatum Sanctum*. In the Oriental Church it is called the "Sacred and Great Saturday." Most European nations use the term "holy," except in parts of eastern Europe, where the term "the Great Saturday" is in vogue. The German people say "Saturday of mourning" (*Karsamstag*). On the Island of Malta, where Arabic is spoken, Holy Saturday bears the name *Sibt il Glorja* (Saturday of Glory). The Christians in Iraq and Iran employ the popular term *Sabt al-Noor* (Saturday of Light).

OBSERVANCE · Holy Saturday commemorates Christ's rest in the tomb. There is no service at all during the daylight hours, since the body of the Lord enclosed in the Sepulcher shared the fate and humiliation of human burial. As Christ rested in the grave the whole Sabbath day, so the faithful waited in prayer and fasting until the evening star announced the beginning of the Easter Vigil.

In ancient days a strict fast called the "Passion fast" was kept until the morning of Easter Sunday; not even children were dispensed from observing it.[61] Both the Eastern and Western Churches called Holy Saturday the "Day of Rest of the Lord's Body in the Tomb." In the fourteenth century the original night service of the Easter Vigil was transferred to the morning of Holy Saturday, but in 1955 Pope Pius XII restored the ancient custom, and it is once more held as a Holy Saturday night service, leading directly into Easter Sunday.[62]

In the early centuries the catechumens would assemble in the church during the afternoon, the men on one side, the women on the other. After an instruction by the bishop, the priests performed on them those rites which are still practiced in the baptism of infants and adults: the exorcism of the powers of evil, the touching of ears and nostrils as a symbol of opening their minds to the word and grace of God, and the solemn pledge of conversion. This pledge was accompanied by a dramatic gesture. Turning toward the west and pointing with the forefinger in the direction of sunset, each catechumen uttered these words, "I renounce thee, Satan, with all thy pomps and all thy works," then turning to the east and pointing likewise, they would say, "To Thee I dedicate myself, Jesus Christ, eternal and uncreated Light." After this, each one recited the Creed publicly before the whole congregation; then they were dismissed to spend the last few hours before their baptism in quiet recollection and prayer.[63]

FOLKLORE · On Holy Saturday there is great activity around the house in central Europe. Easter ham and other foods for the feast are cooked, Easter bread and pastry are baked. Many eggs are boiled and painted. The whole house is decked with flowers and finery in preparation for the great feast. In the Slavic countries, baskets of food, especially eggs, are brought to the church to be blessed by the priest on Holy Saturday afternoon. They are then taken home and eaten for breakfast on Easter Sunday,

Monday, and Tuesday. In many regions the priests go from house to house on Holy Saturday to bless the Easter fare, which is neatly arranged on large tables and decorated with flowers.

An amusing custom is practiced in Poland on Holy Saturday. The boys of the villages "bury" the Lenten fare, herring and *zur*, in a mock funeral. The herring (a real one or a wooden image) is first executed by hanging, then a pot of *zur* is shattered against a rock or tree; finally the fish and the pieces of the pot are interred with glee. No longer will these tiresome dishes be eaten, at least not until next Lent.

In the Alpine provinces of Austria, Easter fires burn on mountain peaks after sunset on Holy Saturday, and bands of musicians go through the towns, playing sacred hymns.

[1] Nilles, II, 209, 211 ff.   [2] H. Leclercq, *Semaine Sainte*, DACL, 15.1 (1950), 1151 ff.   [3] SRC, *A General Decree by Which the Liturgical Order of Holy Week Is Renewed* (November 16, 1955), trans., NCWC, Washington, 1956.   [4] Trapp, 120.   [5] Benet, 49.   [6] J. Jahn, *Biblische Archäologie*, Wien, 1805, III, 308.   [7] SSP, 83 ff.   [8] A. De Santi, *La Domenica delle Palme nella Storia liturgica*, in *La Civiltà cattolica*, 2 (1906), 3 ff., 159 ff.   [9] E. Wiegen, *Palmprozession und Palmesel*, Bonn, 1903; OiT, 155 ff.; Gugitz, I, 151 ff. (*Der Palmesel*). [10] DACL, 6.2 (1925), 2911.   [11] *La Dimanche des Rameaux*, DACL, 15.1 (1950), 1154 ff.   [12] J. A. Jungmann, *Die Reform der Karwochen- und Osterliturgie*, LJ, 5 (1955), 211 ff.   [13] Since the liturgical reform (1955), the prayer of blessing mentions not only branches of palms and olives but also "of other trees."   [14] Nilles, II, 202 ff.   [15] TE, I, 617. [16] OiT, 32 ff. (*Palmbesen*); see pictures in Koren (*Bildanhang*). [17] *Cerem. Episc.*, II, 21, 2.   [18] Geramb, 59 ff.   [19] Benet, 49.   [20] Koren, 108 f.   [21] LE, 150.   [22] From *"greinen"*: LE, 148; from *"carena"*: OiT, 318, note.   [23] *Epist.* 54, VII, 10 (ed. Maur.).   [24] Thurston, 80 ff. [25] Nilles, II, 215.   [26] Nilles, II, 220.   [27] TE, I, 623.   [28] F. Cabrol, *La consécration des huiles au jeudi saint*, DACL, 6.2 (1925), 2787 ff. [29] TE, 624.   [30] OiT, 64; TE, 625.   [31] *Cap.* 3; Mansi, 12, 97.   [32] H. Leclercq, *Mandatum*, DACL, 10.1 (1931), 101 f.   [33] Enc. Brit., 15 (1949), 101 f.   [34] OiT, 53 ff.   [35] Thurston, 84 ff.   [36] Nilles, II, 241. [37] P. Vostochny, "Great Lent in the Greek Rite," OF, 13 (1939), 165 ff. [38] Gugitz, I, 158 ff. (*Der Gründonnerstag*).   [39] Koren, 119; OiT, 61; E. and A. Hynes, "Observing Holy Thursday in the Home," WOR, 31

(1957), 247 ff. [40] OiT, 49 f.; Gugitz, I, 168. [41] Epist. 23, 12; PL, 16, 1073. See G. Römer, *Die Liturgie des Karfreitags*, ZKTh, 77 (1955), 39 ff. [42] Nilles, II, 253 ff. [43] SSP, 88 ff. [44] J. Sauer, *Kreuzpartikeln*, LThK, 6 (1934), 254. [45] J. A. Jungmann, *Die Kommunion am Karfreitag*, ZKTh, 75 (1953), 465 ff. [46] SSP, 90. [47] N. C. Brooks, *The Sepulchre of Christ in Art and Liturgy*, in *University of Illinois Studies in Language and Literature*, VII (1921), 2 ff.; H. P. Feasy, "The Easter Sepulchre," AER, 32 (1905), 337 ff., 468 ff.; Gugitz, I, 174 ff. (*Das Hl. Grab und seine Verehrung*). [48] Young, I, 112 ff. [49] Trapp, 126 f.; A. Dörrer, *Heiliggräber*, OiT, 181 ff.; VL, 80 f. [50] J. A. Jungmann, *Die Andacht der vierzig Stunden und das heilige Grab*, LJ, 2 (1952), 184 ff. [51] De Trinit., IV, 6; PL, 42, 894 f. [52] Hist. Eccl., V, 24, 12; PG, 20, 502 f. [53] See note 46. [54] Nilles, II, 255, 270; P. F. Sfeir, "Good Friday and Easter in the Syrian Church," OF, 7 (1933), 266 ff. [55] T. J. Carroll, "The Lost Day of Holy Week," WOR, 31 (1957), 265 ff.; J. A. Jungmann, *Brauch und Liturgie in der Heiligen Woche*, OiT, 315 ff.; G. Bainbridge, *An Analysis of the Restored Holy Week Ritual for Pastoral Use*, Notre Dame, 1956, 40. [56] *The Devotion of the Three Hours of Holy Week* (anon.), London, 1806. [57] VL, 83 ff.; OiT, 68 ff. [58] Trapp, 127; OiT, 62 ff. [59] ES, 134 f.; OiT, 71 ff. [60] ES, 134. [61] DACL, 7.2 (1927), 2498 ff. [62] See note 3. [63] Thurston, 105 ff.

CHAPTER

16   *Easter*

FEAST OF THE RESURRECTION

The joy and exultation over this greatest of all Christian feasts is evident in the writings of the saints and Fathers from earliest times. Easter is referred to as the "peak (*akropolis*) of all feasts" and the "Queen of all solemnities." Saint Gregory of Nazianz (390) wrote, "This highest Feast and greatest celebration so much surpasses not only civic holidays but also the other feast days of the Lord, that it is like the sun among stars." [1]

THE CHRISTIAN PASCH · The feast is called "Pasch" by most nations: Greeks and Romanians (*Pascha*), Italians (*Pasqua*), Spaniards and Portuguese (*Pascua*), French (*Pâque*), Norwegians (*Paskir*), Danes (*Paaske*), Gaels (*casc*). As stated before, this word is taken from the Greek (and Latin) *pascha*, which comes from the Hebrew word *pesach* (passover). The Passover was celebrated by the Jews on the fourteenth day of the month Nisan, which began about a week before the full moon of spring. It was instituted to commemorate the deliverance of the people of Israel the night before their departure from Egypt. The angel of God destroyed the first-born of Egypt but passed over the houses of the Israelites. It was the command of God, announced by Moses, that each Hebrew family should slay a young lamb without blemish, and sprinkle its blood on the frame of the door. In the evening the lamb was to be roasted, no bones were to be broken, and it was to be eaten with unleavened bread and bitter herbs by all members of the family. According to divine ordination, this rite was to be repeated every year in a solemn ceremony on the eve of the feast, and is still celebrated by Jewish people everywhere today.[2] Jesus observed it for the last time on the night before He died.

There is a significant link between the Jewish Passover and the Christian Easter, because Christ died on Passover Day. It is also symbolic because the lamb that had to be sacrificed for the deliverance of Israel is considered by the Church as prophetic of Him Who is the "Lamb of God, who takes away the sins of the world" (John 1, 29). Thus the name and meaning of the Hebrew Pasch was devoutly accepted into the Christian liturgy. Although the death and Resurrection of the Redeemer would have been commemorated by Christians at whatever time they might have occurred, it is of special significance that the Lord actually did die and rise during the days of the Passover celebration.

From the very first, the Resurrection of Christ was celebrated as the greatest and most important festive day of the whole year. In fact, every Sunday is a "little Easter" consecrated to the memory of the Risen Christ. In the Eastern Churches, Sunday bears the name "Resurrection" even today.[3] The Council of Nicaea (325) prescribed that on Sundays and during Easter time all Christians should pray standing, never bend their knees, to indicate "that we are risen with Christ."[4] A relic of this custom is the practice of saying the Angelus (daily prayer commemorating the Incarnation) standing, instead of kneeling, on Sundays. At Easter time the antiphon of the Blessed Virgin, *Regina caeli, laetare* (Queen of Heaven, rejoice) is said standing.

In addition to this weekly celebration of Christ's resurrection, the Church has observed each year from the earliest centuries a special feast at the time of the Jewish Pasch to commemorate the anniversary of the greatest events in the Christian world. Since there is an intimate bond between the Resurrection of Christ and the sacrament of baptism, the Church united these two "resurrections" in a common ritual. It celebrates the "new life" not only of Christ as the Head, but also of His Mystical Body, His faithful followers. This is why the prayers of the liturgy in paschal week constantly reflect those two thoughts: the Resurrection of our Lord and the baptism of the faithful.[5]

OTHER NAMES · The English word Easter and the German *Ostern* come from a common origin (*Eostur, Eastur, Ostara, Ostar*), which to the Norsemen meant the season of the rising (growing) sun, the season of new birth. The word was used by our ancestors to designate the Feast of New Life in the spring. The same root is found in the name for the place where the sun rises (East, *Ost*). The word Easter, then, originally meant the celebration of the spring sun, which had its birth in the East and brought new life upon earth. This symbolism was transferred to the supernatural meaning of our Easter, to the new life of the Risen Christ, the eternal and uncreated Light.

Based on a passage in the writings of Saint Bede the Venerable (735), the term Easter has often been explained as the name of an Anglo-Saxon goddess (*Eostre*),[6] though no such goddess is known in the mythologies of any Germanic tribe. Modern research has made it quite clear that Saint Bede erroneously interpreted the name of the season as that of a goddess.[7]

Some Slavic nations, such as Poland, call Easter the "Great

Night" (*Wielkanoc*); the Ukrainians, Russians, and Serbs say the "Great Day" (*Velik Den*). In Hungary it is referred to as "Feast of Meat" (*Husvet*), because the eating of meat is resumed again after the long fast.[8]

CIVIC OBSERVANCE · In medieval documents Easter is often recorded as the beginning of a new year, especially in France, where this custom prevailed until 1563. At Easter time the Roman emperors, starting with Valentinian in 367, released from prison persons who were not dangerous criminals; this practice was followed by emperors, kings, and popes all through medieval times and up to the present century.

Leading citizens in the Roman Empire imitated the clemency of the emperors at Easter time, granting freedom to slaves, forgiving enemies by ending feuds and quarrels, and discontinuing prosecutions in the courts. These customs, too, prevailed all through medieval times in the Christian countries of Europe.[9]

EASTER GREETING · In the early centuries, the faithful embraced each other with the words "*Surrexit Dominus vere*" (Christ is truly risen), to which the answer was "*Deo gratias*" (Thanks be to God). In the Greek Church the greeting is "*Christos aneste*" (Christ is risen), the answer, "*Alethos aneste*" (He is truly risen). This greeting is still generally used by Russians and Ukrainians (*Christos voskres. Vo istinu voskres*).[10]

In Russia the Easter kiss was bestowed during Matins before the night Mass; people would embrace each other in the church. All through Easter week the mutual kiss and embrace were repeated not only in the homes but also on the streets, even with strangers. The Poles and western Slavs greet each other with the wish "A joyful alleluia to you!" (*Wesolego Alleluja*).

In medieval times, when the bishop celebrated Easter Mass in his cathedral and the clergy received Communion from his hand, the priests and ministers would kiss him on the cheek after Communion, according to the regulations.[11]

EASTER COMMUNION · Another ancient rite of Easter is the solemn Easter Communion. Church law requires the reception of the Holy Eucharist at least once a year, during Easter time.

This edict dates from the fourth Council of the Lateran (1215).[12] The law was not made to inaugurate a new practice but to safeguard the minimum demands of an old tradition. In the early centuries a great deal more was expected from the faithful than Communion only once a year. The Council of Agde (506), for instance, had urged all Christians to receive at least three times a year.[13]

In the beginning, the obligation of Easter Communion had to be fulfilled on the feast day itself. However, the Church gradually extended the time of this obligation, which now officially begins on Palm Sunday and ends on Low Sunday. By provision of canon law, however, and by special indults, this period has been prolonged in most countries (usually from the first Sunday in Lent to Trinity Sunday).[14]

THE EASTER VIGIL

HISTORY · Among early Christians, from the fourth century on, in all cities and towns the mood of quiet, somber expectancy suddenly turned into radiant exultation and joy at the sight of the first stars in the evening of Holy Saturday. Thousands of lights began to illuminate the growing darkness. The churches seemed to burst with the blaze of lamps and candles, the homes of the people shone with light, and even the streets were bright with the glow of a thousand tapers. At a time when electric lights were unknown, this tremendous annual illumination was overwhelming.[15] The deep impressions it created are still reflected in the writings of the Fathers and in the text of our liturgical service. The night was called the "Mother of All Holy Vigils," [16] the "Great Service of Light" (*sacrum lucernarium*), the "Night of Radiant Splendor" (*irradiata fulgoribus*), the "Night of Illumination" (*luminosa haec nox*).[17] We are told that Emperor Constantine (331) "transformed the night of the sacred vigil into the brilliance of day, by lighting throughout the whole city [of Milan] pillars of wax, while burning lamps illuminated every house, so that this nocturnal celebration was rendered brighter than the brightest day." [18] Saint Gregory of Nyssa (394), in one of his Easter sermons, mentioned "this glowing night which links the splendor of burning lamps to the morning rays of the sun, thus producing continuous daylight without any darkness." [19]

Many hymns have been written in praise of this illumination on the vigil of Easter, the best known being the poem *Inventor rutilis* written by Prudentius (405), a layman and government official of the Roman Empire, and a great Christian poet.

> *Eternal God, O Lord of Light,*
> *Who hast created day and night:*
> *The sun has set, and shadows deep*
> *Now over land and waters creep;*
> *But darkness must not reign today:*
> *Grant us the light of Christ, we pray.*[20]

It is difficult to picture today the solemn joy and excitement that filled the hearts of Christians in the early centuries on that night. For them the Easter Vigil was the glorious annual triumph which they celebrated together with Christ over sin, death, and the powers of evil. Their excitement was increased beyond modern comprehension by the universal belief in those days that Christ would return for the Last Judgment during one of these Easter Vigils. Nobody stayed at home, not even the little children. The multitudes crowded into the churches, and thousands thronged around the house of God, joining in prayer with those who had been fortunate enough to find places inside. Gold and silver candelabra shed their cheerful light through the open doors and windows; hundreds of lamps suspended from the ceiling illumined the church with a new splendor.[21]

The custom of spending the Easter Vigil in prayer seems to date from the time of the Apostles. Tertullian (third century) mentions this prayer *per noctem* (through the night), and even earlier writings indicate the practice among the early Christians of spending the night before Easter Sunday in common prayer.[22]

In later centuries the vigil service began with the lighting of the paschal candle, which from the earliest period was considered a sacred symbol of Christ's Person. The *praeconia paschalia* (jubilant Easter songs) which accompanied the lighting of the candle were already performed in the Roman Empire at the end of the fourth century. The earliest manuscript containing the present text of the song (*Exultet*) dates from the seventh or eighth century.[23] After the blessing of the candle, a prayer service was held; passages of the Bible were read (the "prophecies"), then the priests and people recited psalms, antiphons, and orations. This service lasted much longer than today, but the faithful did not mind, since they spent the whole night in church anyway.

Toward midnight the bishop and clergy went in procession to the baptismal font, a large basin built in a structure outside the church. There the baptismal water was consecrated with the prayers and ceremonies still in use today. Once more the catechumens were addressed by their spiritual shepherd. Then, divested of any ornaments or jewelry, they stepped into the "life-giving waters." The bishop, also standing in the water, baptized them one by one, first the men, then the women and children. After baptism they were anointed. Finally they put on sandals and flowing white garments of pure linen. In this attire they appeared at all services until the end of Easter week.

Long after midnight, probably at the first dawn of Easter Sunday, the vigil was concluded with the customary prayers of the litanies and celebration of the Holy Sacrifice.[24]

This basic structure of the ancient Easter Vigil had been altered somewhat and reduced in significance through the practice of anticipating the vigil service on Holy Saturday morning in past centuries.[25] It was restored, however, by Pope Pius XII to its original place and character, so that once more the impressive light symbolism attains its full effect during the darkness of the night, and the faithful may take their active part in it as of old. The solemn baptism of adults is to be administered, if possible, and the Eucharistic service has again become a celebration of the very time and event of Christ's resurrection.[26]

Our restored vigil celebration has retained some rites that were added in the course of later centuries. The most notable of them is the blessing of the Easter fire.

EASTER FIRE · The Germanic nations had a popular tradition of setting big bonfires at the beginning of spring. This custom was frowned upon by the Church because it served a pagan symbolism, and consequently was suppressed when those nations became Christian. As late as 742, the prohibition of such fires was firmly upheld.[27] However, Irish bishops and monks who came to the European continent in the sixth and seventh centuries brought with them an ancient rite of their own: the setting and blessing of big bonfires outside the church on Holy Saturday night. Saint Patrick himself, the Father and Founder of the Church in Ireland, had started this tradition, to supplant the Druidic pagan spring fires with a Christian and religious fire symbol of Christ, the Light of the World.[28]

This Christian usage of an Easter bonfire naturally appealed to the population of the West Frankish kingdom (France), where the Irish monks established flourishing monasteries. In the East Frankish kingdom (Germany) the Easter fires remained suppressed for a long time, mostly because the missionaries of those regions had not come from Ireland, but from England, and thus did not know the custom of a Christian Easter fire. In the course of the eighth and ninth centuries, however, the custom became so popular in the whole Carolingian empire that it was eventually incorporated into the liturgy of Rome during the latter part of the ninth century.[29] Thus the blessing of the fire has now become the opening rite of the ceremonies on the Vigil of Easter.[30]

RESURRECTION SERVICE · In medieval times it was a general custom to celebrate the *Elevatio* (Raising) of the sacred Host or the cross from the shrine of the Sepulcher during the night of Holy Saturday or in the early morning of Easter Sunday. In many places this was done by the clergy alone. A procession would bear the Blessed Sacrament or the cross from the shrine to the main altar. A more solemn variety of this custom was the Resurrection service, widely practiced in central Europe. With the church already decorated for Easter, the priest took the Blessed Sacrament from the shrine, removed the white veil, and holding the monstrance aloft intoned the ancient antiphon "The Lord is risen, alleluia." While the faithful sang their traditional Easter songs and all the church bells rang, the procession moved from the shrine to the main altar. There the *Te Deum* was intoned, and a solemn benediction concluded the service.[31]

FOLKLORE · Christian folklore has adorned the Easter Vigil with a wealth of interesting customs, most of them based on the joyful liturgy of the solemn service.[32] In many sections of Europe the lights at the domestic shrines are extinguished before the vigil service. No fire or light is allowed anywhere in the house. The stoves, lamps, and candlesticks have been cleaned and prepared on the preceding days; now they stand ready to receive the blessed fire. Meanwhile, the boys build a pile of wooden logs in front of the church, each contributing a piece to which a strand of wire is fastened. At this pile the priest strikes the Easter fire and blesses it. As log after log begins to burn, the youngsters draw them out and rush home swinging the glowing pieces. From them the lamps and the stove are lit. Then the faggots are extinguished and put aside; pieces will be placed in the kitchen stove when storms and lightning threaten throughout the year.[33]

In other places people carry the flames of the blessed fire in lanterns back to their homes. A vigil light before the crucifix is lit, and zealously guarded all through the year.

At the moment of the Gloria in the Mass, when suddenly all the bells start ringing again, the people who have to stay at home embrace and wish each other a blessed Easter.[34]

EASTER SUNDAY

"This is the day which the Lord has made, the Feast of Feasts, and our Pasch: the Resurrection of our Saviour Jesus Christ according to the flesh." With these solemn words the official calendar of the Western Church announces the celebration of Easter Sunday. Equally solemn are the words of the calendar (*Pentecostarion*) of the Eastern Church: "The sacred and great Sunday of the Pasch, on which we celebrate the life-giving Resurrection of our Lord and God, the Saviour Jesus Christ." [35]

LITURGY · In the Latin Church there are no special ceremonies other than the Mass itself, which is celebrated in all churches with festive splendor and great solemnity on Easter Sunday.

In the Greek Church, the solemn services in honor of Christ's resurrection begin at midnight. The priest and all the congregation, lighted candles in hand, leave the church by a side door after the Vigil of Easter. The procession walks around to the main door, which has been closed (representing the sealed tomb of Christ). The priest slowly makes the sign of the cross with the crucifix he holds in his right hand. At this moment the doors swing open, the people intone the hymn "Christ is risen," all the church bells start pealing, and the jubilant procession moves into the brightly illuminated church.[36] The candles in the hands of the worshipers fill the building with a sea of sparkling lights. The Matins of Easter are then sung, and the Holy Sacrifice of the Mass, at which all present receive Communion, is celebrated.

After Mass the solemn Easter blessing is bestowed upon the food brought by each family. In the cities of Russia this blessing used to be held outside the church. People would pile the food on tables, around their Easter breads (*Paska*); each bread bore a lighted taper. The priests in their resplendent robes, accompanied by assistants, passed in procession beside the waiting multitude, blessing the food and the people as bells rang and the church choir intoned joyous Easter hymns.

Of particular historical interest in the Latin liturgy is the sequence. The sequences originated in the tenth century as Latin texts to be substituted for the long-drawn final "a" of the alleluia, which is sung at the end of the Gradual.

The sequence of Easter Sunday, *Victimae Paschali Laudes* (Praise to the Paschal Victim) was written by the priest Wipo (about 1030), court chaplain of Emperor Conrad. It soon became part of the official text of the Easter Mass and is sung or recited in all Catholic churches every day during Easter Week.[37]

The significant fact is that the *Victimae Paschali* was the first inspiration for the famous miracle plays that developed into a wealth of religious drama from the tenth century on. All drama performances of sacred subjects, both within and without the churches, are traced back to this Easter sequence.[38] The dramatic question-and-answer structure of Wipo's poem lent itself naturally to this lovely scene:

> *Tell us, Maria, what didst thou see on thy way?*
> *I saw the tomb of the living Christ*
> *And the glory of the Risen Lord,*
> *The angels who gave witness,*
> *The winding-sheet and the linen cloths.*

> *Christ, my Hope, is risen!*
> *He precedes you into Galilee.*
> *Now we truly know that Christ is risen from the dead.*
> *Thou, Victor, Saviour-King, have mercy on us.*
>   *Amen. Alleluia.*

The words of Wipo's text were soon amplified by other phrases from the Bible, and the appealing play was eventually presented with appropriate devotion before the shrine of the Sepulcher on Easter Sunday morning. It was called the "Visit to the Tomb" (*Visitatio sepulcri*). In front of the shrine, now empty (the cross or Blessed Sacrament having been removed), the clergy played the scene of the Gospel that tells of the visit of the holy women to the tomb on Sunday morning. Two young clerics in white gowns, who sat or stood at the shrine, represented the angels and pronounced the Easter message at the end of the play: "He is not here, He is risen as He foretold. Go, tell His disciples that He is risen. Alleluia."

These liturgical Easter plays strongly appealed to the devout in medieval centuries. As time went on, various plays were written for Christmas, Epiphany, and other feast days. They all followed the structure of the Easter play inspired by the *Victimae Paschali*. A large number of these Easter plays, and later similar Christmas and Epiphany plays, are preserved in manuscripts and early prints all over Europe and in some of the museums and private collections in America.[39]

POPULAR OBSERVANCE · Special celebrations were held in most countries during the early morning hours of Easter Sunday. According to legend all running water was blessed with great powers to protect and heal.[40] In rural sections the inhabitants still perform various water rites at the dawn of the feast. In Austria, groups of young people gather long before sunrise in meadows or on hilltops to dance traditional Easter dances and sing their ancient carols.

A universal celebration was held in the Middle Ages at the hour of sunrise. According to an old legend, the sun dances on Easter morning or makes three cheerful jumps at the moment of rising, in honor of Christ's resurrection.[41] The rays of light penetrating the clouds were said to be angels dancing for joy. In Ireland and England people put a pan of water in the east window and watched the dancing sun mirrored in it.

All over Europe people would gather in open plains or on the crests of hills to watch the spectacle of sunrise on Easter Day. The moment of daybreak was marked by the shooting of cannon and the ringing of bells. Bands and choirs used to greet the rising sun as a symbol of the Risen Christ with Easter hymns and alleluia songs. This morning salute is still performed in the Alpine regions of Austria.[42]

On the island of Malta, a quaint custom is practiced at sunrise on Easter Day. A group of men carries a statue of the Saviour from their church to a hilltop of the neighborhood, not in slow and solemn procession, but *running* uphill as fast as they can, to indicate the motion of rising.

In most places the crowds prayed as the sun appeared; often this prayer service was led by the priest, and the whole group would afterward go in procession to the parish church for Easter Mass. From this medieval custom dates our modern sunrise service, held by many congregations on Easter Sunday.

NEW CLOTHES · As the newly baptized Christians in the early centuries wore white garments of new linen, so it became a tradition among all the faithful to appear in new clothes on Easter Sunday, symbolizing the "new life" that the Lord, through His resurrection, bestowed upon all believers. This custom was widespread during medieval times; in many places a popular superstition threatened with ill luck all those who could afford to buy new clothes for Easter Sunday but refused to do so. An ancient saying in Ireland is "For Christmas, food and drink; for Easter, new clothes." This ancient tradition of new clothes is still adhered to, although its meaning and background have long since been forgotten by many.

EASTER WALK · Another picturesque old Easter Sunday custom is the "Easter walk" through fields and open spaces after Mass. This is still held in many parts of Europe. Dressed in their finery, the men and women, especially the younger ones, march in a well-ordered parade through the town and into the open country. A decorated crucifix or, in some places, the Easter candle is borne at the head of the procession. At certain points on the route they recite prayers and sing Easter hymns, interspersed with gay chatting along the way. In some parts of Germany and Austria, groups of young farmers ride on richly decorated horses (*Osterritt*). After the Reformation this medieval Easter walk lost its original religious character and gradually developed into our present-day Easter parade.[43]

On Easter Sunday open house is held in most Christian nations. Relatives, neighbors, and friends exchange visits. Easter eggs and bunnies are the order of the day, and special Easter hams are the principal dish at dinner.[44] In the rural parts of Austria, any stranger may freely enter any house on Easter Sunday; he will be welcomed by the host and may eat whatever Easter food he wishes. Among the Christians in the Near East the whole Sunday (after Mass and breakfast) is spent in visiting friends and neighbors; wine, pastry, and coffee are served, and children receive presents of eggs and sweets.

EASTER LAUGHTER · On Easter Sunday afternoon most people in the villages and towns of central Europe come back to church for the solemn services of Vespers and Benediction. At the sermon that preceded this afternoon service, a quaint custom was practiced in those regions during medieval times. The priests would regale their congregations with funny stories and poems, drawing moral conclusions from these jolly tales (*Ostermärlein:* Easter fables).[45] The purpose of this unusual practice was to reward the faithful with something gay after the many sad and serious Lenten preachings, a purpose easily achieved as the churches rang with the loud and happy laughter of the audience (*risus paschalis:* Easter laughter).[46] This tradition is found as early as the thirteenth century. From the fourteenth to the eighteenth centuries the custom was widespread, and a number of collections of Easter fables appeared in print.[47] The reformers violently attacked the practice as an abuse, however, and it was gradually suppressed by the Church during the seventeenth and eighteenth centuries.

EASTER BELLS · It is an ancient custom in Slavic countries (Russia, the Ukraine, Poland) to ring the church bells with short

intervals all day from morning to night on Easter Sunday, reminding the faithful that it is the greatest feast of the year.[48]

EASTER WEEK

LITURGY · In the early days of Christianity all of Easter Week
was one continuous feast. Although the number of prescribed
holydays differed in various provinces, most people abstained
from their usual work and attended church services every day.
Many went to all three services that at the time of the Roman
Empire were held daily at morning, noon, and night. Priests in
France used to celebrate two Masses every day during Easter
Week. Indeed, a Spanish Missal of the ninth century shows three
Mass texts for each day of the Easter Octave.

Gradually, however, the Church reduced obligatory attendance
to four days, then, in 1094, to three. In many parts of Europe
these three days are still observed, at least as half-holydays,
which means that most of the faithful, although not obliged to
attend Mass, voluntarily do so, as well as abstain from work.
Since 1911, even Easter Monday is no longer a holyday of obligation, though it remains a legal holiday in most European
countries, both Catholic and Protestant.[49]

Because those who were baptized on Holy Saturday wore new
white garments, Easter Week is also called "White Week" in the
Western Church and the "Week of New Garments" in the Oriental Church. During the whole week the newly baptized, in their
linen dress and soft sandals, stood close to the altar at all services
as a separate group within the sanctuary of the basilica. Every
day the bishop would address them with special instructions after
the other worshipers had left. It was the honeymoon of their
new life as Christians, a week of intense happiness and spiritual
joy. On the Sunday after Easter they attended Mass clothed for
the last time in their white baptismal robes. At the end of the
service the bishop solemnly dismissed them from the place of
honor in the sanctuary, so they could mix with their families and
friends in the body of the church. Later, at home, they exchanged
the white garments for the ordinary dress of their station in life.[50]

EMMAUS WALK (MONDAY) · Easter Monday was, in medieval
times, and still is in many countries, a day of rest, relaxation, and

special festivities. First among them is the "Emmaus walk," a custom inspired by the Gospel of the day (Luke 24, 13-35). Families and groups of friends go on outings or long walks into the fields, forests, and mountains, hold picnics and spend the afternoon playing games, dancing, and singing.[51] In Germany and Austria long ago, youngsters would gather in large meadows to play Easter games and Easter sports (*Osterspiele*), and also to perform ancient folk dances accompanied by the music of guitars and mandolins.[52] The piece of land on which these Easter games took place bore the name "Easter field" (*Osteranger*), and many cities still have lots so called, although the custom has long since vanished. In rural regions, however, such ancient traditions have survived, and are practiced every year.

In French Canada, the Emmaus walk takes the form of a visit to the grandparents, which is faithfully adhered to by all children on Easter Monday. The Poles hold their outings and picnics in large groups; often the inhabitants of a whole town will gather in some rural "Emmaus" grove which remains the goal of their excursions for many years. The days from Holy Thursday to Easter Tuesday are observed as public holidays in Norway, and many people spend this period in skiing and other winter sports in the snowy hills. The deep tan acquired in the open air during the Easter holidays is called *Paskebrun* (Easter tan).

FERTILITY RITES (MONDAY AND TUESDAY) · In most countries of northern Europe, Monday and Tuesday are the traditional days of "switching" and "drenching," customs based on pre-Christian fertility rites, previously mentioned. On Monday the boys are supposed to apply this ancient rite to the girls, while on Tuesday the girls retaliate. Actually, both are now performed on Easter Monday in many places. The custom is called *Gsundschlagen* (stroke of health) in Austria and southern Germany, *Dyngus* (ransom) in Poland, *Loscolkodas* (dousing) in Hungary, and *Pomlazka* (willow switch) among the Czechs and Slovaks. In good-natured mischief the boys will surprise the girls with buckets or bottles of water, and douse them thoroughly, often reciting some little rhyme.[53]

Whole processions are formed by youngsters dressed in out-

landish costumes who go from farm to farm and sing or recite
playful ditties. At the end of their performance they suddenly
splash water on their host and his family, whereupon they are
given eggs, pastry, and sweets. In many places the water is merely
sprinkled, instead of splashed, and in cities people have refined
the ancient custom by spraying perfume at each other, with
friendly wishes for good health and happiness.

The "switching" is done with gentleness. Carrying their rods
of pussy willow or leaved branches, the boys go in little groups
from house to house, apply the switch to all women (but never
to children), and receive small presents in reward. Groups of
girls carry a little tree or branch, decorated with flowers and
ribbons. They make the rounds like the boys, and at every home
they sing traditional songs announcing the summer and expressing good wishes for health and harvest.[54] On Quinquagesima
Sunday in Norway young folks visit relatives and friends and
"spank" them with the *Fastelavns-ris* (carnival rod), which is
made of brightly colored paper strips fastened to a painted stick
or handle.

A similar custom of considerable antiquity was that of "heav-
ing," practiced in some sections of England on Easter Monday
and Tuesday up through the nineteenth century. Some small
villages may still do it. On Easter Monday a group of men go
to each house, carrying a chair aloft, and amid much excitement
and joking insist that any lady present get into the chair and be
lifted up three times, demanding a forfeit in the form of a kiss.
On the next day it is the girls' turn to do the same thing to the
men.

HOLY SOULS (THURSDAY) · Among Slavic nations the Thursday
of Easter Week is devoted in a special way to the "Easter memory" of the departed ones. The faithful go to Mass, which on this
particular day is offered for the dead of the parish. Pictures of
deceased relatives and friends are decorated with flowers both
at home and in the cemetery (many tombstones carry images of
the deceased, usually a framed photograph). No farmer would
work on this day, for the memory of the holy souls demands re-
spectful rest and quiet. According to popular superstition any

man who works his farm on Easter Thursday will meet with ill luck and dire punishment.[55]

EASTER PILGRIMAGE (FRIDAY) · Friday of Easter Week is a favorite day for devout pilgrimages (*Osterwallfahrt*) in many parts of Europe. Praying and singing hymns, the faithful walk many hours through fields and forests, preceded by a cross and many church banners. The goal of the pilgrimage is usually a shrine or church in some neighboring village. There they attend Mass and perform their devotions. At one of these processions, in the Austrian Tyrol, people walk ten hours each way. In some sections of Germany and Austria the farmers make their pilgrimage on horseback, accompanied by a band playing Easter hymns.[56]

LOW SUNDAY · The Sunday after Easter was called the "Octave of the Pasch" from the earliest centuries.[57] Later (in the seventh century) it acquired the name "Sunday in White" (*Dominica in Albis*) because it was the last day on which the white garments were worn by the newly baptized Christians. After attending Mass they changed from their baptismal robes to ordinary dress.[58] The popular name for this Sunday in most European countries is "The White Sunday." The English term "Low Sunday" is derived from the ancient practice of counting the octave day as belonging to the feast, so that Easter actually would last eight days including two Sundays. The primary (high) one is Easter Sunday, and the secondary (low) one the Sunday after Easter.

In the Byzantine Church, Low Sunday bears the title of "second highest" Sunday of the year (*deuteroprote*), or "Sunday following the Pasch" (*Antipascha*). From the Gospel, which tells how the Apostle Thomas touched the wounds of Christ, it is also called Sunday of the Apostle Thomas.[59]

Low Sunday was for centuries, and still is in most parts of Europe, the day when children receive their first Communion. Dressed in white, they enter the church in solemn procession, holding lighted candles. They renew their baptismal vows and assist at Mass, which usually is conducted with great solemnity. In some places a most appealing custom is observed. Each child

receives first Communion with father and mother kneeling beside
him, also receiving the Blessed Sacrament.

[1] *Oratio in Pasch.*, 42; PG, 46, 683. [2] Genesis 13, 1-16; Deuteronomy
16, 1-8. [3] S. Pétridès, *Anastasimos*, DACL, 1.2 (1924), 1926 ff.
[4] Can. 20; Mansi, 2, 678. [5] Schuster, II, 313 ("Easter Sunday").
[6] *De temp. rat.*, 15; PL, 90, 357. [7] Geramb, 63; Gugitz, I, 180.
[8] Nilles, II, 30. [9] Thurston, 236 ff. [10] Nilles, II, 312 ff. (*De saluta-
tione et osculo paschali*). [11] Schuster, II, 317. [12] *Cap.* 21; Mansi,
22, 1008. [13] Can. 18; Mansi, 8, 327 f. [14] CIC, 859, 2. [15] VdM,
423 ff. (*Die Osternacht*). [16] Saint Augustine, *Sermo* 219; PL, 38,
1088. [17] From the *Exultet* (Liturgy of the Easter Vigil). [18] Eusebius,
De Vita Constant., IV, 22; PL, 8, 75. [19] *Oratio IV in S. Pascha;* PG,
46, 681. [20] Trans. by the author. [21] VdM, 425; Schuster, II, 287.
[22] *Ad uxor.*, II, 5; PL, 1, 1296. [23] *Praeconium Paschale*, DACL, 13.2
(1938), 1559 f. [24] VdM, 427 ff. [25] J. A. Jungmann, *Die Vorverle-
gung der Ostervigil seit dem christlichen Altertum*, LJ, 1 (1951),
48 ff. [26] C. Howell, "The Paschal Vigil and the People," WOR, 27
(1953), 172 ff. About changes in the liturgy of the *lucernarium* (Light
service) see LE, 161. [27] *Conc. Germ.*, *Cap. V;* Mansi, 12, 367. [28] L.
Gougaud, *Christianity in Celtic Lands*, London, 1937, 279 ff. [29] R.
Hindringer, *Feuerweihe*, LThK, 3 (1931), 1023. [30] Franz, I, 507 ff.;
LE, 155 f. About the spiritual symbolism of the Easter fire see T.
O'Neill, "The New Fire," WOR, 32 (1958), 268 ff. [31] TE, II, 653;
OiT, 77 ff.; LE, 161. [32] Franz, I, 517-94. [33] Koren, 116; OiT, 74 ff.
[34] OiT, 79. [35] Nilles, II, 304. [36] A. Hammerstede, "On the Symbolism
of Holy Doors," OF, 17 (1943), 337 ff. See also P. F. Sfeir, "Easter in
the Syrian Church," OF, 7 (1933), 266 ff. [37] Schuster, II, 315 (see
text of the fifth stanza, which was suppressed in the sixteenth cen-
tury). [38] Young, I, 201 ff. [39] J. Woerdeman, "The Source of the
Easter Play," OF, 20 (1946), 262 ff. [40] Koren, 126; Benet, 55. [41] ES,
109; Geramb, 70. [42] Geramb, 79. [43] Geramb, 73 (*Das Osterreiten*);
VL, 154. [44] OiT, 79 f.; Geramb, 78. [45] A. Sturm, *Ostermärlein*,
LThK, 7 (1935), 809. [46] Gugitz, I, 180 (*Das Ostergelächter*). [47] J.
Pauli, *Schimpf und Ernst*, Wien, 1522; J. J. Zeller, *Das beschämte
Laster*, Augsburg, 1771. [48] About the "Easter bells" in the Tyrol see
OiT, 79. [49] G. Kieffer, *Ostern (Oktav)*, LThK, 7 (1935), 810.
[50] VdM, 444 ff. (*Die Osteroktav*). [51] Koren, 127. [52] Geramb, 70
(*Osterspiele*). [53] Benet, 56 ff.; R. Hindringer, *Fruchtbarkeitszauber*,
LThK, 4 (1932), 218. [54] Benet, 59 ff.; Nilles, II, 333. [55] Benet,
60 f. [56] Koren, 127; OiT, 93 ff. (*Die Widderprozession*). [57] SSP, 91.
[58] VdM, 446. [59] Nilles, II, 341 ff.

CHAPTER

17 *Easter Songs and Customs*

HYMNS

ANCIENT · The Apostolic Creed contains the phrase "He descended into Hell" (*descendit ad inferos*). This means that the Soul of Christ, after His death, announced to the souls of the just the accomplished redemption which opened for them the gates of eternal bliss. Christian piety has adorned this historical fact with dramatic descriptions of the Lord's victory over Satan: He appears in the glory of His divine majesty, illuminating the kingdom of darkness and breaking down the gates of Hell. He binds Satan and releases the souls of the patriarchs from their long imprisonment.[1] A multitude of hymns and dramatic representations had this "Harrowing of Hell" as their subject. (The familiar pictures of the Risen Christ, holding aloft the banner of victory over death and the Devil, also were inspired by this article of faith.) [2]

Following this apostolic truth, the priest Melito of Sardes (Asia Minor) praised the Resurrection as early as the second century: [3]

> *Trembling for joy cries all creation;*
> *What is this mystery, so great and new?*
> *The Lord has risen from among the dead,*
> *And Death itself He crushed with valiant foot.*
> *Behold the cruel tyrant bound and chained,*
> *And man made free by Him who rose!*

From the fourth century date the magnificent Latin hymns of Easter praise (*praeconium paschale*) which used to be sung at the lighting of the Easter candle.[4] The *Exultet,* still sung in all Catholic churches during the liturgy of the Easter Vigil, is a later formulation of such an ancient hymn. Its origin is unknown, although it has often been ascribed to Saint Jerome or to Saint Augustine. Here are a few lines:

> *This is the Night,*
> *Which throughout the world*
> *Frees all who believe in Christ*
> *From the vices of their time-shackled existence,*
> *From the lightless dungeon of sin,*
> *And restores them to grace: unites them to holiness.*
>
> *This is the Night*
> *In which Christ broke the chains of death*
> *And rose in radiant victory*
> *From the pit of Hades.*[5]

Another fourth-century poem is the Latin hymn of Saint Ambrose, expressing the "paradox of faith" as seen in the death and Resurrection of Christ:

> *O mystery great and glorious,*
> *That mortal flesh should conquer death,*
> *And all our human pains and wounds*
> *The Lord should heal by bearing them.*
>
> *Behold how man, though crushed by death,*
> *Now does arise and live with Christ,*
> *While death, repelled and robbed of might,*
> *Dies from its own malignant sting.*[6]

Early Christian hymns with similar thoughts were written by Saint Gregory of Nazianz and Bishop Synesios of Cyrene (about 414). Another hymn ascribed to Saint Ambrose is now used in the Lauds of Low Sunday: *Claro paschali gaudio.* An English translation may be found in the Protestant Episcopal hymnal of the United States ("That Easter day with joy was bright").[7]

Venantius Fortunatus wrote (about 580) a Latin hymn, *Salve festa dies* (Hail, festive day!), which was later translated into various languages and became a popular Easter song. The first English translation is mentioned in a letter of Archbishop Cranmer to King Henry VIII, in 1544.

An ancient hymn now recited at Vespers during Easter time is the poem *Ad regias Agni dapes* (The royal banquet of the lamb). The present version, based on the text of a sixth- or seventh-century unknown author, was rearranged for the breviary under Pope Urban VIII (1644).

Saint John Damascene (eighth century) wrote a number of beautiful Greek poems in honor of the Resurrection, some of which are now used in the liturgical services of the Greek Church and have been translated into English and become popular Easter hymns:

"Thou hallowed chosen morn of praise" (*Aute he klete kai hagia hemera*). It is sung in the Greek liturgy during Easter night. A free English translation was published by John M. Neale in 1862; the tune for the English text is taken from a German melody composed by Johann H. Schein in 1628.

"Sing all nations" (*Aidomen pantes laoi*). An English adaptation ("Come Ye Faithful, Raise the Strain of Triumphant Gladness") was published by Neale in 1859. The tune was adopted from a German song by Johann Horn, printed in Nürnberg in 1544.

"The day of resurrection" (*Anastaseos Hemera*) is sung in its original Greek text at the midnight service of the Greek Church, when the faithful light their candles before going to Communion. A free translation into English was written by Neale. It is sung to the tune of an old German Madonna hymn (*Ave Maria, klarer und lichter Morgenstern*) which appeared in 1784.[8]

From a German interpolation between the lines of the Easter sequence (*Victimae Paschali*) originated the famous hymn *Christus ist erstanden* (Christ is risen), which is sung to a tune dating from the year 1531. This ancient song is still the most popular Easter hymn in both Catholic and Protestant churches in Germany. It is intoned by the priest and sung by the people at the solemn service of Resurrection (*Auferstehungsfeier*). An English text was written by Isaac Watts (1748).

LATER MIDDLE AGES · Many beautiful Easter songs date from the later Middle Ages. A true carol is the Latin poem *Alleluia! O filii and filiae* (Alleluia, o sons and daughters), written by the Franciscan Jean Tisserand (1494) and first published in Paris in 1525. The earliest English translation ("Young men and maids, rejoice and sing") appeared 1748 in a Catholic manual in London. The tune, composed by an unknown musician, was written in Paris in 1623.

Another carol is the German song *Wir wollen alle fröhlich sein* (Let us all be glad), which appeared in a songbook (*Christlichs Gesangbüchlein*) in 1568. Geoffry Shaw wrote an English text ("Now glad of heart be every one").

Inspired by Wipo's *Victimae Paschali*, Martin Luther (1546) wrote a dramatic Easter hymn which became a favorite church song among the German Lutherans and later in many other Protestant congregations:

> *It was a strange and wondrous war,*
> *When death and Life did battle.*
> *With royal might did Life prevail,*
> *Made death His knave and chattle.*
> *The sacred Book foretold it all:*
> *How death by death should come to fall.*
> *Now death is laughed to scorn.*[9]

In a songbook for students published by the Jesuit Fathers at Cologne in 1695 appeared a Latin Easter hymn (*Finita sunt jam proelia*) that has become a favorite in many countries. An English text was written by Francis Pott in 1861. The modern tune was adapted from Palestrina's *Magnificat Tertii Toni* by William H. Mock in 1861.

> *The strife is over, the battle done,*
> *The victory of life is won,*
> *The song of triumph has begun:*
> > *Alleluia.*

MODERN · Finally, there is a wealth of newer hymns, written in the past few centuries. Charles Wesley (1788) gave us various Easter songs; here is the first stanza of his best-known hymn:

> *Christ the Lord is risen today,*
> *Sons of men, and angels say;*
> *Raise your joys and triumphs high!*
> *Sing, ye heavens, and earth reply!*

Another well-known Easter song is "The world itself" by John M. Neale (1866). It first appeared in his book *Carols for Eastertide,* in 1854:

> *The world itself keeps Easter Day,*
> *And Easter larks are singing;*
> *And Easter flow'rs are blooming gay,*
> *And Easter buds are springing.*
> *Alleluia, alleluia.*
> *The Lord of all things lives anew,*
> *And all His works are living too.*
> *Alleluia, alleluia.*

The Episcopal dean Howard Chandler Robbins wrote an Easter carol for children in 1929, "The Sabbath day was by," that has become a popular hymn in the United States. Another recent carol is the poem "O who shall roll away the stone?" written by Reverend Marion F. Ham, a Unitarian minister. The text was first published in the Boston *Transcript* in April 1936, and the tune composed by the American organist and choirmaster T. Tertius Noble in 1941.

MUSIC · Of liturgical texts set to music, the best known are the Gradual for Easter, *Haec Dies quam fecit Dominus* (This is the day which the Lord has made). This text, both in the original Latin or in translations, has been set to music by several composers and sung in churches of all Christian denominations. This is also true of the Offertory in the Easter Sunday Mass, *Terra tremuit* (The earth trembled).

In Catholic churches the *Regina Coeli Laetare* (Queen of Heaven, rejoice) is prescribed as antiphon of the Blessed Virgin for Easter time. The text is a fourteenth-century Latin poem, and is sung both in Gregorian chant and various musical settings all through the Easter season. Another hymn often used in Catholic churches is *Regina Coeli Jubila* (Queen of Heaven, rejoice). This Latin poem appeared first in 1600; the author is unknown.

Among the great oratorios that glorify the Resurrection of Christ, the earliest is Antonio Scandello's *Auferstehungsgeschichte*

(Story of the Resurrection), composed about 1560. It was first performed in the Royal Court Chapel at Dresden.

The latter part of Handel's *Messiah* deals with the Easter story. Every year at its performance thousands are inspired by "I know that my redeemer liveth," and by the "Hallelujah Chorus," during which all audiences traditionally rise from their seats.

Charles Gounod's *Redemption* is another source of familiar Easter music. This work, once very popular, is now rarely performed, though in many churches Easter Day would not be complete without the resounding chorus "Unfold ye portals." Similar passages of Easter music are found in the famous choral works of César Franck (*Redemption*) and A. R. Gaul (*The Holy City*).

Of the innumerable shorter works, special mention should be made of Johann Sebastian Bach's several cantatas on Easter texts. There are, of course, also many short organ pieces inspired by the Resurrection.

Finally, countless popular Easter songs, as they exist among all nations, celebrate the great feast. Goethe (1832) indicates in the *Osterlied* of his famous poem *Faust,* with classic brevity and clarity of expression, the basic motif of all popular Easter songs:

> *Christ is arisen:*
> *Joy to all mortals*
> *Freed from the threatening*
> *Creeping and deadening*
> *Serpents of evil.*

SYMBOLS AND FOODS

EASTER LAMB · Among the popular Easter symbols, the lamb is by far the most significant of this great feast. The Easter lamb, representing Christ, with the flag of victory, may be seen in pictures and images in the homes of every central and eastern European family.

The oldest prayer for the blessing of lambs can be found in the seventh-century Sacramentary of the Benedictine monastery Bobbio in Italy. Two hundred years later Rome had adopted it, and thereafter the main feature of the pope's Easter dinner for many centuries was roast lamb.[10] After the tenth century, in place of the whole lamb, smaller pieces of meat were used. In some Benedictine monasteries, however, even today whole lambs are still blessed with the ancient prayers.

The ancient tradition of the Pasch lamb also inspired among the Christians the use of lamb meat as a popular food at Easter time, and at the present time it is eaten as the main meal on Easter Sunday in many parts of eastern Europe. Frequently, however, little figures of a lamb made of butter, pastry, or sugar have been substituted for the meat, forming Easter table center-pieces.[11]

In past centuries it was considered a lucky omen to meet a lamb, especially at Easter time. It was a popular superstition that the Devil, who could take the form of all other animals, was never allowed to appear in the shape of a lamb because of its religious symbolism.

EASTER EGG · The origin of the Easter egg is based on the fertility lore of the Indo-European races. To our pre-Christian ancestors it was a most startling event to see a new and live creature emerge from a seemingly dead object. The egg to them became a symbol of spring. Long ago in Persia people used to present each other with eggs at the spring equinox, which for them also marked the beginning of a new year.[12]

In Christian times the egg had bestowed upon it a religious interpretation, becoming a symbol of the rock tomb out of which Christ emerged to the new life of His resurrection. There was, in addition, a very practical reason for making the egg a special sign of Easter joy, since it used to be one of the foods that were forbidden in Lent. The faithful from early times painted Easter eggs in gay colors, had them blessed, ate them, and gave them to friends as Easter gifts.

The custom of using Easter eggs developed among the nations of northern Europe and Christian Asia soon after their conversion to Christianity. In countries of southern Europe, and consequently in South America, however, the tradition of Easter eggs never became popular.

The Roman ritual has a special blessing for Easter eggs: [13]

We beseech thee, O Lord, to bestow thy benign blessing upon these eggs, to make them a wholesome food for thy faithful, who gratefully partake of them in honor of the Resurrection of our Lord Jesus Christ.[14]

In medieval times eggs were traditionally given at Easter to all servants. It is reported that King Edward I of England (1307) had four hundred and fifty eggs boiled before Easter and dyed or covered with gold leaf, which he distributed to the members of the royal household on Easter Day.

The eggs were usually given to children as Easter presents along with other gifts. This practice was so firmly rooted in Germany that the eggs were called *Dingeier* (eggs that are "owed").[15] The children were not slow in demanding what was "owed" to them, and thus developed the many rhymes in France, Germany, Austria, and England wherein youngsters even today request Easter eggs for presents. In England this custom is called "pace-egging," the word "pace" being a corrupted form of Pasch.

In most countries the eggs are stained in plain vegetable-dye colors. Among the Chaldeans, Syrians, and Greeks, the faithful present each other with crimson eggs in honor of the blood of Christ.[16] In parts of Germany and Austria, green eggs alone are used on Maundy Thursday, but various colors are the vogue at Easter. Some Slavic peoples make special patterns of gold and silver. In Austria artists design striking patterns by fastening ferns and tiny plants around the eggs, which show a white pattern after the eggs are boiled.[17] The Poles and Ukrainians decorate eggs with plain colors or simple designs and call them *krasanki*. Also a number of their eggs are made every year in a most distinctive manner with unusual ornamentation. These eggs are called *pysanki* (from *pysac:* to write, to design); each is a masterpiece of patient labor, native skill, and exquisite workmanship. No two *pysanki* are identical. Although the same symbols are repeated, each egg is designed with great originality. The symbols used most are the sun (good fortune), rooster or hen (fulfillment of wishes), stag or deer (good health), flowers (love and charity). As decorative patterns the artists use rhombic and square checkerboards, dots, wave lines, and intersecting ribbons. The *pysanki* are mainly made by girls and women in painstaking work during the long evenings of Lent. At Easter they are first blessed by the priest and then distributed among relatives, friends, and benefactors. These special eggs are saved from year to year, like symbolic heirlooms, and can be seen seasonally in Ukrainian settlements and shops in this country.[18]

In Germany and other countries of central Europe eggs for cooking Easter foods are not broken but pierced with a needle on both ends, and the contents to be used are blown into a bowl. The empty eggshells are given to the children for various Easter games. In parts of Germany such hollow eggs are suspended from shrubs and trees during Easter Week, much like a Christmas tree. The Armenians decorate empty eggs with pictures of the Risen Christ, the Blessed Virgin, and other religious designs, to give to children as Easter presents.

Easter is the season for games with eggs all over Europe.[19] The sport of egg-pecking is practiced in many forms, in Syria, Iraq, and Iran, as well. In Norway it is called *knekke* (knock). In Germany, Austria, and France, hard-boiled eggs are rolled against each other on the lawn or down a hill; the egg that remains uncracked to the end is called the "victory egg." This game has attained national fame in America through the annual egg-rolling party on the lawn of the White House in Washington.

Another universal custom among children is the egg hunting in house and garden on Easter Sunday morning. In France children are told that the Easter eggs are dropped by the church bells on their return from Rome. In Germany and Austria little nests containing eggs, pastry, and candy are placed in hidden spots, and the children believe that the Easter bunny, so popular in this country, too, has laid the eggs and brought the candy.

In Russia and among the Ukrainians and Poles people start their joyful Easter meals after the long Lenten fast with a blessed egg on Easter Sunday. Before sitting down to breakfast, the father solemnly distributes small pieces cut from an Easter egg to members of the family and guests, wishing them one and all a holy and happy feast. Not until they have eaten this morsel in silence, do they sit down to the first meal of the Easter season.[20]

EASTER LILY · The Easter lily is larger than the more generally known Madonna lily. It was introduced in Bermuda, from Japan, at the middle of the last century. In 1882 the florist W. K. Harris brought it to the United States and spread its use here. Since it flowers first around Easter time in this part of the world, it soon came to be called "Easter lily." The American public immediately accepted the implied suggestion and made it a symbolic feature of the Easter celebration. Churches began using it as a decoration on Easter Day, and people adopted it as a favorite in their homes for the Easter solemnities.[21]

Although the Easter lily did not directly originate from religious symbolism, it has acquired that symbolism, and quite appropriately so. Its radiant whiteness, the delicate beauty of shape and form, its joyful and solemn aspect, certainly make it an eloquent herald of the Easter celebration. Besides, lilies have always been symbols of beauty, perfection and goodness. The Holy Scriptures, both of the Old and New Testaments, frequently make use of this symbolism.

Jesus once showed the Apostles some lilies and said: "Not even Solomon in all his glory was arrayed like one of these" (Matthew 6, 28). Now, since the Lord Himself stated that lilies are more glorious than the greatest earthly splendor, it certainly is fitting that we use these beautiful flowers to glorify Him on the day of His resurrection.

EASTER BUNNY · The Easter bunny had its origin in pre-Christian fertility lore. Hare and rabbit were the most fertile animals our forefathers knew, serving as symbols of abundant new life in the spring season.[22] The Easter bunny has never had religious symbolism bestowed on its festive usage, though its white meat is sometimes said to suggest purity and innocence. The Church has never performed special blessings for rabbits or hares, and neither in the liturgy nor in folklore do we find these animals linked with the spiritual meanings of the sacred season. However, the bunny has acquired a cherished role in the celebration of Easter as the legendary producer of Easter eggs for children in many countries.

What seems to be the first mention of the Easter bunny and his eggs is a short admonition in a German book of 1572: "Do not worry if the bunny escapes you; should we miss his eggs, then we shall cook the nest." In a German book of the seventeenth century the story that the Easter bunny lays eggs and hides them in the garden is called "an old fable." [23]

In many sections of Germany the Easter bunny was believed to lay red eggs on Maundy Thursday and eggs of other colors the night before Easter Sunday. The first Easter bunnies made of pastry and sugar were popular in southern Germany at the beginning of the last century. They are now a favorite delicacy for children in many lands.

EASTER HAM · The pig has always been a symbol of good luck and prosperity among the Indo-Europeans. Many traces of this ancient symbolism are still alive in our time. In some German popular expressions the word "pig" is synonymous with "good luck" (*Schwein haben*). In Hungary the highest card (ace) in card games is called "pig" (*disznó*). Not too long ago it was fashionable for men to wear little figures of pigs as good luck charms on their watch chains. Savings boxes for children in the figure of a pig (piggy banks) carry out the ancient symbolism of good luck and prosperity.

It is an age-old custom, handed down from pre-Christian times, to eat the meat of this animal on festive occasions. Thus the English and Scandinavians ate boar meat and the Germans and Slavs roast pork on Christmas Day. Also, in many parts of Europe roast pork is still the main dish at weddings and on major feast days. Hungarians eat roasted piglets on New Year's Day. The French Canadians have their traditional pork pie on festive occasions. At Easter, smoked or cooked ham, as well as lamb, has been eaten by most European nations from ancient times, and is the traditional Easter dish in America, too. The first records on the liturgical blessing of Easter ham date from the tenth century.[24]

EASTER TABLE · The nations of central and eastern Europe have other traditional Easter foods, prepared on the last days of Holy Week, blessed by the priest on Holy Saturday or Easter Sunday, and solemnly displayed on a festive table for Easter Week meals. This blessed Easter fare is called *Weihessen* (blessed food) in Germany and Austria, *Swiecone* or *Swieconka* (sanctified) among the Ukrainians and Poles.[25] The figure of the Easter lamb, which rests on a bedding of evergreen twigs, is surrounded by colored Easter eggs. Around this centerpiece are arranged other foods in great variety and large amounts: Easter breads, meats, sausages, salads, cheese, pastry, spices, and fruit. The whole table and every dish on it are decorated with garlands and clusters of leaves, herbs, and flowers.[26]

EASTER PASTRY · Many nations have distinctive Easter breads and pastries which are blessed by the priest and eaten during Easter Week. Among the Slavic people this Easter bread is called *Paska*. The Russian *paska* is made of flour, cottage cheese, sugar, raisins, eggs, and milk. It is put in a mold and shaped in firm, square pieces, about eight inches high, with a cross on each side, and the letters J. C. (Jesus Christ) imprinted in relief. In Germany and Austria the Easter bread is made with milk, eggs, and raisins, and baked in oblong loaves of twisted or braided strands (*Oster-stollen*). Another kind of Austrian Easter bread is the *Osterlaib* (Easter loaf), a large, flat round loaf marked with the cross or an image of the lamb. In some parts of Ireland people eat on Easter Sunday "Golden bread," which is very similar to our French toast.

A favorite Easter pastry in Poland are the *mazurki*, originating in the province of Mazuria, which are very sweet cakes made with honey and filled with nuts and fruit. A South German pastry is the *Weihkuchen* (blessed cake) made of flour, oil, milk, butter, and honey. The people of Transylvania bake their ham in a cover of bread dough. The Hungarian Easter meat loaf is made of chopped pork, ham, eggs, bread, and spices.[27]

[1] A. Grillmeier, *Der Gottessohn im Totenreich*, ZKTh, 71 (1949), 1 ff., 184 ff.; H. Leclercq, *La descente du Christ aux enfers, d'après la liturgie*, DACL, 4.1 (1920), 682 ff.   [2] K. Young, "The Harrowing of Hell in Liturgical Drama," in *Transactions of the Wisconsin Academy of Sciences, Arts and Letters*, 16.2 (1909), 889 ff.   [3] H. Rahner, *Oster-lyrik der Kirchenväter*, in *Schweizerische Kirchenzeitung*, 110 (1942), 169 ff.   [4] *Praeconium Paschale*, DACL, 13.2 (1938), 1559 ff.   [5] Trans. by the author.   [6] Trans. by the author. For this and the following hymns see H. A. Daniel, *Thesaurus Hymnologicus*, Halle, 1841-56, *passim*.   [7] HPEC, hymn 90.   [8] HPEC, hymns 93, 94, 95.   [9] See note

5. [10] TE, I, 655 f.; Franz, I, 582. [11] Geramb, 73; Benet, 54. [12] H. Hepding, *Ostereier und Osterhase,* in *Hessische Blätter für Volkskunde,* 26 (1927). [13] The blessing of eggs became fairly common in the twelfth century. See TE, I, 656; Franz, I, 589 f. [14] RR, *Bened. ovorum, praesertim in Pascha.* [15] Gugitz, I, 188. [16] Nilles, II, 314. [17] Trapp, 128. [18] Sr. Josepha, "Ukrainian Easter Eggs," in *The Ark,* 1 (1946), 19 f.; Benet, 50 f. [19] OiT, 80, 87 (*Die Ostereier*); VL, 154; Gugitz, I, 187 f. [20] Benet, 55 f. [21] F. X. Weiser, "Speaking of Easter Lilies," in *Horticulture,* 33.4 (1955), 210 f. [22] Gugitz, I, 187 ff. (*Der Osterhase und sein Ei*). [23] *De ovibus paschalibus, Von Oster-Eyern, Satyrae medicae,* 1682; see Gugitz, I, 188 f. [24] Franz, I, 582. [25] Benet, 53 f.; C. Goeb, "Easter Blessings," OF, 5 (1931), 216 ff. [26] OiT, 82 ff. (*Österliche Speisenweihe*); Geramb, 93 ff.; Koren, 120. [27] M. Höfler, *Ostergebäcke,* in *Zeitschrift für österreichische Volkskunde,* 12 (suppl. IV, 1906), 17 ff.

CHAPTER

18

Feast of the Ascension

HISTORY AND LITURGY

On Thursday of the sixth week after Easter (forty days after Easter Sunday), the Church celebrates the Feast of the Ascension. According to the Bible, on that day the Lord commissioned His Apostles to preach the Gospel to all nations; then, having blessed them, "He was lifted up before their eyes, and a cloud took him out of their sight" (Acts 1, 9).

ORIGIN · The feast is of very ancient origin. As a mere commemoration of the event it certainly dates from apostolic times, since the Bible expressly mentions the day and its happenings. However, it seems that the Ascension was not celebrated as a separate festival in the liturgy of the Church during the first three cen-

turies, but was included in the Feast of Pentecost.¹ The first one
to mention it as an established and separate feast is Eusebius,
Bishop of Nicomedia (341).² At the end of the fourth century
it was universally celebrated in the whole Roman Empire. Saint
Augustine (430) attributed its origin to the Apostles themselves,
probably because by his time it already was of such high traditional standing that it ranked with the greatest liturgical celebrations. He mentions as "solemn anniversaries" of the Lord the
"passion, resurrection and ascension, and the coming of the Holy
Spirit." ³ In the Greek Church, Saint Gregory of Nyssa (394) and
Saint John Chrysostom (407) preached sermons on Ascension
Day, which proves that at the end of the fourth century the
feast was well established in the East, too.⁴ From those early
centuries the festival has remained a holyday of obligation up
to this day.⁵

VIGIL · Ascension Day did not receive a vigil celebration until
well into the seventh century, when it was first mentioned in
some Roman lists of holydays.⁶ The reason for this delay was
the fact that a penitential observance like the vigil was actually
out of harmony with the festive season of joy between Easter
and Pentecost, which did not admit of fasting and penitential
exercises in the ancient Church. In the ninth century this vigil
celebration came from Rome to the Frankish empire and was
thus established as a universal custom in the liturgy of the Latin
Church.⁷ The Greek Church has never observed a vigil of As-
cension.⁸

The vigil Mass clearly betrays its late origin. If the vigil had
been in existence at the time of Saint Gregory I (604), that
great pope would have given it a liturgy of its own. As it is, the
Mass text shows no originality; it is borrowed from the preceding
Sunday (with the exception of Epistle and Gospel).⁹

The law of vigil fast was gradually rescinded during the past
centuries. The new Code of Canon Law does not list the vigil of
Ascension among the fast days of obligation.¹⁰

CELEBRATION OF THE FEAST · As with the other feasts of the
Lord, the early Church celebrated not so much the memory of

the historical event of Christ's ascension, but its theological significance. Saint John Chrysostom expressed it in these words:

Through the mystery of the Ascension we, who seemed unworthy of God's earth, are taken up into Heaven. . . . Our very nature, against which Cherubim guarded the gates of Paradise, is enthroned today high above all Cherubim.[11]

A similar thought is expressed in the words of the festive Preface in the Mass: "Christ was lifted up to Heaven to make us sharers in His divinity." [12]

Perhaps the same theological aspect, in preference to the merely historical one, explains the interesting fact that in Jerusalem the earliest celebration of Ascension Day (in the fourth century) was not held on the Mount of Olives (although Saint Helena had built a splendid basilica there), but in the Church of the Nativity in Bethlehem, as if the end of Christ's visible presence on earth would have to be honored in the very place of its beginning.[13] By the eight century, however, the Ascension feast in Jerusalem was solemnly kept on the Mount of Olives.[14]

PROCESSION · From the very beginning of its observance as a separate festival, the Ascension had a distinctive feature in the liturgical procession which went outside the city, and usually to the top of a hill, in imitation of Christ's leading the Apostles "out towards Bethany" (Luke 24, 50).[15] In Jerusalem it was, of course, the original path that Christ took to the summit of the Mount of Olives. In Constantinople the suburb of Romanesia, where Saint John Chrysostom had preached his sermons on the Ascension, was chosen.[16] In Rome, the pope was crowned by the cardinals in his chapel after the morning service, and in solemn procession conducted to the church of the Lateran. From there, after the Pontifical Mass, toward noon, the procession went to a shrine or church outside the walls. The Epistle of the Ascension was read and a prayer service held.[17]

This custom of the procession was introduced as a fairly universal rite in the Latin Church during the eighth and ninth centuries, but finally was replaced by the nonliturgical pageants of the High Middle Ages. The only relic still extant in our present liturgy is the simple but impressive ceremony in every Catholic church, after the Gospel of the Mass has been sung, of extinguishing the Easter candle. In some sections of Germany and central Europe, however, semiliturgical processions are still held after the High Mass. Preceded by candles and cross, the faithful walk with prayer and song through fields and pastures, and the priest blesses each lot of ground.[18]

ASCENSION WEEK · The Feast of the Ascension received an octave only in the fifteenth century.[19] Before that time, the Sunday after the Ascension was called in the Roman books "Sunday of the Rose" (*Dominica de Rosa*). On that Sunday the popes preached and held the solemn service at the church of Santa Maria Rotonda (the Pantheon), and, in token of the Lord's promise that He would send the Paraclete soon, a shower of roses was thrown from the central opening of the church immediately after the pope's sermon.[20]

Even today, the Mass of Sunday is mainly devoted to the thought of the coming Feast of Pentecost. In the Epistle, Saint Peter describes the greatest gift of the Holy Spirit, the virtue of charity (1 Peter 4, 7-11); and, in the Gospel, Christ promises to send the Paraclete (John 15, 26-16, 4).

In the Greek Church this Sunday forms the Feast of the Three Hundred and Eighteen Holy and Godly Fathers of Nicaea. It is a solemn commemoration of the great council of 325 in which the Arian heresy was condemned and Mary's title as "Mother of God" was unanimously confirmed.[21]

Some hermits and ascetics in the early centuries claimed (against the general practice of the Church) that from Ascension Day on they could and should return to their penitential exercises and fasts, because Christ was with the Apostles for only forty days.[22] Thus the Octave of the Ascension was turned by them into a period of fasting and penance. The Council of Elvira (about 303) condemned this claim and insisted on the universal practice of keeping the time of joy (without fast and penance) up to Pentecost.[23]

NAMES · All Christian nations have accepted the liturgical term of "Ascension" for the feast (*Ascensio* in Latin, *Analepsis* in Greek). The German word *Himmelfahrt* has the same meaning

(Going up to Heaven). The Hungarians have a popular term, "Thursday of the Communicants" (*Aldozó esütörtök*), because in past centuries Ascension was the last day for receiving the annual Easter Communion in that country.[24]

A second liturgical title is used in the Byzantine Church: "Fulfilled Salvation" (*Episozomene* in Greek, *Spasovo* in Slavonic).[25] This term signifies what Saint Gregory of Nyssa expressed in one of his sermons: "The Ascension of Christ is the consummation and fulfillment of all other feasts and the happy conclusion of the earthly sojourn of Jesus Christ."[26]

FOLKLORE

ASCENSION PLAYS · During the tenth century some dramatic details were added to the liturgical procession on Ascension Day in the countries of central and western Europe.[27] In Germany it became a custom for priests to lift a cross aloft when the words *Assumptus est in coelum* (He was taken up into Heaven) were sung at the Gospel.[28]

From the eleventh century on, the procession was gradually dropped in most countries and in its place a pageant was performed in church. These "Ascension plays" have never been accorded official approval or liturgical status by the Roman authorities.[29]

By the thirteenth century it had become a fairly general custom to enact the Ascension by hoisting a statue of the Risen Christ aloft until it disappeared through an opening in the ceiling of the church.[30] While the image, suspended on a rope, moved slowly upward, the people rose in their pews and stretched out their arms toward the figure of the Saviour, acclaiming the Lord in prayer or by hymn singing. Hundreds of reports in old books from the fourteenth to the seventeenth centuries contain vivid descriptions of this ancient custom.

One of the most charming examples is the Ascension play of the Bavarian monastery in Moosburg, recorded by the priest and poet Johann von Berghausen (1362).[31] In the center of the church, directly underneath an opening in the ceiling, a platform decorated with colored cloths and flowers was erected. On this platform stood a little tent, open at the top, which represented the Mount of Olivet. Inside the tent was placed a statue of the Risen Christ, holding high the banner of victory. A strong rope that hung down from the ceiling was fastened to a ring on top of the wooden image. After Vespers (in the afternoon), a solemn procession moved from the sacristy to the platform. It was led by two boys in white dresses. They impersonated angels; on their shoulders they wore wings and on their heads little wreaths of flowers. They were followed by a young cleric who represented the Blessed Virgin, "dressed in the robes of holy and honorable widowhood." To his right and left walked clerics enacting Saint Peter and Saint John. Behind them came ten other clerics in Oriental gowns; they were barefoot, and on their foreheads they carried diadems inscribed with the names of the Apostles. The altar boys and priests, vested in festive garb, concluded the group. In front of the platform, the deacon sang the Gospel of Ascension Day, and the choir intoned the antiphon, "I ascend to my Father and your Father, to my God and your God" (John 20, 17). The priests then venerated the image of Christ with inclinations and incense. Finally, while the choir sang *Ascendit Deus in altum, alleluia* (God rose on high), the statue was slowly pulled aloft. As it rose higher and higher, a few figures of angels holding burning candles came down from "Heaven" to meet the Lord and to accompany him on his journey. From a large metal ring that was suspended below the opening, there hung cloths of silk representing clouds. Between these "clouds" the image of the Saviour slowly and solemnly disappeared. A few moments later, a shower of roses, lilies, and other flowers dropped from the opening; then followed wafers in the shape of large hosts. The schoolchildren were allowed to collect these flowers and wafers, to take them home as cherished souvenirs. Father Berghausen explains this custom as follows: "The little ones collect the flowers which symbolize the various gifts of the Holy Spirit. The wafers indicate the presence of Christ in His eucharistic Body, which remains with us, under the species of bread, to the end of time." While the congregation stood with eyes raised to the ceiling, the two "angels" intoned the final message of Ascension Day, which predicts the triumphant coming of the Lord on the clouds of Heaven, for the great judgment at the end of the world: "Why do you stand looking up to heaven? This Jesus, who has been taken up from you into heaven, shall come in the same way as you have seen him going up to heaven" (Acts 1, 11). The celebration was concluded with solemn Benediction.[32]

The Lutheran reformers violently attacked not only occasional abuses in these plays, but the whole institution. However, Luther himself seems to have later regretted the hasty condemnations of earlier years, for in a message to his preachers he wrote in 1530: "If such customs had remained as pageants for the sake of youth and school children, to furnish them with a presentation of Christian doctrine and Christian life, then it could well be allowed that Palm donkeys, Ascension plays, and many similar traditions might be admitted and tolerated; for by such things conscience is not led into confusion."[33]

OTHER CUSTOMS · It was a widespread custom in many parts of Europe during the Middle Ages to eat a bird on Ascension Day, because Christ "flew" to Heaven. Pigeons, pheasants, partridges, and even crows, graced the dinner tables.[34] In western Germany bakers and innkeepers gave their customers pieces of pastry made in the shapes of various birds. In England the feast was celebrated with games, dancing, and horse races. In central Europe, Ascension Day is a traditional day of mountain climbing and picnics on hilltops and high places.[35]

Popular superstitions threaten dire punishments to anyone who works on Ascension Day in field and garden, but especially to women who do their sewing on the feast. Any piece of garment that has been touched by a needle on the Ascension will attract lightning before long, and many stories are told of how people were killed that way. In some sections of Europe it is said that weddings should not be held on Ascension Day because one of the partners would die soon. Those who go bathing in rivers and lakes are exposed to the danger of drowning more than on other days. It seems that all these superstitions are relics of the pre-Christian lore of the demons of death who were said to roam the earth and kill people around this time of the year.[36]

---

[1] Kellner, 106. [2] *De Soll. Pasch.*, 5; PG, 24, 699. [3] *Epist. ad Inquis. Januarii*, 54, 1; PL, 33, 200. [4] Greg.: *In Ascens. Christi*; PG, 46, 689.

Chrysost.: *Hom. in Ascens.*, 2; PG, 50, 444. [5] CIC, 1247, 1.
[6] Schuster, II, 373. [7] TE, I, 662. [8] Nilles, II, 340. [9] See note 6.
[10] CIC, 1252, 2. [11] *Hom. in Ascens.*, 2; PG, 50, 444. [12] MR, *Praefatio de Ascensione Domini.* [13] SSP, 93 f. [14] Adamnan, *De Locis Sacris,* I, 23, 24; CSEL, 39, 249 ff. [15] Dur., VI, 104, 1. [16] Kellner, 108.
[17] Schuster, II, 374. [18] Gugitz, I, 255. [19] TE, I, 662. [20] Schuster, II, 378. [21] N. Nilles, *Die Concilienfeste der orientalischen Kirche,* ZKTh, 6 (1882), 195 ff. [22] Kellner, 109. [23] Can. 43; Mansi, 2, 13.
[24] Nilles, II, 369. [25] ZKTh, 17 (1893), 527. [26] *In Ascens. Christi;* PG, 46, 689. [27] Nilles, II, 370; F. Cabrol, *Ascension,* DACL, 1.2 (1924), 2934 ff. [28] TE, I, 662, note. [29] E. Krebs, *Himmelfahrt Christi,* LThK, 5 (1933), 51. [30] A. Molien, *Ascension,* in *Catholicisme,* I (1948), 888 f. [31] N. C. Brooks, *Das Moosburger Himmelfahrtsspiel,* in *Zeitschrift für deutsches Altertum,* 50 (1925), 91 ff. [32] See also M. Grass-Cornet, *Von Palmeseln und tanzenden Engeln,* OiT, 155 ff.
[33] *Vermahnung an die Geistlichen zu Augsburg,* 1530. [34] Geramb, 87.
[35] Gugitz, I, 236 ff. (*Das Christi-Himmelfahrtsfest*). [36] ES, 20; Gugitz, I, 257.

CHAPTER

19   *Feast of Pentecost*

HISTORY AND LITURGY

"And when the days of Pentecost were drawing to a close, they were all together in one place. And suddenly there came a sound from heaven, as of a violent wind coming, and it filled the whole house where they were sitting. And there appeared to them parted tongues as of fire, which settled upon each of them. And they were all filled with the Holy Spirit and began to speak in foreign tongues, even as the Holy Spirit prompted them to speak" (Acts 2, 1-4).

Whitsunday (Pentecost), with Christmas and Easter, ranks among the great feasts of Christianity. It commemorates not only the descent of the Holy Spirit upon the Apostles and Disciples, but also the fruits and effects of that event: the completion of the work of redemption, the fullness of grace for the Church and its children, and the gift of faith for all nations.[1]

NAMES · The official name of the feast is "Pentecost." This word was used in the Old Testament. It comes from the Greek *pentekoste* (the fiftieth), meaning the fiftieth day after Easter. On this day the Jews celebrated a great religious festival of thanksgiving for the year's harvest, the Feast of Firstfruits (Exodus 23, 16). It was also called the "Feast of Weeks" because the day was reckoned by counting seven weeks after the Pasch (Leviticus 23, 15-21). Being the second in importance of the festivals of the Old Testament, it annually drew large crowds of Jewish pilgrims from the Diaspora (dispersion) into Jerusalem. This fact is mentioned in the report of Saint Luke: "There were staying at Jerusalem devout Jews from every nation under heaven . . ." (Acts 2, 5-11).

The Jews used the word Pentecost to indicate not only the feast itself, but also the whole season of fifty days preceding it. In this sense Saint Luke mentions it in his Acts (2, 1): "When the days of Pentecost were drawing to a close . . ." The early Christian Church accepted the Jewish usage and called the whole season from Easter to Whitsunday "Pentecost." It was a festive time of religious joy, no fasts were kept, and the faithful prayed standing in honor of Christ's resurrection.[2]

In most European languages the name of the feast comes from the ecclesiastical term: *Pentecôte* in French, *Pentecostés* in Spanish, *Pfingsten* in German, *Binkosti* in Slovenian, *Pünkösd* in Hungarian, *Pintse* in Danish, *Pentikosti* among the Slavs of the Eastern Church, and *Pentiqosti* in Syrian. A word meaning "Feast of the Holy Ghost" (*Duhovi, Turice*) is used by some Slavic nations, including the Serbs, Croats, and Slovaks, and by the Romanians (*Domineca Spiritului Santu*). The English word Whitsunday (White Sunday) originated because of the fact that the newly baptized appeared in white garments for the services of the day. Among the Arab-speaking Christians of the

Near East the festival is called '*id el-'uncure* (Feast of the Solemn Assembly), the word coming from the Hebrew '*asereth* (festive meeting).[3]

Some nations have appropriately named the feast after the ancient custom of decorating homes and churches with flowers and boughs. This practice goes back to the nature lore of the Indo-European races. At the time of full spring, when trees stood in their early foliage and flowers blossomed in abundance, our pre-Christian ancestors celebrated a gay festival, with maypole, May Queen, and May dance, during which they adorned their homes with flowers and branches of pale-green tender leaves. This custom was retained in Christian times, and some of its features were transferred to the Feast of Pentecost. Thus the festival is called the "Green Holyday" (*Zielone Swieta*) in Poland and among the Ukrainians, "Flower Feast" (*Blumenfest*) in Germany, "Summer Feast" (*Slavnost Letnice*) among the Czechs. In the Latin countries a similar term is used: *Pascha Rosatum,* in Latin, meaning "Feast of Roses." The Italian name *Pascua Rossa* (Red Pasch) was inspired by the color of the liturgical vestments.[4]

ORIGIN · Pentecost was held annually from a very early date. Since the liturgical celebration of the Lord's feasts started with Easter in apostolic times, Pentecost must have naturally suggested itself as a complementary festival commemorating the fulfillment and fruit of Christ's redemptive task and of His resurrection.

If and how Pentecost was observed in the first two centuries as a separate feast is not known.[5] The first mention of it as a great feast was made in the third century by Origenes and Tertullian.[6] The latter mentioned it as a well-established Christian feast and as the second date for the solemn baptism of catechumens (the first being Easter).[7] Bishop Eusebius of Caesaria (339) called it "all-blessed and all-holy [*panseptos kai panhagia*], the feast of feasts."[8] Saint John Chrysostom (407) used similar phrases in his sermons on Pentecost: "Today we have arrived at the peak of all blessings, we have reached the capital [*metropolis*] of feasts, we have obtained the very fruit of our Lord's promise."[9]

During the early centuries, just the day itself was celebrated in the Western Church. After the seventh century, however, the whole week came to be considered a time of festive observance.

Law courts did not sit, and servile work was forbidden during the entire octave.[10] The Council of Constance (1094) limited this prohibition to three days.[11] Pope Clement XIV, in 1771, abolished Tuesday as a prescribed holyday. Finally, in 1911, Pope Saint Pius X abolished Monday as a holyday of obligation; but most European countries, both Catholic and Protestant, still observe it as a legal holiday.

LITURGICAL OBSERVANCE · There are no special liturgical ceremonies on Whitsunday apart from the Holy Sacrifice, which is usually celebrated with festive splendor and solemnity. In the Latin Church the color of the liturgical vestments is red, symbolizing the love of the Holy Spirit Who descended upon the Apostles in tongues of fire.

After the Gradual of the Mass the ancient sequence *Veni Sancte Spiritus* (Come, Holy Spirit) is recited or sung on each day of Pentecost week. This hymn appeared first in liturgical books around the year 1200. It has been variously ascribed to Pope Innocent III (1216), to King Robert of France (1031), and even to Saint Gregory the Great (604). Most probably, however, its author was Cardinal Stephen Langton (1128), Archbishop of Canterbury. The poem has been known from medieval times as the "Golden Sequence" because of its richness in thought and expression. Each one of the short stanzas is a sentence in itself, thus facilitating meditation.[16]

Another liturgical hymn used in the Divine Office is the prayer poem *Veni Creator Spiritus* (Come, Creator Spirit). It was probably written by Rabanus Maurus (856), Archbishop of Mainz, and has been widely used from the end of the tenth century on.[18] Perhaps the best known among more than sixty English versions is the translation that John Dryden (1700) published in his book *Examen Poeticum* (1693).

In addition to its place in the Pentecost liturgy, the *Veni Creator* has also been assigned as the official opening prayer for Church councils and synods. It is recited and sung by the faithful all over the world at the start of important undertakings, such as the beginning of a school year, at conventions, missions, retreats, and on many similar occasions. It is interesting to note that the *Veni Creator* is the only ancient breviary hymn that has

been retained in the official prayer book of the Protestant Episcopal Church (in the service of ordination).

In the churches of the Byzantine Rite a moving Vesper service
is held on the evening of Whitsunday. After the joyful and festive
note of the day, this evening service suddenly assumes the character of a sorrowful, penitential ceremony. In simple vestments
of dark color the priests recite prayers of contrition and penance accompanied by humble prostrations and genuflections
(*gonuklisia*). The purpose of this ancient ritual is to atone, at
the end of the festive season, for all negligences and excesses
that might have been committed during the fifty joyful days
between Easter and Pentecost.[14]

In the Latin Church, a similar motive of atonement is ascribed
by Pope Saint Leo I (461) to the fast of the Ember Days in
Pentecost week. The fasting should be a penance for faults committed during the feasting and joyful celebrations of the Easter
season.[15]

No Octave Day · Pentecost is the only one of the high feasts
having an octave (*octava*) without an octave day (*dies octava*).
The following Sunday has always been called "First Sunday after
Pentecost." The liturgical notation in the breviary (after the None
of Saturday) also proclaims this fact: "End of the Easter season"
(*explicit Tempus Paschale*). This lack of an octave day is explained by the liturgical character of Pentecost, which in itself
concludes and terminates the great chain of commemorative celebrations connected with the Feast of the Resurrection.[16]

For the purpose of Easter Communion, however, the Church
has allowed the extension of "Easter time" to include the Sunday
after Pentecost (Trinity Sunday).[17]

Pentecost Vigil · As early as the third century the vigil service
of Whitsunday included the solemn rite of baptism in the Latin
Church. On Saturday afternoon the catechumens gathered in
church for prayers and preparation. The baptismal water was
blessed by the bishop. All these ceremonies followed quite closely
the ritual of the Easter Vigil.[18] In some churches they even blessed
a large candle and sang a hymn of praise (*praeconium*) as was

done during the Easter Vigil. These rites are no longer performed today.

In the Eastern churches Pentecost Vigil is not a fast day as it is in the Latin Church. They adhere to the ancient tradition of keeping the full fifty days from Easter to Pentecost as a time of joy, without penance or fast. A solemn and joyful vigil service is kept during the evening or night in the Byzantine Rite. The churches are brightly illuminated, and the congregation takes part in the hymns, prayers, and lessons of the vigil office (*pan-nychida:* all-night service), since they understand the language of the liturgy.[19]

Like Saturday before Septuagesima, this Saturday, in the countries of the Byzantine Rite, is also devoted to special prayer for the souls of the departed (*psycho-sabbaton:* Saturday of the Souls).[20] Before the vigil service starts (during and after the Office of the day), a fourfold blessing is bestowed upon a bowl of cooked wheat cereal mixed with ground nuts, spices, and honey. Cakes and breads of wheat flour, which the people bring, are also blessed.[21] These foods, called *Kollyba* (fine pastry), are a symbol of the resurrection of the body (see John 12, 24). They are offered by the faithful to friends and strangers, and are received with the words "May God grant them [the holy souls] the beatitude of Heaven." [22]

After the blessing of the *Kollyba*, a solemn procession is made to the cemetery, where the graves, decorated with flowers, are blessed by the priest. A joyful meal in the style of the ancient Christian *agape* (love feast) follows the ceremonies.[23]

FOLKLORE

HOLY GHOST DOVE · From the earliest centuries of the Christian era preachers and writers have mentioned the dove as a symbol of the Holy Spirit.[24] This symbolism, of course, was inspired by the Gospel report of Christ's baptism (Luke 3, 21-22). The dove, as a symbol of the Holy Spirit, may be seen in churches, on priestly vestments, on altars, tabernacles, sacred utensils, and in many religious paintings.

In medieval times the figure of a dove was widely used to enact in a dramatic way the descent of the Holy Spirit on Pentecost

Sunday. When the priest had arrived at the sequence, he sang the first words in a loud and solemn voice: *Veni Sancte Spiritus* (Come, Holy Ghost). Immediately there arose in the church a sound "as of a violent wind blowing" (Acts 2, 2). This noise was produced in some countries, like France, by the blowing of trumpets; in others by the choirboys, who hissed, hummed, pressed windbags, and rattled the benches. All eyes turned toward the ceiling of the church where from an opening called the "Holy Ghost Hole" there appeared a disc the size of a cart wheel, which slowly descended in horizontal position, swinging in ever-widening circles. Upon a blue background, broken by bundles of golden rays, it bore on its underside the figure of a white dove.

Meanwhile, the choir sang the sequence. At its conclusion the dove came to rest, hanging suspended in the middle of the church. There followed a "rain" of flowers indicating the gifts of the Holy Spirit, and of water symbolizing baptism. In some towns of central Europe people even went so far as to drop pieces of burning wick or straw from the Holy Ghost Hole, to represent the flaming tongues of Pentecost. This practice, however, was eventually stopped because it tended to put the people on fire externally, instead of internally as the Holy Spirit had done at Jerusalem. In the thirteenth century in many cathedrals of France real white pigeons were released during the singing of the sequence and flew around in the church while roses were dropped from the Holy Ghost Hole.[25]

Like all such religious pageants this dramatic addition to the liturgy of Whitsunday was attacked and ridiculed by the Lutheran reformers. Among other instances there is a report from the town of Biberach in Germany describing how in 1545 children broke the Holy Ghost Dove of the local church and carried the pieces in a mock procession through the streets.[26]

A fairly general custom in medieval times, and one still practiced in many sections of central and eastern Europe, is the use of artfully carved and painted wooden doves, representing the Holy Spirit. Usually this figure is suspended over the dining table. Often it is encased in a globe of glass, into which it has been assembled with painstaking effort, a constant reminder for the members of the family to venerate the Holy Spirit.

OTHER CUSTOMS · Like Easter night, the night of Pentecost is considered one of the great "blessed nights" of the year. In many sections of Europe it is still the custom to ascend hilltops and mountains during the early dawn of Whitsunday to pray. People call this observance "catching the Holy Ghost." Thus they express in symbolic language the spiritual fact that only by means of prayer can the divine dove be "caught" and the graces of the Holy Spirit obtained.

In rural sections of northern Europe superstitions ascribe a special power of healing to the dew that falls during Pentecost night. To obtain these blessings people walk barefoot through the grass on the early morning of the feast. They also collect the dew on pieces of bread which afterward are fed to their domestic animals as a protection against disease and accidents.[27] In many places, all through Whitsunday night can be heard the noise of shooting (*Pfingstschiessen*) and cracking of whips (*Pfingstschnalzen*).[28] In pre-Christian times this observance was held to frighten harmful powers away from home and harvest; in Christian times it assumed the character of a salute to the great feast.

The modern version of the ancient spring festival (maypole and May Queen) is connected with Pentecost in many sections of Europe. The queen is called "Pentecost Bride" (*Pfingstbraut*). Other relics of the Indo-European spring festival are the games, dances, and races held at Whitsuntide.[29] This tradition used to be most popular everywhere in the Middle Ages, and still is in central Europe. In England, Pentecost Sunday was a day of horse races, plays, and feasting (Whitsun ale). In Germany, too, people would hold banquets (*Pfingstgelage*) and drink "Pentecost beer." Finally, there exists a Christian version of ancient nature lore in the custom of blessing flowers, fields, and fruit trees on the Vigil of Pentecost.[30] In German-speaking countries the red peony (*paeonia officinalis*) bears the name *Pfingstrose* (Rose of Pentecost), and the oriole (*oriolus oriolus*) is called *Pfingstvogel* (Pentecost bird).

[1] H. Leclercq, *Pentecôte*, DACL, 14.1 (1939), 260 ff. [2] Nilles, II, 340. [3] The Arabic *'uncure* actually means "origin," but in this case

the term is an assimilation from the Hebrew *'asereth,* which was a name for solemn celebrations (assemblies) among the Jews. See Nehemias 8, 18 and Joel 1, 14. [4] Nilles, II, 397 f.; Benet, 66 f. [5] Kellner, 111. [6] *Contra Celsum,* 8, 22; see P. Koetschau (ed.), *Origenes (Die Griechischen christlichen Schriftsteller),* II, Leipzig, 1899, 239. [7] *De Bapt.,* 19; PL, 1, 1223. [8] *Vita Constantini,* IV, 64; PG, 20, 1220. [9] *In Pentec. hom.,* 2; PG, 6, 465. About Pentecost celebration in ancient Jerusalem see SSP, 93 f. [10] *Conc. Mogunt.,* 36; Mansi, 14, 73. [11] *Acta Conc. Constantin.;* Mansi, 20, 795 B. [12] A. Manser, *Veni Sancte Spiritus,* LThK, 10 (1938), 532 f. [13] G. C. Parabene, *Veni Creator Spiritus,* EI, 35 (1937), 117. [14] Nilles, II, 405. [15] CICI, *Decr. Gratiani, dist.,* 76, c. *Igitur,* 4. [16] Kellner, 115. [17] CIC, 859, 2. [18] TE, I, 663 f. [19] Nilles, I, 55. [20] Nilles, II, 381 ff. [21] Nilles, II, 379 f. [22] A. Gaudin, *Colybes,* DACL, 3.2 (1948), 2342 ff.; N. Nilles, *Eulogesis ton Kollybon,* ZKTh, 16 (1892), 350 ff. [23] Nilles, II, 380 f. [24] H. Leclercq, *Le Saint Esprit,* DACL, 5.1 (1922), 525 ff. [25] Gugitz, I, 287 (*Das Heiligengeistschwingen*). [26] Gugitz, I, 290. [27] Koren, 141; Geramb, 98. [28] Geramb, 89 ff. (*Die weltlichen Pfingst- bräuche*). [29] Gugitz, I, 280 ff. [30] Benet, 69; Koren, 141 f.; VL, 155 ff.

CHAPTER

20   *Feast of the Holy Trinity*

HISTORY AND LITURGY

ORIGIN · The greatest dogma of the Christian faith is the mystery of the Holy Trinity. (Mystery, in this connection, means a super- natural fact revealed by God which in itself transcends the natural power of human reasoning.) During the first thousand years of Christianity there was no special feast celebrated in honor of this mystery, but, as Pope Alexander II (1073) declared, every day of the liturgical year was devoted to the honor and adoration of the Sacred Trinity.[1]

However, to counteract the Arian heresy, which denied the fullness of divinity to the Son, a special Mass text in honor of the Holy Trinity was introduced and incorporated in the Roman liturgical books.[2] This Mass was not assigned for a definite day but could be used on certain Sundays according to the private devotion of each priest. (Such Mass texts which are not prescribed but open to choice on certain days are now known as "votive Masses.") From the ninth century on, various bishops of the Frankish kingdoms promoted in their own dioceses a special feast of the Holy Trinity, usually on the Sunday after Pentecost. They used a Mass text that Abbot Alcuin (804) is said to have composed.

Thus the custom of observing a special feast in honor of the Trinity became increasingly popular in the northern countries of Europe.[3] Several synods prescribed it for their respective territories in France, Germany, England, and The Netherlands. In the thirteenth century the orders of the Benedictines and Cistercians adopted the annual celebration of the feast. It was kept on different Sundays in different places, until in 1334 Pope John XXII accepted the festival into the official calendar of the Western Church and ordered that henceforth it should be held everywhere on the Sunday after Pentecost.[4]

A new Mass text was written and published. It is interesting to note that the beautiful Preface of the Trinity as read today is the same one that appeared in the first text of the Sacramentary of Saint Gregory the Great.[5] Most of the other prayers are of later origin. The Divine Office in its present form was arranged under Pope Saint Pius V (1572). It is one of the most sublime offices of the breviary.

The Feast of the Holy Trinity now belongs among the great annual festivals of Christianity. Although it is not observed with additional liturgical services outside the Mass, its celebration quickly took root in the hearts and minds of the faithful, and in all countries of Europe popular traditions are closely associated with this feast.

SIGN OF THE CROSS · The making of the sign of the cross, which professes faith both in the redemption of Christ and in the Trinity, was practiced from the earliest centuries. Saint Augustine (431) mentioned and described it many times in his sermons and letters.[6] In those days Christians made the sign of the cross (Redemption) with three fingers (Trinity) on their foreheads. The words ("In the name of the Father and the Son and the Holy Ghost") were added later. Almost two hundred years before Augustine, in the third century, Tertullian had already reported this touching and beautiful early Christian practice:

In all our undertakings—when we enter a place or leave it; before we dress; before we bathe; when we take our meals; when we light the lamps in the evening; before we retire at night; when we sit down to read; before each new task—*we trace the sign of the cross on our foreheads.*[7]

DOXOLOGY · The ancient Christian doxology (prayer of praise) "Glory be to the Father, and to the Son, and to the Holy Ghost" was used in the Oriental Church. The second part ("as it was in the beginning . . .") seems to have been added at the time of Emperor Constantine.[8] During the fifth century this beautiful short prayer came into the Western Church and spread very quickly. Since then it has been in constant use in both liturgical and private devotions. Finally, the Council of Narbonne (589) prescribed that it should be added after every psalm and hymn in the Divine Office.[9] It is an ancient tradition that in poetical hymns of the liturgy the Gloria Patri is rendered in a paraphrase (free version) within the last stanza.

EASTERN RITES · The churches of the Byzantine Rite do not celebrate the Feast of the Holy Trinity. Instead, they observe the Sunday after Pentecost as the Feast of All Saints (*Kyriake Ton Hagion Panton*). The official calendar of the Greek Church announces this feast with the interesting words "Today, on the first Sunday after Pentecost, we celebrate the festive day of all Saints everywhere in the world: in Asia, Lybia, in northern and eastern Europe." [10] As may be seen from the territories mentioned, the term "whole world" applies only to the countries of that rite. The Uniate Armenians keep the Feast of the Holy Trinity on the same day as the Latin Church.[11]

FOLKLORE

SYMBOLS · During the first centuries of the Christian era the Holy Trinity was sometimes represented in paintings by three young men of identical shape and looks. By the sixth century, however, it had become an accepted practice that only the Father and Son should be shown in human form; the Holy Spirit is represented by the figure of a dove.[12]

In medieval times there were many imaginative and symbolic pictures, as well as designs, to indicate the great mystery of the faith. The Church has not officially accepted any of them, has tolerated some, forbidden others. One of the best-known symbols of this kind is the trefoil (shamrock). A second plant to which this symbolism is attached is the pansy (*viola tricolor*), which even today is called "Trinity flower" in many parts of Europe. In Puerto Rico a delicately perfumed white flower with three petals is called *Trinitaria*. Another symbol is the figure of a triangle (Trinity) surrounded by rays (divinity) with the picture of an eye inside the triangle (omniscience and providence). This design became very popular and may be found all over Europe in homes, on wayside shrines, and even in churches. An interesting version of this symbol may be seen in the Great Seal of the United States (reproduced on every one-dollar bill).

Centuries ago, architecture made use of many, and sometimes strange, symbols to indicate the Trinity, like three animals (hares, stags, birds) in a circle, or three interlocked rings, or a candle with three flames. Some churches display an architectural number symbolism in honor of the Trinity. One of the most remarkable examples of this kind is the Holy Trinity Church of Stadl-Paura, Austria, built in 1722. It has three aisles, three towers, three doors, three windows on either side, three altars, three bells, and three rows of pews.[18]

SHRINES AND COLUMNS · From the fourteenth century on, the Holy Trinity was generally invoked for help against the dreaded epidemics of the Black Death. Hundreds of Trinity churches in Europe owe their existence to public vows made in time of pestilence and cholera. In subsequent ravages of those terrible diseases, these churches became much-frequented pilgrim shrines. Later, during the seventeenth and eighteenth centuries, public columns in honor of the Holy Trinity were placed in the main squares of cities and towns in central Europe.[14] Sculptured in marble or granite, they carry the traditional image of the Trinity and statues of the saints who were patrons against epidemics. Many of these columns are outstanding examples of late baroque art. The city of Vienna alone has eleven such Trinity columns which were erected during the epidemics of 1679 and 1713.[15]

POPULAR CELEBRATION · During the late Middle Ages and up to the eighteenth century, the Feast of the Holy Trinity was celebrated with popular manifestations of solemnity, special honor, and joy. As an example may serve the festival at the Trinity column of downtown Vienna, in 1680, where the famous Augustinian preacher Abraham a Santa Clara (1709) delivered a sermon before many thousands in the festively decorated square. At the end he appealed to the choir band to express with their instruments the honor, adoration, and gratitude of all to the Holy Trinity, "upon which the whole group of many trumpets and kettle-drums right joyfully broke out in a ringing fanfare." [16]

A proof of the great devotion to the Trinity was the Holy Trinity Confraternities, which flourished to such a degree during the seventeenth century that they surpassed most of the other similar organizations both in the number of local groups and in membership.[17]

SUPERSTITIONS · Whatever the weather on Trinity Sunday, it is said to be good and wholesome. "Trinity rain" is credited with special powers of health and fertility. Ghosts and witches are prevented from doing harm. Magic flowers blossom at midnight, bestowing on their finders all kinds of miraculous benefits like the healing of diseases, discovery of hidden treasures, protection against accidents, and freedom from pain for the rest of the year.[18]

On the other hand, in popular fantasy the neglect or desecration of this great Sunday is punished with dire misfortune. Those who refuse to attend service or who do menial work will suffer sickness, accidents, or even death within the year. Any work with metal instruments (including sewing needles) will bring the additional punishment of drawing lightning upon the house for the rest of the season. This superstition derives (as does that of Ascension Day) from the ancient lore of the death demons roaming the earth at this season of the year.[19]

---

[1] *Decret. Quoniam;* Latin text in Nilles, II, 460.   [2] *Lib. Sacram.,* 103; PL, 78, 116 ff.   [3] Jgn GK, 226; Rup. Tuit., *De divin. offic.,* 11, 1; PL, 170, 293.   [4] Nilles, II, 461.   [5] *Sacram. Gregor.;* PL, 78, 116. [6] VdM, 415 ff.   [7] *De Corona,* 3; PL, 2, 80.   [8] Nilles, II, 462 f.   [9] Can. 2; Mansi, 9, 1015.   [10] Nilles, II, 424 (Greek and Latin text).   [11] Nilles, II, 579.   [12] K. Künstle, *Ikonographie der christlichen Kunst,* Freiburg, 1928, I, 221 ff.   [13] Gugitz, I, 294 ff. (*Verehrung und Brauchtum der Hl. Dreifaltigkeit*).   [14] VL, 62.   [15] Gugitz, I, 298.   [16] F. Loidl, *Menschen im Barock,* Wien, 1938, 16.   [17] VL, 63.   [18] Gugitz, I, 295 f. [19] ES, 20.

CHAPTER

21   *Feast of Corpus Christi*

HISTORY AND LITURGY

ORIGIN · On Maundy Thursday, the day on which the Church commemorates the institution of the Holy Eucharist, it is impossible to honor the Blessed Sacrament with appropriate solemn and joyful rites. Such a festival is precluded by the sad and sorrowful memories of the day—the betrayal of Judas, Christ's agony and arrest, Peter's denial—and by the fact that other prescribed ceremonies are already occupying the time of clergy and faithful on Holy Thursday.[1]

It was a humble nun in Belgium, Saint Juliana (1258), Prioress of Mont Cornillon, who first suggested and advocated a special feast in honor of the Blessed Sacrament to be celebrated on a day other than Maundy Thursday.[2] From her sixteenth year she had often in her prayers beheld a strange sight: it was as if the full moon appeared to her in brilliant light, while a part of its disc remained black and lightless. Finally, in a vision, Christ showed her the meaning of this picture. The moon represented the ecclesiastical year; the black spot indicated the lack of a festival in honor of the Blessed Sacrament. She was to announce to the authorities of the Church that God wished such a feast to be established.

In 1230 Juliana communicated her secret to a small group of learned theologians. As her message became publicly known, she had to suffer scorn and ridicule for some years. But the bishop of her diocese (Liége) and some of his canons eventually lent a willing ear to her appeals. A diocesan synod in 1246 decided in her favor and prescribed such a feast for the churches of Liége.[3]

Was it mere coincidence that one of the men who had supported her efforts in Belgium later became pope? He was Jacques Pantaléon, Archdeacon of Liége. Upon his election to the papal office he assumed the name of Urban IV (1261-1265). On September 8, 1264, six years after Juliana's death, he established for the whole Church that festival in honor of the Holy Eucharist which the saintly nun had proclaimed to be willed by God. It was to be celebrated with great solemnity on the Thursday after Pentecost week, and indulgences were granted to all who would receive Holy Communion or attend special devotions in addition to hearing Mass.[4]

Urban IV commissioned the great Dominican scholar Saint Thomas Aquinas to compose the texts of Mass and Divine Office for the new feast. The splendor, depth, and devotion of the prayers and hymns that Saint Thomas wrote have enriched the liturgy with one of its most beautiful rituals. They are still in use today, admired and appreciated by people of all faiths.[5]

The bull of Urban IV had no immediate effect because he died soon after its publication, and the succeeding popes did not urge the matter. Finally, however, Pope Clement V, in 1314, renewed the decrees in a bull of his own, and then the feast spread quickly throughout the Latin Church.[6] Later it was also accepted by some parts of the Oriental Church (Syrians, Armenians, Copts, and Melchites).[7] The churches of the Greeks, Ukrainians, and Russians (of the Greek Catholic Rite) do not celebrate this feast.[8]

Corpus Christi is a holyday of obligation. In the United States, however, the faithful are exempt from the obligation by a special dispensation of the Holy See.[9]

NAMES · The official title of the feast is, in the Latin Church, *Festum Sanctissimi Corporis Christi* (Feast of the Most Holy Body of Christ). In Greek it is called *Tou Somatos Tou Kyriou Heorte* (Feast of the Body of the Lord). From these ecclesiastical terms many Christian nations have adopted popular names for the feast, like the English and Spanish *Corpus Christi,* the German *Fronleichnam* (Body of the Lord), the Slavic *Boze Telo* (Body of God), the Syriac *pagre d' maran* (Body of the Lord), and the Arabic *'id el-jesed el-ilahi* (Feast of the Body of God). Other names are *Fête Dieu* (Feast of God) in French, *Úrnapja* (Day of the Lord) in Hungarian, *Brasancevo* (Sacred Bread) among the southern Slavs.[10]

PROCESSION · Very early (in the fourteenth century) the custom developed of carrying the Blessed Sacrament in a splendid procession through the town after the Mass on Corpus Christi Day. This was encouraged by the popes, some of whom granted special indulgences to all participants.[11] The Council of Trent (1545-1563) solemnly approved and recommended the procession on Corpus Christi as a public profession of the Catholic faith in the real presence of Christ in the Holy Sacrament.[12]

During the later Middle Ages these processions developed into splendid pageants of devotion and honor to the Blessed Sacrament. They are still publicly held, and often with the ancient splendor, in Italy, France, Spain, Portugal, Austria, Belgium, Ireland, in the Catholic sections of Germany, Holland, Switzerland, Canada, Hungary, and in the Slavic countries and South America. Sovereigns and princes, presidents and ministers of the state, magistrates, members of trade and craft guilds, and honor guards of the armed forces accompany the liturgical procession while the church bells peal, bands play sacred hymns, and the faithful kneel in front of their homes to adore the Eucharistic Lord. The houses along the route of the procession are decorated with little birch trees and green boughs.[13] Candles and pictures adorn the windows; and in many places, especially in Latin countries, the streets are covered with carpets of grass and flowers, often wrought in beautiful designs.[14]

A special and appealing ritual in the procession is an adaptation of the ancient Roman usage of "Stations." Stops are made at various points along the route, the Blessed Sacrament is put on an altar table, and a passage of the Gospel is sung, followed by a hymn and a liturgical prayer for God's blessing upon the town, the people, and the harvest. A Eucharistic benediction concludes each Station. This ritual, approved by Pope Martin V (1431),[15] is still observed everywhere in the Catholic sections of central Europe and in some Latin countries.[16]

HYMNS · The solemnity of the Corpus Christi festival is enhanced by the additional use of Alleluia in the prayers of the liturgy (as at Easter time). Saint Thomas Aquinas has magnificently expressed the jubilant character of the day in his famous hymns, especially in *Sacris Solemniis,* which is recited during the matins of the feast and sung at the procession:

> Sacris solemniis juncta sint gaudia,
> Et ex praecordiis sonent praeconia;
> Recedant vetera, nova sint omnia,
> Corda, voces et opera.[17]

Great is the festive day, joyful and jubilant,
Let us with loving hearts offer the song of praise;
Freed from the sinful past, may we renew in grace
All our thoughts and words and deeds.

The fifth stanza of *Sacris Solemniis* has been used for centuries as a separate hymn in honor of the Blessed Sacrament. As *Panis Angelicus* (Bread of the Angels) it is known and cherished widely among Christians of many denominations. The best musical settings are those of César Franck (1890), of the French Jesuit Louis Lambilotte (1855), and the powerful four-part setting usually ascribed to C. Casiolini which, however, should be more correctly credited to Jacopo Tomadini (1883).

Another hymn by Saint Thomas, *Pangue Lingua Gloriosi Corporis Mysterium* (Praise, o tongue, the mystery of the glorious Body), contains the two stanzas which are sung all over the world at every Eucharistic service, *Tantum Ergo* and *Genitori*.[18] The best known, and perhaps most beautiful, of any musical settings has remained the Gregorian chant tune (Mode III).

For the Lauds of Corpus Christi, Aquinas wrote the hymn *Verbum Supernum Prodiens* (The Divine Word coming forth).[19] Again the last stanza preceding the customary conclusion in praise of the Trinity has become a favorite song and prayer in itself:

O salutaris hostia,
Quae caeli pandis ostium,
Bella praemunt hostilia:
Da robur, fer auxilium.

O saving host, o bread of life,
Thou goal of rest from pain and strife,
Embattled are we, poor and weak:
Grant us the strength and help we seek.

Finally, there is the sequence of the Mass, *Lauda Sion Salvatorem* (Sion, praise thy Lord and Saviour).[20] Saint Thomas enumerates in unmistakable words the main truths of Christ's revelation and the Church's teaching about the Holy Eucharist. In many countries a translation of this sequence into the vernacular is sung by the people as a popular church hymn in honor of the Blessed Sacrament.

The most famous nonliturgical hymn in honor of the Blessed Sacrament is the ancient prayer poem *Ave Verum Corpus* (Hail, true Body). It appeared first in manuscripts at the end of the fourteenth century and is ascribed to Pope Innocent VI (1362).[21] Its original purpose was to serve as a private prayer for the faithful to be said at the elevation of the sacred Host during Mass (*In elevatione Corporis Christi*). This jewel of sacred poetry soon spread through most Catholic countries of Europe. It became famous also among other Christians through the musical setting of exquisite beauty written by Mozart (1791). Other familiar musical arrangements are those of Gounod (1893) and Saint-Saëns (1921).

FOLKLORE

PAGEANTS · In most European countries mystery plays used to be performed after the procession in public squares or in churches. The Corpus Christi pageants were highly popular, especially in England, Germany, and Spain. Perhaps the most famous of them are the *Autos Sacramentales* (Plays of the Sacrament) by the Spanish priest and poet Pedro Calderón de la Barca (1681). They are still performed today on special occasions, such as centenary celebrations, Eucharistic congresses, and ecclesiastical jubilees.[22]

By the seventeenth century, the Corpus Christi processions had developed unusual features which appealed to the mood of baroque piety and were highly favored in all European countries where processions could be held. Saint George and his dragon (in many places Saint Margaret, too), the main characters of the famous mystery pageant of medieval days, now appeared in the procession itself.[23] In Bavaria, impersonations of demons ran along, expressing in vivid pantomime their fright and fear of the Blessed Sacrament.[24] In Belgium and France boys and girls dressed as ancient gods and goddesses, sitting on figures of wild animals, rode in the procession to symbolize the fact that even the pagan past had to rise again and pay tribute to the Eucharistic Lord.[25]

All kinds of symbolic pictures and representations were carried (or walked) in the Corpus Christi processions of western and southern Germany: Moses with the brazen serpent; David and Goliath; the synagogue, symbolized by a withered tree from which hung a broken scepter; the Easter lamb, blood running from its open wound; the figure of Christ wrapped in burial linen and carried by angels dressed in black; the Sorrowful Virgin, followed by thirty mourning women and forty men who walked with outstretched arms, and others.[26]

Especially favored was the attendance of children dressed as angels. Already in 1496, at the great children's procession in

Florence, Savonarola had all of them appear in white or garbed as angels. This custom quickly spread all over Europe in the following centuries. At the Corpus Christi procession in Mainz in 1613 hundreds of children, impersonating the nine choirs of angels, marched before the Blessed Sacrament while many other "angels" strewed flowers in front of the Eucharistic Lord.[27]

These manifestations of baroque piety were gradually restricted and most of them suppressed during the second half of the eighteenth century, not without some resistance and much complaining on the part of the population. In some cities even Lutherans protested against the suppression because, not having processions of their own, they had enjoyed watching these features of the Catholic pageant.[28]

In Spain many figures of gigantic size and other figures with immense masks (*Gigantes y Cabezudos*), representing famous persons of the Old Testament, took part, and still do, in the procession.[29] They perform traditional dances in the street, accompanied by the quaint strains of an ancient melody. In the churches of Spain groups of choirboys danced before the altar in honor of the Blessed Sacrament. The most famous of these Eucharistic dances, still practiced today, is performed on Corpus Christi and some other feast days in the Cathedral of Seville.[30]

DAY OF WREATHS · In central Europe, and also in France, Corpus Christi Day is the "Day of Wreaths" (*Kranzeltag*) and of huge bouquets of flowers borne on the top of wooden poles (*Prangtag*).[31] Wreaths and bouquets of exquisite flowers in various colors are attached to flags and banners, to houses, and to the arches of green boughs that span the streets. The clergy and altar boys wear little wreaths on their left arms in the procession; girls carry wreaths on their heads. Even the monstrance containing the Blessed Sacrament is adorned with a wreath of choice flowers on Corpus Christi Day.[32] In Poland these wreaths are blessed by the priest on the eve of the feast day. After the solemnities people decorate their homes with them. Some are suspended on the walls of the houses or affixed to doors and windows. Others are put up in gardens, fields, and pastures, with a prayer for protection and blessing upon the growing harvest.[33]

AMERICAN PLACE NAMES · In the New World the Feast of Corpus
Christi was celebrated during the sixteenth and seventeenth centuries, with the usual solemn observance, by the missionaries and
their native converts in Florida, California, Texas, New Mexico,
and in the missions of New France (Canada and the Great Lakes
region). In honor of the festival the Franciscans named a bay
of the Gulf of Mexico "Corpus Christi Bay." Later a town,
founded on the shore of that bay, was given the same title—
Corpus Christi, Texas. In a similar way the capital of California
was named Sacramento after the river on which it is situated,
which had been named by the missionaries in honor of the Holy
Eucharist.[34]

[1] A. Browe, *Die Verehrung der Eucharistie im Mittelalter,* München,
1933.   [2] *Vita S. Julianae,* in *Acta SS. Boll.,* April 1, 473 (*Prolegom.,*
442 ff.).   [3] Kellner, 121.   [4] Bull *Si Dominus* of Clement V, containing
the text of the bull *Transiturus* of Urban IV. Latin text in Nilles, II,
469 ff.   [5] *Officium de Festo Corporis Christi,* ed. R. Spiazzi, Turino,
1954 (*Opuscula Theologica,* II), 275 ff. About Saint Thomas's authorship of the hymn *Adoro Te* see 274 (bibliography).   [6] The final
establishment of the Feast of Corpus Christi is often ascribed to the
Council of Vienne (1311); however, it was the pope himself (Clement
V) who decreed it. See Nilles, II, 464 f. and K. Hefele, *Konzilien-
geschichte,* Freiburg, VI (1890), 522.   [7] D. Attwater, "An Eastern
Procession at Corpus Christi," OF, 2 (1928), 211 ff.   [8] Nilles, II, 467.
[9] *Responsum,* December 31, 1885; Balt., CV.   [10] Nilles, II, 464.
[11] Especially Eugene IV (1447) in his bull *Excellentissimus* of May
26, 1433. See N. Maurel, *Ablässe,* Paderborn, 1874, 238 f.   [12] *Sess.,*
XIII, *De Eucharistia,* cap. 5; Mansi, 33, 82.   [13] G. Ellard, *Corpus
Christi in St. Andrä,* OF, 4 (1930), 443 ff.; Gugitz, II, 309 ff. (*Fron-
leichnam*).   [14] See pictures and descriptions of flower carpets in *The
National Geographic Magazine,* 107.4 (1955), 491, and in J. L.
Monks, *Great Catholic Festivals,* New York, 1951.   [15] SRC, *Decr.,*
September 23, 1820 (Approval of the Stations). See R. Stepper,
Fronleichnamsprozession, LThK, 4 (1932), 215 f.   [16] Koren, 162;
Trapp, 150 ff.   [17] HRL, 120 f. English trans. by the author.   [18] HRL,
118 f.   [19] HRL, 122 f.   [20] HRL, 124 f.   [21] I. Cecchetti, *Ave Verum
Corpus Natum,* EC, 2 (1949), 535 f.   [22] *Autos sacramentales,* in
Enciclop. Universal, Madrid, s.a., 10, 657.   [23] VL, 84; Gugitz, I,

310 ff. [24] M. J. Rudwin, *Der Teufel in den deutschen geistlichen Spielen des Mittelalters und der Reformationszeit,* Göttingen, 1915, 152 ff. [25] VI., 86. [26] VI., 84. [27] VI., 87 f. [28] VI., 90. [29] See pictures in *Enciclop. Universal,* Madrid, s.a., 10, 134 (*Cabezudos*). [30] W. H. Grattan Flood, "The Corpus Christi Dance in Seville Cathedral," in *The London Tablet,* 145.6 (1925), 756. [31] See pictures in Koren (*Bildanhang*). [32] Koren, 146 ff. (*Fronleichnam*). [33] Gugitz, I, 313 f. [34] Z. Engelhardt, *The Missions and Missionaries of California,* San Francisco, I (1908), 48 ff., III (1910), 27; *Jesuit Relations,* 30, 181; 32, 89 ff.; Enc. Brit., 19 (1949), 799 (*Corpus Christi*).

CHAPTER

22   *Thanksgiving*

HISTORY AND LITURGY

THANKSGIVING RITES · The religious function of giving thanks to Divinity for favors received is as old as humanity. In fact, it is one of the basic elements of worship in all religions, flowing directly from the moral law of nature which governs the relation of man to God and attaches a fourfold purpose to the acts of worship: adoration, petition, atonement, thanksgiving. Thus we find sacrifices and thanksgiving rites as far back as we have documentary and archaeological evidence on the purpose of any forms of worship.

The Jews in the Old Testament had an elaborate ritual of sacrifices and offerings in thanksgiving to God. The details of these thank offerings are prescribed in the Law of Moses (Leviticus 1, 2, 3, 7, etc.). They were either private acts of thanksgiving on the part of individuals or public acts of worship offered in the name of the whole community. The gifts offered consisted of the sacrifice of animals or the presentation of ritual loaves, cakes, and wafers.

In the New Testament, also, the Sacrifice of the Mass contains the same fourfold purpose prescribed by natural law. The function of thanksgiving has never been overlooked. The early Christians were so much aware of it that they called the Blessed Sacrament, which is offered in the Mass, *Eucharist* (thanksgiving). Due to the fact that the Holy Sacrifice is the greatest act of thanksgiving that could possibly be offered to God, the Church has refrained from instituting any special feast or liturgical ceremony of thanksgiving other than the Mass. In the Catholic Church, liturgically speaking, every day of the year is "Thanksgiving Day." [1]

SPECIAL OCCASIONS · There is, however, the psychological need of special manifestations of thanksgiving for the people on certain occasions. In such cases, as at the end of an epidemic, or liberation from a threatened disaster, or signing of a peace treaty, great celebrations of thanksgiving have been held since medieval times. As far as their religious significance is concerned, they consist either in a Mass of thanksgiving celebrated with unusual splendor and solemnity or in a service of Benediction of the Blessed Sacrament. At the end of such services it is customary to recite or sing the ancient (fourth-century) hymn *Te Deum Laudamus* (God, we praise Thee), and to add the liturgical Mass prayer of thanksgiving.[2]

A free translation in the vernacular, "Holy God, we praise Thy name," is often sung on such occasions. The English text is a translation from the German. The author of this hymn was Johann Franz (1790), and the tune is taken from a cantata of K. Bone (1852):

> *Holy God, we praise thy name,*
> *Lord of all, we bow before thee;*
> *All on earth thy sceptre claim,*
> *All in Heav'n above adore thee.*
> *Infinite thy vast domain,*
> *Everlasting is thy reign.*

HARVEST FESTIVALS

PRE-CHRISTIAN FEATURES · One special, and yearly, thanksgiving celebration going back to ancient times took place at the successful conclusion of the harvest. That is why we find harvest festivals with thanksgiving rites everywhere as far back as we can go in our knowledge of religions and cultures. Among the Indo-European races it was the great "Mother of Grains" to whom these rites were addressed. Within the various ancient nations this common mythological Mother of Fields was represented as a national god or goddess of vegetation (Astarte, Osiris, Tammuz, Demeter, Ceres). Great festivals were held every year in their honor in thanksgiving for the harvest. The most famous of all these feasts were the Eleusinian Mysteries in Greece, held every September as a tribute to the grain goddess Demeter.[3]

Among the Slavic, Germanic, and Celtic races the ancient belief in the great Mother of Grains has persisted to our day in the form of many superstitious practices connected with fall harvesting, especially with the "last sheaf" in every field. Sometimes the sheaf is personified, molded into the form of a straw doll and, as "harvest baby," carried in joyful procession from the field to the village.[4] In Austria it is shaped into a wreath and placed on the head of a girl who then is designated at the harvest festival as "queen" or "bride" (*Erntebraut*). Similar customs were universally practiced in England, where the last load brought home with great rejoicing bore the name "horkey cart," and in Scotland, where the last sheaf is called "kirn [grain] doll." [5]

In northern France harvesters, seated on top of the last load brought home from the fields, chant an ancient traditional tune to the text *Kyre-o-ôle*. This is an interesting relic of folklore from Carolingian times, when shepherds and field workers cheered their solitary toil by singing the Kyrie eleison as they had heard the monks sing it at High Mass. In southern France the last sheaf was tied in the form of a cross, decorated with ribbons and flowers, and after the harvest celebration was placed in the best room of the house to be kept as a token of blessing and good fortune.

JEWISH CELEBRATIONS · Moses instituted among the Jews two great religious feasts of thanksgiving for the harvest: the Feast of the Spring Harvest (*Hag Shavu'oth,* Feast of Weeks, or Pentecost; Leviticus 23, 15-21) and the Feast of the Fall Harvest (*Sukkoth,* Feast of Tabernacles; Leviticus 29-43): [6]

Thou shalt celebrate the festival of weeks to the Lord thy God, a voluntary oblation of thy hand which thou shalt offer according to the blessing of the Lord thy God. And thou shalt feast before the Lord thy God, thou and thy son, and thy daughter, and thy manservant, and thy maidservant, and the Levite that is within thy gates, and the stranger and the fatherless, and the widow, who abide with you in the place . . . (Deuteronomy 16, 9-11).

Thou also shalt celebrate the solemnity of tabernacles seven days, when thou hast gathered in thy fruit of the barnfloor and of the winepress. And thou shalt make merry in thy festival time, thou, thy son, and thy daughter, thy manservant, and thy maidservant, the Levite also and the stranger, and the fatherless and the widow that are within thy gates (Deuteronomy 16, 13-15).

CHRISTIAN TRADITIONS · In the Christian era the custom of celebrating a thanksgiving harvest festival began in the High Middle Ages. For lack of any definite liturgical day or ceremony prescribed by the Church, various practices came to be observed locally. In many places, as in Hungary, the Feast of the Assumption included great thanksgiving solemnities for the grain harvest. Delegates from all parts of the country came for the solemn procession to Budapest, carrying the best samples of their produce. A similar ceremony was observed in Poland, where harvest wreaths brought to Warsaw from all sections were bestowed on the president in a colorful pageant.[7] These wreaths (*wieniec*), made up of the straw of the last sheaf (*broda*), were beautifully decorated with flowers, apples, nuts, and ribbons, and blessed in churches by the priests.

The most common, and almost universal, harvest and thanksgiving celebration in medieval times was held on the Feast of Saint Martin of Tours (Martinmas) on November 11. It was a holiday in Germany, France, Holland, England, and in central Europe.[8] People first went to Mass and observed the rest of the day with games, dances, parades, and a festive dinner, the main feature of the meal being the traditional roast goose (Martin's goose).[9] With the goose dinner they drank "Saint Martin's wine," which was the first lot of wine made from the grapes of the recent harvest.[10] Martinmas was the festival commemorating filled barns and stocked larders, the actual Thanksgiving Day of the Middle Ages. Even today it is still kept in rural sections of Europe, and dinner on Martin's Day would be unthinkable without the golden-brown, luscious Martin's goose.[11]

THANKSGIVING DAY IN AMERICA

PILGRIMS' CELEBRATION · The tradition of eating goose as part of the Martin's Day celebration was kept in Holland even after the Reformation. It was there that the Pilgrims who sailed to the New World in 1620 became familiar with this ancient harvest festival. When, after one year in America, they decided to celebrate a three days' thanksgiving in the autumn of 1621, they went in search of geese for their feast. We know that they also had deer (a present from the Indians), lobsters, oysters, and fish. But Edward Winslow, in his account of the feast, only mentions that "Governor Bradford sent foure men on fowling that so we might after a more speciall manner rejoice together, after we had gathered the fruit of our labours." They actually did find some wild geese, but a number of wild turkeys and ducks as well.[12]

The Pilgrim Fathers, therefore, in serving wild turkeys with the geese, inaugurated one of the most cherished American traditions: the turkey dinner on Thanksgiving Day. They also drank, according to the ancient European tradition, the first wine of their wild-grape harvest.[13] Pumpkin pie and cranberries were not part of the first Thanksgiving dinner in America, but were introduced many years afterward.

The second Thanksgiving Day in the New World was held by the Pilgrims two years later, on July 30, 1623. It was formally proclaimed by the governor as a day of prayer to thank God for their deliverance from drought and starvation, and for the safe arrival from Holland of the ship *Anne*.[14]

NATIONAL CELEBRATION · In 1665 Connecticut proclaimed a solemn day of thanksgiving to be kept annually on the last Wednesday in October. Other New England colonies held occasional and local Thanksgivings at various times. In 1789 the federal Congress authorized and requested President George Washington to proclaim a day of thanksgiving for the whole nation. Washington did this in a message setting aside November 26, 1789 as National Thanksgiving Day.[15]

After 1789 the celebration reverted to local and regional observance for almost a hundred years. There grew, however, a strong desire among the majority of the people for a national Thanksgiving Day that would unite all Americans in a festival of gratitude and public acknowledgment for all the blessings God had conferred upon the nation. It was not until October 3, 1863, that this was accomplished, when President Abraham Lincoln issued, in the midst of the Civil War, a Thanksgiving Proclamation. In it the last Thursday of November was set apart for that purpose and made a national holiday.[16]

Since then, every president has followed Lincoln's example, and annually proclaims as a "Day of Thanksgiving" the fourth Thursday in November. Only President Franklin D. Roosevelt changed the date, in 1939, from the fourth to the third Thursday of November (to extend the time of Christmas sales). This caused so much consternation and protest that in 1941 the traditional date was restored.[17]

[1] F. Cabrol, *Eucharistie*, DACL, 5.1 (1922), 686 ff.; M. B. Hellriegl, "Let Us Give Thanks," OF, 15 (1941), 541 ff. [2] HRL, 12 f. On the author of the *Te Deum* see A. E. Burn, *Niceta of Remesiana*, Cambridge, 1905. [3] Frazer, 393 ff. [4] Frazer, 412 ff.; Benet, 80 ff.; Geramb, 140 ff. (*Die Erntefeste*). [5] Hackwood, 206; Frazer, 406 f. [6] Sr. M. Charity, "Thanking for Harvests," OF, 23 (1949), 538 ff. [7] Benet, 81 ff. [8] J. Uttenweiler, *Martin von Tours*, LThK, 6 (1934), 984 ff. [9] Geramb, 182 ff. (*Martinitag*); Hackwood, 201 ("St. Martin's goose"). [10] Hackwood, 207; VL, 167. [11] Gugitz, II, 178 ff. (*Martiniloben*); Koren, 183. [12] Linton, 59 ff. See E. Arber, *The Story of the Pilgrim Fathers*, Boston, 1897 (contains the text of Winslow's relation "Good Newes from New-England"). [13] B. Smith, *Bradford of Plymouth*, Philadelphia, 1951, 162 f. [14] Linton, 72. [15] Linton, 83 ff. (text of Washington's proclamation). [16] Linton, 89 ff. [17] Linton, 94 f.

PART III

23 *Veneration of Saints*

HISTORY AND LITURGY

Interwoven with the festive seasons and the cycles of weekly liturgy is the liturgical system of saints' days. From the beginnings of Christianity there has been no doubt (as there was none among the Jews) that persons who led a life of great holiness or suffered and died for the cause of God enjoyed the glories of a special reward in Heaven and deserved highest esteem and veneration from the faithful on earth. The Bible, in the book of the Apocalypse, mentions various kinds of "saints": the virgins (14, 1-5), the prophets and Apostles (18, 20), the martyrs for the word of God (6, 9), the martyrs of Jesus (17, 6), and all those who died in the Lord and whose good works follow them (14, 13).[1]

MARY · A great and popular veneration of Mary, the Mother of God (*Theotokos*), existed in the early Church long before any special feast was instituted in her honor. To her is accorded a veneration (*hyperdulia*) that transcends the honor given to any other saint (*dulia*).[2] Her dignity as the Mother of the Incarnate Word of God, and the spiritual privileges conferred on her by reason of this dignity, raise her beyond all created spirits to the exalted position of "Queen of all Saints." On the other hand, she still remains a mere creature in all her glory. The Church has never "adored" Mary or accorded her any honors that are reserved for Divinity.

Wall paintings in the Roman catacombs, dating from the first half of the second century, picture her holding the Divine Child, usually with a Biblical scene for background. The earliest apocrypha (legendary Christian literature) of the second century bear eloquent testimony to the veneration that was accorded Mary at the very dawn of Church history. The first known hymns and poetical prayers to her were written by the deacon of the church of Ephesus, Saint Ephrem the Syrian (373). His twenty *madrase* (poems) on Mary breathe not only tender devotion, but classic beauty as well. Here is a translation of a stanza of one of his hymns:

> *Blessed are you, Mary, for in your soul dwelled the*
> *   Holy Spirit of Whom David sang.*
> *Blessed are you who were deemed worthy to be greeted*
> *   by the Father through Gabriel's mouth.*
> *Blessed are you who were made to be the living chariot*
> *   of the Son of God.*
>
> *He stood on your knees,*
> *He lay in your arms,*
> *He drank from the fountains of your breasts.*
> *He rested, a baby, in your embrace:*
> *But His gown was the flaming light of Divinity.*[3]

The feasts of our Lady observed in the universal Church are quite numerous. They form a radiant pattern of festive commemorations through the year. Some of them have affected the public life of communities and countries for many centuries. Others are celebrated only within the confines of liturgical service. All of them cast the light and warmth of their blessing into the hearts of devout Christians everywhere.

Five festivals, called the "major feasts of Mary," were kept as public holydays (and holidays) up to the present century. It was as recently as 1918 that the new Code of Canon Law dropped three of them from the list of prescribed holydays. In the liturgy, however, they still retain their place, and rank as major feasts. Many ancient customs connected with them have survived to our day.

MARTYRS · In addition to the Biblical saints, Christians immediately began to honor the memory of those who died in the persecutions. This was done on a local scale within each Christian community. The tombs of the martyrs were held in high veneration. On the anniversary of their deaths Mass was celebrated over their graves and a sermon preached. Thus it happened, for instance, that Saint Pionius and his companions were seized by Roman soldiers while conducting the anniversary service at the tomb of Saint Polycarp of Smyrna (Asia Minor) in 250 and were themselves put to death and became martyrs of Christ.[4]

The custom of calling the death date of a martyr his "birthday" (*Dies Natalis*) originated in the early centuries. It expresses the truth that any Christian who remained loyal to the Lord unto the death of martyrdom is truly born into eternal glory at the hour of his execution. The official calendars of both the Eastern and Western Churches have retained this practice to our day. When they announce the "birthday" of a saint it means the day of his death. The only exceptions are the natural birthdays of the three persons who were born into this world without original sin: Christ, Mary, and John the Baptist. Of these three the Church celebrates their earthly nativity as well as the day of death.

During the persecutions in the Roman Empire each community commemorated only its local martyrs. Their names and the dates of their execution were carefully recorded, and each church kept the official list of its heroes. In larger places like Rome, Christian notaries were appointed for the various districts (*regiones*) of the city. It was their task to observe and record all cases of executions of Christians in their particular district. Thus came into existence the venerable catalogues of martyrs in the various cities of the Roman Empire. They were not only read at divine service, but were often engraved on tablets of marble and set up as a public notice for the faithful, to remind them to honor and venerate their local saints.[5]

Concerning the graves of the early martyrs, there is no doubt that the great majority of them remained well identified. According to Roman law, up to the time of Diocletian (305), even executed criminals were entitled to an honorable burial, for earthly justice was satisfied by the death of the guilty person. The body usually was granted to relatives or friends to be duly buried.[6] Thus the tombs of the saints were naturally well known to the bishops and faithful, for in many cases they themselves had selected the burial place, given the last honors to the sacred bodies, and laid them to rest with their own hands. A tradition based on the certitude of such direct evidence is not easily lost even in the course of centuries. This was confirmed by the results of recent research and excavations in various places.

However, with the increasing number and scope of persecutions, many martyrs remained unlisted, and all anniversaries could not be kept even within a particular community. For this reason, only the outstanding few received an established annual feast of memorial services. All the others shared one great feast in common, to give due honor and recognition to their memory every year. This was the "Feast of All Martyrs," instituted in the Eastern Church in the fifth century, and adopted by Rome in the seventh century. Its title was later changed to "Feast of All Saints."

OTHER SAINTS · In the third century the bishops began also listing the names of persons who did not reach the point of execution, but died a natural death after having suffered persecution for the sake of Christ, like Saint Nicholas, who had been in prison for many years but was finally released in 312 at the end of the persecutions. These saints were added to the list under the name of "confessors," because they had heroically confessed their faith before the tribunals.[7] This term has remained in official use up to the present. It now designates any male saint who through the practice of heroic virtue gave witness to Christ. Holy women are identified in liturgical usage as "martyrs" or "virgins" or "virgins and martyrs" or "neither virgins nor martyrs" (a somewhat unfortunate negative term meaning those who became saints as wives and mothers).

In the Western Church, the conversion of the Germanic races brought about an extension of the local calendars of saints. Having no Christian past of their own, they adopted the ritual books of the Roman Church and its list of saints as well. It was not long, however, before they added the names of their own national heroes of God to the annual calendar of saints' feasts and thus prepared the way for a more universal calendar. In the course of the succeeding centuries the Roman list of saints' days was gradually widened by the authorities of the Church; it came to include saints of other local churches and other nations, until the Roman Missal and martyrology became truly representative of the universal Church.[8]

In the Mass text, however, a relic of the original practice remains, for the saints mentioned in the Canon of the Mass are taken from the ancient list of the Italian community.[9] The Oriental Rites were even slower than Rome in adopting the feasts of "foreign" martyrs and saints. Up to this day but few saints of the Western Church are celebrated in the East.[10]

HOLYDAYS

GENERAL · In medieval times a much greater number of saints' days were holydays of obligation than are now. First among them ranked the five major feasts of Mary, of which only two have remained prescribed holydays. The days of all the Apostles were raised to the rank of public holydays in 932.[11] The feasts of Saint Michael, Saint Stephen, Saint John the Baptist, and other saints of the early centuries were celebrated in the past as holydays among all Christian nations. Of all these feasts, there remain today as prescribed holydays the following five: Saint Joseph's Day (March 19), Peter and Paul's Day (June 29), Assumption of Mary (August 15), All Saints (November 1), and the Immaculate Conception (December 8).[12]

In the United States, however, two of these saints' feasts (Saint Joseph and Peter and Paul) are exempt from the obligation by dispensation of the Holy See.[13]

PATRONS' FEASTS · Still another group of holydays is made up of the feasts of those saints who were (and are) special patron saints in certain localities. This group comprises hundreds of saints, often little known to the rest of the world. Every parish, diocese, ecclesiastical province, every religious institution and community has its particular heavenly patron. So have most nations, states, regions, cities, and towns. In each place the feast of the patron saint used to be kept as a true holyday.[14] The present canon law provides for the continuation of this practice, though only from the liturgical aspect; the day of the patron saint may be celebrated as a religious solemnity but not as a holyday of obligation (unless prescribed for the whole Church).[15] In many countries people are still accustomed to the patron's feast as it used to be kept in past centuries. It is now usually held on the Sunday following the liturgical feast. They observe it with great devotion and rejoicing. The whole day, after the service, is spent in celebration consisting of processions, parades, and traditional pageants, fairs, amusements, banquets, and dancing. This festival is called *Kirmes* in German, *Bucsu* in Hungarian, *Kermes* in Slovak, *Pokrove* in Russian and Ukrainian, *Fête Patronale* in French, *Fiesta del Patrono* in Spanish.[16]

A permanent civic testimony to the patronage of saints is the names of countless towns and cities in all Christian lands. In the United States over ninety cities, towns, and counties bear the names of saints. As might be expected, the most frequent title is that of the Blessed Virgin (St. Marys, Santa Maria, etc.); then follow the names John (St. Johns, San Juan, etc.) and Saint Clair (St. Clare, Santa Clara, etc.).

The most significant patronal feasts are, of course, the days of national patron saints which are celebrated by the faithful of an entire country or race. Liturgically speaking, they are in most cases "secondary" patrons because the Blessed Virgin is the primary patron in the majority of Christian countries. In Catholic nations, and in Catholic sections of Protestant countries, these days are still observed, in some cases even as legal holidays.

NAME DAY · There is a third group of saints' days that are observed as holydays, but only privately, within the family and among friends and neighbors. It was a general custom before the Reformation, and still is in Catholic countries, to celebrate not so much the birthday, but, rather, the feast of the saint whose name was received in baptism. This "baptismal saint" is considered a special and personal patron all through life. Children are made familiar with the history and legend of "their own" saint, are inspired by his life and example, pray to him every day, and gratefully accept his loving help in all their needs. It is a beautiful custom, this close relationship of an individual to his personal patron saint in Heaven.

On the feast of such a saint, called "Name Day," all who bear that name usually attend Mass. Upon their return from the church the whole family congratulates them, offering not only good wishes but little presents as well. Then all sit down to a festive breakfast at the gaily decorated table. For the one whose feast day it is the rest of the day is free from regular chores and duties in household or farming and is spent in the manner and mood of a true holiday.[17]

The custom of giving children the names of Christian saints

dates from the first millennium. It was especially in the Frankish kingdoms (France and Germany) that people began a more general practice of assuming for themselves, or bestowing upon their children, the names of Apostles and other Biblical saints, of early martyrs and confessors. By the thirteenth century this custom was fairly widespread on the continent of Europe.

In Ireland, however, the Gaelic population did not follow this custom. It is interesting to note that no Christian names are found in the ancient Irish documents. No names of native saints, not even the name of their beloved patron, Saint Patrick, were given to their children in those early centuries. This fact is explained by the devout and humble attitude of the Gaelic people. They would have considered it an act of irreverence to claim such hallowed names for their own. This practice remained an established tradition until after the advent of the Normans. The Continental practice began to prevail by the thirteenth century.

Some Gaelic clans, however, called themselves the "servants" (*gil, mal*) of our Lord and the saints. Hence the modern surnames like Gilmartin (servant of Saint Martin), Malone (servant of Saint John), Gilpatrick (servant of Saint Patrick), Gilmary (servant of Mary), Gilchrist (servant of Christ), Gillis (servant of Jesus).[18]

Another interesting custom is that of the Spanish-speaking people naming boys Jesús after the sacred name of the Lord. All other Christian nations have refrained from doing so through a feeling of special reverence (just as the popes have always refrained from assuming the name of Peter). In similar fashion the Irish used to set apart and keep sacred the original name of Mary (Muire), never bestowing it on their daughters in this form. All girls who received the name of the Blessed Virgin bore it in other forms (mostly Maire).

It is a general custom in Spanish-speaking countries to use not only the name of Mary but also some of her liturgical titles and attributes as girls' names, like Dolores (Our Lady of Sorrows), Luz (Our Lady of Light), Paz (Our Lady of Peace), Concepción or Concha (Immaculate Conception), Asunción (Assumption), Pura (Virgin Most Pure), Victoria (Our Lady of Victory), Consuelo (Our Lady of Good Counsel), Gracia (Our Lady of Grace), Stella (Star of the Sea), and others. Some of these Spanish names, like Dolores, Grace, Stella, and Victoria, have been adopted into English and American usage.

A similar custom prevails among the Chaldeans and Syrians where, besides our Lady's name (Miriam), other names referring to Mary are given to girls in baptism: Kamala (Mary's perfection), Jamala (her beauty), 'Afifa (her purity), Farida (her uniqueness), and similar words expressing her attributes.

In our day, when even Christian parents often choose their children's names without regard to hallowed traditions, the Church still strongly recommends the bestowing of a saint's name in baptism, at least as middle name whenever the chosen first name is not of Christian origin or significance.[19]

POPULAR VENERATION OF SAINTS

PILGRIMAGES · By the first centuries it was already a general custom to visit the graves of martyrs, especially on the days of their anniversaries, and to spend the whole night in prayerful vigil at their tombs.[20] Whole populations of regions and cities would thus honor the martyrs in the Christian empire of Rome, in both the East and West. Since the graves of those saints were usually located out of town, this act of veneration constituted a true pilgrimage. In addition, there are hundreds of testimonies and examples in the writings of the early centuries describing private pilgrimages of individual Christians to the tombs of saints in far-distant countries.[21]

This trend of "pilgrimage" to the martyrs' shrines persisted beyond death in ancient Rome. People wanted to be buried as close as possible to the grave of a hero of God.[22] In the catacombs of Rome, in Italy, France, Spain, Africa, and the Near East, wherever modern archaeologists discover or investigate the tombs of martyrs, they find the ground all around honeycombed with hundreds of Christian graves. In 1955, when Franciscan archaeologists in Nazareth excavated the surroundings of the old church of the Annunciation, they found a very large number of *Loculi* (burial niches), many of them still containing parts of skeletons of Christians who had been buried there from the fourth to the seventh centuries.[23]

In medieval times the practice of pilgrimages to the saints' tombs, or to famous shrines possessing a relic of some saint, became one of the favorite spiritual exercises of pious Christians everywhere. Dressed in pilgrims' garb, men and women would traverse half a continent to pray at the shrine of a favorite saint. Sometimes they combined a number of such pilgrimages in one journey.

The most famous pilgrims' goal (besides the Holy Land) has, of course, always remained the tomb of Saint Peter in Rome, together with all the other sacred places of the holy city. Next to it rank the sanctuaries of the Blessed Virgin, especially her famous national shrines in various countries. In recent times there have been added the two international centers of pilgrimages in honor of Mary: Lourdes and Fatima.[24]

Great places of international pilgrimage in medieval times were the shrines of Saint James the Apostle (Santiago de Compostela) in Spain, the tomb of Saint Nicholas in Bari, Italy, the shrine of the "Three Holy Kings" in Cologne, and the sanctuary of Saint Mary Magdalene in Marseille.[25]

RELICS · The Christian cult of saints' relics originated from the practice of carefully and reverently collecting and interring the remains of the ancient martyrs, of which many instances are mentioned in the Roman martyrology. Very early, reverence to the saints expressed itself in a special cult of their relics.[26] The popular veneration soon also extended to the dust of their graves and to objects that had been touched by the relics. The ancient Fathers, especially Saint Augustine (430), already had to warn Christians against superstitious practices which easily crept into the cult of saints.[27]

In medieval times, when the genuine or legendary bodies (or part relics) of many saints were brought to the newly converted countries of the North (central Europe, Germany, Holland, England), a period of enthusiastic devotion to relics ensued in those regions. The bodies were received with great ceremony by the ecclesiastical and civil authorities, thousands of people gathered for the occasion, solemn processions escorted the relics into town, all church bells rang, and great festivities were held. It was a general custom to dress the skeletons in appropriate and ornate vestments, decorate them with jewelry, gold, and silver, and expose them to the view and veneration of the faithful in gorgeous glass caskets at the altars of churches.[28]

Besides these official forms of veneration of relics, people practiced a thousand personal cult actions, especially with small relics or pseudo relics they had obtained for private use. Many of these features of veneration were objectionable, if not downright superstitious.[29] The Church authorities had to issue stern prohibitions against abuses in all centuries past. Today such abuses have practically disappeared, and the cult of relics is now strictly regulated by the Code of Canon Law.[30]

PATRONAGE · Biographies and legends of saints were universally read in the Middle Ages, or handed down by word of mouth by preachers and parents. Soon the characteristic features of a saint's life, or some detail of his legend, produced the conviction that he would be especially willing and helpful if invoked in similar conditions or circumstances. Thus originated the various "fields of patronage" ascribed to individual saints. In some cases the Church has officially and liturgically acknowledged certain patronages. Most of them, however, are due to popular feeling and inclination.

Thus we have, in popular tradition, heavenly patrons for all individual vocations and occupations (including alchemists, converted criminals, and treasure hunters); for all kinds of groups and organizations (including bowling clubs, skaters, mountain climbers); for justice and law (oath patrons, patrons of prisoners, executions, and executioners, against false accusations, against thieves, murderers, robbers, for just and speedy trials); against sickness and death (hundreds of saints, each one for a special kind of disease or danger); for animals (mostly domestic, but also for deer, hares, birds, fish); for all needs of the farmer (propitious weather, rain, grains, fruit, herbs, vegetables); against all manner of calamity (drowning, shipwreck, fire, floods, earthquakes, hail, storm, traffic accidents).[31]

The above are only a few examples of the many "fields of patronage" cultivated by the faithful for many centuries now, and involving thousands of historical or legendary saints. If practiced in the right spirit, based on the supernatural fact of the "communion of saints," [32] and without unreasonable or super-

stitious elements, this devotion to the saints' patronage is a powerful help and a great consolation in temporal and spiritual needs.
The fact that some patronages are based on mere legendary
events does not infringe on the spiritual aspect of our petition
nor on the saints' power to intercede for us.[33]

LITURGY AND LEGEND · As the devotional cults of relics or patrons, so also many feasts of the year, especially those of the
early saints, are connected with traditional observances based
on mere legendary claims.[34] Hence it might seem to the less-
informed reader that the popular veneration of the saints is but
a sentimental tribute originating from unhistorical, and sometimes ridiculous, legendary beliefs.

Actually, these traditional observances rest on the bedrock of
liturgical piety, which has always remained the source of popular
celebration. Every true Christian knows from childhood that the
basis of his devotion to the saints is not some fictional event or
legendary patronage (although he might celebrate them, too),
but the very real and historical fact of the saints' heroic service
to God and love of men, the radiant perfection of their lives in
Christian virtue and faith.[35]

The liturgical prayers hardly ever mention any of the legendary
elements with which popular tradition abounds, but quote the
historical facts of martyrdom or heroic virtue and perfect faith.
It was on this basis only that the Church tolerated those additional expressions of legendary observance outside the liturgy.
The liturgical Mass prayers of the various feasts, which may be
found at the end of the following sections, will serve as illustration and proof.

---

[1] *Sanctus*, DACL, 15.1 (1950), 373 ff.   [2] St. Thomas, *Summa Theol.*,
III, Q. 25, a. 5, II.2, q. 103.   [3] *S. Ephrem Syri Hymni et Sermones*,
ed. T. J. Lang, Mecheln, 1882, I, 587 (Syrian text and Latin trans.).
[4] DACL, 10.2 (1932), 2430 ff.   [5] H. Leclercq, *Acts des Martyrs*,
DACL, 1.1 (1920), 373 ff.   [6] *Digesta Juris Romani*, XVIIIL, 24, 3.
[7] The liturgical veneration of confessors started about A.D. 500: DACL,
15.1 (1950), 432.   [8] Kellner, 215 f.   [9] About the "foreign" saints in
the Roman Canon see Jgn MS, II, 210 ff., 306 ff.   [10] See note 8.
[11] DACL, 1.2 (1924), 2634.   [12] CIC, 1247, 1.   [13] *Responsum*, De-

cember 31, 1885; Balt., CV. [14] DACL, 13.2 (1938), 2514 ff. [15] CIC,
1247, 2, 1278. [16] F. Cabrol, *Fêtes Locales*, DACL, 5.1 (1922),
1422 ff.; VL, 156 ff.; Geramb, 154 ff. (*Der Kirchtag*). [17] RCF, 28 f.,
30 f. [18] P. Woulfe, *Irish Names and Surnames*, Dublin, 1923, 7 ff.
[19] RR, *De Sacramento Baptismi*, I, 30, 70. [20] DACL, 10.2 (1932),
2434 ff. [21] VdM, 547 (*Der Märtyrerkult*), 577 ff. (*Die Totenmähler*).
[22] H. Leclercq, *Ad Sanctos*, DACL, 1.1 (1920), 479 ff.; VdM, 571 ff.
[23] Personal observation of the author at Nazareth, June 1955. [24] H.
Leclercq, *Pélerinages aux Lieux saints*, DACL, 14.1 (1939), 65 ff.
[25] Gugitz, II, 33; VL, 63 ff. [26] H. Leclercq, *Reliques et Reliquaires*,
DACL, 14.2 (1948), 2294 ff. [27] VdM, 596. [28] VH, 138 ff. [29] VH,
135 ff. (*Die Heiligen im Aberglauben*). [30] CIC, 1255,2, 1276, 1281,1,
1282,2, 1283, 1286, 1289, 2326. [31] VH, 118 ff. (*Besondere
Schutzheilige*). [32] H. Leclercq, *Communion des Saints*, DACL, 3.2
(1948), 2447 ff. [33] VH, 9 ff. [34] VH, 72 f. (*Der Wunderglaube*);
VdM, 610 ff. (*Wunderglaube*). [35] VH, 31 ff. (*Die Form der kirchlichen Heiligenverehrung*).

CHAPTER

24   *Main Feasts of Mary*

THE ASSUMPTION

HISTORY AND LITURGY · The first annual feast day of Mary seems
to have been celebrated in Palestine. In a eulogy on Saint Theodosius (529), Bishop Theodore of Petra wrote that the monks
of Palestine held every year with great solemnity and devotion
a memorial feast of the Blessed Virgin (*Theotokou Mneme:* the
Memory of the Mother of God). Neither the occasion nor the
date of this "memory" is mentioned, but there is little doubt that
it was a celebration on the anniversary of her "falling asleep."
According to ancient tradition the date was August 15.[1]

This annual commemoration of Mary soon spread throughout

the whole Eastern Church. Emperor Mauritius in 602 confirmed the date and established the feast as a public holiday for his entire realm. Its official title was the "Falling Asleep of the Mother of God" (*Koimesis Theotokou*). Almost immediately Rome accepted this festival and celebrated it in the seventh century under the same title (*Dormitio Beatae Mariae Virginis*).[2]

With the memory of Mary's "falling asleep," however, there was everywhere connected the ancient traditional belief that her body did not decay, but soon after the burial was united again with her soul by the miraculous action of Divine Omnipotence, and was taken up to Heaven. In the Latin Church this general belief brought about a change in the title of the feast. Very soon, in the seventh and eighth centuries, it started to be called *Assumptio* (Taking Up).[3]

The universal belief of Mary's assumption has been framed in ancient legends and stories which, though not strictly historical in themselves, confirm the underlying tradition.[4] The most famous of these legends is quoted in an interpolated passage (added by an unknown author) in the sermons of Saint John Damascene (749). It tells how the East Roman Emperor Marcian (457) and his wife, Pulcheria, asked the Bishop of Jerusalem at the Council of Chalcedon, in 451, to have the relics of the Blessed Virgin brought to Constantinople. The bishop is said to have answered, "Mary died in the presence of the Apostles; but her tomb, when opened later on the request of Saint Thomas, was found empty, and thus the Apostles concluded that the body was taken up to Heaven." [5]

Although the above legend was not actually told by Saint John Damascene, in one of his sermons he clearly expressed the same general belief of all Christianity:

Your sacred and happy soul, as nature will have it, was separated in death from your most blessed and immaculate body; and although the body was duly interred, it did not remain in the state of death, neither was it dissolved by decay. . . . Your most pure and sinless body was not left on earth but you were transferred to your heavenly throne, o Lady, Queen, and Mother of God in truth.[6]

It is this fact of Mary's assumption into Heaven that has been formally celebrated from the beginning of the Middle Ages in all Christian countries up to the Reformation, and in the Catholic Church up to this day. The other two events connected with it, her "falling asleep" and her coronation in Heaven, are included in the feast but not expressly commemorated.

When Pope Pius XII, on November 1, 1950, solemnly announced the Assumption of Mary to be a dogma of the faith, he did not establish a new doctrine, but merely confirmed the universal belief of early Christianity, declaring it to be revealed by God through the medium of apostolic tradition.[7] He also introduced a new Mass text which more clearly stresses the fact of the assumption in its prayers and readings.[8]

The feast was given a vigil and liturgical octave by Pope Leo IV in 874. The octave, however, was abolished in 1955, together with the octaves of all feasts except Christmas, Easter, and Pentecost. The Council of Mainz in 813 prescribed the celebration for the whole empire of the West as a public holyday.[9] Soon after, the popes extended this obligation to the entire Latin Church. It has remained ever since. In 1957, however, Pope Pius XII transferred the obligation of vigil fast from the Feast of the Assumption to that of the Immaculate Conception.

The Armenians list the Feast of the Assumption among the five supreme festivals (*Daghavár*) of the year. As such it is preceded by a whole week of fasting and consists of a three-day celebration of which the second day is the actual feast of obligation. It is also followed by a solemn liturgical octave.[10]

NAMES · In the Byzantine Rite the official title of the feast is still the ancient one (Falling Asleep): *Koimesis Theotokou* in Greek, *Uspenije Marii* in Slavonic. Most European nations have adopted the Latin term of *Assumptio*, like Assumption in English, *Assunción* in Spanish, *Assomption* in French. The German *Mariä Himmelfahrt* means "Mary's Going Up to Heaven," as does the South Slavic *Usnesenje* and the North Slavic *Nanebovzatie*. Among the Syrians and Chaldeans the feast is called *'id al-intiqal Marjam* (The Being Transferred of Mary).[11]

Among the Hungarians the Assumption is kept with special solemnity as a great national holiday. According to legend their first king, Saint Stephen (1038), offered the sacred royal crown to Mary, thereby choosing her as the heavenly queen and patroness of the whole country.[12] Consequently, they call it the "Feast of Our Great Lady" (*Nagyboldogasszonynap*), and Mary is referred to as the "Great Lady of the Hungarians" (*Magna Domina Hungarorum*). They observe August 15 with unusual solemnities, pageants, parades, and universal rejoicing.

In France a traditional pageant used to be performed in many places on Assumption Day. Figures of angels descended within the church to a flowery "sepulchre" and reascended again with an image of the Blessed Virgin dazzlingly robed, while boys dressed as angels played, with wooden mallets on a musical keyboard, the tune of a popular Madonna hymn.

PROCESSIONS · From early centuries the Feast of the Assumption was a day of great religious processions. This popular custom seems to have started with the ancient Roman practice, which Pope Sergius I (701) inaugurated, of having liturgical prayer processions (*litaniae*) on the major feasts of Mary. In many places of central Europe, also in Spain, France, Italy, and South America, such processions are held. In Austria the faithful, led by the priest, walk through the fields and meadows imploring God's blessing upon the harvest with prayer and hymns.[13]

In France, where Mary under the title of her assumption is the primary patron of the country, her statue is carried in solemn procession through the cities and towns on August 15, with great splendor and pageantry, while church bells peal and the faithful sing hymns in Mary's honor.

The Italian people, too, are fond of solemn processions on August 15, a custom also practiced among the Italian-Americans in the United States. In the rural sections outside Rome the so-called "Bowing Procession" (*L'Inchinata*) is held, the statue of Mary being carried through the town (symbolizing her journey to Heaven). Under a gaily decorated arch of branches and flowers (representing the gate of Heaven) it is met by a statue of Christ. Both images are inclined toward each other three times as though they were solemnly bowing. Then "Christ" conducts his "mother" back to the parish church (symbolizing her entrance into eternal glory), where the ceremony is concluded with a service of solemn benediction.[14]

In Sardinia the procession is called *Candelieri* because they

carry seven immense candlesticks, each supporting a torch of a
hundred pounds of wax. The procession goes to the church of
the Assumption, where the candles are placed beside Mary's
shrine. The origin of the *Candelieri* dates back to the year 1580,
when a deadly epidemic suddenly stopped on August 15 after
the town had vowed to honor Mary by offering these candles
every year.[15]

BLESSING OF HERBS AND FRUITS · The fact that herbs picked in
August were considered of great power in healing occasioned
the medieval practice of the "Blessing of Herbs" on Assumption
Day.[16] The Church thus elevated a popular belief of pre-Christian
times into an observance of religious import and gave it the character of a Christian rite of deep and appropriate meaning.[17] In
central Europe the feast itself was called "Our Lady's Herb Day"
(*Kräutertag* in German, *Matka Boska Zielna* in Polish). In the
Alpine provinces the blessing of herbs is still bestowed before
the solemn service of the Assumption.[18] The city of Würzburg in
Bavaria used to be a favored center of these blessings, and from
this fact it seems to have received its very name in the twelfth
century (*Würz:* spice herb).[19] The Roman ritual still provides
an official blessing of herbs on Assumption Day which, among
other prayers, contains the petition that God may bless the
medicinal powers of these herbs and make them mercifully effi-
cient against diseases and poisons in humans and domestic animals.[20]

The Eastern Rites have similar blessings. In fact, the Syrians
celebrate a special feast of "Our Lady of Herbs" on May 15.[21]
Among the Armenians, the faithful bring the first grapes from
their vineyards to church on Assumption Day to have them solemnly blessed by the priest. Before breakfast the father distributes them to his family. No one would dream of tasting the new
harvest before consuming the first blessed grapes on Our Lady's
Day.

In Sicily people keep a partial or total abstinence from fruit
during the first two weeks of August (*La Quindicina*) in honor
of the Blessed Virgin. On the feast day itself they have all kinds
of fruit blessed in church and serve them at dinner. They also
present each other with baskets of fruit on Assumption Day.[22]

BLESSING OF NATURE · Finally, there is the old and inspiring custom on August 15 of blessing the elements of nature which are the scene of man's labors and the source of human food. In all Christian countries before the Reformation the clergy used to bless the countryside, its farms, orchards, fields, and gardens. In the western sections of Austria the priests still perform the "Blessing of the Alps," including not only the mountains and meadows but also the farms.

In the Alpine sections of France the parish priests ride from pasture to pasture on Assumption Day or during the octave. Behind the priest on the horse sits an acolyte holding the holy-water vessel. At every meadow the blessing is given to the animals, which are gathered around a large cross decorated with branches and flowers.[23]

In the Latin countries, especially in Portugal, the ocean and the fishermen's boats are blessed on the afternoon of Assumption Day. This custom has also come to the United States, where fishing fleets and ocean are now solemnly blessed in various coastal towns on August 15.

FOLKLORE · In pre-Christian times the season from the middle of August to the middle of September was observed as a period of rejoicing and thanksgiving for the successful harvest of grains. Many symbolic rites were aimed toward assuring man of prosperous weather for the reaping of the fall fruits and for winter planting.[24] Some elements of these ancient cults are now connected with the feast and season of the Assumption. All through the Middle Ages the days from August 15 to September 15 were called "Our Lady's Thirty Days" (*Frauendreissiger*) in the German-speaking sections of Europe. Many Assumption shrines even today show Mary clothed in a robe covered with ears of grain. These images (*Maria im Gerteidekleid,* Our Lady of Grains) are favored goals of pilgrimages during August.[25]

Popular legends ascribe a character of blessing and goodness to Our Lady's Thirty Days. Both animals and plants are said to lose their harmful traits. Poisonous snakes do not strike, poison plants are harmless, wild animals refrain from attacking humans. All food produced during this period is especially wholesome and good, and will remain fresh much longer than at other times of the year.[26]

An ancient custom in England, Ireland, and sections of the European continent is the traditional bathing in ocean, rivers, and lakes on August 15 ("Our Lady's Health Bathing") to obtain or preserve good health through her intercession on whose great feast all water in nature is considered especially blessed.

LITURGICAL PRAYER · *Almighty and eternal God, who hast taken up into the glory of Heaven, with body and soul, the Immaculate Virgin Mary, Mother of Thy Son: grant us, we pray, that we may always strive after heavenly things and thus merit to share in her glory.*[27]

IMMACULATE CONCEPTION

HISTORY AND LITURGY · This is the only one of the Blessed Virgin's festivals that did not come to the Western Church by way of Rome, but spread from the Byzantine province of southern Italy first into Normandy, thence to England, France, and Germany, until it was finally accepted into the Roman liturgy and approved for the whole Latin Church.[28]

Like the other feasts of Mary, it had its origin in the Eastern Church. There it was introduced in various local churches during the eighth century. It bore the title the "Conception [*Syllepsis*] of the Mother of God." More frequently, however, it was called the "Conception of Saint Anne" (meaning that Saint Anne conceived Mary). The feast spread gradually over the eastern empire until Emperor Manuel Comnenus in 1166 recognized it as a public festival and prescribed it as a holiday for the entire Byzantine realm.

The conception of no other saint was ever commemorated by the Church. The reason why Mary was accorded this exceptional honor lies in the general belief of Christianity that she was free from original sin because of her dignity as mother of God. This belief is found in many testimonies from the earliest centuries. It is clearly stated in the famous "Letter of the Priests and Deacons of Achaja" on the martyrdom of Saint Andrew (first century).[29] Many scholars do not consider this document genuine;

however, it could not have been written later than the end of the fourth century, because its text is used in the earliest missals of the Gothic clergy. Thus the letter, whether genuine or not, by its very antiquity proves the belief of early Christians in the Immaculate Conception—in the fact that Mary was free from original sin.

From Constantinople this festival came to Naples in the ninth century, for Naples was then a part of the East Roman Empire. It was celebrated in Sicily, Naples, and lower Italy under the name "Conception of Saint Anne." When the Normans conquered those Byzantine provinces in the eleventh century, they adopted the feast and took it back to Normandy, where it soon became established as a beloved annual celebration. Through Norman influence it came into England in the twelfth century and into various dioceses of France and Germany during the twelfth to fourteenth centuries. The fact that the Normans had brought it into western Europe is indicated by the popular name it bore in medieval times, "Feast of the Normans." [30]

While the feast thus slowly spread in western Europe, Rome neither celebrated nor officially recommended it, but allowed it to be introduced wherever the local church authorities wished to establish it. Saint Thomas Aquinas mentioned this in his famous *Summa Theologiae:* "Although the Roman Church does not celebrate it, she allows other churches to do so." [31] It was precisely for this reason that many bishops and theologians opposed it as an "innovation." Its fate was also intimately connected with the theological disputations that went on for centuries among the learned as to whether Mary was entirely free from original sin even "at the first moment" of her conception.

Meanwhile, the observance of the feast proceeded on its victorious course. The Franciscans made themselves fervent promoters of its celebration. They were soon joined by the Benedictines, Cistercians, and Carmelites. In the religious houses of these orders, both in Rome and elsewhere, the feast was annually kept with great solemnity. By the end of the fourteenth century it was well established in most European countries.

Finally, in 1477, Pope Sixtus IV officially acknowledged the feast and allowed its celebration in the whole Church without, however, commanding it. It was not until the eighteenth century

that Pope Clement XI (1721) prescribed it as an annual feast to
be celebrated on December 8 (but not yet as a holyday of obligation). In Spain, though, it has been kept as a public holyday
since 1644.[32]

The festival obtained its present high rank in 1854, when Pope
Pius IX solemnly declared the dogma of the Immaculate Conception of Mary and at the same time raised its commemoration
to the status of a holyday of obligation for the universal Church.
A new Mass and Office were introduced, and the term "Immaculate Conception" was officially incorporated in the liturgical
books. The churches of the Greek Rite have kept the festival as
a prescribed holyday since 1166, though they still use the ancient title "Conception of Saint Anne." In 1957 Pope Pius XII
transferred the obligation of vigil fast from August 14 to the
vigil of the Immaculate Conception (December 7).

FOLKLORE · Because of its very recent establishment as a holyday
of obligation, this feast has not developed any popular customs
and traditions except in Spain and Spanish-speaking countries,
where it has been a great public feast day for the past three
hundred years.

Since Mary, under the title of the Immaculate Conception, is
the primary patron of Spain, her feast is celebrated everywhere
with great public solemnity. People prepare themselves by novenas and nocturnal vigils for the feast, solemn processions with
the statue of the Immaculate are made after High Mass, and
additional services are held in the afternoon of the holyday. In
many places December 8 is also the day for the solemn first
Communion of children.

In the northern provinces of Spain it is the custom to decorate
the balconies of the houses with flowers, carpets, and flags on
the eve of the feast, and candles burn in the windows all through
the night. In Seville, the famous "Dance of the Six" (*Los Seises*)
is performed in the cathedral on the feast day and during the
octave. Six boys, their heads covered according to special privilege, enact an ancient religious pageant before the Blessed
Sacrament, dancing in the sanctuary and singing hymns in honor
of the Immaculate Conception. This performance annually draws
large crowds of devout natives and curious tourists.[33]

All through Spain December 8 is the traditional day of great school celebrations. Alumni revisit their alma mater and spend the day in joyful reunion with their classmates and former teachers. In many countries of South America it is the day of commencement celebrations, since the long summer vacations start around the middle of December.

Mary Immaculate is also the patroness of the Spanish infantry and civil guard (state police). On December 8 in all towns and cities, troops attend Mass in a body. It is a colorful pageant to watch. Detachments in splendid uniforms march with military precision, brass bands play ancient, stirring music, and the picture of the Immaculate Conception on each regimental flag is held aloft.

Finally, there is the interesting fact that our modern custom of an annual Mother's Day has been associated in Spain with the Feast of the Immaculate Conception. All over Spain December 8 is Mother's Day, and thus the great feast of our Lady has also become an outstanding day of joyful family celebrations in honor of mothers everywhere in that country.

LITURGICAL PRAYER · *O God who, through the Immaculate Conception of the Virgin, didst prepare a worthy habitation for Thy Son: grant us, we pray, as by the foreseen death of Thy Son thou didst preserve her from all stain of sin, so we may be cleansed by her intercession and may come to Thee.*

---

[1] F. Cabrol, *Assomption*, DACL, 1.2 (1924), 2995 ff.   [2] Kellner, 237 f.
[3] For the first mention of the feast as *Assumptio* see in Bishop Sonnatius of Rheims (about 630): *Statuta*, 20; PL, 80, 446.   [4] H. Leclercq, *Mort de Marie*, DACL, 10.2 (1932), 2019 ff.   [5] *Sermo II in Assumpt.*; PG, 96, 749 ff.   [6] *Ibid.*, 715, 719.   [7] K. Rahner, *Das "neue" Dogma*, Wien, 1951.   [8] M. Marx, "Definition of the Assumption," OF, 24 (1950), 529 ff.   [9] *Conc. Mogunt.*, Can. 36; Mansi, 14, 73. [10] Nilles, I, 250.   [11] Nilles, I, 245.   [12] G. Schreiber, *König Stephan der Heilige*, ZKTh, 62 (1938), 502 ff.   [13] Gugitz, II, 75.   [14] EC, 2 (1949), 211.   [15] EC, 3 (1949), 522 f.   [16] TE, I, 703 f.; Nilles, I, 249. [17] Franz, I, 398 ff.   [18] Gugitz, II, 73 f.   [19] *Ibid.*   [20] RR, *Bened. Herbarum in Festo Assumptionis B.M.V.*   [21] Nilles, I, 249.   [22] EC, 2 (1949), 211.   [23] Gugitz, II, 75.   [24] H. Pfannenschmid, *Germanische*

Erntefeste im heidnischen und christlichen Cultus, Hannover, 1878.
[25] Geramb, 144 ff. (*Der Frauendreissiger*); VL, 161.   [26] Gugitz, I,
75; Koren, 165 ff.   [27] The liturgical prayers given at the end of sections are translations of the Collect (official Mass prayer). Each
prayer is followed by the liturgical conclusion "through Christ Our
Lord. Amen," or, "through Our Lord Jesus Christ, Thy Son, Who
with Thee liveth and reigneth in the unity of the Holy Spirit, God,
for ever and ever. Amen."   [28] See the comprehensive historical sketch
in Kellner, 240-62.   [29] Text of the letter in PL, 1, 1220.   [30] Kellner,
253.   [31] *Summa Theol.,* III, q. 27, art. 2.   [32] Kellner, 253.   [33] L.
Gougard, *Dances populaires dans l'églises,* DACL, 4.1 (1920), 251 ff.

CHAPTER

25 *Other Feasts of Mary*

CANDLEMAS

HISTORY · The Law of Moses prescribed that every Jewish mother
after giving birth to a boy child was to be excluded from attendance at public worship for forty days. At the end of that period
she had to present a yearling lamb for a holocaust and a pigeon
for sin offering, thus purifying herself from ritual uncleanliness.
In the case of poor people, two pigeons sufficed as an offering
(Leviticus 12, 2-8). The Gospel reports how Mary, after the
birth of Jesus, fulfilled this command of the law, and how on
the same occasion Simeon and Anna met the newborn Saviour
(Luke 2, 22-38).

Since Christ Himself was present at this event, it came to be
celebrated quite early as a festival of the Lord. The first historical
description of the feast is given in the diary of Aetheria (about
390). She mentioned that the services in Jerusalem began with
a solemn procession in the morning, followed by a sermon on

the Gospel text of the day, and finally Mass was offered. At that time the festival was kept on February 14, because the birth of Christ was celebrated on the Feast of the Epiphany (January 6). It had no special name but was called "the fortieth day after Epiphany." [1]

From Jerusalem the feast spread into the other churches of the Orient. The Armenians call it the "Coming of the Son of God into the Temple" and still celebrate it on February 14.[2] In the Coptic (Egyptian) Rite it is termed "Presentation of the Lord in the Temple." [3] East Roman Emperor Justinian I in 542 prescribed it for the whole country as a public holyday, in thanksgiving for the end of a great pestilence. By that time it was known in the Greek Church under the title *Hypapante Kyriou* (The Meeting of the Lord), in commemoration of Christ's meeting with Simeon and Anna.[4]

According to the Gospel, Simeon, holding the Child in his arms, said, "Now doest thou dismiss thy servant, o Lord. . . ." The word "now" prompted the Christians of the Orient to believe that Simeon, having seen the Saviour, died on the same day. Thus they made Candlemas also the annual feast of Simeon. Hence the Chaldeans and Syrians even today call the festival *'id Sham'oun al-Shaikh* (Feast of Simeon the Old Man).

In the Western Church the commemoration of this event appeared first in the liturgical books (*Gelasianum, Gregorianum*) of the seventh and eighth centuries. It bore the title "Purification of Mary" and was listed for February 2 (forty days after Christmas).[5]

It was Pope Sergius I (701) who prescribed the procession with candles, not only for the Feast of the Purification, but also for the other three feasts of Mary which were then annually celebrated in Rome (Annunciation, Assumption, Nativity of Mary). The procession was first instituted as a penitentiary rite with prayers (*litaniae*) imploring God's mercy; hence the Church uses the penitential color (purple) even now for the blessing of candles and for the procession.[6]

Some scholars explain these light processions on the feasts of Mary in Rome as a Christian substitute for the ancient popular torch parades at various times of the year.[7] In this case the Candlemas procession would have replaced the light parades of

the Lupercalia, a pagan feast celebrated on February 14 and
15.[8] Other scholars, however, claim that there is no historical
connection between the Christian processions and pagan parades,
for the festival of Mary's purification was never kept on February
14 in the Western Church; moreover, there was no procession
of lights in the beginning, and the pagan custom of the Lupercalia
had been discontinued three hundred years before the procession
was inaugurated.[9]

The original rite of Pope Sergius did not provide for any blessing of candles. The celebrant in those early centuries distributed
to the clergy, for the procession, candles that were neither blessed
nor lighted. The ceremony of blessing originated at the end of
the eighth century in the Carolingian Empire, as did most of the
other liturgical blessings (of Easter fire, Easter water, palms).[10]

LITURGY · In present liturgical usage the officiating priest blesses
the candles before the Mass. He sings or recites five prayers of
blessing. The following excerpts show the intention and purpose
for which this blessing is bestowed by the Church:

. . . We humbly implore thee [o God] through the invocation of thy
holy name and through the intercession of Mary, ever Virgin, whose
feast we devoutly celebrate today, also through the prayers of all thy
saints: Deign to bless and sanctify these candles for human use, for
the welfare of body and soul both on land and on water. These thy
servants desire to carry them in their hands while they praise thee
with their hymns: Hear their voices graciously from thy holy Heaven
and from the throne of thy majesty; be merciful to all who cry to
thee, whom thou hast redeemed by the precious blood of thy Son,
who lives and reigns with thee, God for ever and ever. Amen.

Lord Jesus Christ, true light that enlightens every man who comes
into this world, bestow thy blessing upon these candles, and sanctify
them with the light of thy grace. As these tapers burn with visible
fire and dispel the darkness of night, so may our hearts with the help
of thy grace be enlightened by the invisible fire of the splendor of
the Holy Ghost, and may be free from all blindness of sin. Clarify
the eyes of our minds that we may see what is pleasing to thee and
conducive to our salvation. After the dark perils of this life let us be
worthy to reach the eternal light. Through thee, Jesus Christ, Savior
of the world, who in perfect Trinity livest and reignest, God, for ever
and ever. Amen.[11]

After the blessing the celebrant distributes the candles to the clergy and faithful, who carry them in their hands during the solemn procession. Meanwhile, the choir sings the canticle of Simeon, *Nunc Dimittis* (Luke 2, 29-32), and various antiphons. The symbolism of the light procession is obvious from the antiphon that is repeated after every verse of the canticle, *Lumen ad revelationem gentium* (a light of revelation to the gentiles). It represents Christ, the Light of the World, at His presentation in the temple of Jerusalem.

The procession is always held on February 2, even when the Mass and Office are transferred to another day. In most places it is now held inside the church, but in past centuries the clergy used to proceed into the open and walk through the churchyard past the graves of departed parishioners.[12]

NAMES · From the blessing of candles and the procession of lights come the names of the feast in most countries: Candlemas (English), *Lichtmess* (German), *Candelas* (Spanish), *Candelora* (Italian), *Chandeleur* (French), *Hromnice* (Feast of Candles, among the Slovaks and Czechs), *Svijetlo Marijino* (Light Feast of Mary, in Yugoslavia). The Slavs of the Eastern Rite (Russians, Ukrainians) call it "Meeting of the Lord" (*Stretenije Gospoda*).[13]

FOLKLORE · In some countries the faithful use large and adorned candles, which they bring along for the blessing. Among the Syrians and Chaldeans the sexton of the parish church prepares these candles, which are made of unbleached wax and painted with designs of gold. In central and eastern Europe people bring candles and tapers of various colors, decorated with flower motifs, holy pictures, and liturgical symbols. After the blessing they take them home and keep them all through the year as cherished sacramentals, to be lighted during storms and lightning, in sickrooms, and at the bedside of dying persons.[14]

The Poles have a beautiful legend that Mary, the "Mother of God of the Blessed Thunder Candle" (*Matka Boska Gromniczna*), watches on wintry nights around Candlemas, when hungry wolves are on rampage outside the sleeping village. With her thunder candle she wards off the ravenous pack and protects the peasants from all harm.

In ancient times the tenant farmers had to pay their rent at Candlemas. After this disagreeable task they were entertained by the landlord with a sumptuous banquet. Candlemas is also the term day for rural laborers in most countries of central Europe and in England. Both farm hands and maids who have hired themselves out for the coming season move in with their new masters and begin work on February 3.[15]

All over Europe Candlemas was considered one of the great days of weather forecasting. Popular belief claims that bad weather and cloudy skies on February 2 mean an early and prosperous summer. If the sun shines through the greater part of Candlemas Day, there will be at least forty more days of cold and snow. This superstition is familiar to all in our famous story of the ground hog looking for his shadow on Candlemas Day.[16]

In rural sections of Austria it is held an omen of blessing and good luck if the sun breaks through the cloudy skies for just a few minutes to cast its radiant glow over the earth. Children wait for this moment and greet the appearance of the sunlight with little songs like this one from the province of Vorarlberg:

> *Hail, glorious herald, holy light,*
> *God sends you from His Heaven bright.*
> *Your cheerful glow and golden rays*
> *May bring us happy summer days.*
> *Lead us through earthly toil and strife*
> *To everlasting light and life.*[17]

Finally, Candlemas Day used to be, and still is in many countries, the end of the popular Christmas season. Cribs and decorations are taken down with care and stored away for the following Christmas season. The Christmas plants are burned, together with the remnants of the Yule log, and the ashes are strewn over garden and fields to insure wholesome and healthy growth for the coming spring.[18]

LITURGICAL PRAYER · *Almighty and eternal God, we humbly beseech Thy majesty: as Thy only-begotten Son was presented in the temple this day in the substance of our flesh, so let us be presented unto Thee with cleansed souls.*

ANNUNCIATION

HISTORY · This feast, which commemorates the message of the Angel Gabriel to Mary and the Incarnation of Christ (Luke 1, 26-38), bears the official title "Annunciation of the Blessed Virgin Mary." In early medieval times it was called the "Annunciation of the Lord" or the "Conception of Christ," indicating that in those days it was considered more a festival of the Lord.[19] Its date, March 25, is placed nine months before the celebration of Christ's birth (Christmas).

The feast was held in the Eastern Church as early as the fifth century. It was introduced into the West during the sixth and seventh centuries.[20] The tenth Synod of Toledo (656) mentions it as a festival already well known and universally celebrated.[21] It was kept on the same date as in the East, March 25. In many churches of Spain, however, it was annually held on December 18.[22] During the eleventh century the Spaniards adopted the Roman date but also retained their own, so they had two feasts in honor of the Annunciation. In the eighteenth century Rome replaced the Annunciation in December with a feast of the "Expectation of Birth of the Blessed Virgin" (meaning that Mary expected the birth of Christ). The Gospel of the new feast is still that of the Annunciation.

The Annunciation was a feast of obligation and one of the public holydays in the Middle Ages. In Catholic countries it was so celebrated up to 1918, when the obligation of attending Mass and resting from work was rescinded by the new Code of Canon Law. In the liturgy, however, it still enjoys its character as one of the major feasts of Mary.

In the early Christian centuries March 25 was observed in a special way as the Day of the Incarnation. In order to make the Lord's life on earth an exact number of years, even down to the day, an early tradition claimed that it was also the date of the crucifixion. This fact is mentioned in many ancient martyrologies (calendars of feasts) and in the sermons of various Fathers of the Church. Soon other events of the history of our salvation

were placed on this day by legendary belief, and thus we find
in some calendars of the Middle Ages the following quaint "anniversaries" listed for March 25:

> The Creation of the World
> The Fall of Adam and Eve
> The Sacrifice of Isaac
> The Exodus of the Jews from Egypt
> The Incarnation
> The Crucifixion and Death of Christ
> The Last Judgment.[23]

It was an ancient custom of the papal Curia (executive office)
to start the year on March 25 in all their communications and
documents, thus calling it the "Year of the Incarnation." This
practice was also adopted by most civil governments for the legal
dating of documents. In fact, the Feast of the Annunciation, called
"Lady Day," marked the beginning of the legal year in England,
even after the Reformation, up to 1752.[24]

NAMES · The name of the feast in most nations is the same as
the liturgical one, either in its Latin form or in translation, like
Verkündigung in German. In the Greek Church it is called
Evangelismos (Glad Tidings); among the Slavs of the Eastern
Rite, *Blagovescenije Marii* (Glad Tidings of Mary). The Slavs
of the Latin Rite call it *Zvestovanie Panie Marii* (Message to
Lady Mary); the Arabic Christians, *'id al-bishara* (Feast of
Good News).[25]

A popular name in central Europe is "Feast of Swallows"
(*Schwalbentag, Fecskek napja*). It is the general belief (and
usually happens) that the first swallows return from their mi-
gration on or about this day.[26] An ancient saying in Austria
claims:

> *When Gabriel does the message bring,*
> *Return the swallows, comes the spring.*

This coincidence might have been the reason why people in
medieval Europe ascribed to the swallows a certain hallowed
character. They call them "God's birds" in Hungary, "Mary's
birds" in Austria and Germany; and no farmer would ever kill

swallows or destroy their nests.[27] Another reason might well have been the fact (made known in Europe by Crusaders and pilgrims) that the town of Nazareth, where the Annunciation took place, has an abundance of swallows circling the houses all day with their cheerful twittering.[28]

PAGEANTS · The scene of the Annunciation used to be represented in mystery plays. In the cathedrals of France, Italy, Germany, and England, on the feast itself, or on a Wednesday in Lent, the "Golden Mass" (*Missa Aurea*) was celebrated, during which the Blessed Virgin and Gabriel were represented by deacons kneeling in the sanctuary and singing the Gospel of the Mass in Latin dialogue, while another deacon sang the part of the narrator. It is reported that the Golden Mass was inaugurated at Tournay in Belgium in 1231.[29]

In other places the solemn Mass was followed by a procession in which a choirboy representing Mary was led through the church and the churchyard. In western Germany, a boy dressed as an angel and suspended on a rope from the Holy Ghost Hole would slowly descend inside the church and, hanging in midair, would address "Mary" with the words of Gabriel. While the children stared up at the approaching "angel" their mothers put cookies and candy on the pew benches, making their little ones believe that Gabriel's invisible companion angels had brought them these presents from Heaven.[30]

In the city of Rome a colorful and splendid procession used to be held on the feast day at the end of the Middle Ages. A richly decorated carriage bearing a picture of the Blessed Virgin was drawn by six black horses from St. Peter's to Santa Maria della Minerva. There the pope celebrated a pontifical Mass and afterward distributed fifty gold pieces to each of three hundred deserving poor girls to provide them with the necessary means for an honorable and appropriate marriage.[31]

FOLKLORE · In Russia priests would bless large wafers of wheat flour and present them to the faithful after the service. Returning home, the father would hand a small piece of the wafer to each member of his family and to the servants. They received it with a deep bow and ate it in silence. Later on in the day they took the remaining crumbs of the "Annunciation bread" out into the fields and buried them in the ground as a protection against blight, hail, frost, and drought.[32]

In central Europe the farmers put a picture representing the Annunciation in the barrel that holds the seed grain. While doing so they pronounce some ancient prayer rhyme like this one from upper Austria:

> *O Mary, Mother, we pray to you;*
> *Your life today with fruit was blessed:*
> *Give us the happy promise, too,*
> *That our harvest will be of the best.*
> *If you protect and bless the field,*
> *A hundredfold each grain must yield.*[33]

Having thus implored the help of Mary, they start sowing their summer grains on the following day, assured that no inclement weather will threaten their crops, for, as the ancient saying goes,

> *Saint Gabriel to Mary flies:*
> *This is the end of snow and ice.*

LITURGICAL PRAYER · *O God, who didst will that Thy Word take flesh in the womb of the blessed Virgin Mary at the message of the angel: grant us, we pray, to be aided before Thee by her intercession, whom we believe to be truly the Mother of God.*

NATIVITY OF MARY

HISTORY · A feast in honor of Mary's birth seems to have been held in Syria and Palestine in the sixth century. Saint Romanus (457), a native of Syria and later deacon of a church in Constantinople, was probably the first one who brought this feast to the attention of the authorities of the Greek Church. He wrote a hymn in honor of Mary's birth and spread the knowledge of this festival among the population of East Rome.[34] His efforts were highly successful, for in the following centuries mention is made of a celebration of Mary's nativity in many churches of the empire. Saint Andrew of Crete (740), Archbishop, preached sermons in honor of the feast, as did Saint John Damascene.[35]

This celebration was accepted and adopted by the Roman Church at the end of the eighth or ninth century, but not generally celebrated at first. It spread very slowly through the rest of Europe. Saint Fulbert (1028), Bishop of Chartres, mentioned it in one of his sermons as a "recent" feast.[36] By the twelfth century, however, it was observed among all Christian nations as one of the major feasts of Mary, and remained a holyday of obligation until 1918.

The date (September 8) is explained by the fact that on this day a church in honor of Mary was consecrated in Jerusalem and thus September 8 became an annual anniversary festival of the Blessed Virgin.[37] In Europe this reason for the date was unknown. Popular legends of a later period often supplied the missing explanation by miraculous events. The Syrians also observe on this day the solemn memory of the parents of Mary, Saint Joachim and Saint Anna.[38]

FOLKLORE · In many places of central and eastern Europe the Feast of Mary's Nativity is traditionally connected with ancient thanksgiving customs and celebrations. The day itself marks the end of the summer in popular reckoning, the beginning of the Indian summer, which is called "after-summer" (*Nachsommer*), and the start of the fall planting season. A blessing of the harvest and of the seed grains for the winter crops is performed in many churches. The formula of this blessing may be found in the Roman ritual.[39]

In the wine-growing sections of France, September 8 is the day of the grape harvest festival. The owners of vineyards bring their best grapes to church to have them blessed, and afterward tie some of them to the hands of the statue of the Virgin.[40] The Feast of Mary's Nativity is called "Our Lady of the Grape Harvest," and a festive meal is held at which the first grapes of the new harvest are consumed.[41]

In the Alps the "down-driving" (*Abtrieb*) begins on September 8. Cattle and sheep leave their summer pastures on the high mountain slopes where they have roamed for months, and descend in long caravans to the valleys to take up their winter quarters in the warm stables. The lead animals wear elaborate decorations of flowers and ribbons; the rest carry branches of evergreen between their horns and little bells around their necks.[42]

In central and northern Europe, according to ancient belief, September 8 is also the day on which the swallows leave for the sunny skies of the South. A popular children's rhyme in Austria contains the following lines:

> *It's Blessed Virgin's Birthday,*
> *The swallows do depart;*
> *Far to the South they fly away,*
> *And sadness fills my heart.*
> *But after snow and ice and rain*
> *They will in March return again.*

LITURGICAL PRAYER · *We pray Thee, O Lord, grant to Thy servants the gift of heavenly grace: as the child-bearing of the blessed Virgin was the beginning of our salvation, so may the devout celebration of her Nativity accord us an increase of peace.*

[1] SSP, 77.   [2] Nilles, II, 571.   [3] Nilles, II, 701.   [4] Kellner, 174.   [5] Gelas., 165.   [6] DACL, 14.2 (1948), 1723.   [7] Nilles, I, 92 f.; Jgn GK, 21; LE, 173.   [8] PW, 13.2, 1816 (*Lupercalia*).   [9] Kellner, 175; H. Leclercq, *Lupercales et Chandeleur*, DACL, 14.2 (1948), 1724 ff. [10] Franz, I, 445.   [11] MR, February 2: *In Purificatione B. Mariae Virg.* [12] H. Dausend, *Lichterprozession*, LThK, 6 (1934), 935 ff.   [13] Nilles, I, 91.   [14] Koren, 86 f.   [15] Geramb, 52; Gugitz, I, 61.   [16] Koren, 87; Benet, 111; ES, 60.   [17] Gugitz, I, 61.   [18] WC, 173 f.   [19] Kellner, 231. [20] DACL, 12.1 (1935), 927 ff.; LP, I, 376.   [21] *Conc. Tolet., art.* 1; Mansi, 11, 33 f.   [22] DACL, 1.2 (1924), 2249.   [23] H. Thurston, "Christmas and the Christian Calendar," AER, 19 (1908), 174 ff.   [24] Enc. Brit., 13 (1949), 585.   [25] Nilles, I, 126 f.   [26] Gugitz, I, 149.   [27] ES, 33, 232.   [28] From personal observation of the author at Nazareth, June 1955.   [29] Young, II, 245 ff.; Chambers, II, 318 ff.   [30] Gugitz, I, 147.   [31] EC, 1 (1949), 1396.   [32] A. Yermoloff, *Der landwirtschaftliche Volkskalender*, Leipzig, 1905, 243 ff.   [33] Gugitz, I, 148.   [34] P. Maas, *Romanus der Melode,* LThK, 8 (1936), 972 f.   [35] S. Andr., *In Nativit. B. Mariae, Oratio* I; PG, 97, 806 ff.   [36] *Sermo* 4; PL, 141, 320 ff.

[37] Jgn GK, 246.   [38] Nilles, I, 481.   [39] RR, *Bened. Seminum et Segetum in Festo Nativitatis B.M.V.*   [40] Franz, I, 370.   [41] Geramb, 175 f.   [42] WH, 112 f.; Geramb, 158 ff.

CHAPTER

26   All Saints and All Souls

FEAST OF ALL SAINTS

ALL MARTYRS · The Church of Antioch kept a commemoration of all holy martyrs on the first Sunday after Pentecost. Saint John Chrysostom, who served as preacher at Antioch before he became patriarch of Constantinople, delivered annual sermons on the occasion of this festival. They were entitled "Praise of All the Holy Martyrs of the Entire World." [1] In the course of the succeeding centuries the feast spread through the whole Eastern Church and, by the seventh century, was everywhere kept as a public holyday.

In the West the Feast of All Holy Martyrs was introduced when Pope Boniface IV (615) was given the ancient Roman temple of the Pantheon by Emperor Phocas (610) and dedicated it as a church to the Blessed Virgin Mary and all the martyrs. The date of this dedication was May 13, and on this date the feast was then annually held in Rome. [2] Two hundred years later Pope Gregory IV (844) transferred the celebration to November 1. The reason for this transfer is quite interesting, especially since some scholars have claimed that the Church assigned All Saints to November 1 in order to substitute a feast of Christian significance for the pagan Germanic celebrations of the demon cult at that time of the year. [3] Actually, the reason for the transfer was that the many pilgrims who came to Rome for the Feast of the

Pantheon could be fed more easily after the harvest than in the spring.[4]

ALL SAINTS · Meanwhile, the practice had spread of including in this memorial not only all martyrs, but the other saints as well. Pope Gregory III (741) had already stated this when he dedicated a chapel in St. Peter's in honor of Christ, Mary, and "all the apostles, martyrs, confessors, and all the just and perfect servants of God whose bodies rest throughout the whole world." [5]

Upon the request of Pope Gregory IV, Emperor Louis the Pious (840) introduced the Feast of All Saints in his territories. With the consent of the bishops of Germany and France he ordered it to be kept on November 1 in the whole Carolingian empire.[6] Finally, Pope Sixtus IV (1484) established it as a holyday of obligation for the entire Latin Church, giving it a liturgical vigil and octave.[7] The octave was discontinued in 1955.

The purpose of the feast is twofold. As the prayer of the Mass states, "the merits of all the saints are venerated in common by this one celebration," because a very large number of martyrs and other saints could not be accorded the honor of a special festival since the days of the year would not suffice for all these individual celebrations. The second purpose was given by Pope Urban IV: Any negligence, omission, and irreverence committed in the celebration of the saints' feasts throughout the year is to be atoned for by the faithful, and thus due honor may still be offered to these saints.[8]

LITURGICAL PRAYER · *Almighty and eternal God, who hast granted us to venerate the merits of all Thy saints in one celebration: we beg Thee to bestow upon us the desired abundance of Thy mercy on account of this great number of intercessors.*

COMMEMORATION OF ALL THE FAITHFUL DEPARTED

HISTORY · The need and duty of prayer for the departed souls has been acknowledged by the Church at all times. It is recommended in the Scriptures of the Old Testament (2 Machabees 12, 46), and found expression not only in public and private prayers, but especially in the offering of the Holy Sacrifice for the repose of souls. The customary dates for public services of this kind were, and still are, the day of death and burial, the seventh and thirtieth day after death (Month's Mind Mass), and the anniversary. Except for the funeral Mass, the actual observance of these dates is not made obligatory by the Church but left to the piety of relatives and friends of the deceased.[9]

The memorial feast of all departed ones in a common celebration was inaugurated by Abbot Saint Odilo of Cluny (1048). He issued a decree that all monasteries of the congregation of Cluny were annually to keep November 2 as a "day of all the departed ones" (*Omnium Defunctorum*). On November 1, after Vespers, the bell should be tolled and afterward the Office of the Dead be recited; on the next day all priests had to say Mass for the repose of the souls in purgatory.[10]

This observance of the Benedictines of Cluny was soon adopted by other Benedictines, and by the Carthusians. Pope Sylvester II (1003) approved and recommended it. It was some time, though, before the secular clergy introduced it in the various dioceses. From the eleventh to the fourteenth centuries it gradually spread in France, Germany, England, and Spain, until finally, in the fourteenth century, Rome placed the day of the commemoration of all the faithful departed in the official books of the Western Church for November 2 (or November 3 if the second falls on a Sunday).[11]

November 2 was chosen in order that the memory of all the "holy spirits" both of the saints in Heaven and of the souls in purgatory should be celebrated on two successive days, and in this way to express the Christian belief in the "Communion of Saints." Since the Feast of All Saints had already been celebrated on November 1 for centuries, the memory of the departed souls in purgatory was placed on the following day.[12]

LITURGY · In the Byzantine Rite the commemoration of all the faithful departed is held on the Saturday before Sexagesima Sunday, and is called the "Saturday of the Souls" (*Psychosabbaton*).[13] The Armenians celebrate it on Easter Monday, with the solemn Office of the Dead.[14] The Mass, however, is that of the Resurrection. An interesting and moving observance is held in the

Syrian-Antiochene Rite, where they celebrate on three separate days: on Friday before Septuagesima they commemorate all departed priests; on Friday before Sexagesima, all the faithful departed; and on Friday before Quinquagesima, "all those who died in strange places, away from their parents and friends." [15]

Pope Benedict XV in 1915 allowed all priests to say three Masses on All Souls' Day in order to give increased help to the suffering souls in purgatory.[16] The Church has also granted to all faithful special privileges of gaining indulgences for the holy souls on November 1 and 2. The Office of the Dead is recited by priests and religious communities. In many places the graves in the cemeteries are blessed on the eve or in the morning of All Souls' Day, and a solemn service is usually held in parish churches.

The liturgical color at all services on November 2 is black. The Masses are part of the group called "Requiem" Masses because they start with the words *Requiem aeternam dona eis* (Eternal rest grant unto them).[17]

The sequence sung at the solemn Mass on All Souls' Day (and on other occasions) is the famous poem *Dies Irae* (Day of Wrath) written by a thirteenth-century Franciscan.[18] It has often been ascribed to Thomas of Celano (1250), the friend and biographer of Saint Francis of Assisi, though the authorship is not certain.

FOLKLORE

RELIGIOUS CUSTOMS · The custom of decorating graves and praying in cemeteries is general in all Catholic countries, both in Europe and America.[19] On the afternoon of All Saints' Day or in the morning of All Souls the faithful visit each individual grave of relatives and friends. Sometimes the congregation, led by the priest, walks in procession to the cemetery. There they pray for all the holy souls in front of the cemetery chapel, then the priest recites the liturgical prayers for the dead and blesses the graves with holy water. Afterward the families separate to offer private prayers at the graves of their loved ones.

During the week preceding All Saints crowds of people may be seen in the cemeteries, usually in the evening after work, decorating the graves of their dear ones with flowers, tending the lawn, and spreading fresh white gravel around the tombs. Candles, protected by little glass lanterns, are placed around the graves or at the foot of the tombstones, to be lighted on All Saints' eve and left burning through the night. It is an impressive, unforgettable sight to look upon the hundreds and often thousands of lights quietly burning in the darkness and dreary solitude of a cemetery. People call them "lights of the holy souls" (*Seelenlichter*).[20]

To visit the graves of dear ones on All Souls is considered a duty of such import that many people in Europe will travel from a great distance to their home towns on All Saints' Day in order to perform this obligation of love and piety.

It is an ancient custom in Catholic sections of central Europe to ring the church bells at the approach of dusk on All Saints' Day, to remind the people to pray for the souls in purgatory. When the pealing of these bells is heard, families gather in one room of their home, extinguish all other lights save the blessed candle (kept from Candlemas Day), which is put on the table.[21]

In the rural sections of Brittany four men alternate in tolling the church bell for an hour on All Saints' Day after dark. Four other men go from farm to farm during the night, ringing hand bells and chanting at each place: "Christians awake, pray to God for the souls of the dead, and say the *Pater* and *Ave* for them." From the house comes the reply "Amen" as the people rise for prayer.

In most countries of South America All Souls' Day is a public holiday. In Brazil people flock by the thousands to the cemeteries all morning, light candles and kneel at the graves in prayer. The deep silence of so many persons in the crowded cemetery deeply impresses the stranger. In Puerto Rico, people will walk for miles to the graves of their loved ones. The women often carry vases of flowers and water, for they know they can get no water at the cemetery to keep the flowers fresh. They wear their best clothes as they trudge along in the hot sun. Whole truckloads of people will arrive at the cemetery if the distance is too far to walk. The priest visits each grave and says the prayers for the dead as the mourners walk along with him. Sometimes the ceremony lasts for hours and it is near midnight when the tired pastor visits the last graves.

Among the native populations in the Philippines, a novena is held for the holy souls before November 2. In places where the cemetery is close to the town, candles are brought to be burned at the tombs and prayers are said every night. During these nine days the people also prepare their family tombs for the great Feast of the Souls. Tomb niches and crosses are repainted, hedges trimmed, flowers planted, and all weeds are removed from the graves. On the evening of All Saints' Day young men go from door to door asking for gifts in the form of cookies, candy, and pastry, and they sing a traditional verse in which they represent holy souls liberated from purgatory and on their way to Heaven.

In Poland, and in Polish churches of the United States, the faithful bring to their parish priest on All Souls' Day paper sheets with black borders called *Wypominki* (Naming) on which are written the names of their beloved dead. During the evening devotions in November, and on Sundays, the names are read from the pulpit and prayers are offered for the repose of the souls.

The Church has not established any season or octave in connection with All Souls. The faithful, however, have introduced an "octave" of their own, devoting the eight days after All Souls to special prayer, penance, and acts of charity. This custom is widespread in central Europe. People call this particular time of the year "Soul Nights" (*Seelennächte*). Every evening the rosary is said for the holy souls within the family while the blessed candle burns. Many go to Mass every morning. A generous portion of the meal is given to the poor each day; and the faithful abstain from dances and other public amusements out of respect for the holy souls. This is a deeply religious practice filled with a genuine spirit of Christian charity which overshadows and elevates the unholy customs of ancient pagan lore.[22]

PRE-CHRISTIAN ELEMENTS · Our pagan forefathers kept several "cult of the dead" rites at various times of the year. One of these periods was the great celebration at the end of the fall and the beginning of winter (around November 1). Together with the practices of nature and demon lore (fires, masquerades, fertility cults) they also observed the ritual of the dead with many traditional rites. Since All Saints and All Souls happened to be placed within the period of such an ancient festival, some of the pre-Christian traditions became part of our Christian feast and associated with Christian ideas.[23]

There is, for instance, the pre-Christian practice of putting food at the graves or in the homes at such times of the year when the spirits of the dead were believed to roam their familiar earthly places. The beginning of November was one of these times. By offering a meal or some token food to the spirits, people hoped to please them and to avert any possible harm they could do. Hence came the custom of baking special breads in honor of the holy souls and bestowing them on the children and the poor. This custom is widespread in Europe. "All Souls' bread" (*Seelenbrot*) is made and distributed in Germany, Belgium, France, Austria, Spain, Italy, Hungary, and in the Slavic countries.[24]

In some sections of central Europe boys receive on All Souls' Day a cake shaped in the form of a hare, and girls are given one in the shape of a hen (an interesting combination of "spirit bread" and fertility symbols). These figure cakes are baked of the same dough as the festive cakes that the people eat on All Saints' Day and which are a favorite dish all over central Europe. They are made of braided strands of sweet dough and called "All Saints' cakes" (*Heiligenstriezel* in German, *Strucel Swiateczne* in Polish, *Mindszenti Kalácska* in Hungarian).[25]

In western Europe people prepare on All Souls' Day a meal of cooked beans or peas or lentils, called "soul food," which they afterward serve to the poor together with meat and other dishes. In Poland the farmers hold a solemn meal on the evening of All Souls' Day, with empty seats and plates ready for the "souls" of departed relatives. Onto the plates members of the family put parts of the dinner. These portions are not touched by anyone, but afterward are given to beggars or poor neighbors.[26] In the Alpine provinces of Austria destitute children and beggars go from house to house, reciting a prayer or singing a hymn for the holy souls, receiving small loaves of the "soul bread" in reward. There, too, people put aside a part of everything that is cooked on All Souls' Day and give meals to the poor.[27] In northern Spain and in Madrid people distribute and eat a special pastry called "Bones of the Holy" (*Huesos de Santo*). In Catalonia All Souls' pastry is called *Panellets* (little breads).

In Hungary the "Day of the Dead" (*Halottak Napja*) is kept with the traditional customs common to all people in central Europe. In addition, they invite orphan children into the family for All Saints' and All Souls' days, serving them generous meals and giving them new clothes and toys.

In Brittany the farmers visit the graves of their departed relatives on *Jour des morts* (Day of the Dead), kneeling bareheaded at the mound in long and fervent prayer. Then they sprinkle the grave with holy water, and finally, before leaving, pour milk over the grave as a libation "for the holy souls." In every house a generous portion of the dinner is served before an empty seat and afterward given to the hungry.

LEGENDS · Many other customs of the ancient cult of the dead have survived as superstitions to this day. The belief that the spirits of the dead return for All Souls' Day is expressed in a great number of legends and traditions. In the rural sections of Poland the charming story is told that at midnight on All Souls' Day a great light may be seen in the parish church; the holy souls of all departed parishioners who are still in purgatory gather there to pray for their release before the very altar where they used to receive the Blessed Sacrament when still alive. Afterward the souls are said to visit the scenes of their earthly life and labors, especially their homes. To welcome them by an external sign the people leave doors and windows open on All Souls' Day.[28]

In the rural sections of Austria the holy souls are said to wander through the forests on All Souls' Day, sighing and praying for their release, but unable to reach the living by external means that would indicate their presence.[29] For this reason, the children are told to pray aloud while going through the open spaces to church and cemetery, so the poor souls will have the great consolation of seeing that their invisible presence is known and their pitiful cries for help are understood and answered.

LITURGICAL PRAYER · *O God, Creator and Redeemer of all the faithful, grant to the souls of Thy servants departed the remission of all their sins, that through our devout prayers they may obtain the pardon which they have always desired.*

HALLOWEEN

DRUIDIC ELEMENT · Unlike the familiar observance of All Souls, Halloween traditions have never been connected with Christian religious celebrations of any kind. Although the name is taken from a great Christian feast (Allhallows' Eve), it has nothing in common with the Feast of All Saints, and is, instead, a tradition of pre-Christian times that has retained its original character in form and meaning.

Halloween customs are traced back to the ancient Druids. This is attested to by the fact that they are still observed only in those sections of Europe where the population is wholly or partly of Celtic stock. In ancient times, around November 1 the burning of fires marked the beginning of winter. Such Halloween fires are kindled in many places even now, especially in Wales and Scotland.[30]

Another, and more important, tradition is the Druidic belief that during the night of November 1 demons, witches, and evil spirits roamed the earth in wild and furious gambols of joy to greet the arrival of "their season"—the long nights and early dark of the winter months. They had their fun with the poor mortals that night, frightening, harming them, and playing all kinds of mean tricks.[31] The only way, it seemed, for scared humans to escape the persecution of the demons was to offer them things they liked, especially dainty food and sweets. Or, in order to escape the fury of these horrible creatures, a human could disguise himself as one of them and join in their roaming. In this way they would take him for one of their own and he would not be bothered. That is what people did in ancient times, and it is in this very form the custom has come down to us, practically unaltered, as our familiar Halloween celebration: the horrible masks of demons and witches, the disguise in strange and unusual gowns, the ghost figures, the frightening gestures and words, the roaming through the streets at night, the pranks played, and finally the threatening demand of a "trick or treat." The pumpkin "ghosts" or jack-o'-lanterns with a burning candle inside may well be a combination of the demon element and the Halloween fire. These pumpkins are found all over central Europe at Halloween, in France, southern Germany, Austria, Switzerland, and the Slavic countries. So is the custom of masquerading and "trick or treat" rhymes, at least in the rural sections where ancient traditions are still observed.[32]

ROMAN ELEMENT · In those countries that once belonged to the Roman Empire there is the custom of eating or giving away fruit, especially apples, on Halloween. It spread to neighboring countries: to Ireland and Scotland from Britain, and to the Slavic countries from Austria. It is probably based upon a celebration of the Roman goddess Pomona, to whom gardens and orchards were dedicated. Since the annual Feast of Pomona was held on November 1, the relics of that observance became part of our Halloween celebration, for instance the familiar tradition of "ducking" for apples.[33]

[1] PG, 1, 706 ff.   [2] DACL, 15.1 (1950), 438.   [3] Frazer, 633.   [4] Beleth, *Rationale divin. offic.*, 127; PL, 202, 133.   [5] LP, I, 417.   [6] S. *Adonis Martyrol., Nov. 1;* PL, 123, 387.   [7] Kellner, 326.   [8] *Decr. Si Dominum;* Nilles, I, 313 (Latin text).   [9] DACL, 12.1 (1935), 27 ff.   [10] *Statutum S. Odilonis pro Defunctis;* PL, 142, 1038.   [11] H. Leclercq, *La Fête des Mortes,* DACL, 12.1 (1935), 34 ff.   [12] DACL, 4.1 (1920), 427 ff.   [13] Nilles, II, 90 ff.   [14] Nilles, II, 561.   [15] Nilles, II, 643.   [16] C. A. Kneller, *Geschichtliches über die drei Messen am Allerseelentag,* ZKTh, 42 (1918), 74 ff.   [17] DACL, 12.1 (1935), 31 ff.   [18] HRL, 252 f. (excellent commentary on author and poem).   [19] H. Leclercq, *Fleurs pour les défuncts,* DACL, 5.2 (1923), 1693 ff.   [20] M. Kollofrath, *Das Seelenlicht. Eine volkskundliche Studie,* in *Kölnische Volkszeitung,* November 2, 1937; VL, 169.   [21] Geramb, 181; Benet, 84.   [22] Koren, 174; Geramb, 180.   [23] Frazer, 632 ff.   [24] Gugitz, II, 157 f.; ES, 15 ("Soul Cake").   [25] Gugitz, II, 154 ff. (*Der Allerheiligenstriezel*); Koren, 175; Geramb, 180 f.   [26] Benet, 84 f.   [27] Geramb, 190 f.   [28] Benet, 84 f.; VL, 169 f.   [29] Koren, 175 f.; ES, 15.   [30] Frazer, 632 ff. ("Halloween Fires").   [31] Gugitz, II, 158; Frazer, 634 f.   [32] ES, 140; Chambers, II, 228 f.   [33] W. Ehlers, *Pomona,* PW, 21, 1876 ff.

27 *Saints' Days I*

BLAISE (FEBRUARY 3)

This martyr, a bishop in Armenia, suffered and died at the beginning of the fourth century. The legends handed down tell us that he was a physician before he became a bishop and that, while in prison, he miraculously cured a little boy who nearly died because of a fishbone in his throat.[1]

The veneration of Saint Blaise was brought to Europe before the ninth century, and he soon became one of the most popular saints of the Middle Ages. Having been a physician, he was now invoked as a helper in sickness and pain, but especially against evils of the throat. Legends of a later date relate how shortly before his death he had asked God for the power of curing all those who would pray to him for help. "And behold, a voice answered from Heaven that his request was granted by the Lord."[2]

In medieval times many shrines existed in honor of Saint Blaise. In central Europe and in the Latin countries people still are given blessed breads (Saint Blaise sticks: *Pan bendito*) of which they eat a small piece whenever they have a sore throat.[3] The best-known sacramental in his honor, however, is the "Blessing of Throats" with candles. It has been in use for many centuries and was adopted by the Church as one of its official blessings.[4] The priest holds the crossed candles against the head or throat of the person and says: "Through the intercession of Saint Blaise, bishop and martyr, may the Lord free you from evils of the throat and from any other evil."[5] In various places of Italy the priests do not use candles but touch the throats of the faithful with a wick dipped into blessed oil while they pronounce the invocation.

LITURGICAL PRAYER · *O God who grantest us joy by the annual solemnity of Saint Blaise, bishop and martyr: grant also that we may rejoice over his protection, whose birthday we celebrate.*

VALENTINE (FEBRUARY 14)

On February 14, 270, this saint, a priest, died through the persecution of Claudius II. His feast was from earliest times associated with the traditional habit of boys and girls declaring their love or choosing a "steady partner" for the following twelve months. The selection was often done, especially in France and England, by a game of chance, the boys drawing the names of their respective "Valentines." Our greeting cards on Valentine's Day are a modern form of this ancient practice.

How did the saint become associated with this unusual lore? Various explanations have been attempted. It is said that the practice originated because people believed that on Saint Valentine's Day birds started to mate.[6] However, such legends do not explain the custom. Besides, in central Europe the Feast of Saint Agnes (January 21) has always been considered the mating day of birds, although Saint Valentine is venerated as the "patron of lovers" even there.[7]

Another explanation is found in a medieval legend which tells how the saint, shortly before his execution, wrote a kind note to the friendly daughter of his prison master, signing it "from your Valentine." This legend was obviously intended to provide a belated reason for the already existing custom of the day.

There is no doubt that the historical origin of Valentine lore is based on a coincidence of dates. The pagan Romans annually celebrated a great feast on February 15 which they called Lupercalia in honor of the pastoral god Lupercus (an equivalent of the Greek god Pan). On the eve of the Lupercalia, and as part of it, young people held a celebration of their own, declaring their love for each other, proposing marriage, or choosing partners for the following year.[8] (In the Roman republic the new year started on March 1; hence the names of the last four months:

September, October, November, December, which mean, respectively, the seventh, eighth, ninth, and tenth.)

This Roman youth festival with its pledge of love stood under the patronage of the goddess Juno Februata. When the Roman Empire became Christian, all worship and patronage of pagan gods naturally ceased. But the youth festival continued, as affection, love, and marriage are not the prerogative of a pagan cult only. There was but one aspect of the celebration that had to be changed: its patronage. And so, in place of the goddess Juno Februata a Christian saint took over. He was, quite naturally, the saint whose feast day the Church celebrated on February 14—the priest and martyr Valentine.

A proof of the Roman origin of Saint Valentine's lore is the fact that in countries of Roman historical background even the smaller details, like the games of chance, the choice made for the "new year," and similar customs, were continued right into the later Middle Ages, while in other countries these details are missing and only the fact that Saint Valentine is the patron of young lovers is observed. The American custom of sending Valentine cards is unknown in countries of northern Europe. It came from England, where it had developed as a substitute for the ancient Roman "choice" of partners on February 14. This is actually what the traditional words imply: "You are my Valentine," that is, I offer you my companionship of affection and love for the next twelve months, and I am willing to consider marriage if this companionship proves satisfactory for both of us.[9]

LITURGICAL PRAYER · *Grant, we beseech Thee, almighty God, that we may be freed from all threatening dangers through the intercession of Thy holy martyr Valentine, whose birthday we celebrate.*

PATRICK (MARCH 17)

Modern scholars place the birth of Saint Patrick in the year 385, and his death on March 17, 461.[10] A Britannic Celt by race, and Roman citizen by nationality, he was captured by Gaels in a coastal raid and taken from his father's estate on the west coast of England to Ireland, where he served as a shepherd slave for

six years. At the age of twenty-two he escaped on a boat which
carried a cargo of Irish hounds to the Continent. Arriving in
France, a vast desert instead of a peaceful, inhabited country
was found. The Vandals and other Germanic tribes had crossed
the Rhine on New Year's night, 407, and made a wide path of
utter destruction down through France; the population, terror-
stricken, had fled into the Alpine sections. After crossing this
"desert" Patrick separated from his pagan companions and returned to England, for a joyful reunion with his family.

His stay at home did not last very long. Impelled by the grace
of God, he left again for the Continent, to devote his life to religious vocation and sacred ministry. From his own words we
know that he traveled through Gaul (France), Italy, and some
of the islands of the Tyrrhenian Sea. He finally decided to attach
himself to the great bishop of Auxerre, Saint Germanus, under
whose direction he studied the sacred doctrines of the faith and
acquired an unusual familiarity with the Bible. He received minor
orders and gradually rose to the diaconate. All that time he had
in his heart the ardent wish to go back to Ireland and teach the
gospel to the Gaels. His wish had been confirmed by dreams and
other manifestations of God's will.

Before he achieved this goal, a great trial cleansed and sanctified him still more. In 431, when the decision was made to send
a bishop to Ireland, Saint Patrick was suggested but turned down
by the authorities. He was also unjustly defamed by a man who
had been his friend. The choice of the bishopric for Ireland fell
on Palladius, Archdeacon of Pope Celestine. Palladius went to
the Gaels; Patrick stayed behind at Auxerre, still a deacon, deeply
humiliated by the defamation.

However, Palladius died the following year (432), and the
choice then fell on Patrick. What he had so long desired and
prayed for, he obtained suddenly and unexpectedly. Without
delay he was consecrated bishop (after having been ordained a
priest). Some time in the spring or summer of 432 he and his
companions set foot on Irish soil. For almost thirty years Patrick
labored unremittingly at the conversion of the island. He baptized many thousands with his own hands, organized the hier-
archy and clergy, established churches and religious communi-

ties. Toward the end of his life he founded the see of Armagh, which he held as archbishop and primate of Ireland till his death.

Contrary to some popular legends, Patrick encountered much resistance, and many vicious attempts were made to stop his work. These attacks did not come from the people, but from the Druidic "priests," who actually were sorcerers, and from some of the local kings. In all these threats, dangers, calumnies, and hardships Patrick never flinched. Unerringly he went his way, fighting all obstacles with the powerful weapons of prayer, penance, heroic patience, and flaming zeal. When he died, the Church was firmly rooted in the Irish nation. In a short time his disciples completed what was left of the task of making all Ireland a flourishing province of Christianity.

Soon after his death, the inspiring figure of the great saint was embellished with fictional and legendary details. Many of them had a true and historical basis; others, especially miracles and unusual deeds, originated in the desire for overwhelming supernatural confirmation of the saint's work. In this the ancient Gaelic writers were not really different from those of other nations, perhaps only more fertile and imaginative. It is a difficult and wearisome task for modern scholars to separate the historical facts from fictional and legendary details, and it will take many more years before Saint Patrick's figure emerges with some degree of certitude as the "real Patrick," freed from later additions. However, much has been found already, and these historical details make the saint so wonderfully alive, so touchingly great, that not even the wildest legends could render him more attractive.

Saint Patrick was greatly venerated from the earliest times. Among the Irish people this veneration assumed a twofold special character. First, it is not only a direct and personal devotion, which they practice in their great manifestations of piety, but, what is more important and valuable, a sincere imitation of the saint. At the famous shrines of Lough Derg in Donegal and Croagh Patrick in Mayo he is not so much honored by "services" and mere prayers as by the hard and almost heroic penance the faithful perform in imitation of his own fasting, mortification, and prayers.[11]

Second, in the course of centuries the veneration of Saint

Patrick became identified with the patriotic and national ideals
of the Irish people. Thus, March 17 is not only a religious holyday
for them, but, at the same time, their greatest national holiday.

Actually, of course, the saint is venerated by other races and
nations, too. In various parts of the European continent people
invoke him as a local patron, hardly aware of the fact that he is
the national saint of Ireland. In Styria, Austria, for instance, he
is a favored patron of the farmers and their domestic animals.[12]

The popular Saint Patrick's celebration on March 17 consists
of traditional details which are faithfully kept in Ireland and have
found their way to the New World as well: attendance at Mass
in the morning, a solemn parade with subsequent meeting and
speeches, festive meals in the home, and an evening of entertainment (dancing, concerts, plays). The custom of wearing green
on Saint Patrick's Day did not start until over a thousand years
after the saint's death. The charming practice of displaying the
shamrock is based on a legend that the saint taught King Oengus
at Cashel the doctrine of the Holy Trinity by using, as an illustration, a shamrock (trefoil) that he found growing there.

It was the custom in Ireland for men to wear the shamrock on
their hat. Girls wore crosses made of ribbons. "A shamrock on
every hat, low and tall, and a cross on every girl's dress." [13] The
merry drink taken on this day was called "Saint Patrick's poteen."

The saint's day heralded the beginning of spring in Ireland. All
livestock were driven out into the pastures to be kept in the open
until the last day of October (Halloween). It still is regarded
as the proper time in many sections of Ireland for the farmers
to commence sowing and planting potatoes. "Saint Patrick turns
the warm side of the stone uppermost" is an ancient saying.
Another proverb claims that "from Saint Brigid's [February 2]
to Saint Patrick's every alternate day is grand and fine; from then
on, every day is fine."

So many and varied are the legends and legendary "facts"
about Saint Patrick that it would take volumes to record them.
The most famous ones are these: that he freed Ireland from all
venomous snakes and reptiles; that he received a miraculous staff
from Christ in a vision and henceforth carried it with him wherever he went; that he obtained from God the privilege of judging
the Irish race at the end of time; that he lived a hundred and

twenty years, like Moses; that he himself was of the Irish (Gaelic) race.

The most inspiring piece of Saint Patrick's lore is the beautiful prayer called "Breast Plate" (*Lorica*). It is a morning prayer in early Irish. The Book of Armagh (ninth century) ascribes its authorship to the saint. It might well be that Patrick actually composed this prayer. For many centuries now millions of faithful have used it with devotion.[14]

LITURGICAL PRAYER · *O God, Thou didst send the Confessor and Bishop, Saint Patrick, to preach Thy glory to the gentiles, grant us through his merits and intercession to accomplish by Thy mercy what Thou commandest us to do.*

JOSEPH (MARCH 19)

Up to the fifteenth century our Lord's foster father was not honored by a special feast of the Church, and people did not generally venerate him, although many ancient Fathers and writers mentioned him with reverence and high regard. It was only at the time of the Crusades that a practice of private devotion to Saint Joseph spread from the Eastern Churches into Europe. This devotion was greatly encouraged by some saints of the twelfth, thirteenth, and fourteenth centuries, especially Saint Bernard (1153), Saint Thomas Aquinas (1274), and Saint Gertrude (1310).[15]

At the end of the fourteenth century the Franciscans, and soon afterward the Dominicans and Carmelites, introduced a Feast of Saint Joseph into their calendars. Finally, under Pope Sixtus IV an annual feast of the saint was established on March 19 for the whole Church.[16] It was, however, a feast of the lowest rank (*simplex*), imposing no obligation on the clergy to celebrate it. During the fifteenth and sixteenth centuries many religious orders and some national rulers, especially the Hapsburgs of Austria and Spain, appealed to the popes to raise the feast in rank and make it a prescribed holyday. Accordingly, Pope Gregory XV in 1621 made it a holyday of obligation.[17] Pius X in 1911 rescinded the obligation of attending Mass, though it was later restored by the new Code of Canon Law in 1918.[18]

In a short time the veneration of the saint quickly and enthusiastically spread through all Catholic nations. Saint Teresa (1582), who had a special devotion to him, inspired the reformed Carmelites to establish a feast of the "patronage" of Saint Joseph, which was annually celebrated by the order on the third Sunday after Easter. This feast was extended in 1847 to the whole Church.[19] In 1870 Pope Pius IX solemnly declared Saint Joseph as the official patron of the universal Church. In 1956 the feast of Saint Joseph's patronage was replaced by a Feast of Saint Joseph the Worker, to be celebrated annually on May 1.

The popular patronage of Saint Joseph is universal in scope. The words of the Egyptian Pharao, "Go to Joseph" (Genesis 41, 55), were applied to him. Filled with affection, love, and confidence, the faithful turned to him in all their temporal and spiritual needs.[20] Every detail of his life gave rise to a special patronage. He is the patron of tradesmen and workers, of travelers and refugees, of the persecuted, of Christian families and homes, of purity and interior life, of engaged couples, of people in temporal distress (food, home, clothing, sickness), of the poor, aged, and dying.

It was a widespread custom in past centuries for newly wed couples to spend the first night of matrimony (Saint Joseph's Night) in abstinence and to perform some devotion in honor of Saint Joseph that he might bless their marriage.[21] Small round breads (St. Joseph's loaves; *fritelli*) are baked and eaten in many sections of Europe on March 19 to honor the heavenly "bread father." [22] From the seventeenth century on it was customary to have a statue of the saint on the table during the main meal and to "serve" it generous portions, which afterward were given the poor.

In northern Spain it is an ancient tradition for people to make a pilgrimage to a shrine of Saint Joseph on March 19 and there to have a special repast after the devotions. This meal consists of roast lamb, which is eaten, picnic style, outside the shrine in the afternoon (*Merienda del Cordero;* Repast of the Lamb). For this occasion the faithful who make the pilgrimage and then partake of the meal are dispensed from the law of Lenten fast.

In the region of Valencia on the east coast of Spain a strange and interesting tradition developed—the burning of fires in honor of Saint Joseph. It is said to have been started by the carpenters in past centuries, when they cleaned their workshops before March 19 and burned all the litter on the evening of their patron's feast. Today, committees are established which collect and exhibit at street crossings structures made of wood by boys and men during the weeks before the feast. These structures represent houses, figures, scenes, many of them symbolic of some political event of the past year. They are admired and judged by the people, and on the eve of Saint Joseph's Day the best one receives a prize and is put aside. All the others are burned in joyful bonfires. Music, dancing, and fireworks (*traca*) are a part of this celebration in honor of Saint Joseph.

In some parts of Italy ancient nature lore rites are still performed on Saint Joseph's Day, the "burial of winter," for instance, which is done by sawing a symbolic figure (*scega vecchia*) in two.[23] In central Europe the day is celebrated by farmers as the beginning of spring. They light candles in honor of the saint, put little shrines with his picture in their gardens and orchards, and have their fields blessed by the priest.[24]

LITURGICAL PRAYER · *Assist us, O Lord, we beseech Thee, by the merits of the Spouse of Thy most holy Mother, that, what of ourselves we are unable to obtain, may be granted us by his intercession.*

ANTHONY OF PADUA (JUNE 13)

This famous and lovable saint was a native of Lisbon. At an early age he entered the Augustinian order and devoted himself with great zeal to the sacred studies. Ten years later, he left the Augustinians and joined the newly founded Franciscans because he was consumed with the desire of going into their "mission" among the Mohammedans in Africa. Ill-health forced him to return to Europe, where he labored as teacher, and more often as preacher, until his early death near Padua, Italy, in 1231. A year later he was canonized. He had already wrought numberless miracles both during life and after death.[25]

A wave of popular veneration for him soon swept the countries of Europe. His life and legend inspired the faithful everywhere

with confidence and devotion. What attracted them was his kindness to all and his great love for the poor, which made him a
fearless advocate of the common people before the great ones of
his time. What appealed to the faithful most, however, was his
power of help and intercession, the result of a life of utter un-
selfishness, charity, zeal, and deepest familiarity with God in
prayer. With Joseph, he is the only male saint who is pictured
holding the child Jesus in his arms—a favor granted him in a
famous vision.

Many and varied are the patronages ascribed to him. During
the time of the wars against the Turks the Christian land armies
stood under his special protection. His help was invoked by the
troops before every battle. The reason for this patronage was the
conviction that the saint, who had been forced by sickness to quit
his spiritual battle against Islam, would now be glad to assist the
fighters of Christianity in defending their faith and their countries against the cruel attacks of Mohammedans.[26]

In 1668 the Spanish government, by special royal order, made
the saint a soldier of the second regiment of infantry. At every
victory in which the regiment was involved, an official promotion
to higher rank was given him. After two hundred years he had
obtained the rank of colonel. Finally, in 1889, he shared the fate
of so many other great soldiers of our times: he was accorded
the rank of general and retired from active service.[27]

Another patronage of Saint Anthony's is that of the poor. The
faithful soon discovered that a powerful means of obtaining his
special favor was for them to give alms to the poor. The custom
soon spread over Europe, and in 1890 this charity was organized
at Toulon, France, under the official name "Saint Anthony's
Bread," a title which may now be found on poor boxes in many
churches.[28]

In Latin countries (Portugal, Italy, Spain, France) Saint Anthony is the patron of sailors and fishermen. They place his statue
in a little shrine on the ship's mast, pray to him in storms and
dangers, and even "scold" him if he does not answer their petitions for help speedily enough.

In all Catholic countries Saint Anthony holds a special place
in the hearts of women. They turn to him with their problems of
love and espousal, happiness in married life, fertility, good and

healthy children.[29] This patronage was doubtless occasioned by his great kindness and goodness to all, and by the fact that images show him with the Holy Child held tenderly in his arms.

Girls go to his shrines to pray for a husband. They light candles before his image and drink from the fountain in the churchyard (Anthony's Well). In Spain he is called *Santo Casamentero* (the Holy Matchmaker). The Basque girls make a pilgrimage on his feast day to the town of Durango in Biscaya, where they climb a high mountain and pray there in the shrine "for a good boy." Sometimes their prayers are answered immediately; for the young Basque men have the habit of making the same journey, waiting outside the church, and asking the girls to dance after their devotions.

Saint Anthony's best-known gift, however, is his power of restoring all manner of lost things. In little matters and great, he is prayed to constantly by millions of people, and, like Saint Christopher, is often invoked by non-Catholics as well. There is no particular event in his life, nor any legend, that would explain the origin of this patronage. In fact, many explanations have been attempted, and most of them are quite unsatisfactory.

The most logical seems to be the report in an ancient Portuguese book (and the event might well be historical) that a man had stolen a valuable volume of chants from a monastery. Some time afterward, when praying to Saint Anthony, he not only felt sorry for the theft but was also inspired with a great urge to return the book. He did so, revealing that the saint had made him restore the "lost" volume; whereupon people began to invoke Saint Anthony on similar occasions when something belonging to them was lost.[30] The custom of praying to the saint for lost articles actually started in Portugal and spread from there to the rest of Europe, whence immigrants brought it with them to America.

Tuesday is devoted in a particular way to the veneration of Saint Anthony because he was buried on Tuesday, June 17, 1231. In the seventeenth century the practice began of holding weekly devotions to him; and even today most "perpetual novenas" to Saint Anthony are held on Tuesdays.[31]

Portugal and Italy, where the saint was born and where he died, honor his feast day with unusual festive splendor and great devotion. In Portugal the epithet "of Padua" is never used, for to the Portuguese he remains "Anthony of Lisbon" or "of Alfama" (the district of Lisbon where he was born). There every house on June 13 displays, among other decorations, a shrine with a statue of the saint.

LITURGICAL PRAYER · *The solemnity of Saint Anthony, Thy Confessor, may give joy to Thy Church, O God; and let her be ever defended by this spiritual assistance, that she may merit the bliss of eternal joys.*

JOHN THE BAPTIST (JUNE 24)

This saint was highly honored throughout the whole Church from the beginning. Proof of this is, among other things, the fact that fifteen churches were dedicated to him in the ancient imperial city of Constantinople.[32] Being the precursor of our Lord, he was accorded the same honor as the first great saints of the Christian era, although he belonged to the Old Covenant. The fact that Christ praised him so highly (Matthew 11, 11) encouraged, of course, a special veneration. Accordingly, we find a regular cycle of feasts in his honor among the early Christian churches.

It was the firm belief among the faithful that John was freed from original sin at the moment when his mother met the Blessed Virgin (Luke 1, 45). Saint Augustine mentioned this belief as a general tradition in the ancient Church.[33] In any case, it is certain that he was "filled with the Holy Spirit even from his mother's womb" (Luke 1, 15) and, therefore, born without original sin. Accordingly, the Church celebrates his natural birth by a festival of his "nativity," assigned exactly six months before the nativity of Christ, since John was six months older than the Lord. As soon as the Feast of Christmas was established on December 25 (in the fifth century) the date of the Baptist's birth was assigned to June 24.[34]

The question arises of why June 24, and not 25. It has often been claimed that the Church authorities wanted to "Christianize" the pagan solstice celebrations and for this reason advanced Saint John's feast as a substitute for the former pagan festival. However, the real reason why Saint John's Day falls on June 24 lies in the Roman way of counting, which proceeded backward from the calends (first day) of the succeeding month. Christmas was "the eighth day before the Kalends of January" (*Octavo Kalendas Januarii*). Consequently, Saint John's nativity was put on the "eighth day before the Kalends of July." However, since June has only thirty days, in our way of counting the feast falls on June 24.[35]

The Council of Agde, in 506, listed the Nativity of Saint John among the highest feasts of the year, a day on which all faithful had to attend Mass and abstain from servile work.[36] Indeed, so great was the rank of this festival that, just as on Christmas, three Masses were celebrated, one during the vigil service, the second at dawn, the third in the morning.[37] In 1022, a synod at Seligenstadt, Germany, prescribed a fourteen-day fast and abstinence in preparation for the Feast of the Baptist. This, however, was never accepted into universal practice by the Roman authorities.[38]

On August 29 the death of the saint is honored by a Feast of the Beheading. A third festival was celebrated in the Oriental Church in honor of "Saint John's Conception" (on September 23), commemorating the fact that an angel had announced his conception.[39] This feast, however, was not adopted by the Latin Church. The Greek Rite (on the day after Epiphany), and recently also the Latin Church (on January 13), keep a feast in memory of Saint John baptizing the Lord.

The Baptist is patron of tailors (because he made his own garments in the desert), of shepherds (because he spoke of the "Lamb of God"), and of masons.[40] This patronage over masons is traced to his words:

> Make ready the way of the Lord,
> make straight all his paths.
> Every valley shall be filled,
> and every mountain and hill shall be brought low,
> And the crooked shall be made straight,
> and the rough ways smooth. (Luke 3, 4-6.)

All over Europe, from Scandinavia to Spain, and from Ireland to Russia, Saint John's Day festivities are closely associated with the ancient nature lore of the great summer festival of pre-Christian times.[41] Fires are lighted on mountains and hilltops on the eve of his feast. These "Saint John's fires" burn brightly and quietly along the fiords of Norway, on the peaks of the Alps, on the slopes of the Pyrenees, and on the mountains of Spain (where they are called *Hogueras*). They were an ancient symbol of the warmth and light of the sun which the forefathers greeted at the beginning of summer. In many places, great celebrations are held with dances, games, and outdoor meals.

Fishermen from Brittany keep this custom even while far out at sea in the Arctic Ocean. They hoist a barrel filled with castoff clothing to the tip of the mainsail yard and set the contents on fire. All ships of the fishing fleet light up at the same time, about eight o'clock in the evening. The men gather around the mast, pray and sing. Afterward they celebrate in their quarters, and the captain gives each crew member double pay.[42]

Another custom is that of lighting many small fires in the valleys and plains. People gather around, jump through the flames, and sing traditional songs in praise of the saint or of summer. This custom is based on the pre-Christian "need fires" (*niedfyr, nodfyr*) which were believed to cleanse, cure, and immunize people from all kinds of disease, curses, and dangers.[43] In Spain these smaller fires (*fogatas*) are lighted in the streets of towns and cities, everybody contributing some old furniture or other wood, while children jump over the flames. In Brest, France, the bonfires are replaced by lighted torches which people throw in the air. In other districts of France they cover wagon wheels with straw, then set them on fire with a blessed candle and roll them down the hill slopes.

As the first day of summer, Saint John's Day is considered in ancient folklore one of the great "charmed" festivals of the year. Hidden treasures are said to lie open in lonely places, waiting for the lucky finder.[44] Divining rods should be cut on this day. Herbs are given unusual powers of healing, which they retain if they are plucked during the night of the feast.[45] In Germany they call these herbs *Johanneskraut* (St. John's herbs), and people bring them to church for a special blessing.

In Scandinavia and in the Slavic countries it is an ancient superstition that on Saint John's Day witches and demons are allowed to roam the earth. As at Halloween, children go the rounds and demand "treats," straw figures are thrown into the flames, and much noise is made to drive the demons away.[46]

It should be noted, however, that in the Catholic sections of Europe the combination of the ancient festival of nature lore with the Feast of the Baptist has resulted in a tradition of dignified celebration, which has come down to our day. People gather around the fireplace, dressed in their national or local costumes, and sing their beautiful ancient songs. When the fire is lighted, one of them recites a poem that expresses the thought of the feast. Then they pray together to Saint John for his intercession that the summer may be blessed in homes, fields, and country, and finally perform some of the traditional folk dances, usually accompanied by singing and music.[47]

LITURGICAL PRAYER · *O God who hast made this an honored day for us by the birth of Saint John: bestow upon Thy people the grace of spiritual joys, and guide the hearts of all Thy faithful into the way of eternal salvation.*

[1] Wimmer, 237 f.   [2] Simeon Metaphrastes, *Certamen S. Blasii;* PG, 116, 817.   [3] Gugitz, I, 66.   [4] Franz, I, 202 ff., 458 ff.; Koren, 88; TE, I, 689 f.   [5] RR, *Bened. candelarum in Festo S. Blasii Ep. et Mart.* [6] Gugitz, I, 75 f.; Enc. Brit., 22 (1949), 949.   [7] Gugitz, I, 77.   [8] PW, 6.2, 2097.   [9] RCF, 64 ff.   [10] For the following historical details see L. Bieler, *The Life and Legend of St. Patrick,* Dublin, 1949, 108 ff., and H. Leclercq, *Vie et apostolat de saint Patrice,* DACL, 7.2 (1927), 1467 ff.   [11] T. Mathew, *Ireland,* London, 1916, 140 ff.   [12] J. Ryan, *Die Patricksverehrung in Oststeiermark,* in *Wiener Zeitschrift für Volkskunde,* 1934, 83 ff.   [13] *The Diary of Humphrey O'Sullivan,* ed. M. McGrath, London, 1936, I, 237.   [14] English text in *The Catholic Encyclopedia,* 11 (1911), 556.   [15] Kellner, 274; H. Leclercq, *Le Culte du Saint Joseph,* DACL, 7.2 (1927), 2665 ff.   [16] For surmises on the choice of March 19 see Jgn GK, 247 and Wimmer, 269.   [17] Kellner, 275.   [18] CIC, 1247, 1.   [19] TE, I, 709; VL, 70 f.   [20] Wimmer, 270; O. Pfülf, *Die Verehrung des hl. Joseph in der Geschichte,* StML, 38 (1890), 137 ff., 282 ff.   [21] Gugitz, I, 130.   [22] Gugitz, I, 133.   [23] F. Skutsch, *Das Josefsfest in Rom,* in *Mitteilungen der schlesischen Gesellschaft für Volkskunde,* 6 (1927), 32 ff.   [24] Gugitz, I, 131.   [25] Wimmer, 113 f.   [26] E. Schlund, *Antonius von Padua,* Wien, 1931, 268 ff.

²⁷ Gugitz, I, 301; VL, 74.   ²⁸ Wimmer, 114.   ²⁹ Gugitz, I, 303.
³⁰ Gugitz, I, 302 f.   ³¹ VL, 73.   ³² Kellner, 219, note 1.   ³³ Sermo
292, 1; PL, 38, 1320.   ³⁴ See St. Augustine: "On the Nativity of John
the days begin to grow shorter" (*incipiunt dierum detrimenta*): Sermo
288, 5; PL, 38, 1308.   ³⁵ C. A. Kneller, *Heortologie*, ZKTh, 21 (1901),
525 f.   ³⁶ Can. 21; Mansi, 8, 328.   ³⁷ Kellner, 222.   ³⁸ J. Freundorfer,
Johannes der Täufer, LThK, 5 (1933), 461 ff.   ³⁹ Nilles, I, 282
(Byzantine Church), 482 (Syrians), 489 (Maronites), II, 707 (Sept.
26:Copts).   ⁴⁰ Wimmer, 263.   ⁴¹ Frazer, 622 ff. ("Midsummer Fires").
⁴² About St. John's fires in various countries see Geramb, 114-17.
⁴³ Frazer, 638 ("The Need-fire"); ES, 173; VL, 159.   ⁴⁴ Gugitz, I, 360;
Frazer, 705.   ⁴⁵ ES, 156.   ⁴⁶ Benet, 72 f.; ES, 250; Geramb, 108.
⁴⁷ Geramb, 121 ff.; Koren, 156 ff.

CHAPTER

28

Saints' Days II

PETER AND PAUL (JUNE 29)

According to ancient tradition these two Apostles were put to
death by Emperor Nero (64). Peter died by crucifixion in the
public circus or amphitheater at the Vatican hill; Paul was beheaded outside the city.[1]

The special celebrations which the Christians in Rome held
in honor of the "Princes of the Apostles" are known from earliest
times. At the end of the fourth century the faithful thronged the
streets on June 29 going in pilgrimage to the Vatican (Saint
Peter's) and from there to the church of St. Paul's "outside the
walls," praying at the shrines and attending the pontifical Mass
which the pope celebrated first at St. Peter's, then at St. Paul's.[2]

Since the great distance between the two churches made it
quite inconvenient, for both the pope and the people, to perform

the two services on the same morning, the liturgy of the feast was divided in the sixth century, and the Mass in honor of Saint Paul was henceforth celebrated on the following day. This "commemoration of Saint Paul" has remained a liturgical feast on June 30 ever since.[3]

In both the Eastern and Western Churches the Feast of Peter and Paul was observed as a holyday of obligation from the fifth century on.[4] It has remained so through all the centuries since.

Saint Peter is patron of fishermen and sailors, of key makers (because he carries the keys of the Kingdom) and watchmakers (because of the cock's crowing—an ancient time signal). He used to be invoked against fever (because Christ cured his mother-in-law from fever).[5] Above all, however, he was highly venerated from the tenth century on as the heavenly gatekeeper who guards the gates of eternity and admits or turns away souls. This power, of course, is ascribed to him in connection with the "granting of the keys" by Christ and the power of "binding and loosening."

Another "patronage" shared by Peter and Paul seems to be taken from the ancient Germanic mythology of the gods Thor (Donar) and Woden. These two gods had been the leaders of the Germanic group of gods, but after conversion to Christianity the people invested Peter and Paul with the function of the "deposed" gods as far as nature is concerned. Thus Peter and Paul became the "weather makers." Many legends ascribe thunder and lightning to some activity of Saint Peter in Heaven (usually bowling). When it snows, he is "shaking out his feather bed." He sends rain and sunshine, hangs out the stars at night and takes them in again in the morning. Saint Paul is invoked against lightning, storms, hail, and extreme cold. It seems that he is entrusted with the task of persuading Saint Peter to do the "right things" regarding the weather.[6]

Saint Paul alone is venerated as patron of tentmakers and weavers (having been one himself) and of theologians (because of his profound theological writings).[7] Both Apostles have been invoked from ancient times against the bite of poisonous snakes. If you pray very hard on Peter and Paul's Day no snake will bite you all through the year, say people in many places even today.[8]

Various flowers and herbs are under Saint Peter's patronage, especially those with a hairy stem. The "Peter's plant" (*primula hirsuta*) is collected, dried, and kept to be used as a medicine (in tea) against snake and dog bite.

In Hungary, grains are blessed by the priest after Mass on Peter and Paul's Day. People weave crowns, crosses, and other religious symbols from straw, have them blessed, and carry them on wooden poles in procession around the church. Afterward they take them home and keep them suspended from the ceiling over the dinner table. Bread is also blessed in a special ceremony on this day in Hungary.

A moving custom is practiced in rural sections of the Alpine countries. On June 29, when the church bells ring the Angelus early in the morning, people step under the trees in their gardens, kneel down and say the traditional prayer, the "Angel of the Lord." Having finished the prayer they bow deeply and make the sign of the cross, believing that on Saint Peter's Day the blessing of the Holy Father in Rome is carried by angels throughout the world to all who sincerely await it.[9]

LITURGICAL PRAYER · *O God, who has sanctified this day by the martyrdom of Thy Apostles Peter and Paul, grant that Thy Church may in all things follow their precepts, as she has received from them the beginnings of her faith.*

CHRISTOPHER (JULY 25)

Only the name of this saint and the fact of his martyrdom are known. His veneration was widespread in both the Eastern and Western Churches in early centuries. He is supposed to have died in Palestine or Lebanon (Canaan). But very early, too, legends supplied with abundant fantasy what history could not provide, and all kinds of startling details were told about him.[10] He was a giant of no mean proportions; it took four hundred soldiers to take him captive; for twelve hours his body was pierced with arrows until he fell to the ground, but even then he was still alive and had to be beheaded.

Later legends added many other details to the story of his life and conversion. The most familiar one is told in the thirteenth-century *Golden Legend*. Proud of his giant stature, a man, whose original name was Offerus, decided to serve only the strongest lord in the world. He entered the service of the emperor; but on seeing that the emperor was afraid of the Devil, he forthwith served the Devil. One day he saw how the Devil trembled at the sight of a crucifix, so he decided to serve Christ. A hermit told him he should carry Christian pilgrims through a deep and dangerous river. He did so. One night a little boy asked to be carried across. The giant took the little one on his shoulders and started across the churning waters. But as the child on his back grew heavier and heavier Offerus felt that he would break down under the burden. When he reached the other shore, panting and exhausted, he asked in surprise why the child was so heavy. He received the answer: "You have not only carried the whole world on your shoulders but Him Who created it. I am Christ the Lord, whom you serve." Then the Lord Himself took Offerus into the water, baptized him, and gave him the new name "Christoph- orus" (Christ-bearer). He told the saint to ram the tree trunk that he carried as staff into the ground. Christopher did so, and the tree immediately burst forth with leaves and blossoms. The Child had disappeared, and the saint went joyfully to persecu- tion and death for his beloved Lord.[11]

This beautiful legend captivated the hearts of the faithful everywhere and was the inspiration for many devotions. Saint Christopher was venerated as patron against sudden and unpro- vided death, especially during times of great epidemics, when people never knew in the morning whether they would still be alive that evening. They believed that by looking at his picture and saying a prayer to him in the morning they would be safe from death on that day. So they hung his picture over the door of the house, or painted it on the walls outside, to give others the benefit of it, too.

This tradition has been kept in central Europe to the present day, although its meaning has been forgotten by many. Any tourist traveling through southern Germany, Switzerland, Austria, and France will notice the large images of Saint Christopher painted on the outside of houses and churches.[12]

Christopher is the patron of ferryboats and their crews, of pilgrims and travelers, of gardeners (because his staff burst into bloom), and of freight ships. In France all fortresses were put under his protection in centuries past. In England he was invoked against hail and lightning. Since he carried our Lord safely through the waters, he became the patron of all passenger traffic, especially in automobiles. In many countries cars are blessed on his feast day. At churches that bear his name the blessing is usually given in a more solemn way on his feast, and hundreds of automobiles line up in front of the shrine to receive the blessing for that year.[13]

More recently Saint Christopher has also been venerated as the patron of skiing, and appropriately so. Having carried the Christ Child through the waters, he gladly protects children and grownups gliding over the snow. It was a coincidence, but perhaps somewhat providential as well, that the town in the best and most famous ski territory in Austria is named Saint Christopher (*Sankt Christoph am Arlberg*).

Finally, there are the Saint Christopher medals and plaques, which people have blessed by a priest to carry on their persons as a protection against accidents. These medals are now also put in cars and other vehicles and are popular with Christians of all faiths. The custom of using such images of the saint started in the sixteenth century, and their original purpose was to serve as a picture for travelers to gaze on every morning and ask God to save them from sudden death that day.[14] This custom has died out long since but the medals have remained as a token of the saint's generous help and protection in modern traffic, which kills almost as many people as epidemics did in ancient times.

LITURGICAL PRAYER · *Grant us, O Lord, almighty God, as we celebrate the birthday of Saint Christopher, Thy Martyr, that through his intercession we may be strengthened in the love of Thy holy Name.*

ANNE (JULY 26)

Saint Anne, or Ann, is not mentioned in the Bible. It was only in legendary books of the early Christian centuries that the names of Mary's parents were given as Joachim and Anne. Since the Fathers of the Church rejected the use of such legendary sources, the faithful in Europe had no feast in honor of our Lord's grandparents. In the Middle East, however, the veneration of Saint Anne can be traced back to the fourth century.[15]

The Crusaders brought the name and legend of Saint Anne to Europe, and the famous Dominican Jacobus de Voragine (1298) printed the story in his *Golden Legend*. From that time on the popular veneration of the saint spread into all parts of the Christian world. It was encouraged by the religious orders of the Franciscans, Dominicans, Augustinians, and Carmelites. In southern France a Feast of Saint Anne was celebrated as early as the fourteenth century. Pope Urban VI in 1378 extended it to England at the king's request. Not until 1584, however, did the feast become universal, when Pope Gregory XIII prescribed it for the whole Church.[16]

As grandmother of Christ and mother of Mary, Saint Anne soon became the patron of married women, and for childless couples a special aid in obtaining children. According to legend she was married three times, first to Joachim, after his death to Cleophas, and finally to Salomas. This detail of the ancient story inspired young women to turn to her for help in finding a husband. After all, since she had had three husbands herself, should she not be able and willing to provide at least one bridegroom for those who trustingly appealed to her? In the languages of all European nations young women implored her:

> *I beg you, holy mother Anne,*
> *Send me a good and loving man.*

Her patronage of fertility was extended also to the soil. Thus she became a patron of rain. It is a popular saying in Italy that "rain is Saint Anne's gift"; in Germany, July rain was called "Saint Anne's dowry." [17]

Finally, the gentle grandmother of the Lord is everywhere invoked as one of the great helpers for various needs of body and soul. Many churches have been erected to her, most of them becoming famous centers of pilgrimages. One of the best-known shrines in this part of the world is St. Anne de Beaupré in Quebec, Canada.

From the eighteenth century on, Anne, which means "grace," was used more and more as a favorite name for girls. At the beginning of the nineteenth century it was the most popular girls' name in central Europe, surpassing even that of Mary. This preference was based on a famous saying of past centuries, "All Annes are beautiful." Naturally, parents wanted to assure this benefit for their baby daughters by calling them Anne or by adding Anne to a first name. Thus we have the many traditional names containing Anne or Ann (Mary Ann, Marianne, Marian, Ann Marie, Joanne, Elizabeth Ann, Lillian, Martha Ann, Louise Ann, Patricia Ann).[18]

A hundred years ago there still remained the custom in many parts of Europe of celebrating Saint Anne's Day as a festival "of all Annes," meaning all beautiful girls. Dressed in their finery the bevy would parade through the streets with their escorts, bands would serenade them in parks and squares, balls would be held (both Johann Strausses composed "Anne Polkas" for this festival). Saint Anne's Eve was the day of receptions for debutantes at court and in private homes. Public amusements, including fireworks, entertained the crowds. The warm summer night was alive with laughter, beauty, music, and lights. And all of it was still connected in the hearts and minds of the participants with a tribute to Saint Anne, whose feast day shed its radiance upon this enchanting celebration.[19]

LITURGICAL PRAYER · *O God, who didst deign to confer on Saint Anne the grace to be the mother of her who was to give birth to Thy only-begotten Son: mercifully grant us, who celebrate her feast, that we may be helped by her intercession.*

NICHOLAS (DECEMBER 6)

Despite the immense popularity of Saint Nicholas during the Middle Ages, both in Europe and Christian Asia, there is scarcely any definite historical fact known about him except that he was bishop of Myra in Asia Minor; that he was cast into exile and prison during the persecution of Emperor Diocletian and released by Constantine the Great; that he died in Myra about 350, and in the year 1087 his body was brought by Italian merchants from Myra to the city of Bari in Italy, where his relics are still preserved and venerated in the church of San Nicola. The reports of numerous miracles ascribed to the saint, both before and after his death, are based on a long tradition. As early as 450, churches were being built in his honor, and his veneration was general in the Greek Church. From there, at the end of the tenth century, it spread to the German Empire, and reached its height when his relics arrived in Italy during the eleventh century. The Church celebrates his feast day as a bishop and confessor annually on December 6.[20]

By the year 1200, this much-loved saint had captured the hearts and imaginations of all European nations. Many churches, towns, provinces, and countries venerated him as their patron saint. He is patron of Greece, Russia, Sicily, and Lorraine; of many cities in Germany, Austria, Switzerland, Holland, and Italy. Merchants, bakers, and mariners, among others, have made him their patron. But he was always best known as the patron saint of children.[21]

The beautiful legend of Saint Nicholas might be told to children something like this:

Saint Nicholas was born of a rich and noble family in the city of Parara in Asia Minor. When he was very little he lost his mother and father and had to live the sad and lonely life of an orphan. After he had grown to young manhood, he decided to devote his life entirely to the service of God, doing good works for his fellow men. Obeying the words of Christ, he distributed all his possessions to the poor, the sick, and the suffering. He is said to have secretly helped very poor people by putting gifts of money through their windows during the night, when no one could see him (just as he now brings his gifts to you during the night).

His love for the Christ Child inspired him to make a pilgrimage to the Holy Land and offer prayers in those historical and holy places. On this trip a terrible storm arose but, by his prayers, he miraculously saved the already sinking ship as it tossed and turned in the high seas. That is the reason he is now venerated as a patron of mariners by many brave sailors all over the world.

When he returned home from this pilgrimage, the bishops of Asia Minor elected him as successor to the bishop of Myra, who had just died. The whole city rejoiced when they heard of his appointment. Nicholas received the holy orders, modestly and devoutly, and, as bishop, practiced not only great holiness of life, by fasting and prayer, but had boundless love for his fellow men. Having been an orphan himself, he now became the beloved father of widows and orphans. His constant kindness and charity were bestowed especially on the children, whom he often gathered about him, instructing them in the word of God and delighting them with many little gifts.

Under the Roman Emperor Diocletian, who persecuted the Christians, Saint Nicholas was taken from his home, exiled and imprisoned. He suffered hardships of hunger, thirst, cold, loneliness, and chains. He wanted to die as a martyr. But when Emperor Diocletian left his throne and the first Christian Emperor, Constantine the Great, ruled the Roman lands, all Christians who had suffered in prison because of their faith, were released. Among them was Saint Nicholas, who was able to return to Myra, where he lived for many years, a kind father to all his flock, especially to the poor.

One day he became very ill and soon he realized it was time for him to go to Heaven. There he was met by many angels who conducted his soul to the throne of God. Saint Nicholas was very happy.

The whole city mourned his passing, most of all the little children. But very soon they found out that even from Heaven he continued to help them, if only they asked him. So the children started praying to Saint Nicholas and their prayers were answered by thousands of miracles, small ones and great ones. To this day, boys and girls all over the world pray to their patron saint, Saint Nicholas.

In many parts of Europe children still receive his "visit" on the eve of his feast. Impersonated by a man wearing a long white beard, dressed in the vestments of a bishop, with miter and crozier, he appears in the homes as a heavenly messenger. Coming at the start of Advent, he admonishes the children to prepare their hearts for a blessed and holy Christmas. He examines them on their prayers. After exhorting them to be good, he distributes fruit and candy and departs with a kindly farewell, leaving the little ones filled with holy awe.[22]

It was this "visit of Saint Nicholas" on December 5 that the Dutch brought to the New World as an annual cherished custom.

From it later developed the American custom of Santa Claus's visit at Christmas.

LITURGICAL PRAYER · *O God, who didst adorn the holy bishop Nicholas with numberless miracles, grant, we beseech thee, that through his merits and prayers we may be saved from the flames of hell.*

LUCY (DECEMBER 13)

With Catherine and Barbara, Lucy, or Lucia, is one of the three great "girl saints." She died during the persecutions of Diocletian at Catania in Sicily, being beheaded by the sword. Her body was later brought to Constantinople and finally to Venice, where she is now resting in the church of Santa Lucia.[23]

Because her name means "light" she very early became the great patron saint for the "light of the body"—the eyes. All over Christianity her help was invoked against diseases of the eyes, especially the danger of blindness. This is the reason why she is often pictured with a plate in hand on which lie two eyeballs. The lighters of street lamps in past centuries had her as patron saint and made a special ceremony of their task on the eve of December 13. She also is the patron of the gondoliers in Venice, whose familiar song, "Santa Lucia," is an affectionate tribute to her.[24]

Saint Lucy attained immense popularity in medieval times because, before the calendar reform, her feast happened to fall on the shortest day of the year. Again because of her name, many of the ancient light and fire customs of the Yuletide became associated with her day. Thus we find "Lucy candles" lighted in the homes and "Lucy fires" burned in the open. In Scandinavia before the Reformation Saint Lucy's Day was one of unusual celebration and festivity because, for the people of Sweden and Norway, she was the great "light saint" who turned the tides of their long winter and brought the light of day to renewed victory.[25]

This is the reason why her lore has survived in the Scandinavian countries even after the Reformation and calendar reform, which brought the solstice back to December 23. In Sweden and Norway it is still a custom on December 13 for a girl in a white dress (representing the saint), with a wreath on her head in which burning candles are placed, to awaken the family from sleep and offer a tray with coffee and cakes. The impersonation is called *Lussibrud* (Lucy bride) and her pastry is *Lussekattor*.

Another popular custom in Scandinavia on the eve of December 13 is for children to write the word *"Lussi"* on doors, fences, and walls. With the word always goes the picture of a female figure (Saint Lucy). The purpose of this practice in ancient times was to announce to the demons of winter that their reign was broken on Saint Lucy's Day, that the sun would return again and the days become longer.

"Lucy fires" used to be burned everywhere in northern Europe on December 13. Into these bonfires people threw incense and, while the flames rose, trumpets and flutes were played to greet the changing of the sun's course. These fires were greatly valued as a powerful protection against disease, witchcraft, and dangers, and people would stand nearby and let the smoke of the incense reach them, thus obtaining the desired "protection." [26]

After the calendar reform, when the original reason for such celebrations (the solstice) was gradually forgotten, Lucy's figure degenerated into a winter demon in many sections of Europe.[27] In Sweden and Norway, however, the ancient meaning of the feast was essentially preserved and Lussi always remained a friendly, cheerful figure. Thus the attractive little martyr and great saint of the Middle Ages has kept her name and her role as "light bringer" in Scandinavia, although most people today are unaware of the historical background and true meaning of this part of their folklore.

In the liturgy of the Church, Saint Lucy has held, and still holds today, the inspiring position of a saint whose very name reminds the faithful at the middle of Advent that her own "light" is only a reflection of the great "Light of the World" which is to start shining at Bethlehem on Christmas Day. It is as if she would say: "I am only a little flame in Advent showing you the way:

> *Behold, the Lord will come*
> *And all His saints with Him,*

> And on that day
> There will be a great light. Alleluia." [28]

LITURGICAL PRAYER · *Hear us, O God, our salvation, as we rejoice on the feast of Saint Lucy, Thy Virgin and Martyr, and grant us to learn the spirit of pious devotion.*

[1] J. Sauer, *Verehrung des hl. Petrus (und Paulus)*, LThK, 8 (1936), 136. [2] Prudentius, *Perist.*, XII; CSEL, 61 (1926), 420 ff. [3] Kellner, 285. [4] TE, 1, 712. [5] Wimmer, 367. [6] Gugitz, II, 1 ff. (*Verehrung und Brauchtum des hl. Petrus*); ES, 209. [7] Wimmer, 363. [8] Wimmer, 363, 367. [9] Gugitz, II, 5. [10] Wimmer, 148. [11] Gugitz, II, 50 ff. (*Vom Grossen Christoph*). [12] R. Hindringer, *Christophorus*, LThK, 2 (1931), 934 ff. [13] Wimmer, 148 f. [14] Gugitz, II, 51. [15] Kellner, 275. [16] E. Schaumkell, *Der Cultus der hl. Anna am Ausgang des Mittelalters*, in *Der Katholik*, 8 (1893), 14 ff. [17] Wimmer, 109. [18] Gugitz, II, 47 f. [19] Gugitz, II, 40 ff. (*Das Annenfest*). [20] Wimmer, 344. [21] K. Meisen, *Nikolauskult und Nikolausbrauch im Abendlande*, Düsseldorf, 1931; VL, 147. [22] Gugitz, II, 223 ff. (*Sankt Nikolaus der Gabenbringer*); Geramb, 207 ff.; VL, 145 ff. [23] H. Leclercq, *Sainte Lucie*, DACL, 0.2 (1930), 2616 ff. [24] Wimmer, 303. [25] Gugitz, 235 ff. (*Der Lucientag*). [26] Koren, 46; Geramb, 210. [27] Gugitz, II, 236 f. [28] BR, First Sunday of Advent, third antiphon of Lauds.

Dictionary of Terms

Antiphon. A verse recited before and after psalms and Biblical hymns in the prayers of the liturgy. The antiphons usually express key thoughts of a particular feast or celebration.

Apology. A discourse explaining and defending the teachings of the faith and the institutions of the Church.

Armenian Rite. The liturgy (Mass) of the Armenian Rite is a translation of the Greek liturgy of Saint Basil (379) and, among the Catholic Armenians, parts of the Latin liturgy. The language of the rite is ancient Armenian. Of the two million members of this rite, about 100,000 are in union with Rome.

Benediction of the Blessed Sacrament. A liturgical rite in which the solemn blessing is conferred on the faithful with the Eucharistic host (the Body of Christ under the species of bread).

Blessed Sacrament. See *Eucharist.*

Breviary. The book containing the official texts of the Divine Office.

Byzantine Rite. This is the ancient rite of the patriarchate (Church province) of Constantinople (Byzantium) in the former East Roman Empire. The original language of the rite is old Greek, still used in Greece. Various nations accepting this rite, however, retained their own languages (Slavonic among the Russians, Ukrainians, Serbians; Arabic among the Melkites; old Rumanic among the Romanians). To the Byzantine Rite belong over one hundred million Christians, of whom seven million are in union with Rome.

Chaldeans. The Catholic Christians of the East Syrian Rite, mostly in Syria, Iraq, and Iran. Their liturgical language is Syriac. The Malabar Christians in India also belong to this rite, which, however, they modified in various points. Members of the East Syrian Rite not in union with Rome are Nestorians.

Canon. 1. An individual "rule" (law) within a collection of ecclesiastical laws. 2. Member of a community of priests living under a "common rule" at a bishop's church. 3. An honorary title for priests.

Canon of the Mass. The "rule" of the Sacrifice, meaning the prescribed prayers and ceremonies of the sacrificial action in the Mass from the Preface to the Our Father.

Catechumens. Those who attended the official instruction in the faith preparatory to baptism. From the third century on, this instruction was connected with traditional ascetical exercises (fasting, additional prayers) and with liturgical rites of initiation (exorcisms, blessings, anointing, "handing over" of gospels, Our Father, and Creed).

Collect. Liturgical prayer recited by the celebrant, in which he offers to God the collective petitions of the Church for all her members. The Collect of the Mass is offered at the beginning (after the Kyrie or Gloria).

Copts. Members of the ancient native Christian community of Egypt. The language of their rite is Coptic (Egyptian) mixed with Greek and Arabic. Of the 800,000 Copts, 60,000 are in union with Rome.

Council. A meeting of ecclesiastical leaders (bishops) for the purpose of establishing laws and regulations concerning matters of faith, morals, and church discipline. A council intended to represent not merely a province or nation but the whole Church is called ecumenic (general).

Creed. See *Symbolum.*

Divine Office. The daily liturgical prayer-worship prescribed for the clergy (from the order of subdeacon up) and for many religious communities. It is either chanted in common or recited privately.

Eastern Churches. General designation for all the churches of Eastern Europe, Asia, and Africa that do not follow the liturgical rite of Rome but have ancient rites of their own. Communities of these churches are now established also in other parts of the world. The Eastern Churches are either uniate (in union with Rome) or non-uniate (refusing to acknowledge the supreme ecclesiastical authority of the pope).

Eucharist. The sacrament in which Christ is present, under the appearance (species) of bread and wine, as the spiritual food for the souls of the faithful.

Eucharistic Benediction. See *Benediction of the Blessed Sacrament.*

Eucharistic Sacrifice. See *Sacrifice.*

Gradual. Prayer verses recited after the Epistle of the Mass, and followed by one or more Alleluias (except in Lent).

Greek Rite. See *Byzantine Rite.*

Gregorian Chant. The official plain chant at liturgical functions of the Western (Latin) Church. It received its final formulation through Pope Gregory the Great (604).

Indulgence. The pardon of temporal punishment (in this life or in purgatory) for sins already forgiven. This pardon is granted by the Church from the spiritual treasury of the merits of Christ and His saints.

Liturgical. Any text, action, or object that is prescribed or approved for use in the official worship of the Church.

Liturgy. 1. The official worship of the Church as performed in the Holy Sacrifice and ministration of sacraments, in all other official rites, and in the Divine Office. 2. The ceremonies and texts used in the above-mentioned acts of official worship. 3. In the Byzantine Church the term "liturgy" is applied to the Eucharistic Sacrifice as such.

Maronites. Catholics of the West Syrian Rite of Saint Maro (423), mostly in Lebanon, Syria, and Palestine. Their liturgical language is Syriac mixed with Arabic.

Mass. See *Sacrifice.*

Melkites. The Arab-speaking Catholics of the Byzantine Rite (mostly in Syria, Palestine, and Egypt).

Mystical Body of Christ. The union of all those who are incorporated into the true Church of Christ by the profession of her faith and by baptism. The grace of Christ is the life animating this body. Each member is a cell of the body (a living cell if united with Christ by grace, a lifeless cell if separated from Him by sin). All members together, with Christ as the Head, constitute the Church.

Occidental Church. See *Western Church.*

Octave. The liturgical celebration of higher feasts through eight days. The eighth day is called "Octave day"; the intervening days are "days within the Octave."

Oriental Churches. See *Eastern Churches.*

Preface. The ancient solemn prayer of thanksgiving and adoration at the beginning of sacrificial action of the Mass. It starts with the call *"Sursum Corda"* (Lift up your hearts) and ends with the threefold *Sanctus* (Holy). A part of the text was made mutable so that the thoughts of particular celebrations could be expressed. Thus we have a number of Prefaces for various feasts and seasons of the year.

Rite. 1. The prayers and ceremonies of a liturgical function (rite of blessing; rite of baptism). 2. The common system and form of administration and liturgical worship within a certain group of churches (Coptic Rite, Chaldean Rite). 3. The community of all the faithful belonging to a certain rite (Byzantine Rite, Roman Rite).

Rubric. Official note of instruction, regulating the performance of liturgical prayers or ceremonies. In the liturgical books such notes are usually printed in red; hence the name (from the Latin *rubrum:* red).

Sacramentary. A liturgical book of early centuries containing only those texts that the celebrant himself (bishop or priest) had to recite at the celebration of the Mass and at other liturgical functions connected with a Mass.

Sacrifice (The Holy, or Eucharistic, Sacrifice). The sacrifice of the New Testament, instituted by Christ, in which the sacrifice of the Cross is repeated in its full reality and value, but in an "unbloody" way. The sacrament of the body and blood of Christ is made present in the "consecration." Thus Christ becomes the sacrificial victim and offering in this highest act of the liturgy, and is consumed under the Eucharistic species by the celebrant (and the faithful) in Holy Communion.

Sequence. A hymn recited (and sung) after the Gradual of the Mass on certain feasts.

Superstition. There are two, basically different, kinds of beliefs and practices usually called "superstitions." The first attributes preternatural powers to a thing in itself without relation to God; for instance, the "power" of a rabbit's foot to protect from harm. This, if consciously held and practiced, is obviously morally wrong. The second kind, often called "pious superstition," does not ascribe preternatural powers to an object in itself but considers these powers as granted by God. An example is the ancient belief that all running water is blessed with healing powers on Easter Sunday in honor of the Lord's resurrection. Such a "pious superstition" is, of course, not morally wrong in itself, but it is erroneous, since there is no basis in Divine Revelation or in ecclesiastical authority for such a belief. Most superstitions mentioned in this book belong to the second kind.

Symbolum. 1. The formula of profession of the faith that was "given" to the catechumens in a liturgical ceremony, and "returned" by them shortly before baptism. 2. Every formulation of the profession of faith that is acknowledged by the Church and officially used by her.

Synod. See *Council.*

Synoptics. The first three Evangelists: Matthew, Mark, Luke.

Vespers. 1. The official evening prayer of the Church in the Divine Office. 2. A liturgical devotion in the parish church on the afternoons of Sundays and holydays.

Vigil. 1. The religious night watch (with prayer and readings) of the early Christians, which was usually concluded by the Eucharistic Sacrifice. The only vigil of this kind at present is the Easter Vigil.

2. The liturgical preparation for a major feast, observed on the previous day, often with fast and other penitential features of the liturgy.

Votive Mass. 1. A Mass text that may be chosen by the priest according to his wish or upon request of the faithful on certain days when a liturgical feast is not obligatory. 2. A Mass text prescribed on certain occasions (Forty Hours) from the list of Votive Masses in the Roman Missal.

Western Church. All churches belonging to the Roman Rite. Except for a small territory in Dalmatia, they all use the Latin language in their liturgy; hence the "Latin Rite."

Index